Perspectives on the Old Saxon *Heliand*

MEDIEVAL EUROPEAN STUDIES XII
Patrick W. Conner, Series Editor

OTHER TITLES IN THE SERIES:

Via Crucis: Essays on Early Medieval Sources and Ideas
Thomas N. Hall, Editor, with assistance from Thomas D. Hill and Charles D. Wright

Hêliand: Text and Commentary
Edited by James E. Cathey

Naked Before God: Uncovering the Body in Anglo-Saxon England
Edited by Benjamin C. Withers and Jonathan Wilcox

Theorizing Anglo-Saxon Stone Sculpture
Edited by Catherine E. Karkov and Fred Orton

Old English Literature in its Manuscript Context
Edited by Joyce Tally Lionarons

Ancient Privileges: Beowulf, Law, and the Making of Germanic Antiquity
Stefan Jurasinski

The Postmodern Beowulf: A Critical Casebook
Edited by Eileen A. Joy and Mary K. Ramsey

The Power of Words: Anglo-Saxon Studies Presented to Donald G. Scragg on his Seventieth Birthday
Edited by Jonathan Wilcox and Hugh Magennis

Cædmon's Hymn and Material Culture in the World of Bede
Edited by Allen J. Frantzen and John Hines

The Cross and Culture in Anglo-Saxon England
Edited by Karen Jolly, Catherine E. Karkov, and Sarah Larratt Keefer

Cross and Cruciform in the Anglo-Saxon World: Studies to Honor the Memory of Timothy Reuter
Edited by Sarah Larratt Keefer, Karen Louise Jolly, and Catherine E. Karkov

Perspectives
on the Old Saxon *Heliand*

INTRODUCTORY AND CRITICAL ESSAYS, WITH AN
EDITION OF THE LEIPZIG FRAGMENT

Edited By
Valentine A. Pakis
University of St. Thomas

WEST VIRGINIA UNIVERSITY PRESS
MORGANTOWN 2010

West Virginia University Press 26506
© 2010 by West Virginia University Press

All rights reserved.

First edition published 2010 by West Virginia University Press

18 17 16 15 1 4 13 12 11 10   9 8 7 6 5 4 3 2 1

ISBN-10: 1-933202-49-1
ISBN-13: 978-1-933202-49-5
(alk. paper)

Library of Congress Cataloging-in-Publication Data

Perspectives on the Old Saxon Heliand : introductory and critical essays, with an edition of the Leipzig fragment / edited by Valentine A. Pakis.
-- 1st ed. p. cm.
Includes bibliographical references and index.
ISBN-13: 978-1-933202-49-5 (pbk. : alk. paper)
ISBN-10: 1-933202-49-1 (pbk. : alk. paper)
1. Heliand. 2. Old Saxon language. I. Pakis, Valentine A.

PF4000.P47 2010
829'.1--dc22

Library of Congress Control Number: 2009028337

Cover image: Ivory carving from front panel of MS Douce 176m, an early ninth century illuminated gospel. Used with permission of the Bodleian Library, Oxford University.

Contents

Preface vii
Valentine A. Pakis

I. Introductions to the *Heliand* and its Language

The Historical Setting of the *Heliand*, the Poem,
and the Manuscripts 3
James E. Cathey

The Old Saxon *Heliand* 34
G. Ronald Murphy

An Overview of Old Saxon Linguistics,
1992–2008 63
Marc Pierce

II. The Diatessaronic Tradition

The Parable of the Fisherman in the *Heliand*:
The Old Saxon Version of Matthew 13:47-50 93
Tjitze Baarda

(Un)Desirable Origins: The *Heliand* and
the Gospel of Thomas 120
Valentine A. Pakis

III. Orality and Narrative Tradition

Was the *Heliand* Poet Illiterate? 167
Harald Haferland
(Translated by Valentine A. Pakis)

The Hatred of Enemies: Germanic Heroic Poetry
and the Narrative Design of the *Heliand* 208
   Harald Haferland
   (Translated by Erik Baumann)

IV. The Portrayal of the Jews in the *Heliand*

The Jews in the *Heliand* 237
   G. Ronald Murphy

Jesus Christ between Jews and Heathens:
The Germanic Mission and the Portrayal of Christ
in the Old Saxon *Heliand* 254
   Martin Friedrich
   (Translated by Ariane Fischer and James Pasternak)

V. The Discovery of the Leipzig Fragment (2006)

A New *Heliand* Fragment from the Leipzig
University Library 281
   Hans Ulrich Schmid
   (Translated by Valentine A. Pakis)

Plates

1. Leipzig, Universitätsbibliothek, Thomas 4073 (MS),
outer side 303
2. Leipzig, Universitätsbibliothek, Thomas 4073 (MS),
inner side 304

Works Cited 305

Preface

This anthology is the first of its kind since Jürgen Eichhoff and Irmengard Rauch's excellent *Der Heliand* (Wege der Forschung 321), which appeared in 1973, and it is the first collection of *Heliand* scholarship ever to be assembled entirely in English. Some have said that it would be pointless to translate articles from German on such a topic, since anyone interested in Old Saxon literature will necessarily be able to read German scholarship, but my experience has suggested otherwise. The *Heliand* appeals to a wide audience – historians, biblical scholars, linguists, and scholars of medieval literature, for instance, have all had much to say about it – and many of its readers lack the skill or patience to wade through difficult German prose. I have found this to be true, in particular, of many students and scholars of Anglo-Saxon England, whose interest in the *Heliand* is strong for reasons that do not need to be outlined here.

The popularity of the *Heliand* in the English-speaking world has grown considerably over the past two decades, and a few scholars are largely responsible for this. To mention some major works: In 1989, G. Ronald Murphy's *The Saxon Savior: The Germanic Transformation of the Gospel in the Ninth-Century Heliand* reopened the discussion over the synthesis of Germanic and Christian worldviews in the poem, and in 1992 his English translation – *The Heliand: The Saxon Gospel* – was published by the Oxford University Press. In this year, too, Irmengard Rauch's *The Old Saxon Language: Grammar, Epic Narrative, Linguistic Interference* appeared, which is the first grammar of Old Saxon to have been written in English and also the first to shift the focus of Old Saxon linguistics from the phonology of the language to its syntax and semantics. James E. Cathey's *Hêliand: Text and Commentary*, published in 2002, represents the first attempt to make the Old Saxon original more accessible to English speaking students, and should become the standard classroom edition in America and elsewhere.

A number of relevant shorter writings on the *Heliand* have also been printed in English, on the wave of the books named above. These English articles, together with the recent stream of studies in German by Harald Haferland and the discovery of a new manuscript fragment of the *Heliand*, inspired the composition of the present volume. My goal in collecting articles was not to fill in every gap between now and the last collection, but rather to bring together recent scholarship that both addresses new turns in the field and, where possible, engages with the relevant arguments of the past three decades.

With the exception of the study by Tjitze Baarda, originally published in 1992, each of the articles postdates the year 2000. Baarda's work was included because of the freshness of its perspective; seldom does a medieval Germanic poem capture the philological attention of a Semiticist with expertise in New Testament textual criticism. The introductory essays by James E. Cathey and G. Ronald Murphy complement one another and will be especially useful for beginning students. Whereas Cathey focuses on the historical background, meter, and manuscripts of the *Heliand*, Murphy outlines the chief literary themes of the poem. Marc Pierce's survey of work in Old Saxon linguistics, an original contribution to this volume, will bring the reader up to date in the many aspects of this growing field. My own contribution, like Baarda's, is concerned with the relationship between the *Heliand*, Tatian's Diatessaron, and the Coptic Gospel of Thomas. My purpose here is not, however, to debate philological details but rather to examine the ideological motivations that have propelled such debates in the past. A section of this book

Preface

contains two representative essays by Harald Haferland that present unconventional approaches to the way in which the poem was composed. These studies are especially captivating for those who believe, as I do, that oral-formulaic theory has been too rashly cast aside. The representation of Jews in the *Heliand* is the theme of the fourth section of the anthology. Recent scholarship on this topic in Anglo-Saxon England – see the titles by Andrew Scheil and Renate Bauer, for example – demonstrate the liveliness of this issue and also the need to bring together the evidence from Old Saxon, which should be incorporated into larger studies in the future. In this section, Murphy's article offers a cultural and literary analysis and Martin Friedrich's the perspective of a Church historian. In April of 2006, a new manuscript leaf of the *Heliand* was discovered in the Leipzig University Library. The concluding section of this book consists of the initial reaction to this find, the *editio princeps* by Hans Ulrich Schmid.

Although full bibliographical information is provided in the notes of the individual chapters, it seemed appropriate to assemble a complete list of works cited at the end of the book. No comprehensive bibliography of *Heliand* studies has appeared since the 1975 publication of Johanna Belkin and Jürgen Meier's *Bibliographie zu Otfrid von Weißenburg und zur altsächsischen Bibeldichtung*. While the bibliography is limited here to the works cited in the volume itself, it includes enough recent titles to be of use to researchers.

A confluence of support enabled this book to come about. It is my pleasure to thank, first of all, each of the authors for kindly allowing his work to be reprinted (and translated when necessary) for inclusion in the volume, and also for openly accepting my editorial modifications. Marc Pierce deserves special thanks for his original contribution. My gratitude is also due to the editors and publishers who granted the rights to reproduce the articles and the plates, namely Patrick W. Conner and the West Virginia University Press, Brian Murdoch and Camden House, Arend Quak and Rodopi, R. Allen

Preface

Shoaf and *Exemplaria*, Joachim Heinzle and the S. Hirzel Verlag, Wolfgang Adam and the Carl Winter Universitätsverlag, Peter Meister and the Peter Lang Publishing Group, Jochen-Christoph Kaiser and the W. Kohlhammer Verlag, and Ulrich Johannes Schneider of the Leipzig University Library. I am indebted to my fellow translators as well – Erik Baumann, Ariane Fischer, and James Pasternak – for committing to the project before publication was secured and for their finished products. Jeremy Bergerson deserves my thanks for his skillful copyediting. Finally, the West Virginia University Press must be acknowledged for its acceptance of this volume and for its strong support of *Heliand* scholarship in recent years.

Valentine A. Pakis

I

Introductions to the *Heliand* and its Language

The Historical Setting of the *Heliand*, the Poem, and the Manuscripts[1]

James E. Cathey

The Old Saxon telling of the Gospel, titled *Heliand* (Savior) by J. A. Schmeller in his edition of 1830, was not written in a vacuum but was, as is everything, a product of its place and time. The *Heliand* was composed in what is now part of northern Germany in the first half of the ninth century. The time was approximately in the middle of the period extending from the first Christian missions to the north of Europe in the 500s to the end of the 1100s, by which time most Europeans, excepting the Balts and the Prussians, had at least superficially been converted. It is the political and religious background of that period which provides a context in which to understand the missionizing intent of the *Heliand*, and the political as well.

THE SAXONS

The Roman historian Tacitus placed the precursors of the Saxons in southern Denmark, north of the Eider river, in the first century AD. According to the Greek explorer Ptolemaus, they lived in what is now Holstein (between the Eider and Elbe rivers) during the second

---

1 Originally published in James E. Cathey, ed., *Hêliand: Text and Commentary*, Medieval European Studies 2 (Morgantown: West Virginia UP, 2002), 3–28.

century AD. Kathleen Herbert describes them from the point of view of the Angles, ancestors of the English:

> South of [the Angles], in the lands around the lower Elbe and Weser, were the Suebic tribes. The first Roman writer to mention the English makes no reference to the Saxons. Like Franks, it is the name of a later confederation of tribes from this area. The Saxons were of Suebic stock; their earlier English neighbors called them *Swæfe*; later they were known as Old Saxons, to distinguish them from the folk who had crossed to Britain.[2]

The Saxons did not expand their territory beyond the Elbe until the third century but were fighting with the Franks to their south by 350 in the area between the lower Rhine and upper Weser rivers. By the 400s they were plundering the coasts of southern England and of France, and together with the Angles, some of them settled in England beginning around 450. Toward the end of the 600s the continental Saxons were as far south as the Lippe river and in Thuringia, but by the 700s the Franks were able to exert sufficient pressure to contain them to the north in Westphalia

THE EARLY MISSIONS

Up to the time shortly preceding the composition of the *Heliand*, Germanic groups were still in the process of settling their territories and frontiers. Their worldview was by definition pre-Christian. Although the Frankish king Clovis had been converted to Roman Catholicism through baptism in 496, the general population had been left largely undisturbed by missionizing efforts. Only later did the mission come, but not, as we might expect, directly northward from Rome. It rather took a long sweep through time and geography.

The effort to missionize the Saxons had its historical roots with the Celts of Roman Britain, where Christian churches had been

---

2 Kathleen Herbert, *Looking for the Lost Gods of England* (Pinner: Anglo-Saxon Books, 1994), 9.

established during the third century. From post-Roman Britain the effort of conversion proceeded to Ireland in the fourth century. The increasing settlement of England by Anglo-Saxons from the continent during the fifth century interrupted communications between Rome and Britain, and the center of the Celtic Church shifted to Ireland, a land little touched by Roman influence. The Irish, in turn, brought the Church back to Britain by establishing northern monasteries at Iona and Lindisfarne. From these outposts Irish monks preached the Gospel in Scotland and northern England, while the English south remained a mixture of pagan and Anglo-Roman Christian.

The missionizing effort conducted by the Irish did not stop at attempts to convert the Scottish Celts and Anglo-Saxons. The first great missionary to the continent was also Irish. St. Columban (born about 545) left Bangor in northern Ireland reportedly along with the apostolic number of twelve fellow monks in the decade before 600. He (and they) established monasteries adhering to the Celtic Church in what is now eastern France and, later, at Bobbio in northern Italy, where Columban died in 615 on his mission to the Lombards. One companion of Columban, Gall (born in Ireland about 550, died around 630), remained in what is now Switzerland when his patron continued on to Italy. The great monastery at St. Gallen carries his name.

The Franks had long been on the periphery of Roman influence, particularly after they entered northern Gaul, which retained a continuation of Roman administration in the form of the Gallo-Roman Church. The key turning point in the history of this Church in the West came with the conversion of the Frankish king Clovis to Roman Catholicism when, according to the story in the *History of the Franks* by Gregory of Tours, Clovis's god of battle (i.e. Wodan) failed him, whereas his calling upon Christ routed the enemy.[3] From that time on the Franks were at least nominally Catholic.

At about the same time that the Celtic Catholic Columban was establishing his Burgundian monastery at Luxeuil in the French

---

3   J. N. Hillgarth, ed., *Christianity and Paganism, 350–750: The Conversion of Western Europe*, 2nd ed. (Philadelphia: University of Pennsylvania Press, 1986), 82.

Vosges, the Roman Catholic Pope Gregory I in 596 sent a mission in the opposite direction, from Rome to Britain, led by Gregory's appointee as Bishop of London, who was later to be known as St. Augustine of Canterbury (died in 605). Augustine began the work of converting the southern Anglo-Saxons, concentrating first on their leader Ethelbert, king of Kent. His efforts resulted in the nominal baptism of allegedly ten thousand of Ethelbert's followers in the Roman Church. The ground rules for conversion were set down by Gregory in a letter sent from Rome in 601 to give guidance to Augustine. These rules stated, in part, that idols were to be removed from heathen temples, but the temples themselves should be purified by the removal of altars on which sacrifices had been performed, and Christian altars should be set up in their place. In other words, the tactic was to replace the content of the old forms, including the content (semantics) of certain vocabulary.[4] Since the kings were understood in their native, pre-Christian context as intermediaries with the gods, their conversion was always paramount. (As we will see, the ancient poetic form likewise received new content in the *Heliand*, which retains abundant allusions to older conditions.)

THE ARIAN AND MOSLEM THREATS

The great competition within Christian religiosity in Western Europe was between Roman Catholicism and Arianism, which did not hold with the unity of Father, Son, and Holy Spirit. The Burgundians and the Visigoths at the borders of Clovis's territory were Arian in belief, and converting them to Roman Catholicism was virtually equivalent in importance to converting pagan groups like the Alamanni and Saxons. Already in a letter from Bishop Avitus of Vienne to Clovis in about 496 we read the exhortation to go out and subdue pagans

---

4   See Wolfgang Hempel, *Ubermuot diu alte . . .: Der Superbia-Gedanke und seine Rolle in der deutschen Literatur des Mittelatlers*, Studien zur Germanistik, Anglistik und Komparatistik 1 (Bonn: Bouvier, 1970), 82.

(i.e. Arians) for the sake of the Christian mission:

> The followers of [Arian] error have in vain, by a cloud of contradictory and untrue opinions, sought to conceal from your extreme subtlety the glory of the Christian name. [. . .] Since God, thanks to you, will make of your people His own possession, offer a part of the treasure of Faith which fills your heart to the peoples living beyond you who, still living in natural ignorance, have not been corrupted by the seeds of perverse doctrines [that is, Arianism]. Do not fear to send them envoys and to plead with them the cause of God, who has done so much for your cause. So that the other pagan peoples, at first being subject to your empire for the sake of religion, while they still seem to have another ruler, may be distinguished rather by their race than by their prince.[5]

James C. Russell notes, however, that "[f]rom the death of Clovis in 511 until the arrival of the Irish missionary monk Columban in Gaul about 590, the progress of Christianization among the Germanic peoples, aside from the Merovingian court, was negligible," but he asserts further that "the heroic self-discipline and asceticism of Irish monasticism may have appealed to the Germanic warrior spirit" and that "[w]hatever the sources of attraction were, Columban and his followers succeeded in establishing a network of monasteries, free from local episcopal control, on the property of northern Frankish aristocrats."[6] Whether this attraction represents the continuation of pre-Christian religious control by the nobility or new ways of thinking or even so mundane a matter as the teaching of innovative methods of agriculture by the monasteries, the Church had effectively found a method of influencing the Franks and eventually recruiting them to its teaching—or perhaps it was rather that the Frankish aristocracy used the Church for the sanctioning of its domination.

---

5   Hillgarth, ed., *Christianity and Paganism* [note 3], 76–78.
6   James C. Russell, *The Germanization of Early Medieval Christianity* (Oxford: Oxford UP, 1994), 154, 156, respectively.

While England was being missionized, a competing monotheistic religion born on the Arabian Peninsula swiftly rose to power and began to threaten Europe. Mohammed moved from Mecca to Medina, proclaiming that "there is no God but God, and Mohammed is the prophet of God." By the time of his death in 632 Mohammed had kindled a religious fervor that let Islam conquer most of North Africa and Spain within the next eighty years. The Arabs were halted in 732 by Charles Martel, who defeated the Mohammedan forces at Poitiers in the middle of France. It was not obvious during these centuries that Europe as a whole would become and remain Christian. The effort to convert the Saxons approximately one hundred years after the victory at Poitiers was still part of an attempt to consolidate Europe for Christianity.

Power politics and the Church in Rome were inextricably linked during the period under consideration. Rome was under pressure from Byzantium to the east, and Europe as a whole was pressed by the Arabs coming from the south through Spain. Rome had reached a nadir of power. Syria, Palestine, North Africa, and Spain had all converted to Islam. Greece and southern Italy (Sicily and Calabria) came under the influence of the Eastern Rite in Byzantium after 731. The Germanic Lombards, who adhered to Arianism, threatened Rome from the north, and only central Italy and France remained under the Roman Church. Arianism as a rival theology ceased to be a threat to the Roman Church by the middle of the seventh century, but the disposition of the Franks seemed uncertain indeed. The position of the Pope threatened to be reduced to that solely of the bishop of Rome.

The English Mission

From southern England the next great Christian missionary journeyed south. Wynfrith, known as Boniface (born about 675, died in 754), was educated in the abbey of Nursling near Winchester. Upon being elevated to the rank of bishop in 722 he was charged by Pope

The Historical Setting of the Heliand

Gregory II to work in Germany. At Geismar, near Fritzlar in Hessia, Boniface toppled the pillar that supported the heathen worldview, a great oak dedicated to the god Thor. In not being punished by the gods for his heresies, Boniface and his fellow missionaries demonstrated the primacy of the Christian God among the heathen. The foundation by Boniface of the monastery at Fulda in 743 was less dramatic than the cutting down of the oak at Geismar but key to the ongoing effort to missionize the entire north of the continent. Thus were the first blows struck for Christianity on Saxon territory about one hundred years prior to the composition of the *Heliand* at a time when Islam was firmly established in Spain and posed a considerable threat to the Roman Church (then restricted to part of what is now Italy).

It was Boniface who began to change the situation by calling a synod in 747 at which all Thuringian, Bavarian, and Frankish bishops swore allegiance to Rome. Four years later, following the deposition of the last in the line of Merovingian kings, Pippin III (714–768) was anointed as king of the Franks in the presence of Boniface. Pippin subsequently pledged by oath in 754 to Pope Stephen II to protect the Roman Church against the Lombards, thereby effecting the rescue of Rome, which otherwise would probably have sunk to the status of a minor power. The consolidation of Frankish allegiance to and protection of Rome continued under the reign of Pippin's son Karl (768–814), known as Charlemagne, the greatest of Frankish kings.

CHARLEMAGNE AND EUROPE

Charlemagne was not the only son of Pippin III. Charlemagne and his younger brother, Karlmann, were both anointed by Pope Stephan II in 754 and along with their father, Pippin, were granted the honorific title Patricius Romanorum, which almost guaranteed later conflict. In 770 Charlemagne defied the wishes of the Pope and married the daughter of the Lombard king Desiderius in an attempt to isolate

Karlmann politically. Karlmann, however, died suddenly the following year, and Charlemagne (ignoring the rights of inheritance of Karlmann's sons) seized all of the Frankish kingdoms. He sent his wife back to her father in 771 and, now following the wishes of the Pope, he turned against Desiderius in 773. The sons of Karlmann had fled to the Lombard court, and Desiderius urged the Pope to anoint them as kings. Charlemagne prevailed, however, and took the title Rex Langobardorum.

Meanwhile, Charlemagne was also concerned about his southern flank and eventually secured the borders against the Arabs, although not before the first Frankish campaign across the Pyrenees ended with the defeat of Roland in 778. Within the following ten years, however, he extended his realm to southern France and far enough to the east to include the Bavarians.

CHARLEMAGNE AND THE SAXONS

The Saxons were the only large unconverted grouping left in the west of the continent, and Charlemagne led numerous campaigns against them in the period 772–804. Even before then Charlemagne's father Pippin had led expeditions against the Saxons in 743, 744, 747, and according to the *Royal Frankish Annals,* in 758, "went into Saxony and took the strongholds of the Saxons at Sythen by storm. And he inflicted bloody defeats on the Saxon people. They then promised to obey all his orders [. . .]."[7] The Saxons were not a single people but rather a confederation of different groups which occupied the northern German areas of Westphalia, Eastphalia, Engern, and North Albingia with their various political or juridical districts. There was no single king, and Charlemagne had to fight grueling wars against separate entities. The only one unifying instance was

---

7 Bernhard Walter Scholz and Barbara Rogers, trans., *Carolingian Chronicles: Royal Frankish Annals and Nithard's Histories* (Ann Arbor: University of Michigan Press, 1970), 13, 42.

The Historical Setting of the Heliand

an annual assembly at Marklo on the Weser River. Present at the assembly were about 3,700 representatives: the heads of the hundred political districts (*Gaue*) with thirty-six elected representatives from each district, twelve each for the three estates of the nobles, freemen, and tenant farmers. Only the thralls were excluded. During the reign of Charlemagne a strong champion emerged on the side of the Saxons in the person of the Westphalian duke Widukind, who had a strong following among all the people.

The Saxons gained strength under Widukind and took some Frankish territory to the south of Westphalia. Charlemagne recognized the danger and swore in 775 either to Christianize the Saxons or to liquidate them. He penetrated their territory to the east of the Weser for the first time in that year and met the Eastphalians near Goslar and the Engern at Bückeberg, but the Saxons did not resist. Instead Charlemagne showered the leaders of Eastphalia and Engern with gifts, and they delegated hostages to him. The Eastphalians were faced with Slavs on their eastern frontier and could scarcely afford a two-front war. The Westphalians, however, resisted, and Charlemagne was forced to fight them at Lübbecke, after which they offered hostages and swore allegiance to him.

Unfortunately for Charlemagne, this brief foray into Saxon territory and the co-opting of some leaders of the Eastphalians, Westphalians, and Engern did not result in the pacification of the whole area. In 777 he moved with a large army to Paderborn and convened the Frankish assembly there on Saxon territory, at which location he also ordered the Saxons to convene their assembly. Charlemagne required those whose representatives attended to pledge to him and to the Christian faith their fealty or risk losing their freedom and property. Those Saxons then promised loyalty to him and accepted Christianity, which meant in effect that the southern part of Saxon territory became part of Charlemagne's Frankish lands. A mass baptism took place, and Abbot Sturm from the newly-founded monastery at Fulda, with its approximately four hundred monks, took charge of further religious instruction. However, because of the procedure followed by the monks from Fulda in setting baptism as the first goal of their mission—and in mercilessly carrying it out by destroying all heathen cult sites—they triggered a reaction on the part of the Saxons.

Widukind had not challenged Charlemagne up to this point but had instead withdrawn to the protection of the Danish court. After the aggressive behavior of the monks from Fulda, however, the general populace was prepared to resist this strange and seemingly destructive new religion and united in great numbers behind Widukind, who in 778 led a campaign that destroyed churches and cloisters in the west of the territory all the way to Deutz by Cologne and south to the mouth of the river Lahn. Only a defense by the Alemans and East Franconians saved the monastery at Fulda. Charlemagne countered in 779 by moving back into Saxon territory, and all went as before. The Eastphalians and Engern gave hostages and cooperated. Charlemagne reshuffled the structure of the mission, and the situation quieted. He made his next move in 780, when he called together an assembly at the source of the river Lippe at which he partitioned Saxony into missionary dioceses and appointed bishops, priests, and abbots from other parts of his territories to run them: the Bishop of Würzburg went to Paderborn, the Abbot of the cloister at Amorbach went to Verden, and so on. Charlemagne was back in Italy in 781, and all was quiet in Saxony.

In 782 Charlemagne held another assembly at Lippspringe, this time to dissolve the old Saxon political structure. Instead of bringing in Frankish nobility, he installed Saxons from notable families as dukes on the Frankish model in an effort to co-opt at least part of the previously loosely-organized political system.

Widukind and his followers reacted strongly to the confiscation of property, the introduction of mandatory tithing, and the overthrow of the old way of government by annual assembly. This time he and his troops attacked missionaries and the newly-installed dukes and nobles. Charlemagne ordered loyal Eastphalians, Palatinates, and allied Saxons, together with Frankish forces, to meet Widukind. Charlemagne's forces were wiped out almost completely. Charlemagne hurried north and conferred with the leader of his loyal Saxon troops, after which the survivors of the battle against Widukind were marched up, and he had them all executed. Even though Widukind won the battle, he must, however, have also suffered great losses, since he returned to the Danes after this victory.

Charlemagne persevered and in 783 led a campaign to Detmold, where the Saxons had prepared to do battle. He won a bloody victory and withdrew to Paderborn to await reinforcements. His next move was to the river Hase where he won a bitter battle against Saxon forces. In spite of these successes, a new campaign was necessary in 784, but nothing decisive came of it. Charlemagne convened the assembly again in Paderborn in 785, but no record survives of what transpired there. In any case, following the assembly of 785 there were no more hostilities in the middle and southern territories. Charlemagne began negotiations with Widukind, and they exchanged hostages. The result was that Widukind, along with his hostages from Charlemagne, traveled to Attiguy and was baptized there in 785. Charlemagne himself was Widukind's sponsor.

THE CONSOLIDATION OF POWER

The law known as *Capitulatio de partibus Saxoniae* came into force on October 28, 797, in which it was stipulated that only the king, Charlemagne in this case, could convene a Saxon assembly. The position of the Church was strengthened in that the death penalty was imposed for heathen belief and practices. Attendance at mass and the hearing of sermons as well as tithing was made obligatory. The Saxons had to build new churches, each with a house of worship and two manses. For every group of one hundred and twenty men, a servant and a servant girl had to be assigned for work in the church. In other words, the draconian measures that had led to the rebellion in 778 were codified and legally reinforced, but the struggle continued for the northern territories, and Charlemagne was involved until 804 with subduing Saxon groups there.

As in the advice given by Pope Gregory I in his letter of 601, the leader was here again the key figure in the process of conversion. After Widukind submitted to baptism, the missionaries had an easier time converting the populace. The *Heliand* was likely still a part of the effort of persuasion and pacification when it was composed some forty years after Widukind's baptism.

Semantic Hurdles to the Task of Conversion

One overriding concern is the meaning (semantics) of the Old Saxon words in the work of conversion to Christianity. Deep cultural divides had to be crossed on the way to conversion, not the least of which was the gap between a world-accepting native religiosity and a world-rejecting, extra-mundane religion, Christianity.[8] Putting missionaries in the field among uncomprehending or even hostile Saxons was hazardous enough, but perhaps the most difficult practical problem was the translation of Christian concepts, since the pre-Christian Saxon conception of the world and of behavior in it were at considerable odds with the message of Christianity.

The Saxons practiced some form of religion common to Germanic groups. There was no uniform ritual but various forms were tolerated, that is, there was no one specific way to worship but rather many ways to (attempt to) gain the favor of the gods. Sacred springs and trees were worshiped, and there were cult sites. The monk Ruodolf of Fulda (died in 865) reported that the Saxons also worshiped in open air a wooden idol of considerable size that was placed vertically. They called it the *Irmensûl*, a world pillar (as has been worshiped by various groups in various parts of the world). There was a store of

---

8   See Russell, *The Germanization* [note 6].

treasure at the temple, where gods called Saxnot (perhaps another name for Wodan), Thor, and others were honored.[9] To the Saxon mind the world was ruled by forces in it, not apart from it. When the world perished at the end of our time, everything including the gods would go down with it. Thus one of the primary messages to be imparted was of a God that stands eternally beyond the visible.

Perhaps more troublesome were socio-cultural standards that had to be overthrown in order that Christianity might prosper. The very vocabulary with which this new religion had to be described contained meanings at odds with the Christian message, most particularly as regards the place of the individual among other members of society and the attitude of the individual toward God. The missionaries had to persuade converts that the proper attitude was one of humility before God and good will towards their fellow humans, but Old Saxon had no native word to render the Latin term *humilitas*. The pre-Christian mindset was rather the opposite, and the words with which the new message had to be conveyed were in themselves frequently opposite to what was meant. It was thus necessary for the mission to persevere and subvert old words to convey new meanings, since imported words from Latin would necessarily have remained in a foreign realm apart from daily life.

The Germanic ethic required behavior that, according to Christian sensibility was understood as *superbia*. To the traditional Germanic—and thus Saxon—mindset, the egocentric goal of achieving fame in this world as an individual (and proper status for one's family) was all that would live on after one's death. Tales told of dead heroes constituted the only transcendent realm in a world defined merely by what is here and now.

Fame was attained not through good works but rather through glorious and brave deeds on one's own behalf and/or against one's

---

9 A brief description of this is to be found in Achim Leube, "Die Sachsen," in *Die Germanen: Geschichte und Kultur der germanischen Stämme in Mitteleuropa*, ed. Bruno Krüger, 2 vols. (Berlin: Akademie, 1979–83), 2:468

opponents. Positive words for praise, including adjectives like *bald* 'brave, bold', *frôkni* 'bold', *gêl* 'boisterous', and *oƀarmôdig* 'proud', or nouns like *êra* 'honor', *gelp* 'terrifying battle cry', or *hrôm* 'fame', were not matched by words in the Saxon vocabulary like *reticent, modest, gentle,* or *humble*. Belief in one's own might was paramount.

The egocentric native concepts of honor, fame, etc. were not directly confronted by the Church, since this would have been counterproductive. Russell writes:

> The notion of Christian honor, with its goal of individual salvation, directly opposed the supremacy of the Germanic concept of [. . .] the bond of kinship which could be extended to others through an oath of loyalty. [. . .] This bond included the duty to avenge a kinsman or lord's death, as well as the obligation to follow one's lord into battle, even if death was imminent. To survive one's lord in battle was cause for disgrace, exceeded in shamefulness only by acts of cowardice and outright betrayal.[10]

Although the societal context was not chaotic, not "every man for himself," homicide was a common means of achieving individual goals, be it for the maintenance of property rights or in order to gain renown as a member of a fighting troop. Great leaders attained their position through eloquence, bravery, and strength, and their followers gained fame in turn for the same qualities along with their faithfulness to their leader. There was a strong bond to kinship and prestige group, but these bonds were maintained through individual strength instead of humanitarian sympathy. Ethical values were posited on individual qualities instead of considerations for the good of the group. Hempel writes, "The Church is thus required repeatedly to condemn manslaughter, [. . .] vengeance, [. . .] abduction [. . .] as mortal sins and to pay great attention to them in moral teachings as well as law."[11] The Church in its preaching focused on the deadly

---

10 Russell, *The Germanization* [note 6], 121.
11 Hempel, *Ubermuot diu alte* [note 4], 53: "Daher ist die Kirche genötigt, in Morallehre wie Gesetz immer wieder den Totschlag [. . .], die Rache, [. . .], den Raub [. . .] als Totsünden zu brandmarken und ihnen breite Aufmerksamkeit

sins of homicide, revenge, and pillage.

To convey the message of Christian charity and ego-denying *humilitas*, the native words that were negative and pejorative in the context of Christian sensibilities were employed with the (indeed eventually realized) hope that the Christian content would also convert their meanings.[12] Subversion of the vocabulary was the only possible method available to spread the Gospel. As Russell puts it:

> Instead of directly confronting this opposing value system and attempting to radically transform it—an approach which almost certainly would have resulted in an immediate rejection of Christianity—the missionaries apparently sought to redefine the Germanic virtues of strength, courage, and loyalty in such a manner that would reduce their incompatibility with Christian values, while at the same time 'inculturating' Christian values as far as possible to accommodate the Germanic ethos and world-view.[13]

To Saxons presented with the story of Christ in the form of the *Heliand*, a work necessarily written in a way that would appeal to a pre-Christian or newly converted audience, the choice of vocabulary that rang with old associations and carried old meanings must have clashed, at least somewhat, with the religious world of the story.

In some cases, however, the old meanings and cultural values may have actually helped to illustrate the Gospel story that the poet was recasting for his Saxon audience. G. Ronald Murphy, in his analysis of the use of light and bright imagery, argues interestingly that the author of the *Heliand* relied on the use of bright images and light in John's Gospel to portray a path from birth into this "light" and death into the "other light" in analogy with images from Germanic mythology, such as that of *bifröst*, a bridge of light (rainbow) from this world to the abode beyond earthly existence.[14]

---

zu widmen."
12 See ibid., 57.
13 Russell, *The Germanization* [note 6], 121.
14 G. Ronald Murphy, "The Light Worlds of the *Heliand*," *Monatshefte* 89

James E. Cathey

THE POEM

The Old Saxon *Heliand* is preserved in 5,983 lines of verse edited from the M and C manuscripts (see The Manuscripts below). The work was composed during the long period of decline of Germanic culture and slow encroachment of European culture during which Christianity had begun to replace ancient forms of worship, while the poetic forms, although not given up, were abandoning their strict alliterative and metrical constraints everywhere on the continent. The *Heliand* shows a mixture of the more strictly controlled old poetic form and a discursive, prose-like overlay (see Heliand Verse below).

Although the new culture was slowly and against considerable odds being introduced to northern Germany from monasteries at Fulda or Werden (as Richard Drögereit argued) or Corvey (which is Klaus Gantert's position),[15] the old culture had very deep roots indeed. Throughout the corpus of the *Heliand* there are words and phrases whose semantic content at least historically referred to conditions of earlier belief and behavior, although it seems clear that by the time of the composition of the work many of the meanings had changed. Nevertheless, we can wonder what reactions certain words and phrases would have triggered in a contemporary audience still cognizant of (or even still practicing) pre-Christian habits of thought.

The assumption here is that, because of its traditional alliterative form, the *Heliand* was written to be read aloud. Burkhard Taeger discusses the musical notation found over lines 310–313 in manuscript

(1997), 5–17.

15 See Richard Drögereit, "Die Heimat des Heliand," *Jahrbuch der Gesellschaft für niedersächsische Kirchengeschichte* 49 (1951), 1–18, repr. in *Sachsen, Angelsachsen, Niedersachsen: Ausgewählte Aufsätze in einem dreibändigen Werk*, by Drögereit, ed. Carl Röper and Herbert Huster, 3 vols. (Hamburg: Commercium, 1978), 3:51–68; idem, *Werden und der Heliand: Studien zur Kulturgeschichte der Abtei Werden und zur Herkunft des Heliand* (Essen: Fredebeul & Koenen, 1951); and Klaus Gantert, *Akkomodation und eingeschriebener Kommentar: Untersuchungen zur Übertragungsstrategie des Heliandichters* (Tübingen: Narr, 1998).

The Historical Setting of the Heliand

M and tentatively concludes "[. . .] that the *Heliand* can also be viewed as intended for a 'half-liturgical' use."¹⁶ The question of which audience it addressed cannot be settled with finality. Perhaps it was intended as an exercise for monks or even as mealtime devotionals read aloud to them. Perhaps it was written in order to be read (or "sung") in episodes before groups of potential converts who had already suffered baptism by coercion and who now needed to be persuaded of the validity of the new faith. Drögereit hypothesizes that "the unknown poet, probably a Frisian, composed his sermon-epic not for monks but for noble ladies in one of the many religious communities of canonesses, namely in Essen."¹⁷

The question of the site of composition has been debated for a century and a half. The general body of opinion tends to favor Fulda because, among other reasons, the *Heliand* reflects the commentary on Matthew written by the Abbot of Fulda, Hrabanus Maurus, and because there was a copy of the work known as *Tatian* there. A version of *Tatian* was used as a basis for the structure of the *Heliand*. There are, however, arguments in favor of other monasteries. Drögereit favors Werden on paleographic evidence, namely the fact that only at Werden was the letter <ƀ> used, which is characteristic of the M and P manuscripts, and on the evidence of the presence of Frisian monks there. The *Heliand* evinces so-called Frisianisms in the spellings <kiasan> and <niate> in lines 223 and 224. These views are, however, challenged by Bernhard Bischoff, who claims

---

16 Burkhard Taeger, "Ein vergessener handschriftlicher Befund: Die Neumen im Münchener *Heliand*," *Zeitschrift für deutsches Altertum und deutsche Literatur* 107 (1978), 192: "[. . .] daß auch der 'Heliand' vor dem Horizont halbliturgischen Gebrauchs zu sehen sein dürfte."

17 Richard Drögereit, "Die schriftlichen Quellen zur Christianisierung der Sachsen und ihre Aussagefähigkeit," in *Die Eingliederung der Sachsen in das Frankenreich*, ed. Walther Lammers (Darmstadt: Wissenschaftliche Buchgesellschaft, 1970), 465: "der unbekannte Dichter, wohl ein Friese, [verfaßte] sein Predigt-Epos nicht einmal für Mönche, sondern für adlige Damen in einem der zahlreichen Kanonissenstifte, nämlich Essen."

that many manuscripts that Drögereit attributes to Werden were instead brought there from the monasteries at Corbie in France or its Saxon offshoot Corvey, or from elsewhere—or they were never there at all.[18] Another scholar, Willy Krogmann, believes that Fulda must be excluded as a site of composition on the basis of the word *pâscha* instead of *ôstar/ôstarun* for "Easter." The latter word was used only in the Archdiocese of Mainz, and Fulda was in its territory. Werden was under the Archdiocese of Cologne, where *pâscha* was the term for "Easter," and Krogmann also adduces the paleographic evidence of <ƀ> in favor of Werden.[19] Gantert points out that the sons of Saxon nobility had been schooled in Corbie in the Picardy and were then instrumental in founding the monastery at Corvey in 815 on Saxon territory, which at least would have provided a fertile ground for the reception of the *Heliand*.[20]

In any case, whether composed at Fulda or Werden or Essen, the *Heliand* adheres faithfully to the Christian Gospel while the work is couched in terms acceptable to a northern audience familiar with stories of Germanic mythology and historical culture presented in alliterative verse.

HELIAND VERSE

Pre-literate societies preserve their literary monuments in memorized, oral form. Essential to long recitations is a mnemonic code to cue

---

18 Bernhard Bischoff, Review of *Werden und der Heliand: Studien zur Kulturgeschichte der Abtei Werden und zur Herkunft des Heliand*, by Richard Drögereit, *Anzeiger für deutsches Altertum* 66 (1952), 7–12.
19 Willy Krogmann, "Die Praefatio in librum aniquum lingua Saxonica Conscriptum," in *Der Heliand*, ed. Jürgen Eichhoff and Irmengard Rauch, Wege der Forschung 321 (Darmstadt: Wissenschaftliche Buchgesellschaft, 1973), 25–26.
20 Gantert, *Akkomodation* [note 15]. For a summary of paleographic and other evidence (or lack of the same) regarding the provenance of the *Heliand*, see Thomas L. Markey, *A North Sea Germanic Reader* (Munich: Fink, 1976), 259ff.

The Historical Setting of the Heliand

speakers when memory lags. The Germanic code had as a constant, over the span of centuries, alliteration and a fixed number of dynamic stresses per line. In the simplest and perhaps original form, the "long line" consisted of eight syllables containing four stresses, two in each "half line" on either side of a pause (Latin *caesura*; German *Zäsur*). Schematically, we can represent a basic line as

$$/ \smile / \smile \quad / \smile / \smile$$

where the / indicates a stressed syllable and ˘ an unstressed syllable.

Alliteration was superimposed on the pattern of stresses. (A certain leeway in filling the syllables, which is called *Füllungsfreiheit* in German, was allowed.) The term alliteration (German *Stabreim*) indicates an initial "rhyme" of consonants or vowels with each other in such a manner that certain specified stressed syllables each begin either with the same single consonant, with identical clusters of initial *s*- plus a consonant, or with initial vowels of any quality. (End rhyme, which affected unstressed syllables, did not play a role here and—in any case—was a later borrowing, perhaps from Latin hymns.) The key position was the first stress in the second "half line" (the third stressed syllable from the beginning of the "long line"), which should contain a "heavy" syllable defining the alliteration of the whole line. (A "heavy" syllable is one that has a stressed vowel followed by a consonant cluster or one that has a diphthong.) That is, if the third stressed syllable started with /h/, then the first stressed syllable had to, and commonly the second stressed syllable then also started with /h/. The fourth stress (second stress in the second "half line") could not alliterate. An ancient example in North Germanic is found on the Gallehus horn from about AD 400:

> ek hlewagastiR holtijar   horna tawidō
> 'I Hlewagast, son of Holt, made this horn.'

James E. Cathey

In the Gallehus inscription we hear alliteration on the /h/ in /horn-/ in the first and second stressed syllable, and we also find various unstressed syllables, including one before the first stress in /hlewa-/. The presence of an initial unstressed syllable (Greek *anacrusis*; German *Auftakt*), here /ek/, is thus also an ancient feature of the poetic form, which is much used and expanded on in the *Heliand*—also before stressed syllables other than the first.

The *Heliand* does not, on the whole, represent an ideal of alliterative verse. Dynamic stress played less of a role in Old Saxon than in earlier stages of the Germanic dialects, and the author was constrained to proselytize with a theologically sound message as well as to entertain. We are thus confronted with a great mixture of lines varying from what might be termed "pure" alliterative to almost prose-like poetry. Within close proximity of each other one finds a variety of lines, as in the sequence 978–981. An example of a rather well-formed line in the historical alliterative tradition is:

> 978: dôpte allan dag   druhtfolc mikil

In this line we see that the third (and "heavy") syllable /druht/ in *druhtfolc* (a noun: 'retainers, people') sets the alliteration, which is carried through in the verb *dôpte* 'baptized' and *dag* in the phrase *allan dag* 'all day' in the first and second stresses. The fourth stressed syllable, /mi-/ in *mikil* (an adjective: 'great') properly lacks alliteration. Line 979 is also fairly well-formed, although it contains a few extra unstressed syllables. This line alliterates on /w/, here again on a noun phrase (*uualdand Krist* 'ruling Christ') in the key third position:

> 979: uuerod an uuatere   endi ôk uualdand Krist.

The next line, 980, is also a good example, this time alliterating in /h/ on the third stress in the phrase *handan sînun* 'with his hands':

> 980: hêran heƀencuning   handun sînun.

The Historical Setting of the Heliand

An example of a more typical line in the *Heliand* is 981, which properly alliterates in /b/ but shows many more unstressed syllables:

981: an allaro baðo them bezton   endi im thar te bedu gihnêg

In this last example we find a fairly long anacrusis before the first alliterating syllable in *baðo* and a very long unstressed anacrusis before the key alliteration in the third stressed syllable in *bedu* ("and bowed [*gihnêg*] there to him in prayer [*te bedu*]"). Although line 981 alliterates, it is so filled out with unaccented syllables that it is more discursive while yet still true to the poetic convention. David R. McLintock has this to say about the form of the *Heliand*:

> The biblical epic in alliterative verse flourished in England, and the *Heliand* may have been composed in imitation of such works as a consequence of Anglo-Saxon participation in the conversion of the Saxons. A literary link with England is attested not only by the Cotton manuscript but also by the existence of an Old English translation of the *Genesis* (the so-called *Genesis B*). Differences in verse technique may be explained partly by the differing grammars of the two languages. Notable features of Old Saxon verse are density of alliteration and the proliferation of unstressed syllables, especially before the first ictus of the *b* verse [the second half line].[21]

Much has been written about alliterative verse and about the language of the *Heliand*; Winfred P. Lehmann and Alger N. Doane have each provided good overviews of the subject.[22]

---

21 David R. McLintock, "Heliand," in *Dictionary of the Middle Ages*, ed. Joseph R. Strayer et al., 13 vols. (New York: Scribner, 1982–1989), 6:150.
22 Winfred P. Lehmann, "The Alliteration of Old Saxon Poetry," in *Der Heliand*, ed. Jürgen Eichhoff and Irmengard Rauch, Wege der Forschung 321 (Darmstadt: Wissenschaftliche Buchgesellschaft, 1973), 144–76; Alger N. Doane, ed., *The Saxon Genesis: An Edition of the West Saxon Genesis B and the Old Saxon Vatican Genesis* (Madison: University of Wisconsin Press, 1978).

James E. Cathey

The Dating of the Heliand and the Praefatio

The letter <ƀ> is found during a short period *only* in manuscripts from the abbey in Werden, which was founded around the year 800, namely in a Latin-Old Saxon glossary from about 850 and particularly in the tax lists from about 900. We can also reconstruct this <ƀ> from the original manuscript of the third Vita Liudgers, the Frisian founder of Werden, which was written there in about 864.[23]

A certain form of large <N> also appearing in the M and P manuscripts of the *Heliand* was written that way only in Werden up to the period in question.[24] This dating (post 850), which Drögereit first establish in 1951,[25] contradicts the previous accepted dating made on the basis of the Latin *Praefatio*.

The Latin *Praefatio et Versus* is customarily divided into *Praefatio A*, *Praefatio B*, and *Versus*. Although the preface has not been seen physically attached to any manuscript of the *Heliand*—at least since its publication by Flacius Illyricus in 1562—there is internal and external evidence that the two at one time were connected. The *Praefatio A* describes the commissioning of a translation of the New Testament with the words:

> Præcepit namq[ue] cuidam uiro de gente Saxonum, qui apud suos non ignobilis Vates habebatur, ut [uetus ac] nouum Testamentum in Germanicam linguam poetice transferre studeret, quatenus non solum literatis, uerum etiam inliteratis sacra diuinorum præceptorum lectio panderetur.

---

23   Richard Drögereit, "Die Heimat des Heliand" [note 15], 3:53:: "[ƀ] begegnet während einer kurzen Periode nur in Quellen der um 800 gegründeten Abtei Werden, und zwar in einem lateinisch-altsächsischen Glossar von ca. 850 und vor allem in den Werdener Heberegistern von ca. 900. Wir können dieses [ƀ] ferner noch für die etwa 864 dort abgefaßte Originalhandschrift der dritten Vita Liudgers, des friesischen Gründers Werdens, erschließen."
24   Ibid., 3:54.
25   Drögereit, *Werden und der Heliand* [note 15].

> [For he ordered a certain man of the Saxon people who was deemed among them to be no inglorious bard to devote himself to a poetic translation into the German language of the Old and New Testaments so that the holy reading of the divine commandments might be diffused not only to the literate but also to the illiterate.]

This passage has been thoroughly dissected by Krogmann, among others, and revealed to have its faults, including words and phrases added at a date later than its original composition.[26] Thus the phrase *vetus ac* is perhaps among them, although it could be taken to refer to the Old Saxon *Genesis* if the *Praefatio* was introductory to both works. The grammatical subject of *præcepit* is *Ludouuicus pijssimus Augustus*, identified by most scholars as Louis the Pious (Ludwig der Fromme), who ruled from 813 to 840. The *Praefatio* thus seems to establish a *terminus ante quem* of Louis's death date, if the perfect form *præcepit* is understood to mean that the *Heliand* was commissioned during his lifetime—and if *Ludouuicus pijssimus Augustus* indeed refers to the Louis the Pious. Drögereit points out, however, that a son of Louis the Pious, Louis the German, was called *augustus* in the year of his birth in 805, which—if this is the correct *Ludouuicus*—would push the possible dating of composition to his death in 876.[27] Against this argument stand the dating of the manuscripts and fragments, of which three can be restricted to about 850.[28]

The prose *Praefatio B* is a rendering of Bede's story of Caedmon's dream, in which the poet, a simple herdsman, while asleep receives divine impulse to compose in verse. The *Versus* relates basically the same poetically, establishing the modest credentials of the divinely inspired, humble man of the countryside.[29]

---

26 Krogmann, "Die Praefatio" [note 19].
27 Drögereit, "Die Heimat des *Heliand*" [note 15].
28 This introduction was written before the discovery of the Leipzig fragment in 2006. On the significance of the latter, see the articles printed in this volume.
29 See Theodore M. Andersson, "The Caedmon Fiction in the *Heliand* Preface," *PMLA* (1974), 278–84.

The *terminus post quem* for the composition is generally linked to the composition of Hrabanus's commentary on Matthew, which was finished in 822.

The allusion to Caedmon and his dream-inspired talent as a poet serves to set the *Heliand* in a tradition of Germanic divinely-inspired eloquence. Richard North, in discussing the "unflawed gift" of poetry, cites Cynewulf's *Elene* and claims that "Cynewulf's poetic predecessors [...] before the conversion [...] believed in the divinely invested integrity of poetic skill."[30] The *Heliand* makes many allusions to the prestige and importance associated with speaking eloquently, which we can with some certainty view as an attribute of leadership as practiced in earlier times; I have expanded on this topos elsewhere.[31] Of course, the *Heliand* itself was written in alliterative verse for reasons of prestige and as an aid to its reception among the Saxons.

THE MANUSCRIPTS

The surviving manuscripts are the M in Munich, the C in the British Library, the P in Berlin (formerly in Prague), the S found at Straubing, and the V at the Vatican. M and C descend from a common prior manuscript *CM, while P and V seem to stand apart from that and from each other. According to Taeger there are indications for a connection SM as against C but also for CS against M, a finding which demands further clarification.[32] Later, Taeger admits the possibility that identical mistakes in C and M could have been made independently by different scribes, and he also postulates a common line of

---

30 Richard North, *Pagan Words and Christian Meanings* (Amsterdam: Rodopi, 1991), 26.
31 James E. Cathey, "Die Rhetorik der Weisheit und Beredtheit im *Hêliand*," *Literaturwissenschaftliches Jahrbuch* 37 (1996), 31–46.
32 Burkhard Taeger, "Das Straubinger 'Heliand'-Fragment: Philologische Untersuchungen," *Beiträge zur Geschichte der deutschen Sprache und Literatur* 101 (1979), 181–228.

The Historical Setting of the Heliand

descent connecting C and P, evidently posterior to *CM.[33] In any case, he correctly states: "A complete stemma is of course not completely demonstrable when, beyond the two manuscripts, it is constructed only from fragments that do not overlap."[34] From these manuscripts, chiefly C and M, 5,983 lines can be edited to make up our readings of the *Heliand*. There is evidence also for a lost manuscript *L from the library in Leipzig, about which very little is known.

The Monacensis (M) manuscript in Munich dates from the ninth century and still contains seventy-five leafs. The original was larger by at least six, although it is not clear by exactly how many, since the first is missing along with gaps after leafs 33, 37, 50, 57, 67, and a larger one after leaf 75. M is considered the best manuscript in spite of its missing beginning and ending in that its language is relatively consistent and is written in just one hand. Drögereit claims it for the scriptorium at Werden,[35] while Bischoff states flatly that "manuscript M was written at Corvey."[36]

Cotton Caligula A. VII, the C manuscript, is younger than M and is likely to be from the tenth century. C contains more corrections than M and shows less consistency in its forms. Franconian features are more prominent, especially in the diphthongization of Saxon /e:/, spelled <ê>, to /ie/, spelled <ie>, and of /o:/, <ô>, to /uo/, <uo>, and in the third plural present indicative ending *-ent*. Robert Priebsch placed the site of composition of C in England at

---

33 See his introduction in Otto Behaghel, ed., *Heliand und Genesis*, 10th ed., rev. Burkhard Taeger, Aldeutsche Textbibliothek 4 (Tübingen: Max Niemeyer, 1996).

34 Taeger, "Das Straubinger 'Heliand'-Fragment" [note 32], 187: "Ein vollständiger Stammbaum ist natürlich nicht voll erweisbar, wenn er außer aus zwei Handschriften nur aus Fragmenten konstruiert wird, die sich an keiner Stelle überlagern."

35 Drögereit, *Werden und der Heliand* [note 15].

36 Bernhard Bischoff, "Die Schriftheimat der Münchener Heliand-Handschrift," *Beiträge zur Geschichte der deutschen Sprache und Literatur* [Tübingen] 101 (1979), 161: "die Handschrift M ist in Corvey geschrieben."

Winchester, perhaps by a Saxon scribe.[37] C contains the beginning of the *Heliand*, but lacks its ending.

The manuscript in Berlin (P) consists of a single leaf from around the year 850 containing lines 958–1006. As noted above, it is allied to manuscript C and descended along with it from a postulated *CP.

The Vatican manuscript (V) contains excerpts from the Old Saxon *Genesis* along with lines 1279–1358 of the *Heliand* and is from the third quarter of the ninth century. Since only V maintains the original reading of line 1303 as against the shortened version in M and the altered one in C, it is revealed as independent of and anterior to *CM.[38]

Manuscript S, which was discovered only in December of 1977 during a search for fragments of Carolingian manuscripts in the libraries of Straubing, is furthest removed from *CM, descending along with M from a postulated *MS. (A key to the relationship of S with M is line 508, where S has *antheti*—with an accent mark over the <n>—M has *anthehti*, but C has *an ehti*.) The fragment is badly mangled, since it was used in the binding of a *Weltchronik* from 1493, but contains 25 lines grouped in bunches between lines 351 and 722. S can be dated to around the year 850.

THE FITTS

The entire *Heliand* was composed in what perhaps were seventy-five episodes or divisions, called "fitts" (German *Fitten*). The Latin *Praefatio* describes a way in which the *poeta* divided the episodic composition into fitts, using the word in the accusative plural form *vitteas* as a direct loan from Old Saxon, but only the C manuscript indicates the division of the narrative into fitts, which was the Anglo-Saxon practice at the time. Johannes Rathofer, in his

---

37 Robert Priebsch, *The Heliand Manuscript Cotton Caligula A. VII in the British Museum: A Study* (Oxford: Clarendon, 1925).
38 Behaghel, ed., *Heliand und Genesis* [note 33], xvii.

interesting but controversial book, describes a symmetry around the center that involves the thirteen central fitts (symbolizing Christ and the Twelve) with the account of the Transfiguration (fitt 38) in the middle.³⁹ The whole work is, according to Rathofer, divided into thirds by fitts in the proportion 31–13–31. He furthermore sees a second pattern in the form of a cross (a *figura crucis*) that involves the number four.⁴⁰ The first and final twenty-two fitts thus constitute the horizontal bars of such a cross, while the central thirty-one form vertical bars of fifteen each, with fitt thirty-eight again in the center. The first fitt itself is, according to Rathofer, symbolically structured with the numbers three (the Trinity) and four (the Four Evangelists). He adduces much material to support his hypotheses and, taken on their own terms, his arguments seem persuasive. Almost needless to say, Rathofer's views have drawn considerable fire. Alois Wolf concludes that "the author of the *Heliand* gave a numerical structure to this fitt. [. . .] The 'sacred counting' of epic variations can, however, not be confirmed."⁴¹ Gerhard Cordes, in a lengthy review, comes to the blunt conclusion: "If you once again look through the arguments given above, not a single one holds up in spite of all the energy and care invested. The 'plan of construction' cannot be proven for the *Heliand*."⁴²

---

39 Johannes Rathofer, *Der Heliand: Theologischer Sinn als tektonische Form. Vorbereitung und Grundlegung der Interpretation*, Niederdeutsche Studien 9 (Cologne: Bohlau, 1962).
40 Ibid., 561.
41 Alois Wolf, "Beobachtungen zur ersten Fitte des Heliand," *Niederdeutsches Jahrbuch* 98/99 (1975/1976), 20: "der Helianddichter [. . .] [hat] dieser Fitte zahlhafte Struktur verliehen. [. . .] Das [. . .] 'geistliche Zählen' epischer Variationen bestätigte sich aber nicht."
42 Gerhard Cordes, Review of *Der Heliand: Theologischer Sinn als tektonische Form. Vorbereitung und Grundlegung der Interpretation*, by Johannes Rathofer, *Anzeiger für deutsches Altertum* 78 (1967), 78: "Wenn man die obigen Ausführungen noch einmal durchsieht, hat doch eigentlich—bei allem Fleiß und aller Vorsicht—kein einziges Argument Stich gehalten. Der 'Bauplan' ist auch für den *Heliand* nicht

Anatoly Liberman points out that "the poem is too long to be read straight through from beginning to end, so its attractiveness must have been based on something other than number symbolism and the like."[43] Murphy sees the Transfiguration as being at the center of the narrative but that "due to the formal unwieldiness of the Gospel story itself, the poet could not order the entirety of the Gospel's incidents into parallel episodes in his composition, but rather selected a number of them based on the his spiritual insight into their appropriateness."[44] Murphy states in reference to the Transfiguration on the mountaintop that it

> suggests two other mountain scenes in the epic in which the author brings the Gospel story to a striking climax in Germanic imagery: the epic 'battle scene' on Mt. Olivet, in which Peter defends his Chieftain with the sword, and the brilliant recasting of Christ's teachings in Germanic terms in the Sermon on the Mount. The scene on Mt. Olivet is in song 58, exactly twenty songs away from the Transfiguration's song [fitt 38], and the Sermon on the Mount reaches the conclusion of its first part in song 18—also twenty songs away from song 38. I do not think that this placement is accidental.[45]

Murphy then proposes his own scheme of parallel episodes, advocating a structure based on a symmetrical arrangement around the scenes brilliantly illuminated on the three mountains with images of light.[46]

---

zu beweisen."
43 Anatoly Liberman, "Heliand," in *Dictionary of Literary Biography*, vol. 148, ed. Will Hasty and James Hardin (New York: Gale Research, 1995), 194.
44 G. Ronald Murphy, *The Heliand: The Saxon Gospel* (New York: Oxford UP, 1992), 222.
45 Ibid., 224.
46 Ibid., 229.

The Historical Setting of the Heliand

A Comparison of the M and C Manuscripts

Here we present a side-by-side comparison of the same excerpt—lines 2906b to 2919a—in order to illustrate particularly the kinds of orthographic distinctions that obtain between them. The sample is taken from the edition of Eduard Sievers, who provides facing pages that, where possible, show matching lines in manuscripts M and C; also compare these lines with those in the normalization provided in Behaghel and Taeger's edition, which is also printed below.[47]

Manuscript M	Manuscript C
Tho letun sie *an* suidean strom hohhurnid skip hluttron udeon skedan skir uuater. Skred lioht dages, sunne uuard an sedle; the seolidandean naht nebulo biuuarp; nathidun erlos forduuardes an flod: uuard thiu fiorthe tid thera nahtes cuman – neriendo Crist uuarode thea uuaglidand – tho uuard uuind mikil, hoh uueder afhaben: hlamodun udeon storm an strome; stridiun feridun thea uueros uuider uuinde: uuas im uured hugi, sebo sorgono ful: selbon ni uuandun lagulidandea an land cumen thurh thes uuederes geuuin.	Thuo lietun sia an suithean strom hohhurnid scip hluttron uthion scedan scirana uuatar. Scred lioht dages, sunno uuarthe an sedle; thia seolithandiun naht neflu biuuarp; nathidun erlos forthuuardes an fluod: uuarth thiu fiorða tid thera nahtes kuman —neriendi Crist uuaroda thiu uuaglithand –: thuo uuarth uuind mikil ho uueder ahaban: hlamodun uthion, strom an stamne; stridion feridun thia uueros uuidar uuinde: uuas im uureth hugi, seƀo sorogono full: selbon ni uuandun lagolithanda an land cumin thuru thes uuedares giuuin.

The first difference to strike one is in the spelling. Not only do these two versions differ from each other, but they are also different from the following:

---

47   Eduard Sievers, ed., *Heliand* (Halle: Waisenhaus, 1878); Behaghel, ed., *Heliand und Genesis* [note 33].

Thô lêtun *sie suîðean* strôm,
hôh hurnidskip hluttron ûðeon,
skêðan *skîr* uuater. Skêd lioht dages,
sunne uuarðan sedle; the *sêolîðandean*
2910 naht *neƀulo* biuuarp; nâðidun erlos
forðuuardes an flôd; uuarð thiu fiorðe tid
thera nahtes cuman —*neriendo* Crist
uuarode *thea uuâglîðand* –: thô uuarð uuind mikil,
hôh uueder *afhaƀen*: hlamodun ûðeon,
2915 *strôm* an *stamne*; strîdium feridun
thea uueros uuiðer uuinde, uuas im uurêð hugi,
seƀo sorgono ful: selƀon ni uuândun
lagulîðandea an land cumen
thurh thes uuederes geuuin.

A careful comparison will give an inkling into the choices made in the normalized text last edited by Taeger. Note, for example, the spelling <th> in *uuarth* in C (line 2911) as against <d> as in *uuard* in M, which is generally resolved in <ð>; or <b> as against <f> in *nebulo/neflu* in line 2910 that represents the phoneme /ƀ/.

The long vowel phoneme spelled as <ô> in our text appears either unmarked as <o> or as the Franconian diphthong <uo>, for example *Thuo* in line 2906. The same holds for <e> vs. <ie> in *lietun* (2906), which is resolved as long <ê> in the normalized text. It is the presence of the contrasting spellings of <uo> and <ie> that really shows that unmarked <o> and <e> in parallel positions are long. Other factors played a role in normalization, including etymological knowledge from related languages.

As we see from the strange blunder *scirana uuatar* in line 2908 of the C manuscript, with a masculine accusative ending on an adjective referring to a neuter singular noun, editors also had to correct some syntactical problems. The choice between "storm" and "stream" (*storm* and *strom*) and between "on the stream" and "on the stern" (*an strome* vs. *an stamne*) in line 2915 offered a different sort of editorial conundrum.

Walther Mitzka states in the eighth edition of Behaghel's *Heliand und Genesis* (Altdeutsche Textbibliothek 4): "The edition by Sievers, which provides exact reproductions of M and C, must be the point of departure for all linguistic examinations. The two main manuscripts do not agree in their sounds and forms; we do not know which of them is closer to the language of the original."[48] It is somewhat ironic, then, that Behaghel's version has since become the standard to which one appeals.

---

48 Walther Mitzka, Introduction to Otto Behaghel, ed., *Heliand und Genesis*, 8th ed., rev. Mitzka, Altdeutsche Textbibliothek 4 (Tübingen: Max Niemeyer, 1965), xiv: "Die Ausgabe von Sievers, die genaue Abdrücke von M und C liefert, hat für alle sprachlichen Untersuchungen den Ausgangspunkt zu bilden. Die beiden Haupthandschriften stimmen in ihren Lauten und Formen nicht überein; welche von ihnen der Sprache des Originals näher steht, wissen wir nicht."

The Old Saxon *Heliand*[1]

G. Ronald Murphy

Introduction

The *Heliand* is over a thousand years old, and is the oldest epic work of German literature, antedating the *Nibelungenlied* by four centuries. It consists of approximately 6,000 lines of alliterative verse, twice the length of *Beowulf*, which shares just enough imagery and poetic phraseology with the *Heliand* that it might possibly be contemporary. The *Heliand* was written in Old Saxon,[2] possibly at the behest of the emperor Louis the Pious (Ludwig der Fromme), in the first half of the ninth century, around the year AD 830, near the beginning of the era of the Viking raids. That it is in continental Low German has probably been the reason for its neglect within the context of German literary history, but such neglect is hard to justify. The author has never been identified. His purpose seems to have been to make the Gospel story completely accessible

---

1 Originally published in *Early Germanic Literature and Culture*, ed. Brian Murdoch and Malcolm Read, The Camden House History of German Literature 1 (Rochester: Camden House, 2004), 263–83.
2 For selections from the Old Saxon text with annotations and commentary, see James E. Cathey, ed., *Hêliand: Text and Commentary*, Medieval European Studies 2 (Morgantown: University of West Virginia Press, 2002). The standard edition of the entire Old Saxon text is given in note 7. There is a collection of essays on the text edited by Jürgen Eichhoff and Irmengard Rauch, *Der Heliand*, Wege der Forschung 321 (Darmstadt: Wissenschaftliche Buchgesellschaft, 1973).

and appealing to the Saxons through a depiction of Christ's life in the poetry of the North, recasting Jesus himself and his followers as Saxons, and thus to overcome Saxon ambivalence toward Christ caused by forced conversion to Christianity. That forced conversion was effected through thirty-three years of well-chronicled violence on the part of the Franks under Charlemagne, and counter-violence by the Saxons under Widukind, and ended with the final but protracted defeat of the Saxons.[3]

There must have still been resentment among the Saxons at the time of the composition of the *Heliand* since there was a revolt of the Saxon *stellinga*, what we might call the lower social castes, during this period. Whoever the poet of the *Heliand* was, he had his task cut out for him. His masterpiece shows that he was astonishingly gifted at intercultural communication in the religious realm. By the power of his imagination the poet-monk (perhaps also ex-warrior) created a unique cultural synthesis between Christianity and Germanic warrior society – a synthesis that would plant the seed that would one day blossom in the full-blown culture of knighthood and become the foundation of medieval Europe.[4]

The *Heliand* has come down to us in two almost complete manuscript versions, one housed now in Munich at the Bavarian State Library, designated M, and the other in London at the British Library, designated C. Neither is held to be the author's original of circa 830, which was most likely composed by a monk in Fulda acting under the ecumenical aegis of the abbot (H)Rabanus Maurus.[5] It is now

---

[3] For further detail see G. Ronald Murphy, *The Saxon Savior: The Germanic Transformation of the Gospel in the Ninth-Century Heliand* (New York: Oxford UP, 1990), 11–31.

[4] For a description of the mutual influence of Germanic culture and Christianity from a socio-historical point of view, see James C. Russell, *The Germanization of Early Medieval Christianity* (New York: Oxford UP, 1994).

[5] Some further circumstantial evidence for the association of the *Heliand* with Fulda and with the patronage of Rabanus Maurus is the provenance of the very early *Heliand* fragment V (at the Vatican), which is believed to predate

lost. M is the older of the two extant manuscripts and believed to have been written in the second half of the ninth century, circa 850, in Corvey.[6] C is believed to have been written about a hundred years later, circa 950–1000, at an East Anglian monastery in England. Though later than M, C seems to have kept more to the original division of the *Heliand* into *fitts* or songs.

The manuscript in Munich is in such excellent condition that one could almost believe it is a modern reproduction; its excellent condition seems to stem from the high quality calfskin on which it was written. In several places neumes have been inserted above the text, giving sure evidence that the *Heliand* was chanted, as is also implied in the *Praefatio*. Unfortunately, the last two fitts are missing from M. In addition to the two manuscripts, there are also four fragments, named after their place of finding: P from Prague, V at the Vatican, S from the binding of a book held in the Jesuit high school in Straubing, and the recently discovered Leipzig fragment, L.[7] The existence of four separate fragments as well as the two manuscripts, the one copied at Corvey (M) and the other at a monastery in East Anglia (C), as well as the presence of neumes in the texts, give evidence of widespread readership and use both in Germany and England in the ninth and tenth centuries and possibly beyond. We know that Martin Luther had a copy, and that it was used as a justification for the existence of a tradition of translating the Gospels into the

---

M and C, and is much closer to the original, stemming from the first half of the ninth century – V is from Mainz. Rabanus, abbot of Fulda and supporter of Louis the Pious, was made archbishop of Mainz after he had been abbot of Fulda from 822 to 841.

6   See Bernhard Bischoff's discussion in "Die Schriftheimat der Münchener Heliand-Handschrift," *Beiträge zur Geschichte der deutschen Sprache und Literatur* [Tübingen] 101 (1979), 161–70.

7   For a suggestion concerning the relationship of the manuscript texts – L excluded – see Otto Behaghel, ed., *Heliand und Genesis*, 10th ed., rev. Burkhard Taeger, Altdeutsche Textbibliothek 4 (Tübingen: Max Niemeyer, 1996), xviii–xxix. Text citations are from this edition. Italicized words indicate existing manuscript variants.

vernacular. It even seems that Luther admired the *Heliand*'s version of the angel's greeting to Mary as "full of grace." In the *Heliand* this becomes *thu bist thinon herron liof* (literally: *you are dear to your lord*, or *your lord is fond of you*). He uses this example to ridicule the idea of anyone being literally full of grace, as if he or she were a beer vat, and as if grace were something that could be poured into them. He insists instead on his preference for the German *du bist deinem Herren lieb* taken – perhaps – from the *Heliand*, but unfortunately without attribution.

Where was the *Heliand* used? The audience of the *Heliand* was probably to be found in mead hall and monastery. The epic poem seems not to have been designed for use in the church as part of official worship, but seems intended to bring the Gospel home to the Saxons in a poetic milieu, in a more familiar environment like the mead hall, in order to help the Saxons cease their vacillation between their loyalty to the sagas of Wodan and Thor, and loyalty to the epic of the mighty Christ. Some internal evidence, as well as liturgical tradition, would thus indicate that the *Heliand* epic was designed for after-dinner singing – in the poetic tradition of the scop, who sang in the mead hall of the nobility, and in Benedictine tradition in the monastic refectory of the monks.

The *Heliand* was first published by printing press in 1830, by Johann Andreas Schmeller, a millennium after its composition, and immediately had an influence on among others, the work of the Brothers Grimm. The first edition was dedicated by Schmeller to Jacob Grimm, and was read by Wilhelm Grimm when he was working on the editing and composition of the fairy tales. The *Heliand* has also been used by German nationalists in the nineteenth and twentieth centuries for their own pan-Germanic purposes, completely ignoring the great poem's historical context and Christian-Saxon origin.

The poetic technique of the author is centered on the use of analogy. In order to Saxonize the Gospel story, the author needed to find appropriate parallels for places and events of the evangelists' narrative. With regard to Bethlehem and Nazareth, for example, he is not interested in asking pilgrims what these places actually looked like. Instead, he attaches the Saxon word *burg* to each one. A *burg* at that time was a hill-fort, a local hilltop fortified with earthen embankments crowned with a palisade, a heavy wooden wall of sharpened pilings. Inside the fort was the hall of the chieftain. Outside the fort, often at the foot of the hill, were the smaller thatched-roof houses of those who were not of the warrior class. The warrior-nobility prided themselves, if we go by the account in the *Heliand*'s version of the nativity, on being born within the walls of the hill-fort. Some easier geographic analogies are readily provided by the location of Jesus's activities by the Sea of Galilee and the presence of the North Sea. Fishing scenes are frequent enough in the Gospel itself; the *Heliand* strengthens them by adding details of the apostles working on the nets and of implying that they are using the seine technique that must have been popular in the river regions of the north.

Finally the author finds not only cultural equivalencies for the events of the Gospel story, but often he sets them in parallel to a literal translation which he gives in the following line. "Your lord is fond of you" is followed by "woman full of grace." The poetic power of the *Heliand* lies in the unexpected parallel imagery and in the charm created by hearing northern equivalents for the Mediterranean concepts of the Bible in such close proximity to each other. The technique itself is biblical, and can be found in the Psalms. For example, in ancient Hebrew poetry, *mountain* can be "rhymed" with *hill* not on the similarity of sound, but of similarity of image. Likewise, snow can be rhymed with hail, fish with whales, and more familiarly, "he leads me beside the still waters" can be rhymed with "he gave me repose." I call this technique concept alliteration. The Saxons did not know or practice Roman crucifixion, but they did punish criminals and make an offering to Wodan by hanging criminals and animals from the branches of sacred trees.[8] In the *Heliand*, therefore, crucifixion

---

8 See the account by Adam of Bremen who came to Bremen in 1066 and wrote of Germanic religious customs that were still practiced in his time, especially

The Old Saxon Heliand

is "rhymed" in the following line with hanging. The arrogant thief crucified alongside Christ is made in the *Heliand* to say "get down from the cross, slip out of the rope."

The poet worked in a number of categories in order to create a Saxon poetic equivalent to the Gospel. Since he was using the Diatessaron, a synthesis of the four Gospel narratives compiled originally in Greek by Tatian, a second-century Syrian Christian, and subsequently translated into Latin and most of the European vernaculars, including Old High German, he had all the known pericopes ("readings," biblical narrative units) of the story at hand, and he chose to leave out very few, notably those that had to do with examples that seemed to justify the taking of interest on loans. First, warrior equivalencies will be examined; second, mythological incorporations; third, magic; fourth, epic structure; and, fifth, the enormous role of light in the *Heliand*.

Warrior Culture in the Poem

The audience of the *Heliand* lived in an early feudal environment and thus might not have found the concept of a rabbi and his disciples comprehensible. The author changes rabbi to chieftain, *drohtin*, and disciples to *gisiðos*, the young warrior companions of a chieftain. This translation makes the Gospel more at home sociologically, but it also makes the relationship of Christ to his disciples not one of teacher to students, but military leader to personal bodyguard. What is required then of disciples, faith in their teacher, becomes fidelity to one's leader in the *Heliand*. This Germanic reading of faith as personal fidelity will have far-reaching consequences that will extend from the piety of the medieval crusader to the Reformation's notion of faith.

---

at the temple in Uppsala, Sweden: *History of the Archbishops of Hamburg-Bremen*, trans. Francis J. Tschan, Records of Western Civilization (New York: Columbia UP, 1959; repr. 2002), 10–11, 207–08.

The duty of a warrior disciple is laid out both in the birth of John the Baptist and in the scene of Peter's drawing his sword at Jesus's arrest on Olivet. When the angel announces the birth of John the Baptist to his father Zachary in the temple he adds something significant:

> [God] Hêt that ic thi scol sagdi, that it scolde gisîð uuesan
> heƀancuninges, hêt that git it helden uuel,
> tuhin thurh treuua, quað that he im tîras sô filu
> an godes rîkea forgeƀan uueldi. (129–32)

> [God said that I should say to you that your child will be a warrior-companion of the King of Heaven. He said that you and your wife should care for him well and bring him up on loyalty, and that He would grant him many honors in God's kingdom][9]

In this remarkable passage we have the earliest known blending of Germanic warrior virtue with Christian religion. God the All-Ruler is made to request that John be raised specifically to practice the warrior virtue of *treuwa*, unflinching loyalty in battle to one's chieftain. God's reason is that He wishes to make John his *gesið*. In the original Old Saxon there is a truly amazing linkage of two cultural worlds in two words: God wishes to make John a *gesið heƀancuninges*, a warrior companion of the King of Heaven. Discipleship has been reconceived as the author goes on to say that John's chieftain will be Christ, and John will be *Kristes gesið*, a warrior-companion of Jesus.

The feudal world required reciprocity between chieftain and warrior-companion, and the reciprocal relationship on the part of the chieftain was that he care for his men, a care which the *Heliand* calls protection and love. Thus, it does not come as a total surprise that, when Christ is born and the shepherds have come and gone from the Christmas scene in Bethlehem, Mary is described in the Gospel

---

9 All English translations from the *Heliand* are taken from G. Ronald Murphy, trans., *The Heliand: The Saxon Gospel* (New York: Oxford UP, 1992).

The Old Saxon Heliand

and in the *Heliand* as pondering all these things in her heart, and in the *Heliand* the poet adds that Jesus will be raised on the reciprocal virtue to John's *treuwa*, telling us how the mother – the loveliest of ladies – brought up the chieftain of many men, the holy heavenly child, on love, *minnea* (fitt 6).

St. Peter, throughout the *Heliand*, is made into the ideal warrior companion of Christ. When Peter is about to drown due to lack of faith, or when he disowns Christ three times as the cock crows, or when he draws his sword to defend Christ, all are made into major epic scenes in the *Heliand*. From the scene of his walking on the waters:

>   the sêolîðandean
> naht nebulo biuuarp;   nâðidun erlos
> forðuuardes an flod;   uuarð thiu fiorðe tid
> thera nahtes cuman   – neriendo Crist
> uuarode thea uuâglîðand –:   tho uuarð uuind mikil,
> hôh uueder afhaben: hlamodun ûðeon,
> strôm an stamne;   strîdiun feridun
> thea uueros uuiðer uuinde . . .
>   Thô gisâhun sie uualdand Krist
> an themu sêe uppan   selbum gangan,
> faran an fâðion . . .
>   "Nu gi môdes sculun
> fastes fâhen;   ne sî iu forht hugi,
> gibâriad gi baldlîco: ik bium that barn godes,
> is selbes sunu,   the iu uuið thesumu sêe scal,
> mundon uuið thesan meristrôm." (2909–31)

[Night wrapped the seafarers in fog. The earls daringly kept on sailing over the waters. The fourth hour of the night had come – Christ the Helper was guarding the wave-riders – and the wind began to blow powerfully. A great storm arose, the waves of the sea roared against the bow stem post, the men fought to steer the boat into the wind . . . then they saw the Ruler himself walking on the sea, traveling on foot. . . . "Now you should be steadfast and brave, do not be fearful-minded, be courageous! I am the Child of God, his own Son, and I will defend you against the sea and protect you from the ocean waves."]

Jesus proclaims that he is aware of his duty to his men to extend his protection to them, even if the enemy is an ocean storm. Then Peter, his good thane, calls overboard to Christ and asks him to command him to come across the waves to him, ". . . tell me to walk to You across this seaway, dry across the deep water, if You are my chieftain, protector of many people." Not only does Christ as chieftain of St. Peter have the right to tell him to come to him, but as chieftain, he also has the obligation to protect Peter as one of his men. As in the Gospel story, Peter does well walking on the water until he begins to doubt. The *Heliand* author makes the scene more vivid for his North Sea audience:

> . . . he [Peter] *imu* an his môde bigan
> andrâden diap uuater,   thô he driƀen gisah
> thene uuêg mid uuindu: uundun ina *ûðeon*,
> hôh strôm unbihring.   Reht sô he thô an is hugdi tuehode,
> sô uuêk imu that uuater under,   enti he an thene uuâg innan,
> sank an thene sêostrôm,   endi *he* hriop sân after thiu
> *gâhon* te themu godes sunie   endi gerno bad
> that he ine thô *generidi*,   thô he an *nôdiun* uuas,
> thegan an gethuinge.   Thiodo drohtin
> antfeng ine *mid* is faðmum   enti frâgode sâna,
> te huî he *thô getuehodi* . . .
>
>   Thô nam ine alomahtig,
> hêlag bi handun: thô uuarð imu eft hlutter uuater
> fast under fôtun,   endi sie an fâði samad
> bedea gengun,   antat sie oƀar bord skipes
> stôpun *fan* themu strôme. (2942–61)

The Old Saxon Heliand

[... in his emotions Peter began to feel the fear of deep water as he watched the waves being driven by the wind. The waves wound around him, the high seas surrounded the man. Just at that moment doubt came into his mind. The water underneath him became soft and he sank into a wave, he sank into the streaming sea! Very soon after that he called out quickly, asking earnestly that Christ rescue him, since he, his thane, was in distress and danger. The chieftain of peoples caught him with his outstretched arms and asked him immediately why he doubted. ... Then the holy, all-mighty One took him by the hand and all at once clear water became solid under his feet, and they went together on foot, both of them, walking, until they climbed on board the boat from the sea.]

The author has no difficulty recognizing, through Peter, the doubt that lay in the minds of many of the Saxons concerning the ability of their new chieftain, Christ, to protect them, but the author has shown them that Christ is not only willing to rescue them from death, drowning, but is also heartfelt enough to go hand in hand, something the author has touchingly inserted, walking with them, to the boat where all is safe and the storm is over.

The *Heliand* author might have been expected to delete the incident of Peter's triple denial of Christ, but he does not, true as it is to the Saxon warriors' own state of mind and behavior at the author's time. After having related the scene, however, he adds a compassionate explanation of Peter, which is his own creation:

> Than ni thurbun thes liudio barn,
> uueros uundrioan,   behuî it uueldi god,
> that sô lioben man   leð gistôdi,
> that he sô hônlîco   hêrron sînes
> thurh thera *thiuun* uuord,   thegno snellost
> farlôgnide sô lioƀes: it uuas al bi thesun liudiun giduan,
> firiho barnun te *frumu*.   He uuelde ina te furiston dôan,
> hêrost oƀar is hîuuiski,   helag drohtin:

> lêt ina gekunnon, huilike craft haƀet
> the mennisca môd âno *the* maht godes;
> lêt ina gesundion, that he sîðor thiu bet
> liudiun gilôƀdi, huô liof is *thar*
> manno *gihuilicumu*, than he mên gefrumit,
> that man ina alâte lêðes thinges . . . (5023–36)

[People should not be amazed, warriors should not wonder, why God would have wanted such a loveable man and powerful thane to have such an evil thing happen to him (especially in the world of feudal loyalty) as to deny his beloved Chieftain so shamefully because of a servant-girl's words. It was done for the sake of those people, for the sake of the sons of men. The holy Chieftain intended to make Peter the first man in the leadership of his household, and wanted Peter to realize how much strength there is in the human spirit without the power of God. He let Peter commit sin so that afterward he would better appreciate people, how all human beings love to be forgiven when they have done something wrong . . .]

No scene in the *Heliand* makes such a warrior-like impression as when one of Jesus's disciple/warriors finally draws a sword in his chieftain's defense. This scene may well be the one that helped make Peter the poet's favorite, and almost makes Peter sound like a Viking berserker:

> Thô gibolgan uuarð
> snel suerdthegan Sîmon Petrus
> *uuell* imu innan hugi, that he ni mahte ênig uuord sprekan:
> sô harm uuarð imu an is hertan, that man is hêrron that
> binden *uuelde*. Thô he gibolgan geng,
> suîðo thrîstmôd thegan for is thiodan *standen*
> hard for is hêrron: ni uuas imu is hugi tuîfli,
> *blôð* an is breostun, ac he is bil atôh,
> suerd bi sîdu, slog imu tegegnes
> an thene furiston fîund folmo crafto,

> that thô Malchus uuarð   mâkeas eggiun,
> an thea suîðaron half   suerdu gimâlod:
> thiu hlust uuarð imu farhauuan,   he uuarð an that hôƀid uund,
> that imu herudrôrag   hlear endi ôre
> beniuundun brast: blôd aftar sprang
> uuell fan uundun.   Thô uuas an is uuangun scard
> the furisto thero fiundo. Thô stôd that folc an rûm:
> andrêdun im thes billes biti. (4865–82)

[Then Simon Peter, the mighty, noble swordsman flew into a rage; his mind was in such turmoil that he could not speak a single word. His heart became intensely bitter because they wanted to tie up his Lord there. So he strode over angrily, that very daring thane, to stand in front of his commander, right in front of his Lord. No doubting in him, no fearful hesitation in his chest, he drew his blade and struck straight ahead at the first man of the enemy with all the strength in his hands, so that Malchus was cut and wounded on the right side by the sword! His ear was chopped off, he was so badly wounded in the head that his cheek and ear burst open with a mortal wound! Blood gushed out, pouring from the wound! The men stood back – they were afraid of the slash of the sword.]

This is quite an expansion of the modest account in the Gospel, but much more in line with the grim battles in *Beowulf* and the *Battle of Maldon*.[10] To make for a better epic conflict, the religious enemies of Christ in the Gospel, the Sadducees, the Pharisees, and the Torah scholars, have been combined by the author to create one hostile enemy military force, the Jewish army. This combination is required both by good epic form, which requires a powerful antagonist, and by what I presume was the Saxons' general unfamiliarity with the Jews of their day, much less with the Jewish sects of the first century. The *Heliand* author has to give some identity to the Jewish "enemy

---

10   See "The Final Battle" in Murphy, *The Saxon Savior* [note 3], 95–117.

force" and he does so in accord with northern European prejudices by describing them repeatedly as competent warriors but as "southern people, sneaky."[11]

Mythological Incorporations

The poet-monk who wrote the *Heliand* was quite familiar with Germanic mythology. Not only did he incorporate elements into the *Heliand* Gospel, he even tackled the theological problem of the role of fate, the highest Germanic religious power, in his Christian worldview. To begin with a familiar object from later German storytelling, the *Heliand* has the earliest instance of the invisibility cape or *Tarnkappe*, used by Siegfried in the *Nibelungenlied*. In the *Heliand* it is a magic helmet, the *heliðhelm*, and the author finds a place for it in the scene in which Pilate's wife is having bad dreams about her husband's actions toward his famous prisoner. The magic helmet is being worn by Satan to conceal his identity. He has come from hell with it to attempt to prevent the salvation of the world by opposing the crucifixion of Christ (fitt 65). Even hell (*hel* in the *Heliand*), is the damp dark place of Germanic mythology and *Beowulf*'s monsters; it is not the fiery inferno of the Mediterranean tradition. Heaven, too, will be described as a place of light and green meadows (of Valhalla).

Fate as an absolute force beyond gods and men must have been a special challenge to the author. The three blind women, the Norns, who sit under the tree at the edge of the well of time, spin, measure, and cut the thread of all things. It would seem that a missionary would have to treat such a force as antithetical to the Trinity, but the *Heliand*

---

11 The only place in the *Heliand* where contemporary Jews come under condemnation may be in the scene of the cleansing of the temple (fitt 45). Here the author criticizes Jews for being people who accept interest on loans, for practicing usury. Charlemagne had recently forbidden the practice of usury throughout the empire, and the *Heliand* condemns the practice in very absolute terms as *unreht enfald*, pure injustice.

The Old Saxon Heliand

author finds a place for "the workings of fate" and for its invisible spirit, time. When John the Baptist is born the author writes:

> Thô uuarð sân aftar thiu maht godes,
> *gicûðid* is craft mikil: uuarð thiu *quân* ôcan,
> idis an ira eldiu: scolda im erɓiuuard,
> suîðo godcund gumo giɓiðig uuerðan,
> barn an *burgun*. Bêd aftar thiu
> that uuîf *uuirdigiscapu*. Scred the uuintar forð,
> geng *thes* gêres gital. Iohannes quam an
> an liudeo lioht. (192–99)

[Soon thereafter the power of God, his might strength, was felt: the wife (Elizabeth), a woman in her old age, became pregnant – soon the husband, that godly man, would have an heir, an infant boy born in the hill-fort. The woman awaited the workings of fate. The winter skidded by and the year measured its way past. John came to the light of mankind.]

Fate has been allotted a place in the *Heliand*'s scheme of things; it takes care of measuring the nine months of pregnancy. Fate attends to timing and to the accidentals, the color of John's hair, even his fingernails and the fairness of his skin. All the very things, one might reflect, that one day will become the realm of biology and history are not excluded but are "co-workers" with God. Even the time of the passion and death of Christ are determined by the divine will working with fate. In the above scene when Peter draws his sword to prevent Christ's capture, when Christ tells him, in the Gospel, to sheath his sword because he who lives by the sword will die by the sword, this is explained in the *Heliand* to have Christ clearly give fate its due:

> Thô sprak that barn godes
> selɓo te Sîmon Petruse, hêt that he is suerd dedi
> skarp an skêdia: "ef ik uuið thesa scola uueldi," quað he,
> "uuið theses uuerodes geuuin uuîgsaca frummien,

> that manodi ik thene mâreon   mahtigne god,
> hêlagne fader   an himilrîkea,
> that he mi sô managan engil herod   oƀana sandi
> uuîges sô uuîsen,   sô ni *mahtin* iro *uuâpanthreki*
> man adôgen: iro ni stôdi gio sulic megin samad,
> folkes *gefastnod*,   that im iro ferh aftar thiu
> uuerðen mahti.   Ac it haƀad uualdand god,
> alomahtig fader   an oðar gimarkot,
> that uui *githoloian* sculun,   sô huat sô ûs *thius thioda* tô
> bittres brengit: ni sculun ûs belgan uuiht,
> uurêđean uuið iro geuuinne;   huand sô hue sô uuâpno nîð,
> grimman *gêrheti*   *uuili* gerno frummien,
> he suiltit imu *eft*   suerdes eggiun,
> *dôit* im *bidrôregan*:   uui mid ûsun dâdiun ni sculun
> uuiht auuerdian." (4882–4900)

[Then the Son of God spoke to Simon Peter and told him to put his sharp sword back into its sheath. "If I wanted to put up a fight against the attack of this band of warriors, I would make the great and might God, the holy Father in the kingdom of heaven, aware of it so that he would send me so many angels wise in warfare that no human beings could stand up to the force of their weapons. But, the ruling God, the all-mighty Father, has determined it differently: we are to bear whatever bitter things this people does to us. We are not to become enraged or wrathful against their violence, since whoever is eager and willing to practice the weapon's hatred, cruel spear-fighting, is often himself killed by the edge of the sword and dies dripping in his own blood. *We cannot by our own deeds avert anything.*] (emphasis mine)

There is more than a little fatalism that will enter Germanic Christianity through the *Heliand*, since Christ himself is made to express sentiments that come close to equating fate, the events of this world, regardless of their bitterness, as part of the will of God. It is useless to resist them.

The Old Saxon Heliand

Even the raising of Lazarus from the dead, which shows the superiority of Christ over fate, is done with fate's cooperation (fitt 49). The real test of course is the time of the death of Christ, and that is given the same treatment, with a twist. Christ is going to overturn fate by rising from the dead and unlocking the door to the road to heaven. The author knows his audience, and he knows that they want to have more assurance concerning Christ's non-resistance to fate and the attacking Jewish army, so he once again creates an apologetic for Christ's actions:

> Uuerod Iudeono
> sô manag mislic thing   an mahtiga Crist
> sagdun te sundiun.   He suîgondi stuod
> thuru ôðmuodi,   ne antuuordida *niouuiht*
> uuið iro uurêðun uuord: uuolda thesa uuerold alla
> lôsian mid is liƀu: bithiu liet hie ina thia lêðun thiod
> uuêgian te uundron,   all sô iro uuillio geng:
> ni uuolda im opanlîco   allon cûðian
> Iudeo liudeon,   that hie uuas god selƀo;
> Huand uuissin sia that te uuâron,   that hie sulica giuuald habdi
> oƀar theson middilgard,   than uurði im iro muodseƀo
> giblôðit an iro brioston: than ne gidorstin sia that barn godes
> handon anthrînan: than ni uuurði heƀanrîki,
> antlocan liohto mêst   liudio barnon.
> Bethiu mêð hie is sô an is muode,   ne lêt that manno folc
> uuitan, huat sia uuarahtun.   Thiu uurd nâhida thuo,
> mâri maht godes   endi middi dag,
> that sia thie ferahquâla   frummian scoldun. (5379–96)

[The Jewish people said many different sinful things about mighty Christ. He stood there, keeping silent in patient humility. He did not answer their hostile words, he wanted to free the whole world with his life – that is why he let the evil clan subject him to whatever terrible torture they desired. He did not want to let all the Jewish people know openly that he was God Himself. For, if they really knew how much power he had over this middle world, their feelings would turn cowardly within their breasts and they would never dare to lay their hands on the Son of God, and the kingdom of heaven, the brightest of worlds, would never be unlocked to the sons of men. Because of this, he hid it in his heart and did not let the human clan know what they were doing. *Fate was coming closer then, and the great power of God, and midday*, when they were to bring his life-spirit to its death agony.] (emphasis mine)

It seems that the Jews, as a stand-in for the human race, are the instruments of fate, but they could be deflected by intimidation, and so Christ conceals his identity from them. Meanwhile coming closer are fate, God, and midday. As in the case of the date of birth of John the Baptist, the nine-month period was within the realm of fate, and so also is the decision that the crucifixion should be on Friday and at noon.

There is even an iconographic representation of Christ that leans on Germanic religious mythology. Wodan is typically pictured with two ravens, Mind and Memory, *hugin* and *munin*, on his shoulder. They are the heart of his awareness of what is going on in *middelgard*. They fly about during the day observing the comings and goings of men and gods, and then return to their master to whisper in his ear all that they have observed. It seems that the *Heliand* author could not resist feeling that this function of Wodan's ravens seemed quite similar to the role of the dove, the Holy Spirit. The scene that is just made for his use is the incident of the baptism of Christ in the Jordan by John the Baptist. In Luke 3, as Christ comes up out of the waters a voice says "This is my beloved Son," and John says that he saw the Holy Spirit coming down from heaven upon Jesus in the form of a dove which remained above him (*mansit super eum*, in Tatian). In the *Heliand* the dove does not remain vaguely "above him":

The Old Saxon Heliand

> Krist up giuuêt
> fagar fon them flôde, friðubarn godes,
> liof liudio uuard. Sô he thô that land *afstop*,
> sô anthlidun thô himiles doru, endi quam the hêlago gêst
> fon them alouualdon oƀane te Kriste:
> – uuas im an gilîcnissie *lungras* fugles,
> diurlîcara dûƀun – endi sat im uppan uses drohtines *ahslu*,
> uuonoda im oƀar them uualdandes barne. (982–89)

[Christ came up radiant out of the water, the Peace-Child of God, the beloved Protector of people. As he stepped out onto the land, the doors of heaven opened up and the Holy Spirit came down from the All-Ruler above to Christ – it was like a powerful bird, a magnificent dove – and it sat upon our Chieftain's shoulder, remaining over the Ruler's Child][12]

Magical Elements

When it comes to finding equivalents for miraculous or sacramental incidents such as the multiplication of the loaves, or the institution of the Eucharist, or even explaining the divine inspiration of scripture, the poet seems to have had no difficulty. He simply alluded to the magic with which his audience was already familiar. Germanic religion was filled with magic spells and enchantments, magic objects that retained their ability to perform supernatural feats long after their connection to the god who made them had been severed. J. R. R. Tolkien's *Lord of the Rings* trilogy shows how a poet in the twentieth century can still draw successfully upon the ancient Germano-Christian forms of magic. Consider the origin of the runes, which are said to have been seized from the depths of the well of fate as Wodan hung himself as a sacrifice to divine the nature of reality. He

---

12 For a fuller look at the versions in *Tatian* and Old High German, see Murphy, *The Saxon Savior* [note 3], 77–80.

reached down and grasped the runes, later giving them to mankind. Therefore writing itself is a divine institution and each letter can be used for magic. This makes the task of the *Heliand* poet easier. How does he explain that the Lord's Prayer is a divine entity, taught by the God-man himself? He simply alludes to the story of Wodan and the runes. In the Gospel the disciples ask Christ to teach them to pray as John the Baptist taught his disciples to pray. In the *Heliand*, the warrior companions phrase it differently: *gerihti us that geruni*, teach us the secret runes, and suddenly the Our Father becomes a magic spell capable of reaching God.

One might think that the Eucharist would offer more of a challenge to a group accustomed to treating food as something for the mead hall and not really for religion. The *Heliand* once again has Jesus say magic words. After Jesus told his disciples that the bread is truly his body and the wine is truly his blood he adds, following a brief discourse: *thit is mahtig thing*, this is a magic thing, this is a thing that has power. The word *mahtig* has been shown by Stephen R. Flowers to be a word for magic, used to designate performative words (magic words) or performative persons or, here, things that possess an unusual strength, such as the ability of the magic helmet, the *heliðhelm*, to hide its wearer.[13] The magic powers of the Eucharist bread and wine are then explained in a way that enforces what Jesus said at the Last Supper. Where Jesus in the Gospel and in the liturgy asks his disciples to perform the Eucharist in his memory, the

---

13 Stephen E. Flowers, *Runes and Magic, Magical Formulaic Elements in the Older Runic Tradition* (New York: Peter Lang, 1986). For further discussion of Germanic magic, see Jan de Vries, *Altgermanische Religionsgeschichte*, 2nd ed., 2 vols. (Berlin: Walter de Gruyter, 1956–57). For the mutual effect of Germanic and Christian religious concepts and practices upon one another, see Valerie Flint, *The Rise of Magic in Early Medieval Europe* (Princeton: Princeton UP, 1991). Flint maintains that Christianity actually fostered magic rather than suppressing it. The *Heliand* seems to support her thesis in that magic was a convenient and familiar vehicle for expressing the sacred and sacramental mysteries to the Northern European mind.

The Old Saxon Heliand

Heliand explains that the bread and wine of the Eucharist possess the power to help men remember what Jesus is doing out of love to give glory to the Lord. It possesses the magic power to give honor to the Chieftain. Thus repeating these magic words over the bread and wine fulfills a feudal obligation to honor one's Chieftain, and will enable Christ's men to repeat the magic of his words and defy time and the fates: "everyone all over *middilgard*" will come to know what he is doing. Truly a remarkable synthesis of Christianity and a beautiful concept of magic. Catholic sacramental theology will come to be very much influenced by this touching synthesis.

There is even some humor in the *Heliand*'s use of magic. When the disciple/warriors are distributing the miraculously multiplied loaves at the miracle of the feeding of the five thousand, the Gospels say nothing about how or where the multiplication took place. The *Heliand* makes no such omission. As the warrior companions go around among the crowd distributing the loaves they are shocked as they become aware that the bread *undar iro handun uuohs*, that the bread between their hands was growing!

If one were to object that there is no tradition in Christianity for seeing magic in God's words, and performative magic at that, it is easy to see what the response would have been – it is in the first fitt of the *Heliand*. The author describes creation itself as taking place through magic words. *Fiat lux*, Let there be light, and there was light. The words of God effect immediately what they say; that is, they are performative. "Your sins are forgiven you," and they are forgiven. "This is my body," and it is. The task of the Evangelists was to write down

> all so hie it fan them anginne   thuru is *ênes* craht,
> uualdand gisprak,   thuo hie êrist thesa uuerold giscuop
> endi thuo all bifieng   mid ênu uuordo,
> himil endi erða   endi al that sea bihlidad êgun
> giuuarahtes endi giuuahsanes: that uuarð thuo all mid uuordon godas
> fasto bifangan. (38–43)

[all the things which the Ruler spoke from the beginning, when he, by his own power, first made the world and formed the universe with one word. The heavens and the earth and all that is contained within them, both inorganic and organic, everything was firmly held in place by Divine words.]

Looked at through Germanic Christian eyes, the six days of creation in which God uttered the magic words "Let there be . . ."[14] many times, the words of Christ at Cana, to the paralytic, to the blind, even to the three-days-dead Lazarus, "Lazarus, come forth," are all highly powerful magic, they are *mahtig*. The Saxons need not fear that they have been forced into a religion that knows far less of magic enchantment than their former faith. The whole Bible is a magic spell, a *geruni*.

EPIC STRUCTURE

To make his version of the Gospel into a magic and mythic spell, God's spell, the author also put the narrative into an epic structural frame centered on the scene that must have been of great significance for him, the Transfiguration on Mount Tabor. The monumental study made by Johannes Rathofer attempted to establish the existence of four divisions in the *Heliand*, and was unable to do so, since he preferred to concentrate on numerical analysis rather than the content of the individual fitts.[15] His ultimate contention that the *Heliand* is a centered composition with the Transfiguration, fitt 38, as its middle point, has been accepted. If this is the case, then the events of the fitts should end up in a balanced structure on either side of fitt 38. In 1958 Cedric Whitman discovered this structuring pattern in the *Iliad*,[16] and

---

14 In the Latin text of the Bible this would be a single causative word: *Fiat*.
15 Johannes Rathofer, *Der Heliand: Theologischer Sinn als tektonische Form. Vorbereitung und Grundlegung der Interpretation*, Niederdeutsche Studien 9 (Cologne: Bohlau, 1962).
16 See his *Homer and the Heroic Tradition* (Cambridge, Mass.: Harvard UP,

it seems that the author of the *Heliand* was following the same ancient technique that facilitates both memorization and oral delivery.

The form of the arrangement rather nicely gives the events that follow the Transfiguration something of a Germanic feel of being fated by the event prior to the Transfiguration, blending in with the carefully allotted role of fate in the *Heliand*. In fitt 33 we have the death of John the Baptist; in the parallel scene, fitt 43, the death of Jesus is foretold. In fitt 23 the Last Judgment is predicted; in fitt 53 Doomsday is described. In a rather touching parallel in fitt 19 Jesus teaches his disciples the magic runes of the Lord's Prayer so that they can appeal to the Father; in fitt 57 he himself is calling out in his agony in the garden to the Father. Even the nativity and the resurrection have been made parallel by the description of both as a "coming," in the one case as a coming of God's child to this light, and in the other as the spirit of Christ coming back, making its way under the gravestone, to the body. For people whose lives have been influenced from time immemorial by the battles and events that occurred on the crests of their hill-forts, this structure, anchored on three mountains, the mount of the sermon, Mount Tabor, and Mount Olivet, becomes familiar. The events of Christ's life are made by the form of the tale to fit into a more northern religious emotional framework of invisible parallelism, a certain fatedness, in the realm of time.

THE THEME OF LIGHT IN THE POEM

The Transfiguration in the *Heliand* is a scene full of light, it is a key to the spiritual world of the poet and of his *Heliand* epic, and he has placed it in the very center of the *inclusio* structure of the poem so that it cannot be but felt by the hearer or reader.[17] The *Heliand* adds even more radiance to the scene than the Evangelists had done:

1958).
17 For a fuller treatment of the light theme in the *Heliand*, including the role of sight and blindness, see G. Ronald Murphy, "The Light Worlds of the *Heliand*," *Monatshefte* 89 (1997), 5–17.

> Côs imu *iungarono* thô
> sân aftar thiu   Sîmon Petrus,
> Iacob endi Iohannes,   *thea* gumon tuêne,
> bêðea thea gibroðer,   endi imu thô uppen thene berg giuuêt
> sunder mid them gesiðun,   salig barn godes
> mid them thegnum thrim . . .
>   Thô imu thar te bedu gihnêg,
> thô uuarð imu thar uppe   ôðarlîcora
> uuliti endi giuuâdi: uurðun imu is uuangun liohte,
> blîcandi sô *thiu bergte sunne*:   sô skên that barn godes,
> liuhte is lîchamo: liomon stôdun
> uuânamo fan themu uualdandes barne;   uuarð is geuuâdi sô huît
> sô snêu te sehanne. (3107–12, 3123–28)

[Then, soon after that, from among his followers he picked Simon Peter, James and John, the two men who were brothers, and with these happy warrior-companions set out to go up on a mountain on their own – the happy Child of God and the three thanes. . . . As he bowed down to pray up there his appearance and clothes became different ("other-like"). His cheeks became shining light, radiating like the bright sun. The Son of God was shining! His body gave off light, brilliant rays came shining out of the Ruler's Son. His clothes were white as snow to look at.]

In the Gospel account (Matt 17.1–3: "He was transfigured before them. And his face shone as the sun, and his garments became white as snow") there is not quite as much enthusiasm, and there is far less emphasis on the fact that not just his face but his entire body was emitting brilliant radiation. As the *Heliand* poet goes on, he makes a connection between Germanic and Christian images of heaven:

> sô blîði uuarð uppan themu berge: skên that berhte lioht,
> uuas thar gard gôdlic   endi groni *uuang*,
> paradise gelîc.   Petrus thô gimahalde,

The Old Saxon Heliand

> helið hardmôdig   endi te is hêrron sprac,
> grôtte thene godes sunu: 'gôd is *it* hêr te uuesanne,
> ef thu it gikiosan uuili,   Crist alouualdo,
> that man thi hêr an thesaru hôhe   ên hûs geuuirkea,
> mârlico gemaco   endi Moysese ôðer
> endi Eliase thriddea: thit is ôdas hêm,
> uuelono uunsamost.' (3134–43)

[It became so blissful up there on the mountain – the bright light was shining, there was a magnificent garden there and the green meadow, it was like paradise! Peter the steady-minded hero then spoke up, addressed his Lord and said to God's Son, "This is a good place to live, Christ All-Ruler, if you should decide that a house be built for you up here on the mountain, a magnificent one, and another for Moses and a third for Elijah – this is the home of happiness, the most appealing thing anyone could have!"]

The poet has changed the top of the mountain to paradise. He has introduced the notion of a place where the light is always shining, and suggested both the Germanic and biblical images of heaven: the green meadow of Valhalla and the Garden of Eden. The light from heaven and the green of earthly meadows and garden combine to create the *Heliand*'s harmonized image of paradise. Light shines everywhere and it comes both to the meadow of Valhalla and to the garden of Paradise from the shining light-person, Jesus Christ. This radiance is associated with bringing bliss to Peter the "Saxon warrior-companion" so that he is slightly beside himself. Peter's happiness is the "beaming" happiness of human beings that they are enveloped in such a vast world of light, that they are part of the glowing communication between the two worlds of light, earth, this light, and heaven, the other light. At the end of the scene the poet adds his comment: "They saw God's Child standing there alone; that other light though, heaven's, was gone." This image of Germanic-

Christian light and happiness, Paradise, is the center of the *Heliand*. In it Jesus is viewed as a kind of light bridge. He brings the light of the other world to *middilgard*, and makes it as bright as paradise. For a people accustomed by their religious mythology to the image of a shimmering light bridge connecting the two worlds of heaven and earth, *bifrost*, the frosty Milky Way visible at night arching from the horizon across the sky, or the rainbow seen during the day, a bridge of pale light on which the gods, the giants, and souls of the dead travel from this light to the other light, Christianity must have seemed poetically barren of any inspiration from the natural world. The author of the *Heliand* fills in the missing gap and makes Jesus the bridge of light, the *bifrost* bringing otherworldly radiant happiness to our hilltops. In one of his more striking thoughts the author even adds: *so lerde he in liohten uuordun*, he taught them in light-words.

In equidistant parallel on both sides of the Transfiguration scene's light, the author placed the brilliance of the light shining at the Nativity and the Resurrection. As in Luke's Gospel, when Jesus is born, men on night watch in the fields (in the *Heliand* they are not shepherds, they are St. Joseph's "horse-guards"!), see the angels from heaven. In the *Heliand*, though, the awesomeness of the situation is not so much caused by the sudden appearance of the angels as an otherworldy light breaking through the night sky:

> Gisâhun finistri an tuuê
> telâtan an lufte,   endi quam lioht godes
> uuânum thurh thiu uuolcan   endi thea uuardos that
> bifeng an them felda.   Sie *uurðun* an forhtun thô,
> thea *man* an ira môda: gisâhun that mahtigna
> godes engil cumin,   the im tegegnes sprac,
> hêt that im thea uuardos   uuiht ne antdrêdin
> lêðes fon *them liohta* . . . (390–97)

[They saw the darkness split in two in the sky and the light of God came shining through the clouds and surrounded the guards out

The Old Saxon Heliand

in the fields. They saw the mighty angel of God coming toward them. He spoke to the guards face to face and told them they should not fear any harm from the light.]

In Luke's Gospel the angel simply tells the men not to be afraid; in the *Heliand* attention is called to the light by having the angel tell the men not to be afraid of it.

In parallel, during the *Heliand*'s description of the Resurrection once again attention is called to the arrival of the light:

> Sia oƀar themo graƀe sâtun
> uueros an thero uuahtun *uuannom* nahton
> bidun undar iro bordon, huan êr thie berehto dag
> oƀar middilgard mannon quâmi,
> liudon te liohte. Thuo ni uuas lang te thiu
> that thar uuarð thie gêst cuman be godes crafte,
> hâlag âðom undar thena hardon stên
> an *thena* lichamon. Lioht uuas thuo giopanod
> firio barnon te frumu: uuas fercal manag
> antheftid fan *helldoron* endi te himile uueg
> giuuaraht fan thesaro uueroldi. Uuânom *up* astuod,
> friðubarn godes . . . (5765–76)

[The warriors sat on top of the grave on their watch during the dark starlit night. They waited under their shields until bright day came to mankind all over the middle world bringing light to people. It was not long then until: there was the spirit coming, by God's power, the holy breath, going under the hard stone to the corpse! Light was at that moment opened up for the good sons of men; the many bolts on the doors of Hel were unlocked; the road from this world to heaven was built! Brilliantly radiating, God's Peace-Child rose up!]

As Christ rises, the light of paradise itself is transmitted from Christ's radiance at the Transfiguration and communicated to people, including those held captive like Baldr under the earth in the dank realm of Loki's ugly sister Hel. The Christian *bifrost* is now in existence and functioning as He rises up.

Not only is the Christian Resurrection attributed to Christ but it is communicated to all. To the angels as brilliant radiance, to the grave guards as blinding light, to the women as beaming happiness:

> Rincos sâtun
> umbi that graf ûtan,   Iudeo liudi,
> scola mid iro scildion.   Scrêd forthuuardes
> suigli sunnun *lioht* . . .
>
>   sân *up* ahlêd
> thie grôto stên fan them graƀe,   sô ina thie godes engil
> gihueriƀida an halƀa,   endi im uppan them *hlêuue* gisat
> diurlîc drohtines bodo.   Hie uuas an is dâdion gelîc,
> an is ansiunion, sô huem   sô ina *muosta* undar is ôgon scauuon,
> sô *bereht* endi sô blîði   all sô *blicsmun* lioht;
> uuas im is giuuâdi   *uuintercaldon*
> *snêuue gelîcost.* Thuo sâuun sia ina sittian thar,
> thiu uuîf uppan them giuuendidan stêne,   endi fan them uulitie quâmun,
> them idison sulica egison tegegnes . . . (5779–82, 5803–12)

[The Jewish warriors, the fighting men with their shields, were sitting outside around the grave. The brilliant sunlight continued to glide upward. . . . suddenly the great stone lifted up, uncovering the grave, as God's angel pushed it aside. The Chieftain's great messenger sat down on the grave. In his movements and in his face, for anyone who attempted to look directly at him, he was as radiant and blissfully beaming as brilliant lightning (*sô bereht endi sô blîði all sô blicsmun lioht*)! His clothes were like a cold winter's snow. The women saw him sitting there on top of the stone which had been removed, and terror came over them because of the nearness of such radiance.]

The Old Saxon Heliand

With their relief at hearing the news from the angel that Christ is risen, the three Marys who had come to the tomb to anoint the body change from pale to radiant themselves: "The pale women, *bleca idisi*, felt strong feelings of relief taking hold in their hearts – radiantly beautiful women, *uuliti-sconi uuif*" (fitt 69). It is interesting to see the psychological depth that the author attaches once again to *uuliti*. As in modern English, the women are "beaming"! They are "radiant." And that seems to be the chief reason for bringing the poet's fellow Saxons to Christianity, so that they may be a part of this beautiful structure centered on light, and become a part of its radiant happiness.

Where did the author find inspiration for his light-filled version of Germanic Christianity? Though it may have been mediated from the Christian East, I believe it ultimately comes from the first chapter of John's Gospel, in which the Evangelist alludes to the first verses of Genesis. John reminds the reader that "in the beginning" the world was brought into being not by anything done by God, but simply by his speaking performative words, and God's very first word was "Let there be light." Christ is seen in the *Heliand* as one responsible for the magic spoken light-word, "Let there be light," in all its fullness of meaning, both radiation and happiness. It is he who brings himself to *middilgard*, to make Valhalla a Paradise beaming with happiness and light for Peter and his Saxon warrior-companions. For the poet of the *Heliand*, John the Evangelist's words about Christ were shaping and defining:

> In the beginning was the Word, and the Word was with God, and the Word was God. . . . All things were made through Him [and thus the beginning of the *Heliand* in which all things are held together by God's Words]. In Him was life, and that life was the light of men. And the light shines in the darkness and the darkness grasped it not. . . . It was the true light, the light that enlightens every man, that was coming into the world. He was in the world, and the world was made through Him and the world knew Him not, . . . but as many as received Him he gave the power of becoming the sons of God.

The *Heliand* is one of the great hidden treasures, hard to fit into a history of German(ic) literature and thus easily overlooked, yet clearly part of it and a foundational document of Western culture. It deserves much greater attention for the light it can shed on the roots and origins of Germanic culture and Christianity. There is a great deal of value in reading a document like the *Heliand* written at a time when English and North German, Anglo-Saxon and Saxon, were not really two different languages. It is impossible not to feel the power of the work, and there is a great opportunity for those interested in cultural studies to begin to do comparative work between the Anglo-Saxon *Beowulf*, for instance, and the Saxon *Heliand*. In both works there is a confluence of Germanic and Christian culture in the poetry of two epic narratives. It is to be hoped that James E. Cathey's recent annotated edition of the Old Saxon text of the *Heliand* for students, and my translation and commentary, will be a help in making the *Heliand* more accessible, and that admirable philological scholarship continues to be pursued, notably in the work of D. H. Green and others,[18] which will open up ever more of the hidden wealth waiting in the words and worlds of the Old Saxon poem.

---

18 See D. H. Green, *The Carolingian Lord. Semantic Studies on Four Old High German Words: balder, fro, truhtin, herro* (Cambridge: Cambridge UP, 1965). See also the valuable work on cultural confluence in the early medieval world, cited above, by James Russell, Stephen E. Flowers, and Valerie Flint. A recent doctoral dissertation undertaken at Georgetown University, Washington D.C., by Mark Dreisonstock initiates a fascinating new discussion of the opposition in the *Heliand* and in *Beowulf* to money and profit as a threat to the traditional warrior culture's concept of wealth as munificence.

An Overview of Old Saxon Linguistics, 1992–2008

Marc Pierce

The early Germanic languages all tend to appeal to different constituencies. Old English and Old Norse tend to attract significant attention from both literary scholars and linguists; Gothic seems to appeal the most to Indo-Europeanists and theoretical phonologists (as demonstrated by the attention paid to Sievers' Law in Gothic, which seems to be reassessed with every new phonological theory); and Old High German naturally attracts the most attention from those interested in the history of German. Old Saxon, on the other hand, has sometimes been the Cinderella of the early Germanic languages. Admittedly, the study of Old Saxon has not been as neglected as that of some of the others (e.g. Old Frisian and Old Low Franconian), but a good deal of work remains to be done.

Happily, though, there are signs that this traditional neglect is beginning to fade away. Beyond a general increase in the attention paid to Old Saxon, especially to the major Old Saxon text, the *Hêliand*,[1] note (1) the attention paid to the 2006 discovery of a new

---

1 The *Hêliand* ('Savior'), an approximately 6,000 line poem on the life of Christ, was composed in alliterative verse, and written about 830, probably in the monastery at Fulda. For some discussion of the possible place of composition, see James Cathey, *Hêliand: Text and commentary*, Medieval European Studies 2 (Morgantown: U of West Virginia Press, 2002), 17–18. Some sources write

leaf of the *Hêliand* in the Leipzig University library, and (2) the recent presence of a session on the *Hêliand* at the International Congress of Medieval Studies, held yearly at Western Michigan University in Kalamazoo, Michigan. The West Virginia University Press has sponsored this session every year since 2002, and the session has featured papers on a number of *Hêliand*-related topics, by a number of different scholars, both senior and junior.

This paper provides a brief overview of recent work in Old Saxon linguistics, from 1992 to 2008.[2] 1992 was selected as a starting date because that year saw the publication of two major works on Old Saxon, namely a new grammar of the language by Irmengard Rauch and a new translation of the *Hêliand* into English by G. Ronald Murphy. This paper is not comprehensive, and certainly not exhaustive, but instead offers a bird's-eye-view, looking at only a few articles for each linguistic topic. It is also generally limited to works published in English or German, as these are the two languages most commonly used in Old Saxon studies, although this does not mean that Old Saxon studies is the exclusive provenance of these two languages.[3] The focus here is on the Old Saxon *Hêliand*, although works on the Old Saxon Genesis are also considered. Finally, it concentrates on published work and not on recent presentations or unpublished

---

Heliand without a macron; I follow Cathey and write the word with a macron. When quoting I maintain the usage of the source.
2   This limitation means that some important recent works – e.g. Klaus Gantert, *Akkommodation und eingeschriebener Kommentar: Untersuchungen zur Übertragungsstrategie des Helianddichters* (Tübingen: Narr, 1998); Cynthia Zurla, *Medium and Message: The Confluence of Saxon and Frankish Values as Portrayed in the Old Saxon Heliand*, Doctoral Diss. (McGill University, 2005); and Gesine Mierke, *Memoria als Kulturtransfer: Der alsächsische »Heliand« zwischen Spätantike und Frühmittelalter*, Studien zur Literatur und Gesellschaft des Mittelalters und der frühen Neuzeit 11 (Cologne: Böhlau, 2008) – will not be treated here, as they fall into the area of cultural studies, not linguistics.
3   A French translation of the *Hêliand*, for instance, was published in 2008: E. Vanneufville, trans., *Heliand: L'évangile de la mer du Nord* (Turnhout: Brepols, 2008).

manuscripts (though some such works are also covered). It begins with a discussion of the Leipzig fragment of the *Hêliand*, and then turns to handbooks (including translations), phonology, metrics, syntax, morphology, semantics, and etymology, in that order.

As noted above, a new leaf of the *Hêliand* was discovered in the library of Leipzig University in April 2006 by Thomas Döring, an employee of the library. The discovery was entirely accidental: A seventeenth-century book with a cover that Mr. Döring did not recognize happened to catch his eye. The cover was identified by Hans Ulrich Schmid of the Institut für Germanistik at the Universität Leipzig as a fragment of the *Hêliand* on the following grounds: The text was written in Carolingian miniscule, was in alliterative verse, and exhibited some typically Old Saxon lexical items (e.g. *sten* 'rock' and *ik uuet* 'I know'). Schmid confirmed his hunch that it was a fragment from the *Hêliand* by checking the appropriate section of Eduard Sievers's (1878) edition of the poem.[4] The Leipzig fragment "consists of one leaf of *Hêliand* verse line 5823 '. . .ndan' to line 5846 'te' or 'to' (vowel unclear) on the outer side of the book cover, and verse line 5846 'strang' to line 5870 'forahta' on the inner side of the book cover,"[5] and deals with the speech of the women at Jesus's grave (see Luke 24). The fragment has been dated to the ninth century on paleographic and linguistic grounds, making it contemporary to the Monacensis MS M, and to the fragments MS P (Prague), MS V (Vatican), and MS S (Straubing), and approximately one century earlier than the Cotton Caligula MS C, which is the only extant manuscript of the *Hêliand* containing the same section of the text as the Leipzig fragment. Commentaries on the fragment by Rauch, Schmid, and

---

4   Eduard Sievers, ed., *Heliand* (Halle: Waisenhaus, 1878). For details on the discovery of the fragment, see Hans Ulrich Schmid, "Ein neues ‚Heliand'-Fragment aus der Universitätsbibliothek Leipzig," *Zeitschrift für deutsches Altertum und deutsche Literatur* 135 (2006), 309.
5   Irmengard Rauch, "The Newly Found Leipzig *Heliand* Fragment," *Interdisciplinary Journal of Germanic Linguistics and Semiotic Analysis* 11 (2006), 2.

Heike Sahm are available.⁶ Its discovery also received a good deal of mainstream media attention, including coverage in *Die Welt* and the *Berliner Morgenpost*.⁷

The discovery of the Leipzig fragment will have a significant impact on the study of Old Saxon; at the very least it will have a similar effect to the discovery of the "New Leaf" of the Gothic Bible, found in Speyer in 1971,⁸ and at most it will lead to a reinterpretation of traditional thinking about the role of the *Hêliand* in history. Rauch noted the following possible points of linguistic relevance: (1) The Leipzig fragment confirms certain conjectures about readings in some of the other *Hêliand* manuscripts; (2) paleographic considerations of the Leipzig fragment, specifically the initial capital <H>, support the fitt divisions described by the Latin *Praefatio*, but only present in MS C; (3) it supplies additional data, which can only be welcomed, given the relatively limited amount of Old Saxon data available, and (4) the fragment "strengthens the putative association of the Latin prose and verse Prefaces with the *Hêliand*."⁹ Within a broader historical context, Rauch noted that in the mid-sixteenth century, the Reformation theologian Philipp Melanchthon praised "Louis the Pious for commissioning a Gospel harmony, which Melanchthon claims Luther is reading and which is housed in the Leipzig Pauliner Library."¹⁰ The Leipzig fragment

---

6   Ibid., 1–17; Schmid, "Ein neues ‚Heliand'-Fragment" [note 4]; idem, "Nochmals zum Leipziger 'Heliand'-Fragment," *Zeitschrift für deutsches Altertum und deutsche Literatur* 136 (2007), 376–78; and Heike Sahm, "Neues Licht auf alte Fragen: Die Stellung des Leipziger Fragments in der Überlieferungsgeschichte des *Heliand*," *Zeitschrift für deutsche Philologie* 126 (2007), 81–98.

7   Some such articles on the Leipzig fragment were still available online as of May 14, 2008. The press release from the University of Leipzig can be read at the following URL: *http://db.uni-leipzig.de/aktuell/index.php?pmnummer=2006155*.

8   Oswald J. L. Szemerényi, "A New Leaf of the Gothic Bible," *Language* 48 (1972), 1–10.

9   Rauch, "The Newly Found Leipzig *Heliand* Fragment" [note 5], 13–14. The controversy over the *Fitten* is far too wide-ranging to be treated here.

10 Rauch, "The Newly Found Leipzig *Heliand* Fragment" [note 5], 14.

provides evidence for this claim, and allows us to answer, with a tentative "yes," the question posed by Murphy: "Was Luther acquainted with the *Heliand*?"[11]

I turn now to a discussion of the handbooks on Old Saxon.[12] The paucity of handbooks, as well as the delays in updating and reprinting those that do exist, are reasonably clear signs of the relative neglect of Old Saxon.[13] The two standard grammars before 1992 were those by Ferdinand Holthausen (1921) and Johann H. Gallée (1910)[14]; the two main dictionaries were those by E. H. Sehrt (1966) and Samuel Berr (1971).[15] Beyond this, there was Gerhard Cordes's *Elementarbuch* (1973), which was originally planned as the third edition of Holthausen's grammar, but became an almost completely new work (although

---

11   G. Ronald Murphy, trans., *The Heliand: The Saxon Gospel* (Oxford: Oxford UP, 1992), 12n19. Murphy (ibid.) notes the similarity of Luther's rendering of the Latin phrase *gratia plenia* (traditionally rendered as 'full of grace') as *du bist deinem Herrn lieb* to the phrase used in the *Hêliand* (*thu bist thinun herron liof*), whence his question of Luther's acquaintance with the *Hêliand*.

12   Shorter handbook-type works, e.g. the chapter on Old Saxon in Orrin W. Robinson, *Old English and Its Closest Relatives* (Stanford: Stanford UP, 1992), are not treated here. Some other handbooks – e.g. Steffen Krogh, *Die Stellung des Altsächsischen im Rahmen der germanischen Sprachen*, Studien zum Althochdeutschen 29 (Göttingen: Vandenhoeck & Ruprecht, 1996); and Martin Fuss, *Die religiöse Lexik des Althochdeutschen und Altsächsischen* (Frankfurt: Peter Lang, 2000), are also not considered.

13   E. A. Ebbinghaus, Review of *The Old Saxon Language: Grammar, Epic Narrative, Linguistic Interference*, by Irmengard Rauch, *General Linguistics* 33 (1993), 123, cites this lack of appropriate handbooks as one of the reasons for the relative neglect of the study of Old Saxon.

14   Ferdinand Holthausen, *Altsächsisches Elementarbuch*, 2nd ed. (Heidelberg: Carl Winter, 1921); Johann H. Gallée, *Altsächsische Grammatik*, 2nd ed., rev. Johannes Lochner (Halle: Max Niemeyer, 1910). Gallée's grammar was reprinted with minor corrections in 1993: *Altsächsische Grammatik*, 3rd ed., rev. Heinrich Tiefenbach (Tübingen: Max Niemeyer, 1993).

15   E. H. Sehrt, *Vollständiges Wörterbuch zum Heliand und zur altsächsischen Genesis*, 2nd ed. (Göttingen: Vandenhoeck & Ruprecht, 1966); Samuel Berr, *Etymological Glossary to the Old Saxon Heliand* (New York: Peter Lang, 1971).

Cordes retained Holthausen's chapter on syntax).[16] The latter work was received with caution; see the reviews by Herbert Penzl and Heinrich Tiefenbach for some relevant commentary.[17] Since 1992 a number of new handbooks have become available, as follows.

Rauch's *The Old Saxon Language*,[18] as one might expect from the author's previous innovative work on Old Saxon,[19] departed from the traditional Neogrammarian-style grammars of Holthausen, Gallée, and Cordes in several significant ways: its language of composition, since it was the first grammar of Old Saxon written in English; its use of semiotic concepts; and its audience (it was "written for the neophyte as well as the seasoned scholar").[20] Among other innovations, Rauch attempted to introduce students to various concepts from theoretical linguistics and moved away from the historical/comparative grounding of earlier grammars, aiming to introduce students to Old Saxon on its own (synchronic) terms rather than by extensive comparison to the other early Germanic languages.[21]

---

16   Gerhard Cordes, *Altniederdeutsches Elementarbuch: Wort- und Lautlehre* (Heidelberg: Carl Winter, 1973).

17   Herbert Penzl, review of *Altniederdeutsches Elementarbuch: Wort- und Lautlehre*, by Gerhard Cordes, *Language* 52 (1976), 514 praised Cordes's "thorough familiarity with the OS corpus, his careful workmanship, and his philological skill," but felt that the book might "prove too difficult, idiosyncratic, and partly flawed to serve as an introduction to OS for the neophyte." Heinrich Tiefenbach, "Anmerkungen zu einem Altneiderdeutschen Elementarbuch," *Beiträge zur Namenforschung* 10 (1975), 64–75, offered a more negative assessment of the work.

18   Irmengard Rauch, *The Old Saxon Language: Grammar, Epic Narrative, Linguistic Interference*, Berkeley Models of Grammars 1 (New York: Peter Lang, 1992).

19   See for instance Irmengard Rauch, "What Can Generative Grammar Do for Etymology? An Old Saxon Hapax," *Semasia: Beiträge zur germanisch-romanischen Sprachforschung* 2 (1975), 249–60.

20   Rauch, *The Old Saxon Language* [note 18], xxv.

21   This does not mean, however, that Rauch completely left diachrony to one side, as her treatment of Old Saxon umlaut illustrates, in which she distinguished between diachronic and synchronic umlaut rules (I use the term 'rule' here in a non-technical sense).

The motivation for this is clear: native speakers are normally not etymologists. Thus, Rauch argued for a model of "diachronic synchrony," meaning "ongoing variation and/or change within the Old Saxon language era."[22] One concrete example of this model was Rauch's treatment of Old Saxon phonology, which did not trace the development of each particular sound from Proto-Indo-European, but instead analyzed the place of each sound within the synchronic phonological system of Old Saxon.

Rauch's innovative treatment, as one might expect, met with mixed reviews. Richard D'Alquen stated that the book "offers such a wealth of thoughtful scholarly and pedagogic innovation, that it deserves appreciative scrutiny from us all. [. . .] The author deserves our thanks and congratulations."[23] This same innovation drew fire from other reviewers; Ebbinghaus and Hans F. Nielsen both criticized the book for treating Old Saxon in relative isolation, rather than comparing it more extensively with the other early Germanic languages.[24] In addition, both Ebbinghaus and Nielsen felt that the book required more knowledge of theoretical linguistics and more reading sophistication than one could reasonably expect from the absolute beginner in the study of historical Germanic linguistics.

More recently, James E. Cathey has written two handbooks on Old Saxon. His *Old Saxon* is rather short (seventy pages), and focuses mainly on the nuts and bolts of the language, although it does provide a brief synopsis of cultural and literary matters.[25] It is also much more traditionally oriented than Rauch's grammar;

---

22 Ibid., xxxv.
23 Richard D'Alquen, review of *The Old Saxon Language: Grammar, Epic Narrative, Linguistic Interference*, by Irmengard Rauch, *American Journal of Germanic Linguistics and Literatures* 6 (1992), 93–94.
24 Ebbinghaus, review of *The Old Saxon Language* [note 13]; Hans F. Nielsen, review of *The Old Saxon Language: Grammar, Epic Narrative, Linguistic Interference*, by Irmengard Rauch, *Word* 46 (1995), 442–44.
25 James E. Cathey, *Old Saxon*, Languages of the World 252 (Munich: Lincom Europa, 2000).

Cathey explicitly referred to the Neogrammarian pattern of writing grammars, stating that the "sequential presentation of the grammar is arrayed in the pattern set by the *Junggrammatiker* that is familiar to Germanists."[26] Cathey's *Hêliand: Text and Commentary* provided much more detail on cultural and literary matters than his earlier book, although somewhat less detail on grammatical topics (its grammar section is just over thirty pages long).[27] It is designed to fulfill two major purposes: (1) to make Old Saxon and the *Hêliand* accessible to students who do not know German, and (2) to make an English-language edition of the *Hêliand* available. As such, it fills a definite need. There are invariably students who would be interested in Old Saxon but may be put off by the need to work through so much German. Moreover, courses in Old Saxon are sometimes cross-listed with other departments (most commonly English), and one cannot always expect students from such departments to have a good reading knowledge of German. An English-language edition of the *Hêliand* was also a desideratum for English-speaking audiences.[28]

In many ways, both of these works are very successful. Cathey's *Old Saxon* has unfortunately not received as much attention as one might wish, although Joseph F. Eska praised it highly, stating that it "packs copious information into few pages and will serve those with either diachronic or synchronic interests very well."[29] *Hêliand: Text and Commentary* is the culmination of its author's long engagement with Old Saxon and the *Hêliand*.[30] Its commentary is inevitably detailed,

---

26   Ibid., 4.
27   Cathey, *Hêliand: Text and Commentary* [note 1].
28   There are several German-language editions of the text; the standard is Otto Behaghel, ed., *Heliand und Genesis*, 10th ed., rev. Burkhard Taeger, Altdeutsche Textbibliothek 4 (Tübingen: Max Niemeyer, 1996).
29   Joseph F. Eska, book notice of *Old Saxon*, by James E. Cathey, *Language* 79 (2003), 836.
30   See for instance James E. Cathey, "Give Us This Day Our Daily *râd*," *Journal of English and Germanic Philology* 94 (1995), 157–75; idem, "Die Rhetorik der Weisheit und Beredtheit im altsächsischen *Hêliand*," *Literaturwissenschaftliches*

insightful, and careful (thus avoiding some of the problems inherent to more speculative works). It unfortunately does not cover the entire *Hêliand* (only about half the text is included), and may require too high a level of linguistic sophistication to be used by absolute beginners. Reviewers have generally agreed with this positive assessment; John M. Jeep, for instance, lauds Cathey's "rich commentary," but suggests that the incompleteness of the text means that it will have to be used in conjunction with the English translation by Murphy, which is discussed below.[31]

As for translations of the *Hêliand*, an inexpensive translation into German by Felix Genzmer was long available as a separate work (it was reprinted as recently as 1989), and has recently been republished in a dual-language edition.[32] English translations were much less accessible. Mariana Scott's *The Heliand* (1966), the earliest complete translation of the poem into English, sought to mirror the structure and style of the original by using alliterative verse and archaic English words like "weeds" for "clothes," and "quick" for "alive."[33] Scott's translation met with mixed reviews, and it was clear that a new translation of the *Hêliand* into English would be welcome.[34]

Jahrbuch, N. F. 37 (1996), 31–46; and idem, "Interpretatio Christiana Saxonica: Redefinition for Re-education," in *Interdigitations: Essays for Irmengard Rauch*, ed. Gerald F. Carr et al. (New York: Peter Lang, 1999), 163–72.

31 John M. Jeep, review of *Hêliand: Text and Commentary*, by James E. Cathey, *Speculum* 79 (2002), 99–104.

32 Felix Genzmer, trans., *Heliand und die Bruchsücke der Genesis*, 2nd ed. (Stuttgart: P. Reclam, 1989). The dual-language edition is Clemens Burchhardt, ed., *Heliand : Die Verdener altsächsische Evangelium-Dichtung von 830 übertragen ins 21. Jahrhundert* (Verden: Wirtschaftsförderkreis des Domherrenhauses, 2007).

33 Mariana Scott, trans., *The Heliand: Translated from the Old Saxon*, University of North Carolina Studies in the Germanic Languages and Literatures 52 (Chapel Hill: U of North Carolina Press, 1966).

34 On Scott's successes and shortcomings, see George Fenwick Jones, review of *The Heliand*, by Mariana Scott, *Modern Language Notes* 82 (1966), 488–90; and Robert L. Kyes, review of *The Heliand*, by Mariana Scott, *The Modern Language Journal* 52 (1968), 46–47.

In 1992, such a translation was published by Murphy. This, which built on a number of his earlier works,[35] attempted to avoid some of the aspects of Scott's work that had been criticized by other scholars.[36] To that end, he chose to translate the poem into English prose, largely because he felt that attempts to force Old Saxon alliterative poetry into English alliterative poetry sometimes sacrificed meaning for alliteration.[37] Like Scott, Murphy did use more archaic English vocabulary at times, such as "thane" (or sometimes "warrior") instead of "knight" to render Old Saxon *degen*, or when he translated Old Saxon *Nazarethburg* (glossed by Cathey as "Stronghold at Nazareth") as "hill-fort Nazareth" or "Fort Nazareth."[38] And like Scott's earlier translation, Murphy's new translation met with mixed reviews. Gerald F. Carr praised it highly, calling it "most readable" and "skillful,"[39] but Joseph Wilson contended that Murphy's translation is so filled with mistakes that "the careful reader [. . .] can unfortunately have no confidence in anything that Murphy says."[40] Be that as it may, Murphy's translation is both more accessible and readable than Scott's. It remains in print, and will therefore presumably remain a fixture in Old Saxon studies for some time to come.[41]

---

35 See especially G. Ronald Murphy, *The Saxon Savior: The Germanic Transformation of the Gospel in the Ninth-Century Heliand* (New York: Oxford UP, 1989); and idem, "Magic in the *Heliand*," *Monatshefte* 83 (1991), 386–97.
36 Murphy, *The Heliand* [note 11].
37 Ibid., xiv-xv.
38 Cathey, *Hêliand: Text and Commentary* [note 1], 338.
39 Gerald F. Carr, review of *The Saxon Savior: The Germanic Transformation of the Gospel in the Ninth-Century Heliand* and *The Heliand: The Saxon Gospel*, by G. Ronald Murphy, *American Journal of Germanic Linguistics and Literatures* 6 (1994), 99.
40 Joseph Wilson, review of *The Heliand: The Saxon Gospel*, by G. Ronald Murphy, *Journal of English and Germanic Philology* 94 (1995), 455.
41 Tonya Kim Dewey (University of California, Berkeley) has prepared a new translation of the *Hêliand* into English, which is to be published by Edwin Mellen Press, but I have not yet seen this work.

An Overview of Old Saxon Linguistics, 1992–2008

I turn now to the study of Old Saxon phonology. Unlike its closest relative, Old High German, whose phonology has been investigated in great detail over the years, Old Saxon phonology has largely been neglected. Moreover, Old Saxon data has played a much more minor role than data from the other early Germanic languages (especially Gothic) in the development of linguistic theory. Several recent studies, however, do draw on Old Saxon data to illustrate points of more general linguistic interest. Cristian Iscrulescu, for instance, used Old Saxon data in his Optimality Theory analysis of the interaction between grammatical and phonological markedness, leading to what he calls the "Marked in the Marked (MIM) generalization."[42] According to Iscrulescu, "outputs inflected for a marked grammatical category are characterized by equal or greater phonological markedness than outputs inflected for the unmarked category."[43] He argued that MIM allows a better analysis of case marking in Old Saxon, claiming that in the nominative and accusative case, the case suffix -*u* is deleted if its retention would lead to an uneven trochee (a foot consisting of a heavy syllable and a light syllable), as in forms like *luft* 'air' (contrast this with the retention of the -*u* in forms like *heru* 'sword'). In the dative case the case ending is retained no matter what kind of foot results (e.g. *heru* with an even trochee and *luftu* with an uneven trochee). Iscrulescu ascribed this development to the MIM: The dative case is grammatically marked and therefore shows a greater degree of phonological markedness than the grammatical unmarked nominative/accusative case.[44]

In other recent work, Laura Catharine Smith has argued that various phonological phenomena in the West Germanic languages

---

42 Cristian Iscrulescu, *The Phonological Dimension of Grammatical Markedness*, Doctoral diss. (University of Southern California, 2006).
43 Ibid., 263.
44 For another analysis of Old Saxon data (specifically degemination) using Optimality Theory, see Marc Pierce, "Constraints on Syllable Structure in Early Germanic," *Journal of Indo-European Studies* 28 (2000), 17–29.

can best be analyzed in terms of prosodic templates, both "simple templates that are defined in terms of feet alone and complex templates which are based on the interaction of feet with other levels of the prosodic hierarchy."[45] Examples of such phenomena include plural formation in Modern German, diminutive formation in Modern German and Modern Dutch, and the loss of *i* in Old High German *-jan* verbs and Old Saxon *i*-stems. In Smith's view, *i*-loss in the Old Saxon *i*-stems is best accounted for by means of prosodic templates, specifically a simple foot-based template.

The handbook analysis of this phenomena is straightforward: The thematic vowel *i* is lost in long stem nouns but retained in short stem nouns, as the following forms show: *gast* 'guest' and *quân* 'woman' are long stems and thus show deletion, while *stedi* 'city' and *uuini* 'friend' are short stems and thus do not show deletion. Smith argued that the preferred foot in Old Saxon was the moraic trochee (a bimoraic, left-headed foot), and that *i*-loss took place to fit words to this template. Thus, while **gasti* and **quâni* cannot be parsed exhaustively into moraic trochees, *i*-loss ensured that *gast* and *quân* could. Forms like *stedi* and *uuini*, on the other hand, can be parsed exhaustively into moraic trochees, and the *i* is therefore maintained. Smith further argued that this approach successfully accounts for the failure of *i*-loss to occur in trisyllabic words like *friundskepi* 'friendship', since the final *i*, which could be syncopated, can be footed as part of the word and is therefore retained.

Beyond works like this, data from Old Saxon has commonly been invoked for comparative purposes, as in the study of *i*-umlaut in early Germanic. Of the early Germanic languages, *i*-umlaut in Old High German and Old Norse has attracted the most attention,

---

45   Laura Catharine Smith, "The Resilience of Prosodic Templates in the History of West Germanic," in *Historical Linguistics 2005*, ed. Joseph Salmons and Shanon Dubenion-Smith (Amsterdam: John Benjamins, 2007), 350. See also idem, *Cross-Level Interactions in West Germanic Phonology and Morphology*, Doctoral diss. (University of Wisconsin-Madison, 2004).

but Old Saxon data continues to play a role in the discussion; Jens Elmgård Rasmussen and Bo Isakson both drew on Old Saxon data for their discussions of *i*-umlaut in West Germanic.[46] Perhaps the most radical recent use of Old Saxon data in the study of umlaut is by Mervin R. Barnes, who contended that *i*-umlaut originated in Old Saxon and spread from Old Saxon into Old High German.[47] Old Saxon data is also commonly used in the discussion of other West Germanic phonological phenomena, e.g. West Germanic Consonant Gemination, as in a recent dissertation by Craig J. Callender and in Kurt G. Goblirsch's treatment of the development of the Old Saxon consonantal system as part of a broader discussion of Germanic consonants.[48] Other recent treatments of Old Saxon phonology include Yasushi Kawasaki's on the connection between phonology and orthography in the *Hêliand* manuscripts and Michael P. Coffey's on monophthongization.[49]

Old Saxon metrics has received a fair amount of attention in recent years. This was not always the case; in a review written in 1981, Ruth P. M. Lehmann could note that Old English and Old Norse meter had been analyzed in great detail, but a good deal of work needed to be done on Old Saxon (the standard handbooks of

---

46 Jens Elmgård Rasmussen, "The Growth of i-Umlaut in Norse and West Germanic: Thoughts on a Recent Book," *Acta Linguistica Hafniensia* 32 (2000), 143–59; Bo Isakson, "How Primary was the OHG Primary Umlaut?" *NOWELE: North-Western European Language Evolution* 41 (2002), 99–104.
47 Mervin R. Barnes, "Old High German Umlaut," in *Interdigitations* [note 30], 239–46.
48 Craig J. Callender, *Gemination in West Germanic*, Doctoral diss. (University of South Carolina, 2006); Kurt G. Goblirsch, "The Voicing of Fricatives in West Germanic and the Partial Consonant Shift," *Folia Linguistica Historica* 24 (2003), 111–52; and idem, *Lautverschiebungen in den germanischen Sprachen* (Heidelberg: Carl Winter, 2005).
49 Yasushi Kawasaki, *Eine graphematische Untersuchung zu den HELIAND-Handschriften* (Munich: Iudicium, 2004); Michael P. Coffey, *Autosegmental Processes in Early Germanic: Evidence from Northwest Germanic*, Doctoral diss. (University of California-Berkeley, 2005).

course provided brief discussions).⁵⁰ The situation was somewhat remedied by the publication of Dietrich Hofmann's *Die Versstrukturen der altsächsischen Steibreimgedichte Heliand und Genesis*, as well as by works such as Geoffrey Russom's *Beowulf and Old Germanic Metre*, which included a chapter on Old Saxon alliterative verse, and Douglas P. A. Simms's 2003 dissertation on comparative metrics, which examined hypermetric verses in Old Saxon and then offered a comparative study of hypermetric verse in Old English and Old Saxon as opposed to Old Norse *dróttkvætt*.⁵¹ The most significant recent studies on Old Saxon metrics are Seiichi Suzuki's *The Metre of Old Saxon Poetry* and his articles on the same theme, which are in some respects follow-ups to his earlier works (especially his detailed study of the meter of *Beowulf*).⁵²

Unlike Hofmann, who focused on Old Saxon meter on its own terms, Suzuki compared Old Saxon meter with that of Old English,

---

50   Ruth P. M. Lehmann, review of *Zur Heliandmetrik: Das Verhältnis von Rhythmus und Satzgewicht im Altsächsischen*, by Ingeborg Hinderscheidt, *Speculum* 56 (1981), 391–93.

51   Dietrich Hofmann, *Die Versstrukturen der altsächsischen Stabreimgedichte Heliand und Genesis*, 2 vols. (Heidelberg: Carl Winter, 1991); Geoffrey Russom, *Beowulf and Old Germanic Metre* (Cambridge: Cambridge UP, 1998); and Douglas P. A. Simms, *Reconstructing an Oral Tradition: Problems in the Comparative Metrical Analysis of Old English, Old Saxon and Old Norse Alliterative Verse*, Doctoral diss. (University of Texas-Austin, 2003). Geoffrey Russom, "A Bard's-Eye View of the Germanic Syllable," *Journal of English and Germanic Philology* 101 (2002), 305–28, also draws on Old Saxon (as well as evidence from Old Norse) but, as in his earlier study, his focus is on Old English.

52   Seiichi Suzuki, *The Metre of Old Saxon Poetry: The Remaking of Alliterative Tradition* (Cambridge: D. S. Brewer, 2004); idem, "Anacrusis in the Meter of the *Heliand*," in *Interdigitations* [note 30], 189–99; idem, "The Metrical Reorganization of Type E in the *Heliand*," *American Journal of Germanic Linguistics and Literatures* 12 (2000), 281–90; and idem, "The Metrical Organization of the *Heliand*: Gradation and Harmonization," *Interdisciplinary Journal for Germanic Linguistics and Semiotic Analysis* 6 (2001), 11–39. Suzuki's metrical analysis of *Beowulf* culminated in *The Metrical Organization of Beowulf: Prototype and Isomorphism*, Trends in Linguistics 95 (Berlin: Mouton de Gruyter, 1996).

especially that of *Beowulf*. Among other issues, Suzuki rejected the idea defended by various scholars (by Russom, for instance) that the *Hêliand* is a monument to a dying poetic tradition,[53] assumed that Old Saxon meter and Old English meter are rooted in the same Germanic poetic tradition (which Suzuki defined as the meter of *Beowulf*), and argued that the *Hêliand* poet was both aware of the Germanic poetic tradition and revised the metrical system of Old Saxon – based on his knowledge of the Germanic poetic tradition – to accommodate the various changes that were in progress in the language at the time of the composition of the *Hêliand*. He characterizes the *Hêliand* poet as follows:

> In light of the minimal departures from tradition and maximal effects of harmonization that the poet accomplished in his versemaking, we may infer that the Heliand poet would have had a firm working knowledge of traditional metre, a daring spirit of innovation, and a profound sense of balance and symmetry, in conjunction with an admirably sensitive awareness of linguistic differences between Old English and Old Saxon down to their details and subtleties.[54]

In Suzuki's view, then, the *Hêliand* is not the product of "a [poetic] tradition in decline,"[55] but instead represents a poetic tradition at the height of its powers.

Suzuki's is an innovative work in many respects, only a few of which can be touched on here. In addition to offering a thorough synchronic overview of Old Saxon meter, he tackled various differences between Old Saxon meter and Old English meter, such as the obscuration of the

---

53   This view is normally rooted in the idea that various linguistic changes affecting Old Saxon (e.g. changes in the primary stress system and their consequences, including vowel epenthesis in certain contexts and the restoration of historically syncopated vowels, presumably due to analogy) also affected Old Saxon meter.
54   Suzuki, *The Metre of Old Saxon Poetry* [note 52], xvi.
55   Russom, *Beowulf and Old Germanic Metre* [note 51], 170.

difference between Type A1 and type A2 verses in Old Saxon as opposed to their maintenance in Old English, as well as various differences in the systems of resolution and alliteration. Suzuki also accounted for some oddities about hypermetric verses in the *Hêliand*. These verses are significantly more common in the *Hêliand* than elsewhere (0.3% of the verses in *Beowulf* are hypermetric, as compared to just under 3% of the verses in the *Hêliand*, according to Suzuki), just over 10% of the hypermetric verses in the *Hêliand* occur in isolation, and they may be used with anacrusis (neither of these last two generalizations is true of *Beowulf*). Suzuki's account of such verses links them to the reorganization of anacrusis and of verse types by the *Hêliand* poet. Finally, he analyzed the meter of the Old Saxon Genesis and discussed some of the differences between the meter of Genesis and that of the *Hêliand*, which in his view is the result of Genesis hewing more closely to traditional metrical principles than the *Hêliand*.

Suzuki's work met with mixed reviews. Tonya Kim Dewey suggested that it "can be considered a groundbreaking work, possibly the new standard text in Old Saxon metrics," but criticized the text for its "analysis of Old Saxon syntax and its effects on the meter, which does not seem to follow any standard syntactic analysis."[56] Robert D. Fulk called the book "an important and useful contribution to the ongoing study of early Germanic meters, for which metrists will be grateful."[57] Finally, Russom offered a generally positive appraisal of Suzuki's work but criticized it for not going as far as it might have, arguing that it "represents Old Saxon metre as thoroughly restructured [. . .] [but] does not present an explicit rule system for the *Heliand* that distinguishes metrical verses from unmetrical verses

---

56   Tonya Kim Dewey, review of *The Metre of Old Saxon Poetry: The Remaking of Alliterative Tradition*, by Seiichi Suzuki, *Interdisciplinary Journal for Germanic Linguistics and Semiotic Analysis* 11 (2006), 281.
57   Robert D. Fulk, review of *The Metre of Old Saxon Poetry: The Remaking of Alliterative Tradition*, by Seiichi Suzuki, *Journal of Germanic Linguistics* 17 (2005), 153.

across the board."[58] Thus, in Russom's view, Suzuki has formulated "explicit constraints of great interest for individual verse types but has not integrated them into a coherent whole."[59] It does seem, though, that future work on Old Saxon meter will have to take a stand with regard to Suzuki's work, whether for or against it.[60]

Recent studies of Old Saxon syntax and morphology include the following. Dewey treated verb position in Old Saxon as part of a larger study of verb position in the early Germanic languages, drawing her evidence largely from alliterative verse.[61] In Old Saxon, unstressed finite verbs tend to appear in second position (verb second, hereafter V2), which Dewey saw as an inheritance from Proto-Germanic, and also as intonationally conditioned.[62] Various developments in Old Saxon (as well as in Old Norse) eliminated this intonational conditioning, allowing for verb placement according to purely syntactic factors. That is, changes in the stress pattern of Old Saxon and resulting changes in the metrical system, meant that "the inherited tendency for auxiliaries and finite verbs in unbound clauses to occur in second position due to their intonationally weak status was no longer motivated on intonational grounds [...] [and] was reanalyzed as a syntactic pattern based on clause type."[63] She suggested that this

---

58   Geoffrey Russom, review of *The Metre of Old Saxon Poetry: The Remaking of Alliterative Tradition*, by Seiichi Suzuki, *Anglia* 123 (2005), 704–05.
59   Ibid., 705.
60   Other recent works on Old Saxon meter include Ari Hoptman, *Verner's Law, Stress, and the Accentuation of Old Germanic Poetry*, Doctoral diss. (University of Minnesota-Minneapolis, 2002); Thomas Bredehoft, "Old English and Old Saxon Formulaic Rhyme," *Anglia* 123 (2005), 204–29; and Megan Hartman, "Kuhn's Law, Old Saxon, and the Hypermetric Line," Conference paper presented at GLAC 14 (Madison, Wisconsin, 2008).
61   Tonya Kim Dewey, *The Origins and Development of Germanic V2: Evidence from Alliterative Verse*, Doctoral diss. (University of California-Berkeley, 2006).
62   Dewey saw this tendency as similar to, but not identical with, Wackernagel's Law; see Jacob Wackernagel, "Über ein Gesetz der indogermanischen Wortstellung," *Indogermanische Forschungen* 1 (1892), 333–436.
63   Dewey, *The Origins and Development of Germanic V2* [note 61], 106.

change was not completed by the time of the *Hêliand*, but was instead a change in progress. Furthermore, the Old Saxon data, along with data from Old Norse and Gothic, motivated Dewey's claim that V2 in the modern Germanic languages is an inheritance from the older languages, and not an independent innovation.

Other current approaches to syntax have also been brought to bear on Old Saxon data. Carlee Arnett analyzed variation in auxiliary selection within the framework of Cognitive Grammar, specifically the prototype model endorsed by this theory.[64] She examined all of the attestations of the perfect active tense formed with an auxiliary verb and a past participle in the *Hêliand* in order to answer the question of why some verbs use *uuesan* 'to be' as an auxiliary, while others use *hebbian* 'to have', much like the situation in Modern German. In Arnett's view, auxiliary selection is linked to prototypes: "Prototypical mutative events occur with *uuesan*, and prototypical transitive events occur with *hebbian*. Events that are not prototypically mutative or transitive show variation in the auxiliary they select."[65] Thus, verbs like *cuman* 'to come' occur with *uuesan*, while verbs like *sterkian* 'to strengthen' occur with *hebbian*. In a later paper, Arnett used Cognitive Grammar to analyze the passive in Old Saxon.[66] Here she argued that the two types of personal passive constructions found in Old Saxon (one with the subject in the nominative case and one with the participant in the dative case) can be traced to varying amounts of degree of transitivity: The first type of personal passive is highly transitive, while the second type is less so.

---

64   Carlee Arnett, "Perfect Selection in the Old Saxon *Heliand*," *American Journal of Germanic Linguistics and Literatures* 9 (1997), 23–72.
65   Ibid., 51. Arnett (ibid., 30) defines these terms as follows: "Prototypically mutative events involve a single participant that nonvolitionally undergoes a change of state [. . .]. Prototypically transitive events involve two participants such that the subject is highly potent, and the object is totally affected."
66   Carlee Arnett, "A Cognitive Approach to the Old Saxon Processual Passive," *American Journal of Germanic Linguistics and Literatures* 12 (2000), 81–99.

Old Saxon has also been used in grammaticalization studies.[67] For instance, Christopher M. Stevens entered the debate over the status of affixoids,[68] arguing that Old Saxon data, specifically derivational suffixes, can be fruitfully brought to bear on the problem, but also noting that controversy surrounds this question in the relevant literature on Old Saxon. (Among other difficulties, different scholars classify the same forms differently: What one scholar might see as a derivational morpheme, another might see as a stem or a root, and so on). Stevens attributed this controversy to the different approaches taken by different scholars, since some researchers approach the Old Saxon data from a diachronic perspective, while others approach it from a synchronic perspective (much like the situation in studies of Old Saxon phonology, as noted above). Stevens therefore argued in favor of a panchronic approach to the Old Saxon data: synchronic tests can be used to determine the status of a given form (specifically whether it is an affix or an affixoid), and at the same time diachronic considerations can steer one's thinking about the given form.

As to the specifics of his analysis, Stevens outlined some possible tests for affixes and affixoids – e.g. "the meaning of the affixoid is more generalized and abstract than the formally identical

---

67 On grammaticalization, see Paul J. Hopper and Elizabeth Closs Traugott, *Grammaticalization*, 2nd ed., Cambridge Textbooks in Linguistics (Cambridge: Cambridge UP, 2003).
68 Christopher M. Stevens, "The Derivational Suffixes and Suffixoids of Old Saxon: A Panchronic Approach to a Linguistic Category," *American Journal of Germanic Linguistics and Literatures* 12 (2000), 53–79. Stevens, "The Prefixes and Prefixoids of Old Saxon: On the Grammaticalization of the Old Saxon Adverbs and Prepositions," *Leuvense Bijdragen* 93 (2004), 152, defines the *affixoid* as "a linguistic item that is neither a root nor a derivational morph," for instance *-werk* in Modern German words like *Laubwerk* 'foliage', which can be contrasted with the *-werk* in forms like *Kraftwerk* 'power plant' (among other differences, words like *Laubwerk* cannot be pluralized, while words like *Kraftwerk* can). For a more general discussion of affixoids, see idem, "Revisiting the Affixoid Debate: On the Grammaticalization of the Word," in *Grammatikalisierung im Deutschen*, ed. Torsten Leuchner et al. (Berlin: Walter de Gruyter, 2005), 71–84.

parent"[69] – and then applied these tests to the derivational suffixes of Old Saxon listed as such by Cordes and Roland Zanni, e.g. *-fald* (as in *managfald* 'numerous, large, manifold' and *tehanfold* 'tenfold', among other forms), and *-fast* (as in *legarfast* 'bedridden' and *wârfast* 'true').[70] In Stevens's view, *-fald* is a suffix, while *-fast* is a suffixoid. He also hypothesized that the development of the various Old Saxon suffixes and suffixoids can be attributed to grammaticalization, as some of them are possibly "erstwhile roots on their way to becoming affixes."[71]

Stevens later examined the prefixes and prefixoids of Old Saxon in two separate publications.[72] In the first of these, he argued that certain root morphemes in Old Saxon have developed into grammatical morphemes (i.e. have been grammaticalized from root to affixoid). Consider his discussion of *megin* 'strength, power, troop, band, crowd', with 'strength, power' being the primary meaning and 'troop, band, crowd' the secondary meaning, which can be used both as a word on its own and as a prefixoid (as in words like *meginkraft* 'great power' and *meginsundea* 'great sin'). In Stevens's view, *megin* has perhaps developed along the following lines: It was originally a noun meaning 'strength, power, force', and then developed the additional meaning 'troop, band, crowd', at which stage it was used as a classifier. The third stage of its development was the addition of

---

69   Stevens, "The Derivational Suffixes" [note 68], 59.
70   Cordes, *Altniederdeutsches Elementarbuch* [note 16]; Roland Zanni, "Wortbildung des Altniederdeutschen (Altsächsischen)," in *Sprachgeschichte: Ein Handbuch zur Geschichte der deutschen Sprache und ihrer Erforschung*, vol. 2., ed. Werner Besch et al. (Berlin: De Gruyter, 1985), 1094–1102.
71   Stevens, "The Derivational Suffixes" [note 68], 77.
72   Christopher M. Stevens, "More Prefixes and Prefixoids of Old Saxon and Further Examples of the Grammaticalization of the Old Saxon Root," *Leuvense Bijdragen* 91 (2002), 301–318; idem, "The Prefixes and Prefixoids" [note 68]. I focus here on his article from 2002, since the 2004 study follows essentially the same pattern as his article published in 2000, except that it examines prefixes and prefixoids instead of suffixes and suffixoids.

'great' (as in the two examples cited above) to its range of meanings, i.e. it became an intensifier; it also fits his tests for 'prefixoid-hood'. Stevens suggested that this possible path of development is along the lines of the development of *full* in English (which according to him has also developed from noun to classifier to prefixoid). Stevens also argued that, while the Old Saxon suffixoids and prefixoids are both good examples of grammaticalization, they generally are derived from different parts of speech; suffixoids and suffixes tend to come from nouns, adjectives, and adverbs, while prefixoids and prefixes tend to come from prepositions and adverbs. Moreover, their paths of grammaticalization tend to be different. His work shows both that Old Saxon data can be valuable for the study of grammaticalization, and that grammaticalization theory can fruitfully be applied to Old Saxon.

Other recent studies of Old Saxon morphology include the following: Jürg Fleischer examined predicate adjectives and participles in Old High German and Old Saxon, which can occur either as uninflected or inflected forms in certain contexts.[73] He argued that, in Old Saxon, the most important factor connected to the distribution of these forms is its position in the paradigm; for instance, in the masculine plural, the inflected form is more commonly used than the uninflected form, while in the singular the opposite tendency prevails. Grammatical gender in Old Saxon is treated by Frederick W. Schwink as part of a more general discussion of grammatical gender in Germanic. In Schwink's view, grammatical gender in Old Saxon is "in a state of considerable disarray and confusion, reflecting, like later Old English, a breakdown of the older declensional patterns, and a shift to *i*-stems that are not declensionally clear."[74] Another recent study of Old

---

73 Jürg Fleischer, "Das prädikative Adjektiv und Partizip im Althochdeutschen und Altniederdeutschen," *Sprachwissenschaft* 32 (2007), 279–348.
74 Frederick W. Schwink, *The Third Gender: Studies in the Origin and History of Germanic Grammatical Gender* (Heidelberg: Carl Winter, 2004), 55.

Saxon gender is that of Santeri Palviainen, which investigated the gender of the Old Saxon suffix -*skepi*. This suffix forms both masculine and neuter nouns, which is somewhat unexpected. In Palviainen's view, the normal gender of such nouns is masculine, and the unexpected neuter nouns are the result of influence from semantically parallel forms.[75]

A number of etymological studies have appeared in recent years. Alfred Bammesberger presented an etymology of Old Saxon *idis* 'woman, wife' (along with its cognates in Old English and Old High German).[76] He argued that these words all stem from a Germanic form **idis*, which is connected etymologically to Greek words meaning 'burn', and proposed three possible accounts for the semantic development from 'burn' to 'woman': (1) the personification of 'fire' as female divine being, and then the extension of this personification to women in general; (2) the extension of 'fire' to 'house' and 'master of the house' via 'fireplace'; (3) the metaphoric use of 'fire' for 'lover'. Bammesberger dealt with another Old Saxon etymology, this time *thimm* 'dark', a hapax legomenon attested in line 5627 of the *Hêliand*, which he traced to Proto-Germanic **þemma* and ultimately to Proto-Indo-European **temh-s-ó*.[77] Perhaps the most interesting part of his discussion is his treatment of the development of the geminate *m* in the Old Saxon form, which hinges on the shift of the *s* in the reconstructed PIE form to *z* in Proto-Germanic and the assumption that Proto-Germanic clusters consisting of nasal or liquid + *z* resulted in geminates in West Germanic.

Other recent etymological studies include that by Dirk Boutkan, which dealt with an Old Saxon fish name, specifically *hacth* 'pike'

---

75 Santeri Palviainen, "The Gender of the Old Saxon Suffix -*skepi*," *Harvard Working Papers in Linguistics* 12 (2007), n.p.
76 Alfred Bammesberger, "The Etymology of Germanic **idis*," *NOWELE: North-Western European Language Evolution* 52 (2007), 81–89.
77 Alfred Bammesberger, "As. *thimm*: Wortbildung und phonologische Entwicklung," *Amsterdamer Beiträge zur älteren Germanistik* 52 (1999), 3–9.

(attested in the Oxford Vergil glosses).[78] He argued that this word is semantically associated with a family of words meaning 'point, hook' (e.g. Old English *hôc* and Old High German *hako*, both meaning 'hook'),[79] since "the animal [is] named after its sharp teeth," as well as various forms in Uralic (e.g. Finnish *hanka* 'hook, oarlock').[80] In Boutkan's view, the Finnish word cannot be a loan word from Germanic, and he therefore concluded that the Old Saxon form is a borrowing from a non-Indo-European substrate. Whether Boutkan's analysis of the Old Saxon word is correct is debatable (I remain somewhat skeptical), but it is certainly thought-provoking. Finally, W. Wilfried Schuhmacher referred to Old Saxon to account for the development of Low German (Velbert dialect) *jot* 'ihr'.[81] He argued that this form, which has been affected by analogy to the dative-accusative form *onk*, does not go back to its putative ancestor, Old Saxon *git* 'you' (nominative plural), but instead reflects a Proto-Old Saxon form **jut* prior to the operation of vowel lowering.

I conclude with discussion of a few recent works that do not fit neatly into any of the categories mentioned above. An important (etymological) study is Prisca Augustyn's *The Semiotics of Fate, Death,*

---

78   Dirk Boutkan, "II. Pre-Germanic Fish in Old Saxon Glosses: On Alleged Ablaut Patterns and other Formal Deviations in Gmc. Substratum Words," *Amsterdamer Beiträge zur älteren Germanistik* 52 (1999), 11–26. The gloss in question can be found in Elis Wadstein, ed., *Kleinere altsächsische Sprachdendmäler mit Anmerkungen und Glossar* (Leipzig: D. Soltau, 1899). Boutkan's article is one of a series on Germanic fish names; see also idem, "Pre-Germanic Fishnames I: Gmc. 'bream'," *Amsterdamer Beiträge zur älteren Germanistik* 52 (1999), 11–26; and idem, "Pre-Germanic Fishnames III: A New Etymology of 'Herring'," *Amsterdamer Beiträge zur älteren Germanistik* 53 (2000), 1–6.
79   Theo Vennemann, "Key Issues in English Etymology," in *Sounds, Word, Text, and Change*, ed. Teresa Fanego, Belén Méndez-Naya, and Elena Seoane (Amsterdam: Benjamins, 2002), 227–52, argues that the Germanic hook-words themselves are borrowings from "Vasconic" (compare Basque *kako, kakho* 'hook').
80   Boutkan, "II. Pre-Germanic Fish" [note 78], 13.
81   W. Wilfried Schumacher, "LG (Velbert) *jot* 'ihr' < **jut* (oder OS *git*)?" *NOWELE: North-Western European Language Evolution* 45 (2004), 59–60.

and the Soul in Germanic Culture, which examined the overlap between Christianity and pre-Christian Germanic myth and religion, and viewed "Germanic Christianity as a dual religious system" that had synthesized pre-Christian Germanic myth and religion with Christianity.[82] Augustyn focused on four major aspects of this dual system: "the mythopoetic scenario that unifies life and death in Germanic culture," connections between Germanic beliefs and Christianity pertaining to death, "mental-emotional concepts of the self," and "poetic strategies for the redefinition of pagan concepts as the immortal soul."[83] Her carefully argued and detailed discussion surveyed concepts like *dôm*, which in her view has to do with "an underlying notion of something like a 'natural sense of right and wrong'"[84]; *hugi*, which Cathey glosses as 'mind, thought, heart', but about which Augustyn observed: *hugi* "encompasses the entire spectrum of human emotions, and [. . .] is perceived as an emotional center located in the chest"[85]; and *siola* (related to English *soul* and German *Seele*), about which she noted: "The author uses [. . .] *siola* very distinctly to express the Christian dogma of eternal life and introduces a new concept that stands in contrast with existing belief."[86]

---

82   Prisca Augustyn, *The Semiotics of Fate, Death, and the Soul in Germanic Culture:The Christianization of Old Saxon*, Berkeley Insights in Linguistics and Semiotics 50 (New York: Peter Lang, 2002), 175. This idea is not new; for instance, Frederic Henry Chase, *The Lord's Prayer in the Early Church* (Cambridge: Cambridge UP, 1891), 1, argued that "Christianity, absolutely new in its central ideas and aims, employed time-honoured machinery for their furtherance [. . .]. It inherited the powers which were inherent in, or had been won by, Judaism." Cathey, "Give Us This Day Our Daily *râd*" [note 30], 157–58, notes that, once the term "Judaism" is replaced by "pre-Christian religion," Chase's point is also valid for Old Saxon territory, such that "the new [religion] was at least to some considerable extent an overlay upon preexisting customs and expectations."
83   Augustyn, *The Semiotics of Fate* [note 82], 3.
84   Ibid., 86.
85   Ibid., 127.
86   Ibid., 79. For a fuller discussion, see James E. Cathey, Review of *The Semiotics of Fate, Death, and the Soul in Germanic Culture: The Christianization of*

An Overview of Old Saxon Linguistics, 1992–2008

Other relevant studies that do not fit neatly into the above categories include the following: Rauch looked for evidence of "paralanguage" (non-verbal elements used to modify meaning and/or convey emotion, e.g. gestures, facial expressions, etc.) in the early Germanic languages. She argued that "one of the most intractable problems in the grammar of Old Saxon, viz. the phonology of the digraphs <ie> and <uo>" can be accounted for by means of paralanguage, specifically the paralanguage feature *drawl*.[87] Jörg Riecke surveyed eighteen manuscripts containing Old Saxon glosses, which show a total of 128 attestations of 102 medical and/or anatomical words.[88] He then compiled a three-part corpus of these forms, one for body parts, one for diseases, and one for medical cures, and provided information on the meaning of each word, as well as its attestation(s), the Latin word(s) that it glosses, and bibliographical references. Riecke's corpus is a valuable asset for further such projects. Ekaterina Skvairs investigated language contact between Old Saxon and Old Low Franconian and its implications for the history of Dutch and Low German.[89] She also argued against the use of the term "Old Low German" and its equivalents as a synonym for "Old Saxon" (as in the work of Cordes and Fleischer, for instance), since, in her view, this term is more properly applied to the result of Old Saxon and Old Low Franconian language contact.[90] Finally, Heike Sahm discussed

---

Old Saxon, by Prisca Augustyn, *Interdisciplinary Journal of Germanic Linguistics and Semiotic Analysis* 10 (2005), 251–60.

87   Irmengard Rauch, "Paralanguage: Evidence from Germanic," *Semiotica* 135 (2001), 154–55. On paralanguage, see George Trager, "Paralanguage: A First Approximation," *Studies in Linguistics* 13 (1958), 1–12.

88   Jörg Riecke, "Anatomisches und Heilkundliches in altsächsischen Glossaren," *Amsterdamer Beiträge zur älteren Germanistik* 52 (1999), 207–225.

89   Ekaterina Skvairs, "Altsächsisch-altniederfränkisches Kontakterbe und sein Fortleben im Niederdeutschen," *Amsterdamer Beiträge zur älteren Germanistik* 55 (2001), 27–60.

90   Language contact involving Old Saxon has been the subject of a good deal of research over the years, as is demonstrated, for instance, by Thomas L. Markey,

variation in the Old Saxon Genesis and argued that the author of Genesis developed a new strategy for dealing with variation – which she defined as "the resumption of an expression that interrupts the flow of the syntax and emphasizes another aspect of a situation or event that has already been evoked" – namely that "he committed himself to a structure of variation based on the appositive style and with this gradation he arrives at the climactic content-related moments of his text."[91]

As the above discussion has shown, Old Saxon is receiving significantly more attention of late than it traditionally has. It is especially heartening that some recent analyses have synthesized more current formal approaches to linguistics like Optimality Theory with more traditional ideas about Germanic philology. The yearly session at the International Congress of Medieval Studies is also a good sign, as is the increasing number of papers on Old Saxon topics presented recently at conferences like the International Conference on Historical Linguistics and the Germanic Linguistics Annual Conference.[92] But perhaps the best sign of the health of the field

---

Germanic Dialect Grouping and the Position of Ingvæonic, Innsbrucker Beiträge zur Sprachwissenschaft 15 (Innsbruck: Institut für Sprachwissenschaft, 1976), who distinguishes between what he calls "genuine Old Saxon with distinctively Ingvaeonic features" and "Old Saxon influenced by High German." See also Heinrich Tiefenbach, "Altsächsisch und Altniederländisch," *Amsterdamer Beiträge zur älteren Germanistik* 57 (2003), 61–76, for another recent study of language contact involving Old Saxon.

91   Heike Sahm, "Wiederholungen über Wiederholungen: Zur Variation in der „Altsächsischen Genesis"," *Zeitschrift für deutsche Philologie* 123 (2004), 321, 340: "die den Fluss der Syntax unterbrechende, andere Aspekte eines bereits genannten Gegenstandes oder Ereignisses hervorhebende Wiederaufnahme eines Ausdrucks." [. . .] "er [legte] sich auf eine verstechnische gebundene Bauform für die Variation fest und konturiert obendrein durch deren Staffelung einen inhaltlichen Höhepunkt seines Texts."

92   Illustrative titles include, for example: Mike Olson and Shannon Dubenion-Smith, "Towards a Typology of Relativization Strategies in Old Saxon," Paper presented at 18th International Conference on Historical Linguistics (Montreal,

is the variety of scholars involved in it, especially as more junior scholars have begun working on Old Saxon topics. Clearly a good deal of work remains to be done, but the field is healthier today than it has been in some time.

2007); and John D. Sundquist, "Case Attraction and Relative Clause Variation in the Old Saxon *Heliand*," Paper presented at GLAC 13 (State College, PA, 2007).

II

The Diatessaronic Tradition

The Parable of the Fisherman in the *Heliand*:
The Old Saxon Version of Matthew 13:47–50[1]

Tjitze Baarda

INTRODUCTION

The reason for this study is the interesting theory of my Utrecht colleague Prof. Dr. Gilles Quispel concerning the Tatianic background of the *Heliand*.[2] This theory may be illustrated with an example that appeals to our imagination, namely his view

---

1 Originally published in *Amsterdamer Beiträge zur älteren Germanistik* 36 (1992), 39–58.
2 This contribution is one of four articles dedicated to the problem of the text of Matthew 13.47ff. in its relation to the text of the Diatessaron and the Gospel of Thomas; the others are: "Philoxenus and the Parable of the Fisherman: Concerning the Diatessaron Text of Matthew 13.47–50," in *The Four Gospels, 1992: Festschrift Frans Neirynck*, ed. Frans van Segbroeck et al., 3 vols. (Leuven: Leuven UP, 1992), 2:1403–23; "'Chose' or 'Collected': Concerning an Aramaism in Logion 8 of the Gospel of Thomas and the Question of Independence," *Harvard Theological Review* 84 (1991), 373–97; and "Clement of Alexandria and the Parable of the Fisherman: Matthew 13.47–48 or Independent Tradition?" in *The Synoptic Gospels: Source Criticism and the New Literary Criticism*, ed. Camille Focant (Leuven: Leuven UP, 1993), 582–98.

on the parable of the man who cast his net into the sea.³ The text of the poem which Quispel refers to (lines 2628–34) reads thus⁴:

    Ôk is imu that uuerk gelîc
that man an sêo innan   segina uuirpit,
fisknet an flôd   endi fâhit bêðiu,
uƀile endi gôde,   tiuhid up te staðe,
lið̄od sie te lande   lisit after thiu
thea gôdun an greote   endi lâtid thea ôðra eft an grund faran,
an uuîdan uuâg.

One may translate these verses in the following way: "Also is the work like to it: / that a man into the sea cast a seine⁵ / a fishing net

---

3 Gilles Quispel, "Some Remarks on the Gospel of Thomas," *New Testament Studies* 5 (1958/1959), 276–90; idem, "Der Heliand und das Thomasevangelium," *Vigiliae Christianae* 16 (1962), 121–51, repr. in idem, *Gnostic Studies II* (Istanbul: Nederlands Historisch-Archaeologisch Instituut, 1975), 70–97; idem, *Het Evangelie van Thomas in de Nederlanden* (Amsterdam: Elsevier, 1971; repr. Baarn: Tirion, 1991), 117–23 (rev. ed., 150–55); idem, *Tatian and the Gospel of Thomas : Studies in the History of the Western Diatessaron* (Leiden: E. J. Brill, 1975), 95–107, 120, 176. See for Quispel's views on the *Heliand* also his "Jewish Influences on the 'Heliand'," in *Religions in Antiquity: Essays in Memory of Erwin Ramsdell Goodenough*, ed. Jacob Neusner (Leiden: E. J. Brill, 1968), 244–50.

4 Otto Behaghel, ed., *Heliand und Genesis*, 10th ed., rev. Burkhard Taeger, Altdeutsche Textbibliothek 4 (Tübingen: Max Niemeyer, 1996), 97 (fitt 32). See Wilhelm Stapel, ed., *Der Heliand* (Münster: C. Hanser, 1953), 75; Felix Genzmer, ed., *Heliand und die Bruchstücke der Genesis* (Stuttgart: Reclam, 1955; repr. 1977), 90; Quispel, "Der Heliand und das Thomasevangelium" [note 3], 150; idem, *Het Evangelie van Thomas* [note 3], 121 (rev. ed., 154). See also Willy Krogmann, "Heliand, Tatian, und Thomasevangelium," *Zeitschrift für die neutestamentliche Wissenschaft* 51 (1960), 255–68; idem, "Heliand und Thomasevangelium," *Vigiliae Christianae* 18 (1964), 65–73 (with a different spelling of the words, e.g., 'Oc ist im that uuer gilik/. . .seo. . ./fisknett an fluot' etc.).

5 Quispel, *Tatian and the Gospel of Thomas* [note 3], 102 renders "doth cast his nets," but rightly "een net . . . werpt," in *Het Evangelie van Thomas* [note 3], 121 (rev. ed., 154). Cf. idem, "Der Heliand und das Thomasevangelium" [note 3], 150; idem, "Gnosis and the New Sayings of Jesus," *Eranos Jahrbuch* 38 (1969), 273–76. I would like to keep the word used by the *Heliand*, *segina* 'seine' (Dutch *zegen*).

into the flood, and catches both, / evil and good ones, tows (it or them?) up to the shore, / brings them to the land, (and) after that (he) chooses[6] / the good ones on the sand and makes the other go again to the ground, / into the wide waves."[7]

Quispel was not the first scholar who posited the view that a Latin Diatessaron text was to be assumed as the main source of the *Heliand*,[8] but he was the first one to postulate that the Old Saxon poem was dependent on an *archaic* form of the Western Diatessaron which had some remarkable agreements with the so-called Gospel of Thomas, which agreements could only be explained by the assumption of a common Judaic-Christian source. When reading the lines quoted above Quispel was struck by the fact that the *Heliand* did not speak of a fishing-net with which the Kingdom of Heaven was compared (so Matt 13.47f.), but a fisherman, or at least *a man who cast a net*. He referred to several Oriental Diatessaron witnesses (such as Aphrahat, Philoxenus)[9] that seemed to prove that the Diatessaron contained a

---

6 Quispel, *Tatian and the Gospel of Thomas* [note 3], 102, renders "throweth"; idem, *Het Evangelie van Thomas* [note 3], 121 (rev. ed., 154), "verzamelt" (=collects); idem, "Liudger en het Evangelie van Thomas," *Rondom het Woord* 13 (1971), 217 ("verzamelt"). The latter rendering ("collects") is strange, since Quispel has laid some emphasis on the fact that the source of the *Heliand* read *eligit* or *elegit*; see "Some Remarks on the Gospel of Thomas" [note 3], 298: "selects"; "Der Heliand und das Thomasevangelium" [note 3], 150: "liest." The rendering "collects" must have been suggested to him by Juw fon Weringha, *Heliand and Diatessaron*, Studia Germanica 5 (Assen: Van Gorcum, 1965), 101.
7 For "endi . . . eft", see § 11j below (*autem* or *et rursum*?).
8 See especially C. W. M. Grein, *Die Quellen des Heliand. Nebst einem Anhang: Tatians Evangelienharmonie herausgegeben nach dem Codex Cassellanus* (Cassel: Theodor Kay, 1869), esp. 173 (ch. 78). Grein was not the first scholar; see Krogmann, "Heliand, Tatian, und Thomasevangelium" [note 4], 255, who mentions J. A. Schmeller (1840). For a discussion of the problem of the Latin harmony as a source, see Johannes Rathofer, *Der Heliand: Theologischer Sinn als tektonische Form. Vorbereitung und Grundlegung der Interpretation*, Niederdeutsche Studien 9 (Cologne: Bohlau, 1962), 7–10.
9 For the Diatessaron text, see my "Philoxenus and the Parable of the Fisherman" [note 2].

form of the parable which differed from the Greek text of Matthew. In addition, he could also refer to Clement of Alexandria[10] and the Gospel of Thomas[11] to support his thesis that there was a form of the text that was independent from the canonical Gospel text which spoke about a person who cast his net and not of a fishing net that was cast into the sea.

In his view, this Diatessaron reading – now also found in the *Heliand*[12] – and the variations in Thomas 8 and in Clement's allusions ultimately went back to an extra-canonical Jewish-Christian tradition that had contained the more original form of the parable of Jesus. This conclusion confirmed Quispel in his belief that Jesus was a wisdom preacher rather than the eschatological prophet Matthew had made of him.[13] It is clear from this that Quispel's discussion of the verses in the *Heliand* were of great importance, since they form an inseparable link in the chain of his argumentation for the recovery of a primitive tradition. It seems appropriate to ask whether this link holds.

THE RECONSTRUCTION OF THE ORIGINAL LATIN DIATESSARON TEXT

1. In one of the most interesting and provoking studies on the relation between the Diatessaron of Tatian and the Gospel according to Thomas, Quispel made an attempt at presenting the scholarly

---

10 See my "Clement of Alexandria and the Parable of the Fisherman" [note 2].
11 For Thomas, Logion 8, see my "'Chose' or 'Collected'" [note 2].
12 See also H.-W. Bartsch, "Das Thomas-Evangelium und die synoptischen Evangelien," *New Testament Studies* 6 (1960/1961), 259: "[. . .] im Heliand 2628, der, wie Quispel darlegt, die originale Form des Diatessaron bewahrt hat."
13 See Quispel, *Het Evangelie van Thomas* [note 3], 123 (rev. ed., 155): "De tijd is gekomen om Jezus ook als een wijsheidsleraar te beschouwen. Daarom acht ik het niet uitgesloten dat de gelijkenis van de visser, die wellicht nog in de *Heliand* naklinkt, de oorspronkelijke bewoordingen en de eigenlijke bedoeling van Jezus heeft bewaard."

The Parable of the Fisherman in the Heliand

world with the reconstruction of the original text of the Western Diatessaron in the passage Matt 13.47f.[14] His main sources for this reconstruction (which I label as form I) were, besides the *Heliand*, the Middle Dutch or Flemish (T^N) and German harmonies (TTh), the Middle Italian Diatessarons, namely the Venetian (T^V) and Tuscan (T^T) harmonies, and some other Latin witnesses, among which Ludolph of Saxony (Lud.) takes an important place in his research into the *original* Latin Diatessaron. In one of his many other studies Quispel presents his readers with a slightly different reconstruction (which is form II) of the same text.[15]

THE RECONSTRUCTION OF THE LATIN DIATESSARON

2. His reconstructions read thus:

I	Variae lectiones in II
1. Simile est regnum caelorum	
2. piscatori mittenti rete suum in mare	*om.* suum
3. quod ex omni genere piscium congregat.	*om.* quod - congregat
4. Quod cum plenum esset,	sit *l.* esset
5. eduxit de mari,	educit, *om.* de mari
6. et sedit secus litus	sedens *l.* sedit
7. et elegit piscos magnos	*om.* et, eligit *l.* elegit
8 et misit in vasa sua,	ponit *l.* misit
9. parvos autem misit in mare.	mittit *l.* misit

3. Quispel acknowledges that such reconstructions are always dangerous, that they are purely hypothetical and cannot be fully approximate – the more so because the reconstructed text is not found in this form in any of the many witnesses adduced, certainly

---

14 Quispel, *Tatian and the Gospel of Thomas* [note 3], esp. 97f., 102f.
15 Quispel, *Het Evangelie van Thomas* [note 3], 120 (whose faulty text has been corrected in the rev. ed., 154).

not in the Latin witnesses.[16] Therefore, he uses this hypothetical form of the text as a "model" by which the many textual deviations in the medieval vernacular texts can be explained. Now, if we would compare this "model" with the most renowned of the Latin Diatessaron texts, the Codex Fuldensis of Victor of Capua,[17] which was a Vulgatized form of an earlier Latin Diatessaron, we discover no fewer than twenty-one textual variants. Now we have, besides the Fuldensis (T^{Lf}), other Latin harmonies – mostly dependent on this text – that also have variant readings, such as the Codex Casselanus (T^{Lc}),[18] the Codex Sangallensis (T^{Lg}) and its Old High German counterpart (OHG),[19] some other Latin harmonies registered by Heinrich J. Vogels in his study of the Latin Diatessaron (A, D),[20] and the commentary of Zacharias of Besançon (Zach) on the Latin harmony.[21]

Differences between the Reconstruction and the Fuldensis

4. The deviations between T^{Lf} and the reconstruction of Quispel will be listed here:

---

16 Quispel, *Tatian and the Gospel of Thomas* [note 3], 98; *Het Evangelie van Thomas* [note 3], 121.
17 Ernst Ranke, ed., *Codex Fuldensis: Novum Testamentum latine interprete Hieronymo ex manuscripto Victoris Capuani* (Marburg & Leipzig: N. G. Elwert, 1868), esp. 71:31–34.
18 Grein, *Die Quellen des Heliand* [note 8], 173 (ch. 78).
19 Eduard Sievers, ed., *Tatian. Lateinisch und altdeutsch mit ausführlichem Glossar*, 2nd ed., Bibliothek der ältesten deutschen Litteratur-Denkmäler 5 (Paderborn: Ferdinand Schöningh, 1892), 101a and 101b (ch. 76).
20 Heinrich J. Vogels, *Beiträge zur Geschichte des Diatessaron im Abendland*, Neutestamentliche Abhandlungen 8:1 (Münster: Aschendorff, 1919), esp. 101, 103.
21 Zacharias Chrysopolitanus, *De concordia evangelistarum (In unum ex quattuor)*, in PL 186, cols. 11–620, esp. 236.

The Parable of the Fisherman in the Heliand

T^{Lf}	Quispel I and II	Witnesses
1. iterum	om.	(Thomas)
2. sagenae	piscatori	(Thomas) *Heliand* "man"
3. missae	mittenti	(Thomas) *Heliand* "uuirpit"
4. (sagena)	rete	T^V T^T
5. (sagena)	rete suum I	(Thomas)
6. congreganti	quod congregat I	T^T
7. genere	add. piscium I	T^{Lg} T$^{L(AD)}$ Lud. OHG T^T T^V T^N TTh
8. quam	quod	T^V T^T
9. impleta	cum plena esset I	T^V T^T
	(cum plena sit II)	
10. educentes	eduxit I, -cit II	(Thomas) *Heliand*
11.	add. id I	*Heliand* (?), cf. T^V T^T
12.	add. de mari I	Lud. "scilicet, de mari"
13. sedentes	sedens II, sedit I	
14. secus litus sed.	sed. secus litus	
15. elegerunt	et elegit I, eligit II	*Heliand* "*lisit* after thiu"
16. bonos	magnos	(Thomas) T^V "*li grandi* e li buoni"
17.	add. pisces	(Thomas)
18. in vasa	et misit (ponit I), i.v.	cf. T^V "si mete", cf. Peshitta
19. vasa	add. sua	T$^{L(AD)}$ Lud. T^T T^V
20. malos autem	parvos autem	(Thomas)
21. foras miserunt	misit in mare	(Thomas) *Heliand*

5. From this comparison it becomes quite clear that in his "model" text not every deviation from the ordinary Vulgata text as represented in the Fuldensis is supported by an actual variant reading in the sources for his reconstruction. Some are based either on a logical inference from other deviations or on a conjectural guess in which the text of Logion 8 in Thomas seems to have played a dominant role. This is due to Quispel's conviction that the original Diatessaron, and consequently also the original *Latin* version of it,

must have contained a form that showed a close agreement with the text of Logion 8 of the Gospel of Thomas, but was different from the canonical text.[22] Both the Diatessaron and Thomas represent, in his view, a very early Aramaic tradition. This is – he argues – valid also for the *Western* translation of the Diatessaron, which according to Quispel was made by the Manichees who brought the harmony to the West[23]: This original Western harmony was influenced by the ordinary text of the Gospels only to a low degree, since it did not originate in a Catholic environment. In this Western Diatessaron – thus he reasons – the original text of the harmony of Tatian had remained relatively unharmed, which was not the case when Victor of Capua made his thorough Vulgatized revision of the harmony in his Codex Fuldensis. The Manichaean Latin Diatessaron left its traces in the later medieval vernacular texts that came into being in Italy, Flanders, and Germany, moreover in part of the Vetus Latina tradition and in some Latin Fathers. Quispel even holds the view that the original Diatessaron may be reconstructed sometimes in a more adequate way by referring to the Western witnesses than by using the Eastern testimonies. Now this Western branch of the Diatessaron has become – so he argues – an important vehicle through which the independent extra-canonical and even pre-canonical Aramaic tradition could invade the Western world. The vernacular offspring of the original Latin Diatessaron thus reveals to us, to a certain extent, the earliest form of the tradition of the words of Jesus. His conclusion is that the Diatessaron was one of the channels through which this old time tradition flowed, the other source was the Gospel of Thomas. Therefore, Quispel could even posit that the Middle Ages "knew more of this tradition than we did before the discovery of the Gospel of Thomas."[24] To what extent can we accept his view with respect to the

---

22 Quispel, *Tatian and the Gospel of Thomas* [note 3], 103: "The differences from the canonical text must have been enormous."
23 Ibid., 102
24 Quispel, "Gnosis and the New Sayings of Jesus" [note 5], 274.

The Parable of the Fisherman in the Heliand

early Latin Diatessaron as a vehicle of pre-canonical tradition? And to what extent does the text of the *Heliand* contribute to our knowledge of that tradition? These are the questions to be answered.

Some Observations on the Latin Reconstruction

6. In spite of his careful observation that the reconstruction is a hypothetical one, Quispel is convinced that his tentative text was not wide of the mark: "On the other hand, we can be rather confident that our reconstruction of the Latin original and of the primitive text of Tatian is correct."[25] There are, therefore, a few severe objections to be made. One of them is that there is kind of a circular reasoning in the argumentation for this reconstruction. His starting-point was that the eighth Logion of Thomas presented the parable in an independent, pre-canonical form. The second step was that the original Diatessaron was dependent on the same material and therefore a second witness to this pre-canonical form of the parable. The next step was the observation that the Western Diatessaron tradition had preserved a very primitive form of the Tatianic text, so that its reconstruction of necessity would bring out the primitive, pre-canonical form of the word of Jesus. However, if we consider the result of this reconstruction, it appears that among the witnesses that could be called for (see § 4) it is exactly the Gospel of Thomas that plays a dominant role. This is, from a methodical point of view, a very problematic procedure, to say the least. I will present here two illustrations of this procedure.

Out of the Sea

7. In his reconstruction (see § 2) Quispel assumes – in line 5 – that the primitive Latin Diatessaron read "eduxit id *de mari*" (reconstruction 1) instead of the usual "educentes." The main argument

---

25 Quispel, *Tatian and the Gospel of Thomas* [note 3], 103.

for the addition of "de mari" is the reading of Ludolph of Saxony, "educentes, *scilicet* de mari." The average reader would interpret Ludolph's text as a clarification of "educentes," so that the addition was not part of his text, but only a comment. Quispel, however, had in mind the reading of the Gospel of Thomas: "He drew it up from the sea" (ⲁϥⲥⲱⲕ ⲙ̄ⲙⲟⲥ ⲉϩⲣⲁⲓ ... ϩⲛ̄ ⲑⲁⲗⲁⲥⲥⲁ). Although he had to admit that there was not a single trace of such a reading in *any* of the extant Western witnesses, he is still confident that he can prove that this was part of the Diatessaron text in Latin dress, since he writes: "*de mari*, which, as we shall see, is very archaic."[26] His conclusion is that in all other Western witnesses the harmony text was assimilated to that of the ordinary canonical text, the true reading being preserved in Ludolph's reference only.[27] One of the arguments for the correctness of his thesis in this respect is that Mar Ephrem the Syrian in his commentary on the Diatessaron presents us with the same reading for the Diatessaron, in which this author speaks of an election *from the sea*: "The remark about the '*electio quae ex mari est*' suggests that Tatian read: 'he drew it out *from the sea*'."[28] Here again, one must seriously ask whether this conclusion is justified. First of all it is clear from Ephrem's text that he read "they lifted it up to the shores of the sea,"[29] that is, 1. he read the verb in the *plural* form, and 2. he did *not* read the verb "drew," which means that his text is in accordance with that of the Greek Matthew, except for the finite

---

26 Ibid., 97.
27 Ibid., 98, 106, 176; remarkably, this reference fails in the Appendix II on Ludolph (ibid., 153).
28 Ibid., 101; see also his "L'Évangile selon Thomas et le Diatessaron," in *Gnostic Studies II* [note 3], 33: "Thomas: de la mer l. ἐπὶ τὸν αἰγιαλόν," with reference to Ephrem's commentary (Arm: *extra*), the Tuscan Diatessaron (*fuori*), the Dutch Diatessaron (*ut*) – none of these witnesses testifying in favor of the reading which Quispel wants to defend.
29 See L. Leloir, ed., *Saint Éphrem. Commentaire de l'évangile concordant: Texte Syriaque (Mss. Chester Beatty 709)*, Chester Beatty Monographs 8 (Dublin: Hodges & Figgis, 1963), 68.17–23.

form of the verb. This reading almost certainly rules out the reading "from the sea." Secondly, the phrase which Quispel lays emphasis on belongs to the Father's comments: Ephrem has the verb "they chose," where Matthew had "collected"; now he distinguishes *between* the final election, when the good ones and bad ones are separated, *and* an earlier selection from the sea, that is, when the net is taken ashore with all kinds of fish. This is called by Ephrem the selection from the world ("ex mari, quae est ex mundo"), when people become members of the Church. This earlier selection belongs to his *interpretation*, not to the *text* that he read in the harmony. Otherwise he should also have read twice the verb "chose" in his text, both in verse 47 and in verse 48. Such a textual phenomenon is not found in *any* text. And so it is not necessary to assume it for the Diatessaron, if one takes into account that Ephrem's remark is merely part of his theological exegesis. So, both in Ludolph and in Ephrem, "from the sea" belongs to their respective comments on the passage.

Apparently, Quispel's view concerning both these witnesses is prompted by his eagerness to connect Thomas and Tatian in order to have two independent witnesses for his thesis of a deviating pre-canonical form of the parable. "It is not just a historical question," he writes, "whether or not Ludolph of Saxony still read a Jewish-Christian variant in his Diatessaron ('educentes, scilicet *de mari*' – 'he drew it *out of the sea*') [. . .] The real issue is whether or not the Latin Diatessaron has preserved in some cases a primitive and Jewish-Christian version, which leads us back to a stage of tradition before the Gospels and enables us to establish that Jesus preached a realized eschatology."[30] "The present author," Quispel continues, "has reasons to suppose that this question should be answered in the affirmative." Apart from the question whether such a trifling variant as *out of the sea* brings us closer to a different teaching perspective of Jesus, the answering of the second question has to be based on solid textual decisions as far as the recovery of the primitive Latin

---

30 Quispel, *Tatian and the Gospel of Thomas* [note 3], 106f.

Diatessaron is concerned. I have not the conviction that Quispel has succeeded in proving his case here.

SAGENA OR RETE?

8. A second illustration for the problematic procedure behind his reconstruction of the primitive Latin harmony text is found in line 2 (see § 4): "... mittenti *rete* suum" (so I; in II *om*. suum). As I have pointed out elsewhere, this reconstruction, for which Quispel could refer to the medieval Italian harmonies, the Tuscan and Venetian Diatessarons ("rete"),[31] is in fact based on the conviction that the Diatessaron reading was in complete agreement with the Logion of Thomas, "who cast *his net*." This explains also why reconstruction I has "rete *suum*." The idea behind this conjecture of the reading *rete* is that the original saying of Jesus in the early pre-canonical tradition did not speak of a σαγήνη, a trail-net, but of a smaller net that could be handled by one person. This idea was prompted by the study of C.-H. Hunzinger,[32] in which the imagery of Thomas was seen as totally different from that in the parable of Matthew. According to this approach the net in Thomas was meant to have been a *casting* net, not a *trail* net, since there is no mention of several people to

---

31   He also refers to the Hague manuscript (*nette*) of T^N and MS U (*netze*) of TTh (*Tatian and the Gospel of Thomas* [note 3], 98f.), which are very uncertain testimonies, since they could be renderings of *sagena* as well (N.B. In his own rendering of the Liège manuscript, Quispel renders *sagene* with *net*; see *Het Evangelie van Thomas* [note 3], rev. ed., 153). The reading *rete* in *ff*^{2} *q*, *retia* in [*a*] *b c e f gl h*, and *retiaculum* in *k* occur beside *sagena* in the Latin tradition, but it is impossible to say whether the reading *rete* was actually found in the primitive Latin Diatessaron on the basis of the vernacular versions and these Latin texts. The wording *rewse*, *rüsse*, etc. in the Middle High German harmony tradition could have been renderings of *rete* or *sagena*.
32   C.-H. Hunzinger, "Unbekannte Gleichnisse Jesu aus dem Thomas-Evangelium," in *Judentum, Urchristentum, Kirche: Festschrift für Joachim Jeremias*, ed. Walther Eltester (Berlin: A. Töpelmann, 1960), 217f.

The Parable of the Fisherman in the Heliand

handle it: "He does not use a boat and a trawl net, as in Matthew, but a cast net: he stands in the water near the border [. . .]."[33] Apart from the question whether one person can handle a trail net,[34] it is to be observed that the Coptic word used here, ⲁⲃⲱ, presupposes the reading σαγήνη,[35] the very word that is also read by Clement. Oddly enough, σαγήνη is found even in Quispel's *own* reconstruction of the Greek Thomas and of the Diatessaron,[36] in spite of his conviction that Clement-Thomas-Diatessaron were to be seen as three independent witnesses that had preserved the original *pre-canonical* form of the parable, which did not speak of a *trail* net. Now, it is interesting to look here at the text of the *Heliand*: "an sêo innan *segina* uuirpit, / *fisknet* an flôd." Shortly after this we find a similar repetition: "tiuhid up te staðe / liðod sie te lande," a repetition which so often occurs in the Old Saxon poem. In the latter case, *te staðe* is the rendering of the text word (*ad litus*),[37] and *te lande* is caused by a sort of *parallelismus membrorum* so often used in the poem in paraphrasing the source text. Likewise, *segina* is the word of his text (*sagena*), whereas *fisknet* is due to the parallelism, just as *sêo* is his text word (*mare*) and

---

33   Quispel, "Gnosis and the New Sayings of Jesus" [note 5], 273 (= *Gnostic Studies II* [note 3], 190). See also "Der Heliand und das Thomasevangelium" [note 3], 149 (= *Gnostic Studies II* [note 3], 95).

34   See my "'Chose' or 'Collected'" [note 2] for a presentation of material which proves that a σαγήνη could be handled by *one* person; even Clement of Alexandria uses this word, in spite of his allusion to *one* fisherman.

35   See my "'Chose' or 'Collected'" [note 2], in a section on *Hunzinger and the Coptic Text*.

36   See Quispel, *Tatian and the Gospel of Thomas* [note 2], 105; and "Der Heliand und das Thomasevangelium" [note 3], 150.

37   The text of the *Heliand* departs here from the Latin harmonies and the Vulgate in reading ". . . ad litus et" instead of "et secus litus" in Vulgata Q and the majority of Old Latin texts; cf. the Venetian harmony. It is at first sight strange that Quispel completely neglects the *Heliand* and T[V] here, but here again his view that the Diatessaron read with the Gospel of Thomas "and drew it from the sea" forbids him to take cognizance of this variant in the *Heliand*, and so he favors the reconstruction "et sedit secus litus."

flôd is the poetical repetition. This suggests that the *Heliand* is here a replica of the ordinary Latin harmony text with *sagena*, not *rete*.[38] In this respect the wording of the *Heliand* is in agreement with the Latin harmony tradition (see also the Dutch harmonies), the Vulgata, and Old Latin *aur ff¹ l*. Of course, one might suggest that the *Heliand* has been influenced by the Vulgate reading here, but if one wants to make this poem one's crown witness for the Old Latin Diatessaron, one has to acknowledge that it has been contaminated at this point. On the other hand, if one wants to connect, as Quispel does, the text of the *Heliand* as a witness of the Old Latin harmony with the pre-canonical text represented in Clement's allusion (σαγήνη) and in Thomas (ⲁⲃⲱ), its reading *segina* would fit in well.

The Heliand and Quispel's Reconstruction

9. If we compare the text of the *Heliand* with Quispel's reconstruction of the Latin Diatessaron we find the following agreements and differences:

Heliand	*Reconstructions I and II*
1. Ôk = iterum]	*om.*
2. is ... gelîc]	= simile est
3. imu]	regnum caelorum (subj.)
4. that uuerk that]	*om.*
5. man]	piscatori
6. an sêo innan]	in mare (after 7)
7. segina]	rete suum (II *om.* suum)

---

38 Theoretically one could, of course, suggest that the author read *rete* (= *fisknet*) in his text and complemented it with *sagena* (= *segina*), in which case he knew two different readings. But then one should assume also that he found in his text besides *mare* also *fluctus*, besides *ad litus* also *ad terram*, an assumption for which there is no reason whatsoever. Moreover, *fisknet* in itself could have been a good rendering of *sagena*, besides the preceding Latinism *segina*. In the calling of the disciples (lines 1150–1189) the word *netti* is used for Latin *rete*.

The Parable of the Fisherman in the Heliand

8. uuirpit]	mittenti (before 7)
9. fiknet an flôd (parall.)	
10. endi fâhit]	quod ... congregat (II *om.*)
11. bêðiu ubile endi gôde]	ex omni genere piscium (II *om.*)
12. *om.*]	Quod cum plenum esset (II sit)
13. tiuhid]	eduxit (II educit)
14. up te staðe]	de mari (II *om.*)
15. liðod sie te lande (parall.)	
16. *om.*]	et sedit (II sedens) secus litus
17. lisit after thiu]	et elegit (II eligit)
18. thea gôdun]	piscos magnos
19. *om.*]	et misit (II et ponit)
20. an greote]	in vasa sua
21. endi lâtid ... eft ... faran]	autem misit (II autem mittit)
22. thea ôðra]	parvos
23. an grund an uuîdan uuâg]	in mare

Concerning the *Vorlage* of the Heliand

10. If we then make a comparison of the text of the *Heliand* with both Quispel's reconstruction and the Western harmony tradition, we can leave out the figures of parallelism that we listed under 9 and 15, moreover those phrases which all the traditions have in common, namely (2) *simile est*, and (6) *in mare*. Since we will deal separately with the peculiar variant reading that attracted the attention of Quispel as being very primitive, namely "a man cast a net," it will not be mentioned in our comparison here. As we assume that the poet of the *Heliand* abbreviated his source text in 12, 16, and perhaps in 19, we do not register these omissions as specific readings of the *Heliand* epic. Further, we do not interpret the reading (18) *thea gôdun* ... (23) *thea ôðra*, where we would expect a rendering of *bonos-malos*, as a variant reading. We may compare lines 2599–2601: "endi lesat thea hluttron man ... endi *thea ôðra* an hellia grund" (*the others* being the rejected, line 2602). Finally, another freedom of the author may

be found in (11) *bêðiu uƀile endi gôde*, where the Western harmonies read *ex omni genere (piscium)*.[39] In this variant the poet anticipated the separation of the *boni* and the *mali* at the end of the parable (where he speaks, as we have already noticed, of the *good ones* and the *others*). Anyhow, the poet of the *Heliand* does not betray that he had a text before him of the type that Quispel suggested in his reconstruction (*magnos - parvos*).

11. What remains to be registered are the following readings of the *Heliand*:

a) *Ôk*] = *iterum* (Matt πάλιν) is not found in Quispel's reconstruction, but is attested in all Latin and vernacular versions of the Western Diatessaron.
b) *segina*] = *sagena* (Matt σαγήνη), see § 8.
c) *endi (fâhit)*] = *et* (Matt καί) is found in the Sangallensis and its Old High German counterpart (*inti*) and in the Dutch Diatessaron tradition, in part of the Vulgata tradition and the Vetus Latina (*aur d ff¹ l*). The omission of the conjunction is found in the Fuldensis and Casselanus harmonies as well as in part of the Vulgata tradition and Old Latin *c*. The reconstruction of Quispel reads *quod*, in accordance with *ff² q e k* (*quae* in *a b f g1 h*, Vulg. QE), cf. the Tuscan (*la quale*) and Venetian (*en la quale*) harmonies. In any event, the *Heliand* differs from the reconstruction and presents us with a reading that was present in the Latin harmony tradition.

---

39 The addition of *piscium* is found in several manuscripts of the Vulgata and of the Vetus Latina, in some Fathers, in several Western harmonies such as the Tuscan and Venetian Diatessarons, the Dutch and German harmonies, and in the Latin harmony text in MSS G and (Monac.) A D, Zacharias Chrysopolitanus, Ludolph of Saxony, and the Old High German Diatessaron. The free way of quoting in the *Heliand* does not enable us to say whether *piscium* was in its source text or not; if not, his text was of the type of the Fuldensis or Casselanus.

The Parable of the Fisherman in the Heliand

d) *fâhit*] It is impossible to say whether this is a rendering of the verb *congregare* or some other verb such as *colligere* (cf. *collegit*: b *f ff²q*; *collexit*: g¹; *colligat*: k; *colliget*: h). The Dutch ("die g[h]adert") and German ("die sament") harmonies could be either verb, and the Italian harmonies (*ragune* T, *se congrega* V) seem to favor the verb *congregare*.

e) *tiuhid*] Quispel's reconstruction *educit* (II) or *eduxit* (I) might certainly give the verb behind the Saxon word, since both *educere* and *tiohan* may mean 'draw (up)' and 'educate' (*ziehen* and *erziehen*). This reconstruction, however, surprises at first sight, since Quispel assumes that Tatian read a verb like σπᾶν 'to pull up, catch' in his text,[40] since he found *tirarono* in the Persian text, *eli la tirano* in the Tuscan text, *la trassero fuori* in the Venetian text, and *trekkense* in the Dutch harmony. He compares this reading with that of Thomas *trahere* l. *educere* (in agreement with the Dutch, Venetian, Tuscan harmonies, the *Heliand*, the Persian harmony, the Syrus Sinaiticus, and Philoxenus).[41] One would have expected that Quispel would have suggested the reading *trahit* or *traxit*, since *educere* is the verb used in the Vulgate and a great deal of the Old Latin witnesses and in the Latin harmonies (being not an impossible rendering of Matthew's ἀναβιβάζειν in this context), whereas the Venetian might render *trahere*. So it is not clear to me why he did not follow here the witnesses that he rightly or wrongly adduced for *trahere*, the more so because this verb is also found in some of the quotations of the Latin Fathers such as Jerome (*extrahitur*) and Augustine (*trahunt, trahitur*). Apparently, he did not want to deviate from his other crown witness, Ludolph of Saxony. In my view, there is no reason to think that the poet of

---

40 Quispel, "Der Heliand und das Thomasevangelium" [note 3], 150 (= *Gnostic Studies II* [note 3], 95); see also *Tatian and the Gospel of Thomas* [note 3], 105 (ἀνέσπα).
41 See ibid., 176; and *Het Evangelie van Thomas* [note 3], 121 (rev. ed., 154).

the *Heliand* had another verb than *educere* before him, nor the translators of the other Western harmonies. For example, the Dutch does not merely read *trekkense*, but adds to it *ut*, which together might go back to *e-ducere*.

f) *up te staðe*] (see § 7) I am not certain whether the adverb *up* 'hinauf' is to be connected with the verb *tiuhid up* = *e-ducit*, or with *te staðe*. However, in both cases it is clear that the *Heliand* deviates from the ordinary Western Diatessaron witnesses both in Latin and in the vernacular versions, which have the reading *et secus litus sedentes*, that is, the text with *et* (καί) before *secus litus* (ἐπὶ τὸν αἰγιαλόν).[42] The reading of the *Heliand* is in agreement with part of the Greek witnesses of Matthew (e.g., ℵ B D P), the Old Latin [*a*] *b d fff² g¹ h q* and *e-k*, Vulgate Q, the Venetian harmony (*eli la tiranno en la riva*); it is also the order of the text in the Eastern Diatessaron tradition. The reading of the *Heliand* does not conform to Quispel's reconstruction "et sedit *secus* litus," but its source seems to have read: "educit *ad* litus et . . .".

g) *lisit*] The reading of the *Heliand* suggests the verb *eligere*, which is the common Latin rendering in the Vetus Latina and the Vulgate, Fathers like Jerome and Augustine (*colligere* only in *e* and *d k*), where one should expect *colligere* (συνέλεξαν in Matthew), and in the Latin and vernacular harmony tradition.[43]

---

42 This text is found in several Greek manuscripts, Old Latin *aur c ff¹ l*, the Vulgate, some Fathers (Augustine, Jerome), the Tuscan and Dutch harmony tradition and several vernacular versions. The omission of καί is found in some other Greek manuscripts such as L Q fam.13 pc. One might suggest the thesis that the latter reading could be the original one, which led to the placing of καί in different places to make clear to which part of the sentence ἐπὶ τὸν αἰγιαλόν belonged.

43 I disagree with Fon Weringha, *Heliand and Diatessaron* [note 6], 101, who identified *lisit* (line 2632) with *colligit*. The ordinary Latin verb here (*eligere*) explains *lisit* very well. Fon Weringha refers to line 2637, "lisit . . . thea hluttron an he enrîki," where he interprets the verb as meaning 'gathers'; however, it

The Parable of the Fisherman in the Heliand

This reading may have been part of the so-called "Western Text" of the Gospels, since it agrees with the Syriac witnesses, including the Diatessaron, whereas it is also found in Thomas and Clement. However, one cannot suggest that the *Heliand* is *directly* dependent upon the Old Latin Diatessaron, since it is part of the whole Latin tradition, including the Vulgatized Latin harmonies.[44]

h) *thea gôdun*] The *Heliand* is in agreement with the ordinary reading *bonos* in the Latin witnesses of Matthew (= τὰ καλά), including the Latin and vernacular harmonies. The reading differs from Quispel's reconstructed Latin harmony text (*pisces magnos*). His assumption of such a variant reading is based on the observation that the Venetian harmony reads *e li grandi e li buoni*. Although he admits that there is not a trace of the reading *magnos* (T^V does not have *pisces*) in the Latin tradition and in the remaining Western harmonies, he is still convinced that we have here a remainder of the Western Diatessaron. This conviction is based on the assumption that it was not only the reading of the Gospel of Thomas, but also of the Syriac Diatessaron,[45] both of which have preserved

---

might mean 'choose' as well, since the preceding text – "brengid irminthiod, alle tesamne" (line 2636) – speaks of collecting, whereas line 2637 suggests a choice out of what has been collected (cf. Latin *separabunt*). One may compare lines 2599–2600 – "*lesat* thea hluttron man / sundor *tesamne*" (for *colligent*, Matt 13.41) – and lines 2568–2569 ("lesan . . . tesamne"), where the idea of *colligere* is at the background in the Latin text. Fon Weringha (ibid., 102) considers the possibility that *lesan* might mean *alesen* (< *az-lesan*, cf. *arlesan* = *eligere*), but rejects it again.

44 Ibid., 102: "[. . .] on that supposition there would be no deviation from the Vulgate and the Diatessaron to begin with, and therefore no problem to be solved at all." Fon Weringha assumes, however, that when the author had before him the Vulgate rendering, he must have deliberately departed from the literal sense of the Latin text by choosing *lisit*, which according to him can only mean *colligit* (see preceding note), and thus shows the poetic freedom of the author of the *Heliand*.

45 This assumption (see Quispel, *Tatian and the Gospel of Thomas* [note 2], 99,

here again the original Aramaic version of the parable. Quispel argues with respect to the Venetian harmony:

> Every fisherman will confirm that he is interested in big fishes. So this variant seems true to nature and reality. But it is only here that we find it and in no other Diatessaron. Were it not for a passage in the Syrian author Philoxenus of Mabbug [. . .], we would not even know that Tatian has integrated this extra-canonical variant into his Diatessaron. The Venetian harmony is the only one that has preserved this very interesting and archaic reading.[46]

It is my conviction that exactly Quispel's observation that a fisherman is interested in big fish has led to the replacement of *good* by *big* or *great*, when the readers of Matthew no longer understood the possible dietary background (*kashrut*) of the contrast τὰ καλά - τὰ σαπρά 'the good ones – the putrid or rotten ones'. There is no convincing indication that the Diatessaron had a text different from that of Matthew. Anyhow, the *Heliand* has no trace of it, but reads *bonos* (and *malos*) with the Western Diatessaron tradition, and leaves out the word *pisces*, which is found in the Dutch and German harmonies (*vesche, vissche, fische*); cf. *optimos pisces* in [*a*] *b h*, and also in some Eastern Diatessaron witnesses. It agrees with the Latin harmonies and the Italian Diatessaron tradition.

i) *an greote*] 'on the sand'[47] is a peculiar reading, which contrasts

---

100f., 176; and *Het Evangelie van Thomas* [note 3], 119f. [rev. ed., 153]) was based on an allusion of Philoxenus of Mabbug, which he wrongly identified as a Diatessaron text; see my "Philoxenus and the Parable of the Fisherman" [note 2], esp. §§ 8–11.

46 Quispel, *Tatian and the Gospel of Thomas* [note 3], 153; see also *Het Evangelie van Thomas* [note 3], 119f. (rev. ed., 153).

47 Krogmann, "Heliand, Tatian, und Thomasevangelium" [note 4], 263, wants to read here *greote* as if it were **griuteun* (Stein?), which he derives from Old

The Parable of the Fisherman in the Heliand

    the *sand* of the beach with the *sea* of the next line. It is clear that, if this is what the author wished to express, we no longer know whether he read in his text *in vasa* with e.g. the Codex Fuldensis and some Latin harmonies or *in vasa sua* with most of the vernacular harmonies and some other Latin Diatessaron witnesses such as A and D mentioned by Vogels.

j) *endi . . . eft*] It is interesting to note that the *Heliand* begins with *endi = et* instead of *autem*; cf. "malos *autem*" in the Latin texts (= Matt δέ). This "and" is the conjunction found in all Eastern Diatessaron witnesses, but also in the Italian harmonies (*e*) and those in Dutch (*ende*) and German (*vnd*). Quispel's reconstruction maintains "parvos *autem*" in spite of the vast Diatessaron testimony for *et*. Does the *Heliand* also read "and"? I am not quite sure. The word *eft* has the meaning of "rursum," but also could mean "autem."[48] Therefore *endi . . . eft* may go back to *autem* as well.

k) *lâtid . . . faran*] "lâtan faran" means "let go, make go"; it may be an equivalent of *mittere*. It recurs in lines 2638–2639 – "*lâtid thea fargriponon an grund faren* / hellie fiures" – where the verb *mittere* (Matt βαλοῦσιν) has been used. Since the poet repeats the whole expression ("lâtid . . . an grund faren") in these lines – which belong to the exposition of the line under discussion (2633), "endi lâtid thea ôðra eft an grund faran" – one might ask whether the expression "an grund lâtan faran" as such stood for *mittere*. But there is no reason to follow this line of thinking.

Saxon *griutea (a stone pot or jar). I have not the expertise to judge the correctness of this suggestion, which would imply that the author rendered "vasa" here (not "vasa sua" as in Quispel's reconstruction). Fon Weringha, *Heliand and Diatessaron* [note 6], 102n375 rejects Krogmann's conjecture as "not supported by lexical evidence"; he considers the conjecture *grôtun* (in agreement with the Venetian harmony: *li grandi*), but rightly rejects it.

48 See Edward H. Sehrt, *Vollständiges Wörterbuch zum Heliand und zur altsächsischen Genesis*, 2nd ed. (Göttingen: Vandenhoek & Ruprecht, 1966), 91 ("wieder," "andrerseits," "darauf").

In lines 2601–2602, the poet writes "endi thea ôðra an hellia grund, / uuerpad thea faruuarhton an uuallandi fiur." This is the rendering of Matt 13.42 (καὶ βαλοῦσιν αὐτοὺς εἰς τὴν κάμινον τοῦ πυρός "and they will throw them into the furnace of fire"). So he seems to have used *grund* in combination with the place where the rejected are cast down. This may be his understanding of *grund* in lines 2638–2639 as well; in that case *an grund* could be taken as a complement to *lâtid faran*, which already anticipates the *hellia grund* of the exposition.[49]

l) *an grund . . . an uuîdan uuâg*] If our suggestion under k is correct, then we have here an indication of the place where the fish will be cast. *Grund* is 'ground', but also 'bottom'. Is *grund* together with *uuîdan uuâg* an indication that the poet really found in his source the phrase *in mare* of the reconstruction of the original Latin harmony that Quispel had made? In that case we have here a reading that is different from *all* other Western harmonies, and not only that, but also different from *all* other Diatessaron witnesses that suggest that the Diatessaron contained a Syriac reading ܠܒܪ '*foras/foris*' in agreement with Matthew's ἔξω. Quispel's reconstruction (*in mare* = εἰς τὴν θάλασσαν)[50] is based upon his conviction that the Diatessaron contained the same form of the text that he found in the Gospel of Thomas. I do not think that any person involved in the reconstruction

---

49   Except for its occurrence in line 2633, the word *grund* regularly occurs with the idea of *hell* (2601, 2638, 5429); see also *hellegrund* (1491).

50   For the Greek reconstruction, see Quispel, *Tatian and the Gospel of Thomas* [note 3], 105, 176. Quispel also refers to Macarius for this reading; see "The Syrian Thomas and the Syrian Macarius," *Vigiliae Christianae* 18 (1964), 226 (= *Gnostic Studies II* [note 3], 113–23, esp. 113): ὁ θηρατὴς εἰς τὸν βυθὸν ῥίπτει. It is, indeed, striking that Macarius speaks here of *one* fisherman; one might also compare the parallel text in Hom. 15, where Macarius even reads εἰς θάλασσαν, but then speaks of more than one fisherman (ῥίπτουσιν). However, one cannot make Macarius the crown witness here for the Diatessaron against all other Syriac testimonies.

The Parable of the Fisherman in the Heliand

of the Diatessaron would follow Quispel in neglecting *all* the testimonies in the East and in the West and sacrifice them for the paraphrasing phrase of the *Heliand*. When, in his commentary, Pierre Bonnard explains the very text of Matthew, he not only writes in his comments "[. . .] tandis que les autres sont rejetés à la mer," but he even *renders* the Greek text of Matthew (ἔξω) with "et rejettent *à la mer* les mauvais."[51] So one has to consider the possibility that the poet of the *Heliand* is merely paraphrasing a source text with *foras*.

THE MAN WHO CAST A SEINE

12. What still has to be discussed is the remarkable beginning of the parable in the *Heliand*.[52] First of all, the introduction reads: "Ôk is imu that uuerk gelîc that man [. . .]." One cannot paraphrase this phrase with "one can also compare the activity of the kingdom of heaven with the fact that a man [. . .],"[53] since the kingdom is not related to the subject, but is indicated by the dative *imu*; cf. Stapel's rendering: "Auch gleicht ihm (das Himmelreich) das Werk, dass ein Mann [. . .]."[54]

---

51 Pierre Bonnard, *L'Évangile selon Saint Matthieu*, Commentaire du Nouveau Testament 1 (Neuchâtel: Delachaux & Niestlé, 1963), 209. In his comments he even uses the phrase "les autres" in agreement with the *Heliand* (*thea ôðra*), but there will be no reader of Bonnard who will say that he had before him here either the Gospel of Thomas or the *Heliand*.

52 One might avoid the whole discussion if one assumes with Fon Weringha, *Heliand and Diatessaron* [note 6], 103, that the poet "did not render his text mechanically, but visualized what he read, and that his images often depicted familiar scenes of his own environment," a procedure to which he reckons the particulars like those of the single fisherman drawing his net ashore, etc. This might well be the case, but since, in the present discussion, the relation between the *Heliand* and the Latin Diatessaron is at stake, one has to weigh meticulously the arguments that have been brought forward.

53 So Quispel, *Het Evangelie van Thomas* [note 3], 121 (rev. ed., 154).

54 So Quispel, "Der Heliand und das Thomasevangelium" [note 3], 150 (= *Gnostic Studies II* [note 3], 96), following the rendering of Stapel.

One might ask how one has to render *man* in this case: The word may mean 'a man', 'a servant', or 'one' (German *man*, in general: 'they' or 'one'), or 'someone'. The question has been debated by Quispel, Krogmann, and Huisman.[55] Instead of "a man" (defended by Quispel and Huisman) or "one" or "they" (defended by Krogmann), I would prefer the rendering "someone" (*jemand*), since the rendering "Also is similar to it, that is, the Kingdom of Heaven, the activity that someone . . .". is quite possible and avoids the dilemma under debate. This, however, means that the poet thinks – as Quispel assumed – of only *one* person who cast a seine. On the other hand, there is no necessity to suppose that that he, in fact, read in his source "Iterum simile est regnum caelorum *homini* mittenti . . .".[56] He might have read the text that is found in all Latin and vernacular harmonies in agreement with the Eastern Diatessaron tradition: "Iterum simile est regnum caelorum *sagenae missae* in mare," interpreting "sagenae missae" as a process in which some person was involved. The poet may merely have paraphrased these words and more or less revived the static phrase by introducing somebody who did the work. This seems to me the more natural explanation for the text in the *Heliand*.

13. Yet another question requires an answer, and that is about the application of the parable that is found in the *Heliand* (which in its own way resembles the text of Matt 13.48f.). In lines 2634–2639 the

---

55 See Quispel, "Some Remarks on the Gospel of Thomas" [note 3], 289; idem, *Tatian and the Gospel of Thomas* [note 3], 102f., 176; idem, "Der Heliand und das Thomasevangelium" [note 3], 150 (= *Gnostic Studies II* [note 3], 96); Krogmann, "Heliand, Tatian, und Thomasevangelium" [note 4], 264; J. A. Huisman, Afterword to "Der Heliand und das Thomasevangelium," by Gilles Quispel, *Vigiliae Christianae* 16 (1962), 151–52; Krogmann, "Heliand und Thomasevangelium" [note 4], 72f. Since I have no expertise in this area, I do not weigh the arguments. I merely conclude that the lexica presented under the lemma *man* already included the renderings *Mensch, Mann, Dienstmann, man,* and *jemand* before this question arose.
56 See Quispel, "Der Heliand und das Thomasevangelium" [note 3], 150 (= *Gnostic Studies II* [note 3], 96).

poet writes: "Sô duod uualdand god / an themu mâreon dage men-niscono barn: / brengid irminthiod, alle tesamne, / lisit imu than thea hluttron an heɓenrîki, / lâtid thea fargriponon an grund faren / hellie fiures."[57] Here again the *Heliand* paraphrases and abbreviates the text, but it is clear that this rephrasing of Matthew is clearly of his own and not based upon any Diatessaron manuscript. He even omits the angels that are mentioned in Matthew. This is different from the text of the *Heliand* in the explanation of the parable of the wheat and the tares, lines 2595ff., where the Son of Man has been replaced by "the berhto drohtin," but the angels are maintained here as the active servants of the Lord. This is not the case in our text, which seems to prove that he adjusted the explanation of the parable to the new form of the introduction that he presented in line 2639 (*man*).[58] This suggests that one rather should not render with "one" or "they" (German *man*), but with "a man"[59] or – what I would prefer – "someone." This does not mean, however, that the poet had a text before him with *homini*.

14. But let us suppose for a moment that Quispel were correct in his verdict that the *Heliand* has preserved here a very archaic reading. In this case we are faced with a very difficult problem. If we had to assume that *man* in the *Heliand* preserved the Diatessaron reading here, it would mean that the harmony text read *homini*, a read-

---

57 Cf. Krogmann, "Heliand, Tatian, und Thomasevangelium" [note 4], 263.
58 Fon Weringha, *Heliand and Diatessaron* [note 6], 102, seems to suggest that it was the other way around: "We then find that the whole parable appears to be adapted to the idea that not the angels, as in the canonical version, but God gathers the good in heaven, and sends the bad to hell." In that case the form of the parable (with *one* person) was fashioned by the application that the poet wished to make.
59 So Quispel, "Der Heliand und das Thomasevangelium" [note 3], 150f. (= *Gnostic Studies II* [note 3], 96f.). However, his remark "Und setzt die Anwendung des Gleichnisses auf den einen Gott nicht voraus, dass im Gleichnis *einer, nicht* 'man' gemeint ist?" would plead in favor of my translation with *someone*.

ing only attested by Clement of Alexandria (ἀνθρώπῳ).⁶⁰ His own reconstruction of the primitive Latin Diatessaron reads *piscatori*.⁶¹ This in turn was the reading that he (in my view, wrongly) assumed to have been that of the Syriac Diatessaron, or rather, as he once supposed, ἀνθρώπῳ ἁλιέι or the Syriac equivalent of it.⁶² Now, the Coptic text of the Gospel of Thomas has "like a wise fisherman" (ⲧⲛ̄ⲧⲱⲛ ⲁⲩⲟⲩⲱϩⲉ ⲡ̄ⲣⲙⲛ̄ϩⲏⲧ). The problem of Quispel's discussion of the respective witnesses is obvious: The Latin Diatessaron behind the *Heliand* has *homini* in agreement with Clement, while the primitive Latin Diatessaron and its Syriac counterpart has *piscatori* in agreement with Thomas. Now, Quispel does not give us any clue to its solution, since he himself apparently does not see a difficulty here. The only thing he sees is that in all these texts the kingdom is compared with *one* person (a man or a fisherman) who casts a net, and not with a net that has been cast. But he should have given us some kind of genealogy of the variant readings that are found here. What is the relation between Thomas (*fisherman*), the Diatessaron (*a man* [=*some fisherman*]) as reconstructed at one place – *or* perhaps the Diatessaron (*a fisherman*) as reconstructed at another place – the reading of Clement (*a man*), and the *Heliand* (*a man*, according to his view)? I cannot draw that genealogy, and I am certain that neither could he. Therefore it is too early for me to back up his views. I am reluctant to follow him when he says that the *Heliand* is so much nearer to the original version of Tatian's work than even Ephrem's commentary on the Diatessaron, and that in the *Heliand*, as in Tatian, it was the parable of the fisherman, and not of the fishnet, that "makes all the difference."⁶³

---

60 Ibid., 149 (*Gnostic Studies II*, 95), as regards *Stromata* 6.11.95.
61 Ibid., 150 (*Gnostic Studies II*, 96); see also *Het Evangelie van Thomas* [note 3], 121 (rev. ed., 154).
62 See Quispel, "Der Heliand und das Thomasevangelium" [note 3], 149 (= *Gnostic Studies II* [note 3], 95.).
63 See Quispel, *Tatian and the Gospel of Thomas* [note 3], 102. In other studies he

The Parable of the Fisherman in the Heliand

Conclusion

This contribution has been written by someone who has a vivid interest in the problems of the reconstruction of the Eastern and Western Diatessaron, not by someone who has any experience in the area of Old Saxon literature. This may explain possible weaknesses in the present author's judgment. However, since the reconstruction of the Diatessaron does not allow us to discard the contribution of the Old Saxon poem to the reconstruction of the Latin Diatessaron, I have ventured to take the risk and enter an area in which I am not qualified.

It is the merit of Quispel that he has renewed the interest of theologians in the text of the *Heliand*, especially in its value to the reconstruction of the Latin Diatessaron, but this cannot prevent us from examining the trustworthiness of the outcome of his research into the poem. This has been the only purpose of this contribution. In the case of the parable of the fishing net or fisherman the result is negative as far as the *Heliand* is concerned. There is only one distinctive and remarkable reading in which the *Heliand* betrays knowledge of an independent Latin source, namely in the verse *tiuhid up te staðe*, a verse in which the *Heliand* differs from Quispel's own reconstruction of the primitive Latin Diatessaron, as it does in so many respects. Was the poet led here by a variant reading either in his text or in some early commentary? It is worthwhile, therefore, to read the *Heliand* beside the other vernacular and Latin witnesses of the Western Diatessaron in order to discover possible characteristic readings that may have had their origin in one of the Latin Diatessarons that were current in the time of the *Heliand* poet or were present in the commentary tradition that he was acquainted with.

---

is more careful with his verdict; see for instance *Het Evangelie van Thomas* [note 3], 121 – "het is niet uitgesloten" – and "Der Heliand und das Thomasevangelium" [note 3], 149 (= *Gnostic Studies II* [note 3], 95): "Ist es, [. . .] wirklich nicht erlaubt, zu vermuten?"

(Un)Desirable Origins:
The *Heliand* and the Gospel of Thomas[1]

Valentine A. Pakis

> "The search for origins is never disinterested; those wishing to trace an idea or tradition to its historical, linguistic, and textual beginnings have always done so with a thesis in mind, and the origin they have found has often been an origin they have produced."[2]

The appellation "Fifth Gospel" betrays the anxiety that has surrounded the Gospel of Thomas since its discovery, not sixty years ago, among the Nag Hammadi codices. The Fifth Gospel occupies a liminal position, since Western efforts to exteriorize this text, compelled by its "exotic" and "heretical" origins, are offset by its antiquity and content, which threaten the authority of the Christian canon. The possibility, in other words, that the Gospel of Thomas preserves an older tradition of the sayings of Jesus frustrates its comfortable place among Eastern apocrypha. From the Christian West, the prologue and opening Logion incite a defensive reading: ⲚⲀⲈⲒ ⲚⲈ Ⲛ̄ϢⲀϪⲈ ⲈⲐⲎⲠ ⲈⲚⲦⲀ Ⲓ̄Ⲥ̄ ⲈⲦⲞⲚϨ ϪⲞⲞⲨ ⲀⲨⲰ ⲀϤⲤϨⲀⲒⲤⲞⲨ Ⲛ̄ϬⲒ ⲆⲒⲆⲨⲘⲞⲤ ⲒⲞⲨⲆⲀⲤ ⲐⲰⲘⲀⲤ (1) ⲀⲨⲰ ⲠⲈϪⲀϤ ϪⲈ ⲠⲈⲦⲀϨⲈ ⲈⲐⲈⲢⲘⲎⲚⲈⲒⲀ

---

1 Originally published in *Exemplaria: A Journal of Theory in Medieval and Renaissance Studies* 17 (2005), 215–53.
2 Allen J. Frantzen, *Desire for Origins: New Language, Old English, and Teaching the Tradition* (New Brunswick: Rutgers UP, 1990), xii.

(Un)Desirable Origins

ⲚⲚⲈⲈⲒϢⲀⲬⲈ ⲈⲦϨⲎⲠ ⲈⲚⲦⲀ ⲒⲎⲤ "These are the secret words that the living Jesus spoke, and Didymus Judas Thomas wrote them. (1) And he said, 'He who finds the interpretation of these words will not taste death'."[3]

On October 7, 1956, three years before Thomas would be edited,[4] the following headlines appeared in the *New York Times*: "Scholars Study a 'Fifth Gospel': 13 Volumes Dug Up in Egypt Are Only Apocryphal Works, Coptic Expert Says Here,"[5] and "Apostolic Authorship Denied."[6] The former article, which despite its subheading made no mention of apocrypha, explained that the Nag Hammadi texts "are themselves translations from books written in the Aramaic language that Jesus spoke." The latter assured the public that the artifact is "in no genuine sense another Gospel." Reassurance would come in two later articles, one of which announced that the Sayings, which now follow a Greek exemplar, "are capable of enriching and furthering our understanding of the canonical Gospels," but are no cause for "sensationalism."[7] The other, which repeated the remark about the discovery's capabilities, also noted:

> As far as writings as a whole are concerned, our four canonic Gospels are the only ones on which we can rely. Again and

---

3 Bentley Layton, ed., *Nag Hammadi Codex II, 2–7*, Nag Hammadi Studies 20 (Leiden: E. J. Brill, 1989), 52. The word separation and numeration of the Gospel of Thomas are editorial. Unless otherwise indicated, English translations are my own throughout this paper.
4 A. Guillaumont et al., eds., *The Gospel According to Thomas: Coptic Text Established and Translated* (Leiden: E. J. Brill, 1959). It should be noted that, before the *editio princeps*, a partial facsimile of the Gospel of Thomas was published in Pahor Labib, ed., *Coptic Gnostic Papyri in the Coptic Museum at Old Cairo* (Cairo: Government Press, 1956).
5 "Scholars Study a 'Fifth Gospel': 13 Volumes Dug Up in Egypt Are Only Apocryphal Works, Coptic Expert Says Here," *New York Times*, October 7, 1956, 34.
6 "Apostolic Authorship Denied," *New York Times*, October 7, 1956, 34.
7 "114 in Coptic Script of 'Thomas Gospel' Described Here," *New York Times*, March 19, 1959, 1.

again we must marvel at the fact that from the large number of primitive Christian writings only those were accepted as canonic which really came from the oldest time and which were free from heretical tendencies.⁸

This opinion would recur in a book review on April 3, 1960: "[T]he Gospel of Thomas has little, if any, independent value as a source for the teaching of Jesus. [. . .] Its value is for the history of the church rather than for the interpretation of the New Testament."⁹

In the spring of 1959, the Dutch patristic scholar Gilles Quispel responded to the media in a lecture entitled "Some Remarks on the Gospel of Thomas," which he would publish later that year.¹⁰ Here he not only discredited the "very inadequate and incompetent items"¹¹ printed in American and British newspapers but also made, as it seemed to him, a shocking announcement:

> The excitement of the general public, especially in the Anglo-Saxon world, seems to be considerable. Great expectations, I am afraid, will be followed by still greater disillusionment. And yet it seems to me that this discovery is much more important than even the wildest of reporters dream of, if only we are willing to apply the methods of scholarship. The *importance of the Gospel of Thomas lies in the fact that it contains an independent and very old Gospel tradition.*¹²

---

8 "Excerpts From Talk on Jesus' Sayings," *New York Times*, March 19, 1959, 12.

9 Robert C. Dentan, "From the Gospel of Thomas," review of *The Secret Sayings of Jesus*, by Robert M. Grant and David Noel Freedman, *New York Times*, April 3, 1960, BR26.

10 Gilles Quispel, "Some Remarks on the Gospel of Thomas," *New Testament Studies* 5 (1958/1959), 276–90. The lecture was delivered between the seventh and seventeenth of April in Aarhus, Copenhagen, Lund, Uppsala, and Oslo.

11 Ibid., 276.

12 Ibid., 277. The italics are Quispel's.

(Un)Desirable Origins

In certain readings of the Gospel of Thomas, Quispel detected the influence of a Judaic-Christian Gospel, composed in Aramaic and independent of the canonical writings, which he identified as the Gospel according to the Hebrews. Traces of the latter, according to Quispel, show themselves in four ways: 1) through Aramaisms in the Coptic text, 2) through parallels from Judaic-Christian literature, 3) through the efforts of form criticism, and 4) through parallels from Diatessaronic witnesses. These traces, Quispel remarked, are of great importance, since they reflect an early and independent account of the canonical narrative; they have, in fact, "some consequences for our assessment of the value of our Gospels."[13]

It is to the connection between the Gospel of Thomas and the Diatessaron, which share more than a hundred non-canonical readings, that Quispel, here and elsewhere, devoted the most energy.[14] His argument that the parallels between Thomas and Tatian derive from a Judaic-Christian Gospel, which found early critics,[15] relied heavily on evidence from Western Diatessaronic witnesses. Among these his favorite was the Old Saxon *Heliand*, the poet of which, he

---

13   Ibid., 278.
14   For the culmination of his research on the topic, see Gilles Quispel, *Tatian and the Gospel of Thomas: Studies in the History of the Western Diatessaron* (Leiden: E. J. Brill, 1975).
15   See Tjitze Baarda, "Thomas and Tatian," in *Early Transmission of Words of Jesus: Thomas, Tatian and the Text of the New Testament*, ed. J. Helderman and S. J. Noorda (Amsterdam: VU Boekhandel, 1983), 49. Originally published as "Thomas en Tatianus" in *Het Evangelie van Thomas*, by R. Schippers and Tjitze Baarda (Kampen: Kok, 1960): "Quispel's solution is most attractive at first sight, not only because the points of agreement between Thomas and Tatian would be adequately accounted for in this way, but because there are then no difficulties of chronology. Nevertheless, there are objections to Quispel's solution. Namely that it has become apparent to us that the Coptic Gospel of Thomas is descended, not from a (West-)Aramaic, but a Syriac text. Tatian wrote his harmony in Syriac, too. Now we can date Tatian's harmony fairly accurately, but not the Syriac text of the Gospel of Thomas. So it is impossible as yet to decide the issue of dependency with any certainty."

thought, "used a very primitive text of Tatian's Diatessaron."[16] In a number of studies, beginning with the lecture from 1959, Quispel tied the *Heliand* to the Gospel of Thomas by way of the Diatessaron and, from there, the Gospel according to the Hebrews.[17] His introduction

---

16 Quispel, "Some Remarks" [note 10], 284.

17 See ibid, 285: "[T]he Gospel of Thomas has left nowhere in the Diatessaron tradition such clear traces as in the *Heliand*"; idem, "Der Heliand und das Thomasevangelium," *Vigiliae Christianae* 16 (1962), 151: "We believe we have proved that the *Heliand* is based on a very deviant and ancient text of the Diatessaron that has variants in common with the Gospel of Thomas. And if the scholars are correct who say that the Gospel of Thomas contains an independent, Jewish-Christian tradition, it is possible that a reverberation of this voice may be felt in the *Heliand*" [Wir glauben bewiesen zu haben, dass der Heliand auf einem sehr abweichenden und altertümlichen Text des Diatessarons beruht, welcher Varianten mit dem Thomasevangelium gemein hat. [. . .] Und wenn die Forscher recht haben, die meinen, dass das Thomasevangelium eine unabhängige, judenchristliche Tradition enthält, dürfte sogar im Heliand noch ein Nachklang dieser Stimme zu spüren sein."; idem, "Jewish Influences on the 'Heliand'," in *Religions in Antiquity: Essays in Memory of Erwin Ramsdell Goodenough*, ed. Jacob Neusner (Leiden: E. J. Brill, 1968), 246: "But then we must not forget that the *Diatessaron* of Tatian contained Jewish Christian Gospel tradition [*sic*]. The same is the case with the *Gospel of Thomas*: if the two writings have so many variants in common, it is because they used the same source, an independent Aramaic Gospel tradition, brought by Jewish missionaries to Mesopotamia, where both Tatian and the author of the *Gospel of Thomas* lived. And so the *Heliand*, based as it is upon a Tatianic Gospel harmony, has preserved distinct echoes of this Palestinian tradition."; idem, "The Latin Tatian or the Gospel of Thomas in Limburg," *Journal of Biblical Literature* 88 (1969), 328: "One finds agreements with the Gospel of Thomas in all versions of the Diatessaron, even in those of the West. This means therefore that the OL [Old Latin] Diatessaron, on which are based the Heliand, the Limburg Life of Jesus, and the Venetian harmony, have preserved readings not alone from Tatian but also from his Jewish-Christian source"; idem, *Tatian and the Gospel of Thomas* [note 14], 29: "Moreover, it was established that the Heliand had many variants in common with the Jewish-Christian Gospel tradition as contained in the *Gospel of Thomas*, the Pseudo-Clementine writings, and the Jewish-Christian Gospel fragments. From this it was deduced that the Heliand preserved quite a few interesting variants of the

(Un)Desirable Origins

of the Fifth Gospel to medieval studies caught the attention of the *Heliand* scholar Willy Krogmann, who, in two articles, denied the connection.[18] The Germanist offered an alternate explanation for each of Quispel's readings, arguing that the latter "had not considered that the *Heliand* is not a word for word translation of its Latin *Vorlage* but rather an epic poem based on it."[19] A typical reading and riposte concerned the repetition of the canonical Ἀπόδοτε 'give' in the Old Saxon (*gebad, selliad*) and Coptic (ϯ, ϯ) versions of Matt 22.21:[20]

MATT 22.21

τότε λέγει αὐτοῖς, Ἀπόδοτε οὖν τὰ Καίσαρος Καίσαρι καὶ τὰ τοῦ θεοῦ τῷ θεῷ.

[Then he says to them, "Give, then, the things of Caesar to Caesar, and the things of God to God."]

Sayings of Jesus not preserved elsewhere." For remarks on Quispel's inconsistent labeling of the Judaic-Christian source, see Baarda, "Tatian and Thomas" [note 15], 49; and William L. Petersen, *Tatian's Diatessaron: Its Creation, Dissemination, Significance, and History in Scholarship*, Supplements to Vigiliae Christianae 25 (Leiden: E. J. Brill, 1994), 279n55.

18 Willy Krogmann, "Heliand, Tatian und Thomasevangelium," *Zeitschrift für die neutestamentliche Wissenschaft und die Kunde der älteren Kirche* 51 (1960), 255–68; idem, "Heliand und Thomasevangelium," *Vigiliae Christianae* 18 (1964), 65–73.

19 Krogmann, "Heliand, Tatian und Thomasevangelium" [note 18], 258: "[hatte] nicht berücksichtigt, daß der Heliand keine wörtliche Übersetzung der lateinischen Vorlage, sondern eine aus ihr gestaltete epische Dichtung ist." For surveys of this debate, see Petersen, *Tatian's Diatessaron* [note 17], 279–81, 288–90, which I shall discuss below, and Juw fon Weringha, *Heliand and Diatessaron* (Assen: Van Gorcum, 1965), 37–38.

20 The Greek, Coptic, and Old Saxon texts are from the following editions: Barbara Aland et al., eds., *The Greek New Testament*, 4th ed. (Nördlingen: C. H. Beck, 2001; repr. 2004); Bentley Layton, ed., *Nag Hammadi Codex II,2–7* [note 3]; Otto Behaghel, ed., *Heliand und Genesis*, 10th ed., rev. Burkhard Taeger, Altdeutsche Textbibliothek 4 (Tübingen: Max Niemeyer, 1996).

Valentine Pakis

Gospel of Thomas 100	Heliand 3829b–3832a
ⲡⲉϫⲁϥⲛⲁⲩ ϫⲉ † ⲛⲁ ⲕⲁⲓⲥⲁⲣ ⲛ̄ⲕⲁⲓⲥⲁⲣ † ⲛⲁ ⲡⲛⲟⲩⲧⲉ ⲙ̄ⲡ ⲛⲟⲩⲧⲉ	'Than uuilliu ik iu te uuârun hêr,' quað he, / 'selƀo seggian, that gi imo sîn geƀad, / uueroldhêrron is geuunst, endi uualdand gode / selliad, that thar sîn ist [...]'
[He said to them, "*Give* those things of Caesar to Caesar, *give* those things of God to God..."]	["Then I myself shall here tell you truthfully," he said, "that you *give* to him his, to the lord of the world his due, and *give* to the ruling god that which is his."]

Quispel notes that this variation, which never occurs in the canonical tradition, appears in other Diatessaronic witnesses, namely the *Tuscan Harmony*, Ephrem Syrus's *Commentary*, and the *Persian Harmony*, and must therefore reflect a Judaic-Christian source.[21] Krogmann responded, "The repetition of the verb before the second relative clause in different texts by no means allows us to assume a common source," and attributed the repetition of the verb to the epic (appositive) style of the Old Saxon poem and, more specifically, to the need for alliteration with *sin*.[22] Thus they argued, without yielding, over ten passages.

---

21 Quispel, "Der Heliand und das Thomasevangelium" [note 17], 148. Later, in *Tatian and the Gospel of Thomas* [note 14], Quispel would add two Middle Dutch witnesses to this reading (see Appendix III, p. 189). For criticism of the claim that Thomas and Tatian borrowed this passage from a common source, see Tjitze Baarda, "Het Evangelie van Thomas: vier korte studies," in *Het Evangelie van Thomas*, by Baarda et al., VU-segmenten 5 (Zoetermeer: Meinema, 1999), 37–44.

22 Krogmann, "Heliand und Thomasevangelium" [note 18], 70–1: "Die Wiederholung des Verbums vor dem zweiten Relativsatz in verschiedenen Texten läßt aber keineswegs auf eine gemeinsame Quelle schließen."

(Un)Desirable Origins

Whether source or style accounts for certain readings in the *Heliand* cannot be known for sure; it is debatable, after all, whether the poet could read.[23] That neither Krogmann nor Quispel admit the indeterminacy of the question suggests that unspoken motives underlay their arguments. I intend to discuss their positions as contrary, yet complementary, reactions to the alterity of the Gospel of Thomas and the familiarity of the *Heliand*. While Quispel sought to define the Coptic text, Krogmann warded it off; while Krogmann sought to define the *Heliand*, Quispel belittled it as an object of study. Their methods reflect the romantic, reconstructive, and positivistic philology that has, especially since the work of Bernard Cerquiglini,[24] come under much criticism. At stake in this debate was, above all, the authority of two disciplines, *Germanistik* and biblical studies, and the texts that each had constructed.

JESUS CHRIST IN GERMAN CLOTHES

"Sang uuas gisungan,   Uuīg uuas bigunnan"[25]

Though the "charm" of the *Heliand*, as G. Ronald Murphy puts it, lies in its synthesis of Saxon cultural values and the Christian Gospel story,[26] no feature of the poem has received more attention than its

---

23 For surveys of this debate, see Gustav Ehrismann, *Geschichte der Deutschen Literatur bis zum Ausgang des Mittelalters. Erster Teil: Die althochdeutsche Literatur* (Munich: C. H. Beck, 1918), 155–56; J. Knight Bostock, *A Handbook on Old High German Literature*, 2nd ed., rev. K. C. King and D. R. McLintock (Oxford: Clarendon, 1976), 177–78. For the most recent contribution, see Harald Haferland, "War der Dichter des 'Heliand' illiterat?" *Zeitschrift für deutsches Altertum und deutsche Literatur* 131 (2002), 20–48.

24 Bernard Cerquiglini, *Éloge de la variant: Histoire critique de la philologie* (Paris: Seuil, 1989).

25 *Das Ludwigslied*, line 48, in Wilhelm Braune, *Althochdeutsches Lesebuch*, 17th ed., rev. Ernst A. Ebbinghaus (Tübingen: Max Niemeyer, 1994), 137: "The song was sung, the battle was begun."

26 G. Ronald Murphy, *The Heliand: The Saxon Gospel* (New York: Oxford UP,

Germanness. It is with this in mind that I consider its familiarity and offer the following sketch. Since the middle of the nineteenth century, studies of the poem have served romantic and nationalistic ends and have, until the present, contributed to the formation and validation of Germanic identity. In *Deutsche Altertümer im Hêliand*, which first appeared in 1845, A. F. C. Vilmar does not hide his effort to conflate the culture of the medieval Saxons with his own, to define and affirm, through cultural reconstruction, the values of his fellow countrymen:

> What we are faced with here is Christianity in German clothes, dressed in the poetics and manners of a noble German tribe, described with unmistakable love and faithful devotion, equipped with everything great and beautiful that the German people, the German heart and life have to offer. It is a German Christ, it is in the most special sense *our* Christ, our beloved Lord and powerful King, that the poetry of this folksinger represents to us.[27]

Toward the end of the nineteenth century, Emil Lagenpusch thanks the poet of the *Heliand* for not renouncing his true Germanic identity. I have left the antecedent of "his" ambiguous, since it is, to some extent, for the opportunity to reconstruct his own Germanic origins, and therefore to define himself, that Lagenpusch is grateful: "Countless are the echoes from Teutonic culture – we find them in

---

1992), xiii.

27 A. F. C. Vilmar, *Deutsche Altertümer im Hêliand als Einkleidung der evangelischen Geschichte*, 2nd ed. (Marburg: N. G. Elwert, 1862), 1: "[E]s ist das Christentum im deutschen gewande, eingekleidet in die poesie und sitte eines edlen deutschen stammes, welches uns hier entgegentritt, mit unverkennbarer liebe und treuer hingebung geschildert, mit allem grossen und schönen ausgestattet, was das deutsche volk, das deutsche herz und leben zu geben hatte. es ist ein deutscher Christus, es ist im eigensten sinne *unser* Christus, unser lieber herr und mächtiger volkskönig, welchen die dichtung des volkssängers uns darstellt." The emphasis is Vilmar's.

(Un)Desirable Origins

nearly every line. The poet, even though he is a faithful Christian, cannot escape from his Teutonic skin, and we thank him for his devotion to his gods, to his Germanness. Countless are the echoes [. . .]."[28] In *Die echte Germanisierung der Kirche*, published in 1935, Otto Dibelius discusses the *Heliand* in terms of its Germanic spirit, and so participates in the ideologically powerful *Deutschkunde* of his time: "A translation of the story of Jesus in the Teutonic spirit! Did not this translation take the hearts of the Germanic tribes by storm?"[29] Occasionally, the emphasis of *Heliand* scholarship shifts from the *Germanisierung des Christentums* to the *Christianisierung des Germanentums*,[30] but the effect remains the same, reflecting only, it seems, whether the scholar regards him or herself to be a Christian German or a German Christian. In an article from 1937 – "Wollte der Dichter des Heliand nichts anderes als ein Künder germanischen Lebensgefühles sein?" – Herman Wicke concludes that the poet, an

---

28 Emil Lagenpusch, "Walhallklänge im Heliand," in *Festschrift zum siebzigsten Geburtstage Oskar Schade, dargebracht von seinen Schülern und Verehrern* (Königsberg: Hartung, 1896), 152: "Zahllos sind die Anklänge aus dem alten Germanentum, fast in jeder Zeile finden wir sie wieder. Der Dichter kann, obgleich er ein gläubiger Christ ist, aus seiner alten Germanenhaut nicht heraus, und wir danken ihm diese Anhänglichkeit an seine Götter, an sein Germanentum. Zahllos sind die Anklänge [. . .]."
29 Otto Dibelius, *Die echte Germanisierung der Kirche* (Berlin: Kranz, 1935), 32: "Also eine Übersetzung der Jesus-Geschichte in germanischen Geist! Mußte diese Übersetzung sich die Herzen der germanischen Stämme nicht im Sturm erobern?"
30 In a recent article, Harald Haferland consciously avoids such hierarchizing terms: "Both tendencies to Germanize and tendencies to Christianize are therefore detectable in the *Heliand*, and this is, in processes of acculturation in general, fundamental and to be expected" [Sowohl Germanisierungstendenzen wie auch Christianisierungstendenzen lassen sich deshalb im *Heliand* nachweisen, und dies ist, wie bei Prozessen der Akkulturation überhaupt, grundsätzlich auch nicht anders zu erwarten]. See Harald Haferland, "Der Haß der Feinde: Germanische Heldendichtung und die Erzählkonzeption des *Heliand*," *Euphorion* 95 (2001), 241.

"an inwardly upstanding German man,"[31] intended rather to be a "Germanic preacher of God's Word."[32]

That the Germanness of the *Heliand* accounts for much of its appreciation also comes to light in commentaries on the *Evangelienbuch*, which is made to be the literary foil of the Saxon poem. To the tastes of medievalists, not surprisingly, the art of the *Heliand* poet is far superior to that of Otfrid, who by un-Germanizing Germanic poetry has earned his reputation as a literary drudge: "An outstanding poetic gift, this Otfrid did not possess."[33] In his romantic *Geschichte der deutschen Litteratur*, Wilhelm Scherer notes, "Strangely enough, the monk from Weißenburg did not want simply to produce a book to be read but also songs to be sung – songs with which he intended to displace the secular folk music that was so detestable to him. He lacked the simple gravity that distinguishes the writer of the *Heliand*."[34] According to Anton E. Schönbach, in an article published in 1896, the *Heliand* poet Germanized the Gospels to a greater extent than did the Frank "because his nature was stronger and bolder than that of Otfrid."[35] Heinz Rupp concludes a more

---

31 Hermann Wicke, "Wollte der Dichter des Heliand nichts anderes als ein Künder germanischen Lebensgefühles sein?" *Zeitschrift der Gesellschaft für niedersächsische Kirchengeschichte* 42 (1937), 229: "innerlich hochstehender germanischer Mann." The phrase is originally in the genitive.
32 Ibid., 238: "germanischer Verkündiger des Wortes Gottes."
33 Ehrismann, *Geschichte der deutschen Literatur* [note 23], 195: "Eine hervorragende poetische Begabung besaß Otfrid nicht."
34 Wilhelm Scherer, *Geschichte der deutschen Litteratur*, 10th ed. (Berlin: Weidmann, 1905), 48: "Seltsam genug, daß der Weißenburger Mönch damit nicht bloß ein Buch zum Lesen, sondern auch Lieder zum Singen liefern wollte, mit denen er den weltlichen Volksgesang, der ihm ein Greuel war, zu verdrängen gedachte. Er hat nicht den schlichten Ernst, welcher den Verfasser des 'Heliand' auszeichnet." Scherer's evaluation of Otfrid's poetry is criticized in W. P. Lehmann, *The Alliteration of Old Saxon Poetry*, Norsk Tidsskrift for Sprogvidenskap, Suppl. Bind 3 (Oslo: H. Aschenhoug, 1953), 7–8.
35 Anton E. Schönbach, "Deutsches Christentum vor tausend Jahren," *Cosmopolis* 1 (1896), 615: "weil sein Wesen kräftiger und derber war als das Otfrids."

recent article: "[T]he marvellous thing about the *Heliand* is that the poet has succeeded in making, [*sic*] Christian doctrine and the life of Jesus understandable to a wide audience. The wonderful thing about Otfrid's *Evangelienbuch* is that it could be written at all."[36] In a letter to a colleague, dated February 2, 1990, Ernst A. Ebbinghaus provides the following (comical) assessment: "The answer to your question about Otfrid is very simple. He wrote the 'poem' so that, as Helm said, we have sufficient text for *Staatsexamen*. I have never found a better explanation. I once undertook to read the entire cursed piece merely because it was there and I was learning OHG. I have regretted it ever since, and I see no reason why we do not read Heliand with our students. That is certainly a better piece of literature."[37]

The Ur-Resistible Heliand

"La philologie médiévale est le deuil d'un Texte, le patient travail de ce deuil. Quête d'une perfection toujours antérieure et révolue [. . .]"[38]

Willy Krogmann lived from 1905 to 1967. He gained his doctorate in 1928 – his advisor was Wolfgang Golther – at the University of Rostock, where he would remain as a lecturer until 1933. For the next seven years he worked as a lexicographer, first in Berlin and then in Hamburg, where he also held seminars in Low German and

---

36 Heinz Rupp, "The Adoption of Christian Ideas into German, with Reference to the 'Heliand' and Otfrid's 'Evangelienbuch'," *Parergon* 21 (1979), 40.

37 This excerpt from Ebbinghaus's personal correspondence is published in the latter's obituary by Anatoly Liberman: "Ernst A. Ebbinghaus (1926–1995): Portrait of the Linguist as an Old Man," *American Journal of Germanic Linguistics & Literatures* 9 (1997), 123.

38 Cerquiglini, *Éloge de la variante* [note 24], 58: "Medieval philology is the mourning for a text, the patient labor of this mourning. It is a quest for a perfection that is always anterior and bygone."

Frisian. In 1940 he had to leave Germany for Holland, where he was stationed, until 1945, as a *Sonderführer* in the German army. After the war he returned to the University of Hamburg, where he taught and wrote about Germanic philology until his death.[39]

In addition to contemporary Low German poetry, Goethe, Shakespeare, and Etruscan etymology, Krogmann's publications address all aspects of early Germanic language and culture, from runology to Minnesang. It might be accurate to place him among the Germanists of his time known today as *innere Emigranten*, who avoided Nazi hegemony by retreating into an "ivory tower of humanistic idealism."[40] The attitude finds expression in the reminiscences of Karl Otto Conrady: "The choice to study German and Latin literature sprang from the wish to step away, pull out, and flee from the squabbles of the present, from the uncertainty of the historical situation of the time, from the necessity of having to understand what was happening, toward the distant, the foreign, toward the supposedly apolitical, and into the realm of inwardness."[41] With such an approach, as Henry J. Schmidt points out, scholars occupied what they thought to be "an ideology-free, morally neutral position, which allowed them to uphold the values of the 'other Germany' by shielding the unspoiled, eternal German *Geist* of the classics from Hitler's *Staat*."[42] Krogmann, however, retreated even further, his interests

---

39 See Ulrich Pretzel, "Krogmann," in *Neue deutsche Biographie*, vol. 13 (Berlin: Duncker & Humblot, 1982), 67–68.
40 Henry J. Schmidt, "What is Oppositional Criticism? Politics and German Literary Criticism from Fascism to the Cold War," *Monatshefte* 79 (1987), 294.
41 Karl Otto Conrady, "Reminiszenzen und Reflexionen," in *Wie, warum und zu welchem Ende wurde ich Literaturhistoriker?* ed. Siegfried Unseld (Frankfurt: Suhrkampf, 1972), 62: "Die Wahl der Fächer Germanistik und Latinistik [. . .] entsprang dem Wunsch wegzutreten, auszuscheren, zu flüchten aus den Querelen der Gegenwart, aus der Ungewißheit der geschichtlichen Situation damals, aus der Not, das Geschehene begreifen zu müssen, hin zum Fernen, Fremden, zum vermeintlich Unpolitischen, ins Reich der Innerlichkeit." Quoted in Schmidt, "What is Oppositional Criticism" [note 40], 294.
42 Ibid., 295.

(Un)Desirable Origins

being not so much the classics as their origins. His writings include, to name a few: *Untersuchungen zum Ursprung der Gretchentragödie* (his dissertation), *Goethes 'Urfaust', Die Heimatfrage des Heliand im Lichte des Wortschatzes, Der Rattenfänger von Hameln: Eine Untersuchung über das Werden der Sage, Der Name der Germanen, Das Hildebrandslied: In der langobardischen Urfassung hergestellt, Die Kultur der alten Germanen, Der althochdeutsche 138. Psalm: Forschungsgeschichtlicher Überblick und Urfassung*, "Die Vorlage des 'Reynke de Vos'," and "Eine 'Ackermann'-Handschrift zwischen Urschrift und Archetypus."[43] Typical of such works is *Das Hildebrandslied*, in which Krogmann, ignoring the criticism of Bostock,[44] restores the difficult poem to what he considered its Lombardic archetype. Given the paucity of Lombardic records,[45] remarkable confidence pervades this study: "If in the *Hildebrandslied*

---

43 Willy Krogmann, *Untersuchungen zum Ursprung der Gretchentragödie* (Wismar: Willgeroth & Menzel, 1928); idem, *Goethes 'Urfaust'* (Berlin: Emil Ebering, 1933); idem, *Die Heimatfrage des Heliand im Lichte des Worschatzes* (Wismar: Hinsdorff, 1937); idem, *Der Rattenfänger von Hameln: Eine Untersuchung über das Werden der Sage* (Berlin: Emil Ebering, 1934); idem, *Der Name der Germanen* (Wismar: Hinsdorff, 1933); idem, *Das Hildebrandslied: In der langobardischen Urfassung hergestellt* (Berlin: Erich Schmidt, 1959); idem, *Die Kultur der alten Germanen* (Konstanz: Athenaion, 1960); idem, *Der althochdeusche 138. Psalm: Forschungsgeschichtlicher Überblick und Urfassung* (Hamburg: F. Wittig, 1973); idem, "Die Vorlage des 'Reynke de Vos'," *Niederdeutsches Jahrbuch: Jahrbuch des Vereins für niederdeutsche Sprachforschung* 87 (1964): 29–55; idem, "Eine 'Ackermann'-Handschrift zwischen Urschrift und Archetypus," *Zeitschrift für deutsche Philologie* 86 (1967): 80–90.

44 Two years before Krogmann's publication, J. Knight Bostock, *Handbook on Old High German Literature* (Oxford: Clarendon, 1955), 65–66, remarked: "The efforts of many scholars to devise a scheme of evolution which would afford a logical explanation of all the contradictory details have led to elaborate constructions, some of which reflect more credit on the ingenuity than on the common sense of their authors."

45 See Wilhelm Braune, *Althochdeutsche Grammatik*, 9th ed., rev. Walter Mitzka (Tübingen: Max Niemeyer, 1959), § 6a. Ingo Reiffenstein has omitted information about Lombardic from the most recent, 15th edition of Braune's grammar (see § 2n1).

the word *hēr* still only occurs with the meaning 'gray-haired, old', which Middle Irish *cīar* 'dark', Old Church Slavonic *čerz* 'gray', Sanskrit *śīra-bha-*, *śera-bha-* 'boa' prove to be the original meaning of Germanic *+haira-*, then it could have meant nothing else in Lombardic."[46]

His other work aside, Krogmann wrote more about the *Heliand* than anyone has before or since.[47] Even before Quispel's articles, he defended the canonical purity of the poem against those who had found apocryphal readings. In "Apokryphes im Heliand?" he contests the opinions of a number of scholars, including Behaghel and Sievers, and holds fast to his thesis: "Wherever the poet deviated from Tatian, he either relied on his commentaries or let his own imagination take over."[48] Though much of the *Heliand* is the poet's own making,[49] Krogmann's appeal to the poet's *Phantasie*, however valid, would beckon criticism. Even more convenient, perhaps, was his own (learned) fancy, which permitted him at one point to accuse the poet of forgetfulness[50] and, at others, to reconstruct verses in defense of his argument. This he does, for instance, to refute Frederick Pickering's claim that the apocryphal Pseudo-Matthew influenced

---

46   Krogmann, *Das Hildebrandslied* [note 43], 15–16: "Wenn im Hildebrandslied *hēr* nur noch in der Bedeutung 'grauhaarig, alt' vorkommt, die mir. *cīar* 'dunkel', abg. *čerz* 'grau', ai. *śīra-bha-*, *śera-bha-* 'Boa' für germ. *+haira-* als ursprünglich erweisen, so kann es sich nur um langobardischen Sprachgebrauch handeln."
47   See Johanna Belkin and Jürgen Meier, eds., *Bibliographie zu Otfrid von Weißenburg und zur altsächsischen Bibeldichtung (Heliand und Genesis)*, Bibliographien zur deutschen Literatur des Mittelalters 7 (Berlin: Erich Schmidt, 1975).
48   Willy Krogmann, "Apokryphes im Heliand?" *Niederdeutsches Jahrbuch: Jahrbuch des Vereins für niederdeutsche Sprachforschung* 79 (1956), 35: "Wo er [the poet] über den Tatian hinausgegangen ist, hat er sich entweder auf seine Kommentare gestützt oder aber seine eigene Phantasie walten lassen."
49   See Haferland, "Der Haß der Feinde" [note 30], 247.
50   Krogmann, "Apokryphes im Heliand?" [note 48], 28: "The mixing of both biblical verses can only be explained by a slip of the poet's memory" [Die Vermengung der beiden Bibelstellen läßt nur die Erklärung zu, daß der Dichter sich auf sein Gedächtnis verließ].

(Un)Desirable Origins

the *Heliand*'s account of the flight to Egypt,[51] the canonical account of which makes no mention of Joseph's companions:[52]

MATT 2.14

ὁ δὲ ἐγερθεὶς τὸ παιδίον καὶ τὴν μητέρα αὐτοῦ νυκτὸς καὶ ἀνεχώρησεν εἰς Αἴγυπτον

[And he, having risen up, took the child and his mother at night and withdrew into Egypt.]

Pseudo-Matthew, Ch. 18	Heliand 754b-757b
erant autem cum Ioseph tres pueri et cum Maria quaedam puella simul iter agentes.	Than habde ina craftag god / gineridan uuið iro nîðe, that inan nahtes thanan / an Aegypteo land erlos antlêddun, / gumon mid Iosepe an thana grôneon uuang.
[There were, moreover, *three boys with Joseph* and a certain girl with Mary going along on the journey.]	[Then powerful God had saved him against their hate, so that *earls*, at night, led him thence to the land of Egypt, *men with Joseph*, to the green meadow.]

The chances are slim that the *Heliand* poet relied on the Gospel of Pseudo-Matthew, according to Krogmann, first because nothing from the poem reflects the content of the infancy story and second because, in this particular passage, "the wording that has come down

---

51 Frederick P. Pickering, "Christlicher Erzählstoff bei Otfrid und im Heliand," *Zeitschrift für deutsches Altertum und deutsche Literatur* 85 (1954/1955), 274.
52 The text of Pseudo-Matthew is quoted from Constantinus de Tischendorf, ed., *Evangelia Apocrypha*, 2nd ed. (Leipzig: Hermann Mendelssohn, 1876), 85.

to us has been corrupted by a scribe. In the original text there was certainly no mention of Joseph's servants."[53] Krogmann undoes the corruption by emending *erlos antlêddun* (756b) to *erlon antledda*. He then explains *mid Iosepe* (756a) as instrumental, and points to the confusion of the scribe, who did not regard *craftag god* as the subject of the *that*-clause. His reconstruction, then, may be translated: "Then powerful God had saved him against their hate, so that he led him at night, the earl [acc.] thence to the land of Egypt, the man [acc.] by means of Joseph to the green meadow." Though plausible, this *Urtext* is more awkward than the manuscript reading. Reference to the infant Jesus as *erl* 'earl' and *gumo* 'man' is anachronistic, and the use of *mid* with a person normally indicates accompaniment, not instrument.[54] Like many of his philological predecessors, Krogmann was confident in the terrain between origins and textual beginnings, so much so that he would sooner reconstruct passages than admit the possibility of apocryphal influence on the *Heliand*. Behind his methods, it seems, lay his ideological investment in the canonical purity, both biblical and Germanic, of the Old Saxon poem. He reacted to the claims of Pickering and others, his fellow Germanists, as if to a threat; the claims of Quispel, an outsider, would raise the stakes.

---

53 Krogmann, "Apokryphes im Heliand?" [note 48], 30: "[d]er überlieferte Wortlaut ist durch einen Schreiber verderbt worden. In der Urschrift war von Mannen Josephs gar keine Rede."

54 Such anachronisms occur in the *Heliand* and are not uncommon in Germanic biblical literature in general. The newborn Christ, for instance, is called *luttilna man* (381b) and *bald endi strang* (599a). In the Old High German *Christus und die Samariterin* (line 8), the woman of Samaria uses the interjection *uuizze Christ* 'Christ knows', before she knows with whom she is speaking (Braune, *Althochdeutsches Lesebuch* [note 25], 136). For a discussion of anachronisms in medieval biblical literature, see Erich Auerbach, *Mimesis: The Representation of Reality in Western Literature*, trans. Willard R. Trask (Princeton: Princeton UP, 1953; repr. 1991), 157–58. For the uses of *mid* in Old Saxon, see F. Holthausen, *Altsächsisches Elementarbuch* (Heidelberg: Carl Winter, 1900), § 510.

(Un)Desirable Origins

On three occasions, following the work C. W. M. Grein, William Foerste, and Walter Henß,[55] Krogmann voiced his belief that the chief source of the *Heliand* was not the Codex Fuldensis but another, now lost, Latin Diatessaron.[56] This is strange, as it was this very idea, as mentioned above, that allowed Quispel to link the *Heliand* to Thomas; it was in fact central to the latter's argument, and the only reason why he had given the Saxon harmony as much attention as he had. One cannot at once agree with Foerste and Henß – who in fact praise the Diatessaron scholars Anton Baumstark and Daniël Plooij[57] – and dismiss Quispel's ideas as groundless. Had Krogmann believed, in other words, that the source of the *Heliand* was not the vulgatized Codex Fuldensis but another Tatianic harmony, which shared non-canonical readings with other Diatessaronic witnesses, and some of these readings also occurred in the Gospel of Thomas, then

---

55 C. W. M. Grein, *Die Quellen des Heliand. Nebst einem Anhang: Tatians Evangelienharmonie herausgegeben nach dem Codex Cassellanus* (Cassel: Theodor Kay, 1869), 129: "That the Codex Fuldensis had perhaps lain before our poet is certainly to be rejected: The Tatian codex that he used certainly resembled our Codex Cassellanus more closely" [(D)aß vielleicht der Codex Fuldensis unserem Dichter zur Benutzung vorgelegen habe, ist jedenfalls zurückzuweisen: der von ihm benutzte Tatiancodex stand jedenfalls unserem Codex Cassellanus näher]; William Foerste, "Otfrids literarisches Verhältnis zum Heliand," *Niederdeutsches Jahrbuch: Jahrbuch des Vereins für niederdeutsche Sprachforschung* 71/73 (1950), 40n4, which contains a list of *Heliand* readings that deviate from the Codex Fuldensis; Walter Henß, "Zur Quellenfrage im Heliand und ahd. Tatian," *ibid.* 77 (1954), 2: "Like the Old High German Tatian across from its Latin column, and the Latin column itself, the *Heliand* truly contains a source-tradition that is independent from the Victor codex" [Tatsächlich besitzt der Heliand, wie der ahd. Tatian gegenüber seiner lateinischen Kolumne und diese selbst, eine vom Victor-Codex unabhängige Quellentradition].
56 See Willy Krogmann, "Eine fremde Fitte im Heliand," *Niederdeutsches Jahrbuch: Jahrbuch des Vereins für niederdeutsche Sprachforschung* 78 (1955), 10–11; idem, "Heliand, Tatian und Thomasevangelium" [note 18], 256; idem, "Heliand und Thomasevangelium" [note 18], 66.
57 Foerste, "Otfrids literarisches Verhältnis" [note 55], 40n4; Henß, "Zur Quellenfrage im Heliand" [note 55], 1.

Quispel's thesis should have appealed to him. Despite his espousal of Foerste and Henß, it seems that Krogmann, though convinced that the Codex Fuldensis never lay before the *Heliand* poet, regarded the *Vorlage* to be a no less "Vulgatized" recension.[58] In any case, he treated the Diatessaron problem as secondary. Whereas in "Heliand, Tatian und Thomasevangelium" he rejected Quispel's *Heliand*-Diatessaron parallels,[59] in "Heliand und Thomasevangelium," as the title suggests, he ignored Tatian altogether. Even though, according to Quispel, readings from the Gospel of Thomas appeared in Old Saxon *by way of* the Diatessaron, the Coptic text was, for Krogmann, the more urgent matter:

> The question about what version of the Gospel Harmony the Heliand poet used requires, on the other hand, an examination of its own. In such an examination Quispel's comparisons would be tested and a short glance would doubtless reveal the same methodological weaknesses as those seen in his "parallels" between the Heliand and the Gospel of Thomas. Here I shall limit myself to the few new things he has supplied in this regard.[60]

These remarks concern "Der Heliand und das Thomasevangelium," in which Quispel displayed, table after table, more than seventy Diatessaronic readings in the *Heliand*.[61] Krogmann, having faced only five of these from Quispel's lecture, was overwhelmed; his choice to insult rather than refute these findings did little to disguise this.

---

58 I discuss the concept of Vulgatization below.
59 Krogmann, "Heliand, Tatian und Thomasevangelium" [note 18], 258–60.
60 Krogmann, "Heliand und Thomasevangelium" [note 18], 66: "Anderseits bedarf die Frage nach der vom Helianddichter herangezogenen Fassung der Evangelienharmonie einer eigenen Untersuchung. In ihr werden auch Quispels Zusammenstellungen zu prüfen sein, die nach [. . .] einer flüchtigen Durchsicht allerdings dieselben methodischen Schwächen zeigen wie seine Parallelen zwischen dem Heliand und Thomasevangelium. Hier beschränke ich mich auf das Wenige, was er in dieser Beziehung neu beigebracht hat."
61 Quispel, "Der Heliand und das Thomasevangelium" [note 17], 121–39.

(Un)Desirable Origins

He would never, in fact, refute them, his *flüchtige Durchsicht* being enough to detect their error.[62]

Regardless of his neglect of Tatian, Krogmann's arguments against the proposed connection between the *Heliand* and the Gospel of Thomas were, at least to one camp, convincing. While Quispel and other Diatessaron scholars would criticize his frequent "recourse to the particularly Germanic qualities of the poet,"[63] Germanists, none of whom has since taken up the question, seem to have been satisfied. Many of Krogmann's counterpoints are indeed persuasive, though, again, their soundness is beyond determination. The following passages, for instance, concern the Coptic and Old Saxon deviations from Matt 12.35/Luke 6.45, where, according to Quispel, there is no mention of hearts (ⲉⲧϨⲚ̄ ⲡⲉϥϨⲎⲦ; *umbi is herte*) or wicked speech (Ⲛ̄ϥⲭⲱ Ⲛ̄ϨⲚ̄ⲠⲞⲚⲎⲢⲞⲚ; *inuuitrâdos, balusprâca*):[64]

MATT 12.35

ὁ ἀγαθὸς ἄνθρωπος ἐκ τοῦ ἀγαθοῦ θησαυροῦ ἐκβάλλει ἀγαθά, καὶ ὁ πονηρὸς ἄνθρωπος ἐκ τοῦ πονηροῦ θησαυροῦ ἐκβάλλει πονηρά.

[The good man brings out good things from the good storehouse, and the bad man brings out bad things from the bad storehouse.]

---

62 In a note to the quotation above (in "Heliand und Thomasevangelium" [note 18], 66n8), Krogmann rejects one more Tatianic reading, namely *Heliand* 3071b-3072a – "ni mugun uuið them thinun [Peter's] suîðeun crafte / anthebbien hellie portun" – which, he thinks, follows only the canonical text: "[. . .] and the gates of Hades will not prevail against it [the Church]" (Matt 16.18). Krogmann also addresses this passage in *Absicht oder Willkür im Aufbau des Heliand* (Hamburg: Friedrich Wittig, 1964), 94.

63 Quispel, "Der Heliand und das Thomasevangelium" [note 17], 142: "Rekurs auf die germanische Sonderart des Dichters."

64 Quispel, "Some Remarks on the Gospel of Thomas" [note 10], 286; idem, "Der Heliand und das Thomasevangelium" [note 17], 146.

Gospel of Thomas 45	Heliand 1755a-1758b
ογαγαθος ⲡ̄ⲣⲱⲙⲉ ϣⲁϥⲉⲓⲛⲉ ⲛ̄ ογαγαθον ⲉⲃⲟⲗ ϩ̄ⲙ ⲡⲉϥⲉϩⲟ ογ ⲕⲁⲕ(ⲟⲥ) ⲡ̄ⲣⲱⲙⲉ ϣⲁϥⲉⲓⲛⲉ ⲛ̄ϩⲛ̄ⲡⲟⲛⲏⲣⲟⲛ ⲉⲃⲟⲗ ϩ̄ⲙ ⲡⲉϥⲉϩⲟ ⲉⲑⲟⲟⲩ ⲉⲧϩ̄ⲛ ⲡⲉϥϩⲏⲧ ⲁⲩⲱ ⲛ̄ϥϫⲱ ⲛ̄ϩⲛ̄ⲡⲟⲛⲏⲣⲟⲛ ⲉⲃⲟⲗ ⲅⲁⲣ ϩ̄ⲙ ⲫⲟⲩⲟ ⲙ̄ⲫⲏⲧ ϣⲁϥ ⲉⲓⲛⲉ ⲉⲃⲟⲗ ⲛ̄ϩⲛ̄ⲡⲟⲛⲏⲣⲟⲛ	ac cumad fan them uƀilan man inuuitrâdos, / bittara balusprâca, sulic sô hi an is breostun haƀad / geheftid umbi is herte: simbla is hugi cûðid, / is uuilleon mid is uuordun, endi farad is uuerc aftar thiu.
[... A good man brings forth good from his storehouse; an evil man brings forth evil things from his evil storehouse, which is *in his heart*, and *says evil things*. For out of the abundance of the heart he brings forth evil things.]	[From an evil man will come *malicious advice, bitter slander*, just what he keeps within his breast chained *around his heart*. His thoughts and his will always make themselves known in his words, and then his actions come travelling along behind.]

Quispel's assertion that these readings are "absent from our canonical Gospels"[65] indicates that he had in mind only Matthew's version. Krogmann simply pointed to Luke 6.45,[66] which refers to both the heart and, by implication, wicked speech: ὁ ἀγαθὸς ἄνθρωπος ἐκ τοῦ ἀγαθοῦ θησαυροῦ τῆς καρδίας προφέρει τὸ ἀγαθόν, καὶ ὁ πονηρὸς ἐκ τοῦ πονηροῦ προφέρει τὸ πονηρόν· ἐκ γὰρ περισσεύματος καρδίας λαλεῖ τὸ στόμα αὐτοῦ "The good man brings forth a good thing from the good *storehouse of his heart*, the bad brings forth a bad thing from the bad. For his mouth *speaks* out of an overflowing of heart." The chances are high that the phrasing of the *Heliand* here reflects the Lucan reading and not a Judaic-Christian Gospel tradition.

---

65 Quispel, "Some Remarks on the Gospel of Thomas" [note 10], 286.
66 Krogmann, "Heliand, Tatian und Thomasevangelium" [note 18], 267.

(Un)Desirable Origins

Elsewhere Krogmann is on less secure ground. The accounts of the parable of the sower (Matt 13.3–9, Mark 4.3–9, Luke 8.4–8) in the *Heliand* and the Gospel of Thomas share a number of deviations from the canonical versions. Whereas in the Synoptics, for instance, seeds fall *along* the road (παρὰ, Vulgate *secus*),[67] where birds then *eat* them up (κατέφαγεν), in Coptic and Old Saxon, according to Quispel, they fall *onto* the road (ⲉⲭⲛ̄, *an*), and the birds *gather* them (ⲁⲩⲕⲁⲧϥⲟⲩ, *alâsun*).

MATT 13.3–4

Ἰδοὺ ἐξῆλθεν ὁ σπείρων τοῦ σπείρειν. καὶ ἐν τῷ σπείρειν αὐτὸν ἃ μὲν ἔπεσεν παρὰ τὴν ὁδόν, καὶ ἐλθόντα τὰ πετεινὰ κατέφαγεν αὐτά.

[Behold, a sower came out to sow. And while sowing it, some fell along the road, and the birds, having come, ate them up.]

Gospel of Thomas 9	Heliand 2398b-2403b
ⲉⲓⲥϩⲏⲏⲧⲉ ⲁϥⲉⲓ ⲉⲃⲟⲗ ⲛ̄ϭⲓ ⲡⲉⲧⲥⲓⲧⲉ ⲁϥⲙⲉϩ ⲧⲟⲟⲧϥ̄ ⲁϥⲛⲟⲩϫⲉ ⲁϩⲟⲉⲓⲛⲉ ⲙⲉⲛ ϩⲉ ⲉⲭⲛ̄ ⲧⲉϩⲓⲏ ⲁⲩⲉⲓ ⲛ̄ϭⲓ ⲛ̄ϩⲁⲗⲁⲧⲉ ⲁⲩⲕⲁⲧϥⲟⲩ	Sum eft bifallen uuarð / an êna starca strâtun, thar stôpon gengun, / hrosso hôfslaga endi helîðo trâda; / [. . .] thô it eft thes uuerodes farnam, / thes folkes fard mikil endi fuglos alâsun.
[Now the sower went out, took a handful and scattered them. Some fell *onto* the road; the birds came and *gathered* them]	[Some, in turn, had fallen *onto/along* a strong road, where footsteps went, the hoofbeat of horses and the tread of men. . . . Then the travelling of people, of folk, destroyed it, and birds *gathered it up*.]

---

67 Quotations of the Vulgate are from Bonifatius Fischer et al., eds., *Biblia Sacra iuxta Vulgata versionem*, 4th ed. (Stuttgart: Württembergische Bibelanstalt, 1994).

Against Quispel's understanding of Old Saxon *an* 'onto', Krogmann points out that the preposition may also have the meaning of its Modern German counterpart, and is therefore a fitting translation of *secus* 'along, beside'.[68] Though this is true, Quispel maintains that the *Heliand* poet did not read *secus viam* but rather *supra* or *in viam*, and so agrees with four other Diatessaronic witnesses.[69] This possibility is also supported by the emphasis the *Heliand* places, quite freely, on the trampling of the seeds. Perhaps the poet would not have made this embellishment had he been following the inconsistent canonical reading[70] – such traffic, it seems, would take place *on* the road, not beside it. About the verb *alasun* (< *alesan*) 'gather up, pick up', which ends the verse line *thes folkes fard mikil endi fuglos alâsun*, Krogmann writes, "Why he wrote *ālāsun* and not *frātun* is explained simply by the fact that he could not use another word beginning with *f*. In the long line, the words *folken*, *fard* and *fuglos* already alliterate with this letter."[71] Outside of Coptic and Old Saxon, *gather* also appears in the Syriac tradition.[72] Recourse to the hypothetical laws of Germanic verse is in this case a feeble crutch; it assumes too much about the act of composition. Moreover, *fretan*, though it almost certainly existed, is unattested in Old Saxon, and the verb *etan* may just as well have been used. In Old English, this passage appears

---

68 Krogmann, "Heliand, Tatian und Thomasevangelium" [note 18], 261.
69 Quispel, "Der Heliand und der Thomasevangelium" [note 17], 147. For a convenient list of the Diatessaronic parallels, see Quispel, *Tatian and the Gospel of Thomas* [note 14], 176.
70 Only Luke 8.5 mentions that the seeds were trampled: ὃ μὲν ἔπεσεν παρὰ τὴν ὁδόν, καὶ κατεπατήθη "some fell along the road and were trampled down." I quote from Matthew's version above because it is Quispel's and Krogmann's chief point of reference.
71 Krogmann, "Heliand, Tatian und Thomasevangelium" [note 18], 261: "Daß er *ālāsun* und nicht *frātun* schrieb, erklärt sich einfach daraus, daß er kein mit *f* anlautendes Wort gebrauchen konnte. In der Langzeile stabten ja bereits *folken*, *fard* und *fuglos* auf *f*."
72 Quispel, "Der Heliand und das Thomasevangelium" [note 17], 147; idem, *Tatian and the Gospel of Thomas* [note 14], 176.

(Un)Desirable Origins

as *fuglas comun and æton ða* 'birds came and ate them'[73]; in the Old High German Tatian, the herd of swine (Matt 8.30) was *ezenti* 'eating', and the Canaanite woman (Matt 15.27) says that whelps, too, *ezzant fon bromun* 'eat of crumbs'.[74]

For Krogmann, the desirable origins of the *Heliand* were the canonical Gospels, the commentaries of Bede and Hrabanus, and the poetic fancy of the Saxon poet. His inflexible thesis compelled him to reconstruct verses in its defense and to rely on the presumed tenets of Old Saxon poetry. That his motivation was not so much the establishment of the likely *Vorlagen* of the poem as it was the defense of its Germanic and Christian canonicity shows itself in at least two ways. First, *Übersetzungskunst* can just as well account for the poet's free rendition of the canonical Gospels as it can for his or her use of any other sources. Second, his choice to disprove the proposed common readings between the Saxon epic and the Gospel of Thomas without first demonstrating the poem's independence from the Diatessaron betrays his defensive stance against the alterity, the "raw novelty," in Said's words, of the Oriental, Coptic text.[75] Krogmann's work underscores the intimacy between race and nation, nation and literature[76]; an Egyptian apocryphal text would not, under his watch, pierce the *Germanenhaut* 'Germanic skin' of the "Saxon Gospel." He compensates for the problematic aspects of his arguments with vitriol – Quispel's position is *schwach* 'weak' and *bedeutungslos* 'meaningless'[77] – and with isolationist appeals to

---

73 R. M. Liuzza, ed., *The Old English Version of the Gospels*, EETS Original Series 304 (Oxford: Oxford UP, 1994), 26.
74 Eduard Sievers, ed., *Tatian. Lateinisch und altdeutsch mit ausführlichem Glossar*, Bibliothek der ältesten deutschen Litteratur-Denkmäler 5 (Paderborn: Ferdinand Schöningh, 1892), chapters 53.9 (p. 75) and 85.4 (p. 117), respectively.
75 Edward W. Said, *Orientalism* (New York: Pantheon, 1978), 59.
76 See Kwame Anthony Appiah, "Race," in *Critical Terms for Literary Study*, ed. Frank Lentricchia and Thomas McLaughlin, 2nd ed. (Chicago: University of Chicago Press, 1995), 274–87.
77 Krogmann, "Heliand und Thomasevangelium" [note 18], 66 (quoted above),

disciplinary authority: "Our determination that the *Heliand* offers no support to Quispel's view will, if nothing else, spare scholars from preliminary work who might find the task more difficult than a Germanist would who is intimate with the character of the Old Saxon epic,"[78] and, "The benefit of such an opinion escapes me. Since Quispel's thesis has not, in my opinion, proved itself valid, it should be abandoned."[79]

Manus profanae emendationis:
DETECTIVE WORK OR CHIROMANCY?

ⲘⲚⲦⲢⲈϤⲞ ⲚϬⲒ ⲠⲈⲦϢⲒⲚⲈ ⲈϤϢⲒⲚⲈ ϢⲀⲚⲦⲈϤϬⲒⲚⲈ[80]

Owing to "a number of obstacles of a political and scholarly sort,"[81] nearly fifteen years separate the discovery of the Nag Hammadi codices and the publication of the Gospel of Thomas. During this period – the history of which, according to several accounts, involves haunted jars, blood vengeance, a one-eyed outlaw, black-market antiquities dealers, something called "the Jesus curse," a safety deposit box with a secret password, a French graduate student, the Suez Canal crisis, an expatriate American philanthropist, and Carl

---

and 71: "After Quispel's last argument also proved to be meaningless . . ." [Nachdem sich somit auch das letzte Argument Quispels als bedeutungslos erwiesen hat].

78 Krogmann, "Heliand, Tatian und Thomasevangelium" [note 18], 268: "Unsere Feststellung, daß der Heliand keine Stütze für Quispels Auffassung darstellt, wird ihnen aber Vorarbeiten abnehmen, die für sie schwieriger gewesen wäre als für einen Germanisten, der mit der Eigenart des altsächsischen Epos vertraut ist."

79 Krogmann, "Heliand und Thomasevangelium" [note 18], 73: "Den Nutzen einer solchen Stellungnahme sehe ich nicht ein. Da Quispels These sich meines Erachtens nicht bewährt hat, ist sie aufzugeben."

80 The Gospel of Thomas, Logion 2, in Layton, *Nag Hammadi Codex II,2–7* [note 3], 52: "Let him who seeks not stop seeking until he finds."

81 Marvin W. Meyer, Preface to *The Nag Hammadi Library in English*, ed. Marvin W. Meyer et al. (Leiden: E. J. Brill, 1977), ix.

(Un)Desirable Origins

Jung – few names feature more prominently than Gilles Quispel.[82] He played an instrumental part in the identification, acquisition, editing, and translation of several of the manuscripts. It was from his hand, at a café in Brussels in 1952, that a representative of Simone Eid, the widow of an antiquities dealer, accepted a check of thirty-five thousand Swiss francs for what would later be known as the Jung Codex. In 1955, he became the first scholar to photograph and decipher a large portion of the Gospel of Thomas; a year later, he was appointed as one of three non-Egyptians to a ten-member committee given exclusive access to the Nag Hammadi library. He also, with four others, collaborated on the first edition of the Fifth Gospel, *The Gospel of Thomas: Coptic Text Established and Translated*, which appeared in 1959.[83] The institutionally mandated dominance of Quispel and his few colleagues over the Nag Hammadi discovery has not escaped criticism. In 1960, for instance, Gerard Garitte wrote "Such childishness will end by creating around the gnostic manuscripts an extremely unpleasant atmosphere and by making one suspect one hardly knows what personal drives and what pretensions to monopolize documents that belong only to science, that is to say, to all."[84] Seventeen years later, commenting specifically on the Jung Codex, James M. Robinson was no less bitter: "What other than the monopoly and hence four positions on the Egypt-UNESCO

---

82 For the history of events surrounding the discovery of the Nag Hammadi codices and the early scholarship devoted to them, see John Dart, *The Laughing Savior: The Discovery and Significance of the Nag Hammadi Gnostic Library* (New York: Harper & Row, 1976), 3–54; James M. Robinson, "The Jung: Codex: The Rise and Fall of a Monopoly," *Religious Studies Review* 3 (1977), 17–30; idem, Introduction to *The Nag Hammadi Library in English* [note 81], 21–25; Elaine Pagels, *The Gnostic Gospels* (New York: Random House, 1979), xiii-xxxvi.
83 See note 4 above. This is not a critical edition, rather a text edition with a facing English translation; it lacks an introduction, apparatus, notes, and glossary.
84 Gerard Garitte, "Bibliographie," *Le Muséon* 73 (1960), 214, quoted and translated in Robinson, "The Jung Codex" [note 82], 28.

Committee (Kasser, Puech, Quispel, Wilson) was achieved by keeping the Jung Codex in the Leu Bank vault until publication? [. . .] Should not scholars in the field make it unmistakably clear to those with exclusive rights that such a situation cannot be tolerated?"[85]

It is as a creator and expert, an authority in several senses, that Quispel announces the importance of the Gospel of Thomas, an importance, again, greater "than even the wildest of reporters dream of."[86] His position enables him to claim, without hesitating to universalize, that the (his) Coptic text might affect "our assessment of the value of our Gospels."[87] This implies, in general, that value is an intrinsic quality of texts, that it is not variously created by readers of different social and discursive contexts. Particularly, this implies that the value of the canonical Gospels lies in their trustworthy accounts of Jesus's words and deeds, an idea undermined by the canon's fourfold composition, by *canonized* inconsistency. For Quispel, then, the Gospel of Thomas is important because it preserves an older tradition of the sayings of Jesus, because it brings us closer to his "original" words. The occurrence in the *Heliand* of a number of these "more primitive" features, he thinks, confirms his argument. How this is possible deserves a closer look.

As mentioned above, Quispel links the *Heliand* to the Gospel of Thomas by way of Tatian's Diatessaron. The latter, he argues, shares with Thomas an extra-canonical source from an independent Judaic-Christian tradition, which he occasionally refers to as the Gospel according to the Hebrews. It is important to note that, though they are known to have existed, both the Diatessaron and the Gospel according to the Hebrews are lost.[88] The connection between the Coptic and Old Saxon texts depends upon the existence of a hypothetical Old Latin

---

85 Robinson, "The Jung Codex" [note 82], 27, 29.
86 Quispel, "Some Remarks on the Gospel of Thomas" [note 10], 277.
87 Ibid., 278.
88 For early Christian references to Tatian and his Diatessaron, see Petersen, *Tatian's Diatessaron*, [note 17], 34–67; for references to scholarship on Judaic-Christian Gospels, see ibid., 29–31.

(Un)Desirable Origins

harmony – a faithful translation of the original Syriac Diatessaron and the source of the *Heliand* – and a hypothetical Judaic-Christian Gospel, which was known to both Tatian and the author of Thomas. The complications surrounding the relationship between Thomas and the Diatessaron are beyond the scope of this paper; Quispel's idea that both texts reflect the same Judaic-Christian source has, to my knowledge, never been popular.[89] Without going into detail, however, it is appropriate to cite a later article by Baarda, "The Parable of the Fisherman in the Heliand,"[90] that shows the unreasonable emphasis accorded the Gospel of Thomas and the *Heliand* in Quispel's Old Latin reconstruction of Matt 13.47–50. About the latter's use of the Gospel of Thomas, Baarda remarks:

> [T]here is kind of a circular reasoning in the argumentation for this reconstruction. His starting-point was that the eighth Logion of Thomas presented the parable in an independent, pre-canonical form. The second step was that the original Diatessaron was dependent on the same material and therefore a second witness to this pre-canonical form of the parable. The next step was the observation that the Western Diatessaron tradition had preserved a very primitive form of the Tatianic text, so that its reconstruction of necessity would bring out the primitive, pre-canonical form of the word of Jesus. However, if we consider the result of this reconstruction, it appears that among the witnesses that could be called for [. . .] it is exactly the Gospel of Thomas that plays a dominant role.[91]

---

89   I have already noted Baarda's early criticism; see note 15 above.
90   Tjitze Baarda, "The Parable of the Fisherman in the Heliand: The Old Saxon Version of Matthew 13:47–50," *Amsterdamer Beiträge zur älteren Germanistik* 36 (1992), 57. It must be noted that Baarda's position in this debate is entirely different from Krogmann's. In the conclusion to this article he writes, "This contribution has been written by someone who has a vivid interest in the problems of the reconstruction of the Eastern and Western Diatessaron, not by someone who has any expertise in the area of Old Saxon Literature."
91   Ibid., 45.

The illogical centrality of the Gospel of Thomas in Quispel's reconstruction suggests that his reassessment of the *value of our canonical Gospels* is not detached from his personal investment in the Coptic text. As regards the *Heliand*, Quispel's "crown witness for the Old Latin Diatessaron,"[92] Baarda concludes that nothing in the Old Saxon version of this parable philologically supports Quispel's reconstruction. It is important, from the perspective of the debate at hand, to examine the methods by which Quispel discovers "primitive" readings in the *Heliand*, that is, the methods of those hoping to reconstruct Tatian's Diatessaron or, at least, the archetype of the Western Diatessaronic tradition.

The oldest extant manuscript containing a Gospel harmony, from East or West, is the Latin Codex Fuldensis, which was commissioned by Victor of Capua in the middle of the sixth century. The preface to this harmony,[93] written by the bishop himself in 546, is of great importance to Diatessaron scholars. Victor identifies what follows as *unum ex quattuor euangelium compositum* "the one Gospel composed out of four" written by *tatianus eruditissimus* "the most learned Tatian." More importantly, he notes that the original title of the work was not Diatessaron but *diapente*, thus "confirming" other reports that Tatian had used a non-canonical source,[94] and remarks that Tatian's writings reflect the work of a *manus profanae emendationis [. . .] corruptionis* "hand of profane emendation, of corruption." The problem with the Fulda harmony is that, though its arrangement is for the most part Tatianic, it has not preserved the textual variants characteristic of other Diatessaronic witnesses; it is, in the words of one scholar, "a fine example of an early Vulgate text."[95] The Codex

---

92 Ibid., 48.
93 Ernst Ranke, ed., *Codex Fuldensis: Novum Testamentum Latine interprete Hieronymo ex manuscripto Victoris Capuani* (Marburg: N. G. Elwert, 1868), 1–2.
94 The title *diapente*, however, can be interpreted in various ways, and does not necessarily mean that Tatian used a fifth source. See Petersen, *Tatian's Diatessaron* [note 17], 49–51.
95 Ulrich B. Schmid, "In Search of Tatian's Diatessaron in the West," *Vigiliae*

(Un)Desirable Origins

Fuldensis, though thought by Eduard Sievers to be the "archetype of all extant Tatian codices,"[96] cannot, according to Diatessaron scholars, account for the many Diatessaronic readings found in Western harmonies such as the *Heliand*. This "discrepancy" lies at the heart of their work, which, since Theodor Zahn,[97] has relied on two conveniently flexible hypotheses. First, as mentioned above, an Old Latin harmony, a faithful witness to Tatian's original work, existed in the West and, second, a process called "vulgatization," the substitution of Vulgate for Diatessaronic readings, accounts for the nature of the Fulda text and the haphazard distribution of Diatessaronic features among vernacular harmonies. Victor of Capua's text, then, "is a 'degenerate,' vulgatized recension, which has grown away from the Diatessaron's text and sequence. Codex Fuldensis' lost archetype contained a more primitive form of the Diatessaron."[98] Other Western harmonies, such as the *Heliand*, are supposedly more faithful to this archetype.

Searching for the Latin *Urtatian* is a field of its own. Non-vulgatized readings in Western vernacular texts, like a scientific anomaly in the Kuhnian sense, have, since Zahn, attracted more and more attention from more and more scholars.[99] If a western harmony contains a reading that differs from the Codex Fuldensis, and this reading has parallels in another Western harmony, it is thought to stem from the Old Latin archetype. Following this two step procedure, scholars have discovered, in the West, Diatessaronic vestiges in Middle Italian, Old and Middle High German, Old and Middle

---

Christianae 57 (2003), 177.
96 Sievers, *Tatian* [note 74], xviii: "Stammhandschrift aller erhaltenen Tatiancodices."
97 Theodor Zahn, *Tatian's Diatessaron*, Forschungen zur Geschichte des neutestamentlichen Kanons und der altkirchlichen Literatur 1 (Erlangen: A. Deichert, 1881).
98 Petersen, *Tatian's Diatessaron* [note 17], 129.
99 See Thomas Kuhn, *The Structure of Scientific Revolutions*, 2nd ed. (Chicago: University of Chicago Press, 1970), 82.

English, Middle Dutch, Old Saxon (of course), and several Latin texts.[100] The chief critic of this undertaking, which proceeded against negligible resistance for over a century,[101] is Ulrich Schmid, who in recent articles has questioned the basic premises of Diatessaron studies, especially with respect to Western harmonies.[102] Diatessaron scholars, he points out, theorize about the Latin harmony tradition almost exclusively from the evidence of vernacular harmonies; they ignore the vast number of Latin harmonies still extant.[103] The excuse for this neglect, he notes, is the false assumption that the Latin Vulgate is a "tight, cohesive, and strictly homogeneous tradition for all its history."[104] The number of manuscripts comprising the Vulgate tradition is so great that "textual scholarship simply has not yet been able to cope with the mass of data; in fact it has not even tried to tackle the matter."[105] He demonstrates that putative Tatianisms need not derive from a "(hypothetical!) Old Latin harmony"[106] but might rather originate from the marginal and interlinear glosses found in various manuscripts of the Fulda, i.e., "vulgatized," type, which *actually exist*. Further, he notes that the Old Latin hypothesis and the concept of vulgatization create more problems than they solve. Given that different Diatessaronic readings appear in different vernacular harmonies, how can each of these texts stem from the same Old Latin archetype? "The Old-Latin harmony," Schmid

---

100 For a complete list of Western Diatessaronic witnesses, see Petersen, *Tatian's Diatessaron* [note 17], 463–89.

101 Exceptional in this regard is the work of Johannes Rathofer, see note 107 below.

102 See esp. August den Hollander and Ulrich Schmid, "Middeleeuwse bronnen van het Luikse «Leven van Jezus»," *Queeste* 6 (1999), 127–46; and Ulrich B. Schmid, "In Search of Tatian's Diatessaron" [note 95].

103 Schmid, "In Search of Tatian's Diatessaron" [note 95], 184.

104 Ibid.

105 Ibid.

106 Den Hollander and Schmid, "Middeleeuwse bronnen" [note 102], 135: "(hypothetische!) Oudlatijnse harmonie."

(Un)Desirable Origins

summarizes, "can only survive with the auxiliary hypothesis of its postulated textual tradition." Last, following Johannes Rathofer,[107] he mentions the embarrassing fact that many variants regarded as "genuine Tatianisms" have been shown to derive not from manuscript readings but from the *faulty transcriptions* of modern editors.[108] The methods of Diatessaron scholarship provide a reductive solution to the philological problem of variation; the hypothetical Old Latin harmony allows scholars to ignore both this variation and *l'enterprise désespérante* of sorting it out.[109]

In *Tatian and the Gospel of Thomas*, published eight years after Krogmann's death, Quispel records four Coptic-Old Saxon parallels that he did not discuss in his earlier articles. One of these concerns the singular forms *sinc* 'treasure' and ⲡ{ⲉϥ}ⲉϩⲟ 'his/the treasure',[110] which deviate from the canonical θησαυροὺς 'treasures' at Matt 6.20:

MATT 6.20

θησαυρίζετε δὲ ὑμῖν θησαυροὺς ἐν οὐρανῷ, ὅπου οὔτε σὴς οὔτε βρῶσις ἀφανίζει, καὶ ὅπου κλέπται οὐ διορύσσουσιν οὐδὲ κλέπτουσιν

[And store away for yourselves treasures in heaven, where neither moth nor rust effaces and where thieves neither dig through nor steal.]

---

107 Johannes Rathofer, "Die Einwirkung des Fuldischen Evangelientextes auf den althochdeutschen 'Tatian': Abkehr von der Methode der Diatessaronforschung," in *Literatur und Sprache im europäischen Mittelalter. Festschrift für Karl Langosch zum 70. Geburtstag*, ed. A. Önnerfors et al. (Darmstadt: Wissenschaftliche Buchgesellschaft, 1973), 256–308.
108 Schmid, "In Search of Tatian's Diatessaron in the West" [note 95], 190.
109 The phrasing is from Cerquiglini, *Éloge de la variante* [note 24], 62.
110 Layton, *Nag Hammadi Codex II, 2–7* [note 3], 80, provides the following note: "[C]opyist first wrote ⲡⲉϥϩⲟ, then added another ⲉ above the line (ⲡⲉϥⲉϩⲟ) and neglected to cancel the superfluous letters ⲉϥ."

Gospel of Thomas 76	Heliand 1641b–1646a
ⲚⲦⲰⲦⲚ̄ ϨⲰⲦ ⲐⲎⲨⲦⲚ̄ ϢⲒⲚⲈ Ⲛ̄ⲤⲀ ⲠⲈϤ ⲈϨⲞ ⲈⲘⲀϤⲰⲬⲚ̄ ⲈϤⲘⲎⲚ ⲈⲂⲞⲖ ⲠⲒⲘⲀ ⲈⲘⲀⲢⲈ ϪⲞⲞⲖⲈⲤ ⲦϨⲚⲞ ⲈϨⲞⲨⲚ ⲈⲘⲀⲨ ⲈⲞⲨⲰⲘ ⲞⲨⲆⲈ ⲘⲀⲢⲈ ϤϤⲚ̄Ⲧ ⲦⲀⲔⲞ	Ef gi uuilliad mînum uuordun hôrean, / than ne samnod gi hîr sinc mikel siloƀres ne goldes / an thesoro middilgard, mêðomhordes, / huuand it rotat hîr an roste, endi regintheoƀos farstelad, / uurmi auuardiad, uuirðid that giuuâdi farslitan, / tigangid the golduuelo.
[You also, seek for his/the *treasure*, unperishing and enduring, where moths do not approach to eat and worms do not destroy.	[If you want to obey my words, then do not collect here great *treasure*, neither of silver nor of gold in this middle earth, a jewel hord, for it will tarnish here with rust, and thieves will steal it away, worms will corrupt it, the clothing will rip apart, golden riches will pass away.]

In addition to the *Heliand*, Quispel cites two other Western harmonies that share this reading, the Middle Dutch *Liège Diatessaron* (*schat* 'treasure') and the early Italian *Venetian Harmony* (*thesauro* 'treasure').[111] Following one aspect of Schmid's criticism, it is instructive to tally the supposed Diatessaronic witnesses from the West that do *not* contain this variation. These include, if their absence from Quispel's collation is trustworthy, Ludolph of Saxony's *Vita Jesu Christi*, the *Vita Beate Virginis Marie et Salvatoris Rhythmica*, the Middle High German *Leben Jhesu*, Matthias von Beheim's *Evangelienbuch*, and *Saelden Hort*, the Italian *Tuscan Harmony*, the Middle English *Pepysian Harmony*, the *Anglo-Saxon Gospels*, Jacob von Maerlant's *Rijmbijbel*, and several

111 Quispel, *Tatian and the Gospel of Thomas* [note 14], 185.

(Un)Desirable Origins

other harmonies from the Middle Dutch tradition. Keeping in mind that various "Tatianisms" appear haphazardly in each of these texts, and that each is several centuries younger than the hypothetical Old Latin archetype, which must predate the Codex Fuldensis, several traditions are unaccounted for. We would expect, that is, to find a Latin manuscript that reflects at least one tradition of vulgatization, but none exists. "[A] scholarly postulate," as Schmid remarks, "should not explain some data at the expense of other data."[112]

Though I can only guess at how he might have responded, Krogmann's argument that the poetics of the *Heliand* can explain such readings, a position endorsed by Schmid without reference,[113] is also useful in this case. Old Saxon *sinc* (*sink*) 'treasure', which occurs seven times in the poem, is not attested in the plural.[114] That its sense is collective is clear by its apposition, later on, to *diurie mêðmos* 'precious jewels': *endi uuili imu thar sinc niman, / diurie mêðmos, endi geƀen is drohtin uuið thiu* "and he wants there to take treasure for himself, precious jewels, and betray his lord for this."[115] Outside of Old Saxon, *sinc* exists in Old English, where it appears, except for one occurrence in Ælfric, only in poetry. Here, too, the evidence suggests that the word is far more comfortable in the singular, since only one of its approximately fifty attestations is in the plural, and this in the formulaic epithet *baldor sinca* 'lord of treasures'.[116] One cannot be certain that the source of the *Heliand* read *thesaurum* and not *thesauros*, as it stands in the Vulgate and the Codex Fuldensis.

---

112 Schmid, "In Search of Tatian's Diatessaron in the West" [note 95], 181.
113 See ibid., 192–93.
114 See Edward H. Sehrt, *Vollständiges Wörterbuch zum Heliand und zur altsächsischen Genesis*, 2nd ed. (Göttingen: Vandenhoek & Ruprecht, 1966), 465.
115 *Heliand*, lines 4578b-4579b.
116 J. B. Bessinger, Jr., ed., *A Concordance to the Anglo-Saxon Poetic Records* (Ithaca: Cornell UP, 1978), 1061. For the reference to Ælfric, see the entry in T. Northcote Toller, Supplement to *An Anglo-Saxon Dictionary*, by Joseph Bosworth (London: Oxford UP, 1955).

The importance of the Gospel of Thomas would come to light, Quispel proclaimed, "if only we are willing to apply the methods of scholarship."[117] Using evidence from the *Heliand*, he confirms his belief that Thomas preserves precanonical readings and therefore challenges the value of the canonical Gospels. As we have seen, both his notion of value and his scholarly methods are problematic. His orientalist role as producer of the Gospel of Thomas, as its usher to the West, is constitutive of his evaluation of the Coptic text. In his search for *profanae emendationes*, for the Diatessaron and its hypothetical sources, it seems as though an urgent desire for reconstruction overlies the problem, as it is for his purposes, of textual variation.

TATIANKULTUS

Dū hapest mir de zungun   sō fasto piduungen,
daz ih āne dīn gipot   ne spricho nohein uuort.[118]

I have already mentioned how Krogmann, having bitten off more than he was willing to chew, resorts to slander and, more interestingly, appeals to the authority of his field. The sole purpose of his articles, he makes it seem, is to dismember Quispel's argument, as only a Germanist can, in order to spare non-Germanists, i.e. *Theologen*, the effort of reaching the same conclusion as his own. Quispel and, later, his student William Petersen act similarly; the conspicuous elitism in their discussions of the *Heliand*-Thomas problem is the subject of the present section.

In the introduction to "Der echte Tatiantext," an article published in 1924, Adolf Jülicher refers to the few scholars engaged in Diatessaron studies as a *Tatiankultus*.[119] A quarter century later, Georg

---

117 Quispel, "Some Remarks on the Gospel of Thomas" [note 10], 277.
118 Old High German *Psalm 138*, lines 9–10, in Braune, *Althochdeutsches Lesebuch* [note 25], 138: "You have so firmly oppressed my tongue that I, without your command, speak not a word."
119 Adolf Jülicher, "Der echte Tatiantext," *Journal of Biblical Literature* 43

(Un)Desirable Origins

Baesecke calls the same group an "order within and order."[120] In 1962, having repeated Jülicher's remark, Baarda notes, "To this it must be immediately added that only a few have any dealings with this cult."[121] Petersen, a more recent initiate, describes his field so: "Diatessaronic research is nothing if not arcane."[122] The study of the Diatessaron, which demands the knowledge of numerous languages and cultures, is indeed challenging and, as with any field, no scholar can master all of its aspects. Words such as *Kultus, Orden, inlaten*, and *arcane* imply, however, that the difficulty of field is not singularly responsible for its exclusivity. Rather, Diatessaron scholars, the initiates, contribute to the validation of their exclusive (powerful) position; certain aspects of their scholarship restrict the availability of their "occult" subject to outsiders. Following Mieke Bal, I find these aspects indicative of the problematics of domination:

> "The burden of domination is hard to bear. Dominators have, first, to establish their position, then to safeguard it. Subsequently, they must make both the dominated *and* themselves believe in it. Insecurity is not a prerogative exclusively of the dominated. The establishing of a justifying 'myth of origin' [. . .]," which in this case is the Diatessaron itself, "is not that simple a performance."[123]

(1924), 132.
120 Georg Baesecke, *Die Überlieferung des althochdeutschen Tatian*, Hallische Monographien 4 (Halle: Max Niemeyer, 1948), 1: "Orden innerhalb eines Ordens."
121 Tjitze Baarda, "Op zoek naar de tekst van het Diatessaron," *Vox Theologica* 32 (1962), 107: "[T]och moet daar direct aan toegevoegd worden, dat slechts weinigen zich met deze cultus inlaten."
122 William Petersen, "New Evidence for a Second Century Source of the Heliand," in *Medieval German Literature: Proceedings from the 23rd International Congress on Medieval Studies*, ed. Albrecht Classen (Göppingen: Kummerle, 1989), 31.
123 Mieke Bal, *Lethal Love: Feminist Literary Readings of Biblical Love Stories*, Indiana Studies in Biblical Literature (Bloomington: Indiana UP, 1987), 110.

Valentine Pakis

In his 1959 lecture, Quispel proposes that several readings in Luke might also stem from a Judaic-Christian Gospel tradition. About Luke 5.36, where we read that no one patches an old garment with a new patch, he writes, "One would rather expect that an old patch does not match a new garment. For, as we can learn from our wives, a new patch will tear an old garment, but an old patch does not go with a new garment."[124] Later in the lecture he describes the Old Saxon epic so: "The *Heliand* [. . .] told the Life of Christ to our barbarian ancestors in the primitive and childish concepts they could understand and in this respect reminds us of the film 'Green Pastures'."[125] The film, which debuted in 1936 and was banned from certain American and English theaters, retells stories from the Old Testament from the perspective of African Americans. "A Sunday-school teacher," as one reviewer summarizes its plot, "describes a heaven populated by black stereotypes."[126] Quispel's words are telling of his esteem for Krogmann, whose research places him, by association, among those who know only trifles and childish concepts, namely women and the African-Americans of *Green Pastures*. These people cannot comment on the arcane texts with which Quipel is so comfortable; they cannot grasp the big issues threatening the value of the canonical Gospels. As literature, the *Heliand* is close to home and childish. It is *valuable* to Quispel as nothing but a treasury of (hypothetical) Diatessaronic readings, which are easily accessible to anyone willing to look.

In "Der Heliand und der Thomasevangelium," Quispel responds to Krogmann's stubbornness with his own: "When Krogmann emphasizes the Germanic character of the *Heliand* to such an extent that he denies its every connection with Tatian and Thomas, he should keep

---

124 Quispel, "Some Remarks on the Gospel of Thomas" [note 10], 281.
125 Ibid., 283.
126 Dave Kehr, review of *The Green Pastures*, directed by Marc Connelly, *The Chicago Reader*, http://onfilm.chicagoreader.com/movies/capsules/4254_GREEN_PASTURES (accessed April 19, 2004).

(Un)Desirable Origins

in mind that there are many different versions of the Diatessaron, and that the continuity of Christian culture, from Syrian to Saxon, is no less impressive than this Germanic character."[127] So concerned is Quispel about the authority of his position that he entrusts J. A. Huisman, a Dutch Germanist, with the task of writing a supportive afterword to his article. In an effort to bring *Heliand* scholars round to Quispel's point of view, Huisman remarks that Krogmann's criticism, however persuasive, does not settle the case:

> It seemed, after the criticism of Willy Krogmann, that Quispel's proposed source relationship between the Heliand and the Gospel of Thomas could not stand up to close examination. Given the great scientific importance of the question, however, it seems appropriate to me as a fellow specialist to say that, from the perspective of *Germanistik*, the question can in no way be regarded as settled.[128]

He also notes that Quispel's wide-reaching expertise cannot be used against him; for the Diatessaron scholar, medieval Germanic poetry is child's play: "Furthermore, Quispel's reputation and expertise in certain areas does not at all mean that he moves about with less

---

127 Quispel, "Der Heliand und das Thomasevangelium" [note 17], 151: "Wenn Krogmann so sehr die germanische Eigenart des Heliands benachdruckt, dass er jede Verbindung mit Tatian und Thomas leugnet, möge er bedenken, dass es eben verschiedene Versionen des Diatessarons gibt, und dass die Kontinuität der christlichen Kultur, vom Syrer bis zum Sachsen, nicht weniger eindrucksvoll ist als die germanische Eigenart."
128 J. A. Huisman, Afterword to "Der Heliand und das Thomasevangelium," by Gilles Quispel, *Vigiliae Christianae* 16 (1962), 152: "Nach der Kritik Willy Krogmanns [...] hatte es den Anschein, dass die von Quispel angesetzte quellenmässige Beziehung zwischen Heliand und Thomasevangelium einer näheren Prüfung nicht standhalten könne. In Anbetracht der grossen wissenschaftlichen Bedeutung der Frage erscheint es mir angebracht, von fachkollegialer Seite einmal auszusprechen, dass sie vom germanistischen Standpunk aus keineswegs als erledigt betrachtet werden darf."

certainty in the unfamiliar forest of *Germanistik*."[129] Quispel felt that, though he could encroach upon Krogmann's field, Krogmann had no right to reciprocate. His final word on the debate appears in *Tatian and the Gospel of Thomas*, a book, it seems, that he considered ideologically neutral: "One would have expected Krogmann to have welcomed the results of the Diatessaron studies which confirmed his views. But for several reasons he violently reacted against the opinion that the Heliand showed influences of the Syrian Tatian, in unfortunate articles which, inspired as they were by ideological biasses [sic], would have been better unpublished."[130] Krogmann never acted so violently as to say that the works of his critic should not have gone to the press. As regards Quispel, Said's criticism of the orientalist Bernard Lewis comes to mind: "[S]ince he is so sensitive to the nuances of words, he must be aware that *his* words have nuances as well."[131]

William Petersen refers to himself as "another of Quispel's *promovendi*,"[132] and now, *promotus*, he repeats the opinions of his teacher; his conservativism affirms the exclusivity of his field. In his discussions of the *Heliand*,[133] he never misses a chance to degrade Krogmann's articles, which in turn come to stand for the general shortcomings of *Germanistik*:

> Quispel's evidence pointed to the dependence of the Heliand upon the Diatessaron, specifically a Diatessaron which deviated

---

129 Ibid.: "'Auch könnte Quispels Ruf und Meisterschaft auf eigenem Gelände nicht verhüten, dass er sich im unbekannten Wald der Germanistik weniger sicher bewog."
130 Quispel, *Tatian and the Gospel of Thomas* [note 14], 27.
131 Said, *Orientalism* [note 75], 316. The emphasis is original.
132 Petersen, *Tatian's Diatessaron* [note 17], 341.
133 See Petersen, "New Evidence for a Second Century Source" [note 122], *passim*; idem, *Tatian's Diatessaron* [note 17], 279–81, 288–90; idem, "The Diatessaron of Tatian," in *The Text of the New Testament in Contemporary Research: Essays on the Status Quaestionis*, ed. Bart D. Ehrman and Michael W. Holmes, 77–96 (Grand Rapids: W. B. Eerdmans, 1995), 85.

(Un)Desirable Origins

from Codex Fuldensis. But his evidence also – for the first time – linked readings in the Heliand with the extra-canonical Gospel tradition. This did not sit well with Germanists, who were not accustomed to having readings in the Old Saxon Heliand – one of the oldest, most revered jewels in the crown of Germanic literature – traced back to Aramaic, Judaic-Christian extra-canonical Gospels."[134]

There are several problems with this statement. Quispel was not the first to suggest an extra-canonical source for the *Heliand*; I have already noted, for instance, the work of Pickering.[135] By "Germanists" Petersen means only Krogmann, since he goes on to mention no other and, for that matter, there is no one else to mention. Finally, his hyperbolic assessment of the *Heliand* – the oldest, most revered jewel in the crown – tempts a sarcastic reading in light of Quispel's comment about the poem's childishness. About Krogmann's inability to contribute to Diatessaron studies, Petersen remarks, "As a Germanist, he would have been poorly equipped for the task; here one sees the necessity of 'spoon feeding' the readers the parallels, in order to make one's case."[136] How Krogmann, a professional philologist and careful researcher, was "unequipped" to hunt for Tatianisms is difficult to understand. If it is because he was not an expert in Eastern languages, then Petersen places himself into an awkward position. The context of this remark is a discussion of the Gospel of Thomas, and Petersen does not know Coptic.[137]

Petersen's chief contribution to the debate is the observation that another poem, the *Vita Beate Virginis Marie et Salvatoris Rhythmica*, also

---

134   Petersen, *Tatian's Diatessaron* [note 17], 281.
135   See note 51 above.
136   Petersen, *Tatian's Diatessaron* [note 17], 289n85.
137   It is Petersen's practice in *Tatian's Diatessaron* to quote a text in its original language – for which he provides his own translation – only if he knows the language of that text. For Coptic texts, he provides the English or German translations of others.

contains Diatessaronic readings.[138] In "The Diatessaron of Tatian," where he incidentally misspells Krogmann's name (*Willi*),[139] he mentions this for the third time:

> Ignoring the long history of research into the matter, Krogmann asserted that the Heliand's agreements with Diatessaronic witnesses were due to chance, poetic license, and cultural factors. [. . .] R. van den Broek's discovery of Diatessonic readings in the Vita Rhythmica – some of which were shared with the Heliand – showed that a distinct, common tradition lay behind the readings. Since the Vita Rhythmica was also a poem, Krogmann's claim that the 'poetic license' exercised by the Heliand's author was responsible for the agreements crumbled.[140]

There are problems, too, with this statement. Krogmann did not ignore any scholarship; he reviews all of the early arguments and then chooses to address only the proposed connection between the *Heliand* and the Gospel of Thomas. Second, the Old Saxon and Latin poems only share *some* readings, a fact that brings Schmid's criticism into play. Finally, Petersen's logic is hard to follow. Krogmann does not deny that the *Heliand* and Thomas share readings because the *Heliand* is a poem – he never argues that *poems* cannot contain Diatessaronic readings – but rather that what seem to be parallel readings can be explained by the style of Old Saxon poetry. It is unclear how Krogmann's argument *crumbles* because of a few lines from a Latin poem that postdates the *Heliand* by nearly half a millenium.

Because of the broadness of Diatessaron studies, Petersen occasionally stresses the need for interdisciplinary cooperation. His pleas, however, underscore the fact that, as Irene Kacandes has pointed out, "Even when

---

138 These readings were first published in Roelof van den Broek, "A Latin Diatessaron in the 'Vita Beate Marie et Salvatoris Rhythmica'," *New Testament Studies* 21 (1974), 109–32.
139 Petersen, "The Diatessaron of Tatian" [note 133], 85.
140 Ibid. For the same comment, see Petersen, *Tatian's Diatessaron* [note 17], 323; idem, "New Evidence for a Second Century Source" [note 122], 29.

(Un)Desirable Origins

discussing interdisciplinarity, one does so from within a discipline."[141] In a paper delivered at the International Congress on Medieval Studies, presumably to an audience of Germanists, he declaims:

> One of the striking features of research into the sources of the Heliand has been the isolation of the Patristiker from the Germanist. Indeed, the exchange of Quispel and Krogmann does not even find mention in Rathofer's 1962 study. The reasons are not hard to find. Scholarly specialization is an ever-present obstacle, and the field of Diatessaronic research is nothing if not arcane. Nevertheless, it seems proper to describe the methods used by Patristic scholars in Diatessaronic research, and to offer an example which demonstrates the connection which experts in *Diatessaronforschung* have found between the Diatessaron and the Heliand.[142]

Beyond his use of the German word for Diatessaron studies, this is not very endearing. The only example he provides for interdisciplinary neglect is the work of a Germanist, Johannes Rathofer's *Der Heliand: Theologischer Sinn als tektonische Form*.[143] Specialization is an obstacle and the Diatessaron is arcane – inaccessible – to everyone, it seems, but Diatessaron scholars. As an expert Diatessaron scholar, he considers it proper to offer a taste of arcana to the uninitiated. Five years later, in *Tatian's Diatessaron*, he does not sweeten his message: "The student of the Diatessaron will need to be *au courant* with Germanic studies, and – although they would seem outside his or her field – the Germanist should not neglect Diatessaronic studies."[144] However difficult it might be, in other words, the Germanist must

---

141 Irene Kacandes, "German Cultural Studies: What Is at Stake?" In *A Users Guide to German Cultural Studies*, ed. Scott Denham, Irene Kacandes and Jonathan Petropoulos (Ann Harbor: University of Michigan Press, 1997), 14.
142 Petersen, "New Evidence for a Second Century Source" [note 122], 31-2.
143 Johannes Rathofer, *Der Heliand: Theologischer Sinn als tektonische Form. Vorbereitung und Grundlegung der Interpretation*, Niederdeutsche Studien 9 (Cologne: Bohlau, 1962).
144 Petersen, *Tatian's Diatessaron* [note 17], 439.

make an effort to participate in the all-encompassing study of the Diatessaron. Petersen expresses his interdisciplinary intentions in a rhetoric that betrays his sense, as a Diatessaron scholar, of academic superiority. By modeling himself so painstakingly on his teacher, he brought along the latter's prejudices: that the work of Diatessaron scholars addresses the value of the Gospels, that the subject is arcane and unapproachable to the uninitiated, and that outsiders are unfit – unequipped – to question the hypotheses of the experts.

Conclusion

My criticism does not detract from the great contributions of the scholars in question, and it would be vain to think that it could. Willy Krogmann has perhaps taught us more about the *Heliand* than anyone else; Gilles Quispel is one of the premier Church historians of our time, and the breadth of his erudition is hard to imagine; William Petersen's survey of Diatessaron studies, a project befitting a team of scholars, is indispensable to anyone interested in the topic. My goal has been to expose unacknowledged ideological motivations and how these have fortified disciplinary boundaries. In this respect, I do not pretend to be breaking new ground. Classical, medieval, and biblical scholars have had great success reexamining their fields and canonical texts from various critical perspectives.

I promised in my introduction to discuss the positions of Krogmann and Quispel as contrary, yet complementary, approaches to the familiarity of the *Heliand* and the alterity of the Gospel of Thomas. To clarify, the familiar and the "other" beckon similar reactions from those in positions of power. The "other," in this case the Gospel of Thomas, can inspire fascination or fear. If fascinated, its beholder will familiarize and define it to his or her liking, as Quispel did with the Coptic discovery. If frightened and threatened, its beholder will, as Krogmann did, fend it off. Regarding the Gospel of Thomas, their arguments complement each other in that they are both enabled by the privilege of (Western) academic authority. As regards the familiar, in this case the *Heliand*, it can inspire scorn on account of its blatancy or it can be embraced as constitutive of cultural identity. As we have seen, the debate about the origins of the Saxon epic unfolded along these lines; whereas Krogmann had a great interest in the Germanness and canonicity of the poem, Quispel saw only a witness to a distant Eastern tradition.

Though criticism of philology has typically kept romanticism and positivism apart, I am not alone in thinking that they overlap.[145] The studies of Quispel and Krogmann are positivistic to the extent that, in them, hypotheses and methods are taken to guarantee the truth of their conclusions. Quispel's argument depends on several hypothetical texts, the existence of which he never doubts. His confidence stems from his assumption that the methods devised to identify these texts are foolproof. Krogmann begins with the hypothesis that the *Heliand* poet did not use extra-canonical sources. This he confirms by explaining Quispel's findings as stylistic variations in Old Saxon, the knowledge of which depends on the hypothetical laws of Germanic alliterative poetry. Their studies are romantic because of the primacy they accord the past, without acknowledging the subjectivity of this investment, in the establishment of present value and identity. Their urgent production (reconstruction) of origins would have made Schiller proud: "Whoever does not venture beyond reality will never conquer the truth."[146]

---

145 See, for instance, Peter Richardson, "The Consolation of Philology," *Modern Philology* 92 (1994), 1–13.
146 Friedrich Schiller, *Über die ästhetische Erziehung des Menschen in einer Reihe von Briefen* (Stuttgart: Reclam, 1965), 41: "[W]er sich über die Wirklichkeit nicht hinauswagt, der wird nie die Wahrheit erobern."

III

Orality and Narrative Tradition

Was the *Heliand* Poet Illiterate?[1]

Harald Haferland

(Translated by Valentine A. Pakis)

INTRODUCTION

The question posed in the title seems outlandish.[2] The *Heliand* has come down to us in several manuscripts and may have been written to be read aloud at monastic tables, especially for the benefit of lay brothers, for whom it would make the Christian message, as it is in the Bible itself, accessible in a familiar form. Moreover, the few neums in the Munich manuscript and other emphases in the text indicate that such readings definitely took place.[3]

---

1 Originally "War der Dichter des 'Heliand' illiterat?" *Zeitschrift für deutsches Altertum und deutsche Literatur* 131 (2002), 20–48.
2 I am indebted to Dieter Kartschoke for discussing the following ideas with me.
3 Burkhard Taeger, "Ein vergessener handschriftlicher Befund: Die Neumen im Münchener *Heliand*," *Zeitschrift für deutsches Altertum und deutsche Literatur* 107 (1978), 184–93. Before the beginning of fitt 54 there is the subtitle *Passio*, which was certainly put there to help the reader find his place in the text. See Burkhard Taeger, *Der Heliand: Ausgewählte Abbildungen zur Überlieferung. Mit einem Beitrag zur Fundgeschichte des Straubinger Fragments von Alfons Huber*, Litterae 103 (Göppingen: Kümmerle, 1985), xv. On the reception of the *Heliand*, see Dieter Kartschoke, *Bibeldichtung: Studien zur Geschichte der epischen Bibelparaphrase von Juvencus bis Otfrid von Weißenburg* (Munich: Fink, 1975), 219–24; Taeger, *Der*

The *Heliand* generally conveys the most relevant information about the life of Christ, just as it had been recorded in the second-century Diatessaron of Tatian, a harmony of the four Gospels and some apocryphal traditions compiled out of the need to have all of the authorized accounts of Jesus together in one work. Boniface brought a copy of a Latin Diatessaron edited by Victor of Capua from Rome to Fulda,[4] where a hundred years later, in the second quarter of the ninth century, a number of hands translated it line by line and often word for word into Old High German.[5]

From such a method the *Heliand* deviates considerably. Only about half of the sections found in Tatian were chosen for the work,[6] and the translations, though close to the sense, are for the most part quite free. Within the framework of the so-called *Variationstil*, the systematically inserted circumlocutions and appositions lead to such

---

Heliand, xi-xvi; Klaus Gantert, *Akkommodation und eingeschriebener Kommentar: Untersuchungen zur Übertragungsstrategie des Helianddichters* (Tübingen: Narr, 1998), 265–77. That a version of the *Heliand* was prepared for monastic recitation cannot be proved conclusively. This assumption is complicated, for instance, by the fact the poet found it necessary to define *nôna* as the ninth hour of the day (see 3420, 3491).

4   See Achim Masser, "Tatian," in *Die Deutsche Literatur des Mittelalters: Verfasserlexikon*, ed. Wolfgang Stammler et al., 2nd ed., vol. 9 (Berlin: Walter de Gruyter, 1995), 620–28, esp. 622.

5   This method of translation, which is visible in the layout of the manuscript, is given due attention in Masser's edition: *Die lateinisch-althochdeutsche Tatianbilingue Stiftsbibliothek St. Gallen Cod. 56*, ed. Achim Masser, Studien zum Althochdeutschen 25 (Göttingen: Vandenhoeck & Ruprecht, 1994).

6   I am relying here on the numbered sections of the Old High German text in Sievers's edition: *Tatian: Lateinisch und altdeutsch mit ausführlichem Glossar*, ed. Eduard Sievers, 2nd ed, Bibliothek der ältesten deutschen Litteratur-Denkmäler 5 (Paderborn: Ferdinand Schöningh, 1892; repr. 1966). These section numbers are cited in the column titles of the following edition, from which I shall quote throughout this paper: Otto Behaghel, ed., *Heliand und Genesis*, 10th ed., rev. Burkhard Taeger, Altdeutsche Textbibliothek 4 (Tübingen: Max Niemeyer, 1996).

Was the Heliand *Poet Illiterate?*

a swelling in size that passages in the *Heliand* are often twice as long as their exemplars. The scope of the translation is further expanded in those occasional places where elliptical accounts in the Gospels are filled out and where those parts lacking in clarity are colored in. Nevertheless, the section divisions of Tatian are always recognizable in the poem, as are often single verses from the Gospels.

We should conclude, then, that the poet had before him a Latin manuscript of the Diatessaron, which he followed section by section, omitting some and rearranging a few others. There are also a number of places worthy and in need of exegesis that the poet explicates with reference to learned commentaries, which he uses for his interpretations.[7] When compared, here too the corresponding places in the *Heliand* and the commentaries share clearly recognizable sentence boundaries, so that, since precise sources can be identified with some certainty, the method and style of the poet show through the text. Independent additions of the poet's own making constitute only about a tenth of the *Heliand*'s content,[8] and they are, though in the guise of orally composed heroic poetry, closely connected to the material of the Gospels. According to this structure, then, the *Heliand* is, in whole as in part, a carefully drafted and thoughtfully worked out text, and it must therefore seem entirely absurd to suspect that the poet was unable to read and write. On the contrary, he must have been able to read Latin and he must have spent some years, if not

---

7 The commentaries in question are essentially that of the Venerable Bede on Luke, Alcuin's on John, and Hrabanus Maurus's on Matthew. See Ernst Windisch, *Der Heliand und seine Quellen* (Leipzig: F. C. W. Vogel, 1868); C. A. Weber, "Der Dichter des Heliand im Verhältnis zu seinen Quellen," *Zeitschrift für deutsches Altertum und deutsche Literatur* 64 (1927), 1–76. An overview of source research is provided by Wolfgang Huber, *Heliand und Matthäusexegese: Quellenstudien insbesondere zu Sedulius Scottus*, Münchener Germanistische Beiträge 3 (Munich: M. Hueber, 1969), 12–58.

8 These places are mentioned in Harald Haferland, "Der Haß der Feinde: Germanische Heldendichtung und die Erzählkonzeption des *Heliand*," *Euphorion* 95 (2001), 246n30.

his whole life, in a monastery, which would have been the only place where he could have acquired the prerequisite training that enabled him to deal with his sources as independently as he did.

Yet the *Heliand* also has another side. Since its form is that of alliterative verse, the specifically Germanic form of heroic and panegyric poetry, the poet must also have acquired a knowledge that encompasses not only alliterative meter and technique but also the language and worldview of this type of poetry. For now I shall concentrate on a small but distinctive example from the large sphere of knowledge and skills that such composition entailed. Whoever glances at the index of poetic formulas appended to Sievers's edition of the *Heliand*, which is often unclear and incomplete, will encounter an abundance of formulations that the poem shares with Old English, Old Norse, and even Old High German alliterative poetry.[9] The poet could hardly have come up with these independent of this tradition. Even if you restrict yourself to a single type – that which bears two alliterating letters and is therefore especially likely to be used in the A-verse of a long line – you will find an adequate number of examples (around 200!) to suggest that the different poets were drawing from the same reservoir of poetic formulas.

From this it is possible to assume that they inherited these formulas from each other. A novel formula, that is, would appear in a single text and would be disseminated to others through readings and re-use. This can be shown with a short example: Whereas less specific formulas such as *mit uuordun endi mit uuerkun* 'with words and deeds' (5, 541, 2107; see *Beowulf* 1833: *wordum ond weorcum*) could have been thought of independently,[10] those that evidence the

---

9 Eduard Sievers, ed., *Heliand, Titelauflage vermehrt um das Prager Fragment des Heliand und die Vaticanischen Fragmente von Heliand und Genesis*, Germanistische Handbibliothek 4 (Halle: Waisenhaus, 1935), 389–464. Such an index arranged according to the alliterating consonants remains a desideratum. With respect to Old High German, there is an interesting correspondence between *scarpun scûrun* 'sharp weapon' (5136) and *scarpen scurim* in the *Hildebrandslied* (64).

10 This formula appears about twenty more times in the *Heliand* in different

Was the Heliand *Poet Illiterate?*

creativity and succinctness of a kenning, such as *thes billes biti* 'the bite of the sword' (4882, 4903; see *Beowulf* 2060: *billes bite*), were doubtless passed on through the immediate knowledge of texts. They are unique formulations, and a poet must have heard or read them somewhere in order to have made use of them himself. There are no other explanations for the *Heliand* poet's use of *thes billes bite*, it seems, than that he had read this formula in *Beowulf* or a related text, or that the *Heliand* and *Beowulf* owe this reading to a common literary source. In light of the broad dissemination of these formulas in early Germanic alliterative poetry, however, such an assumption might require, in addition, the acceptance of other, rather improbable assumptions. Loans between monastic libraries, for instance, would have to have included secular texts from very early on and, what is more, an astonishingly broad range of such texts. It is therefore more likely that the inventory of formulas used in alliterative verse was passed on by another means.

In purely oral transmission, the knowledge of formulas – now gained by hearing them – would in principle seem the same as that gained by reading, only that the number of intermediaries would have to be multiplied. I should cite some additional formulas, which, according to Sievers's index, the *Heliand* shares exclusively with *Beowulf*. These the *Heliand* poet could not have borrowed from the Anglo-Saxon Christian poetry whose manuscripts, as is often assumed, had lain ready at hand in monasteries such as Fulda: *berht bôcan godes* 'bright beacon of god [=star]' (661; see *Beowulf* 570: *beorht bēacen godes*); *bôta bîdan* 'expect relief' (5873; see *Beowulf* 934: *bōte gebīdan*); *ferran gefregnan* 'to learn from afar' (3752; see *Beowulf* 2889: *feorran gefricgean*); *grim endi grâdag* 'fierce and greedy' (4368; see *Beowulf* 121: *grim ond grædig*); [*uuirthid*] *môd mornondi* 'his mood

---

cases and with different prepositions and conjunctions. Quotations of *Beowulf* are from Gerhard Neckel, ed., *Beowulf und die kleineren Denkmäler der altenglischen Heldensage: Mit Text und Übersetzung, Einleitung und Kommentar sowie einem Konkordanz-Glossar. In drei Teilen*, Germanistische Bibliothek, Reihe 4: Texte (Heidelberg: Carl Winter, 1976).

became troubled' (721; see *Beowulf* 50: [*him wæs*] *murnende mōd*); *sebo mit sorgun* 'with a worrisome spirit' (608; see *Beowulf* 2600: *sefa wið sorgum*); [*hebbian*] *uuordo geuuald* 'to possess the authority of words' (4978; see *Beowulf* 79: [*habban*] *wordes geweald*); *uuið that uureðe uuerod* 'against the hostile people' (4904; see *Beowulf* 319: *wið wrað werod*).[11]

Because orally transmitted heroic poetry existed in the Germanic Middle Ages, the probability is high that such formulas stem from a common reservoir that was available, at first, only orally. They would have belonged to a sociolect passed from singer to singer, the dissemination of which can be explained by its traditional character and by the lifestyle of the singers themselves.[12] Again and again, potential singers could be socialized into this group and travel widely with their new knowledge. Even if, for centuries, the oral traditions in England and on the Continent – other cultural contacts between the two aside – had been developing independently of one another, the consistency of this reservoir is hardly improbable. This is true even if it originated very early on. The alliterative meter had only to accommodate the changes in the respective languages, and thus in Old Saxon poetry, for instance, there is a preponderance of function

---

11 For additional, more widely distributed examples, see Robert L. Kellogg, "The South Germanic Oral Tradition," in *Franciplegius: Medieval and Linguistic Studies in Honor of F. P. Magoun, Jr.*, ed. Jess B. Bessinger and Robert P. Creed (New York: New York UP, 1965), 69.

12 This was emphasized strongly in Milman Parry, "Studies in the Epic Technique of Oral Verse-Making," in *The Making of Homeric Verse: The Collected Papers of Milman Parry*, ed. Adam Parry (Oxford: Clarendon Press, 1971), 275–79, 333–37. The same phenomenon has been examined in *Beowulf* by, among others, John Miles Foley, *The Odyssey, Beowulf, and the Serbo-Croatian Return Song* (Berkeley: University of California Press, 1990). Albert B. Lord provided a detailed description of an analogous method of training among the Serbo-Croatian Guslars in *Der Sänger erzählt: Wie ein Epos entsteht*, trans. Helmut Martin (Munich: C. Hanser, 1965), 35–57. On the reservoir of formulas that developed within the sociolect of singers, see also ibid., 82–103.

words. As the example *mit uuordun endi mit uuerkun* demonstrates, the instrumental dative, still preserved in Old English, was slowly obsolescing. Though the instrumental meaning had, more and more, to be expressed by the word *mit*, this addition clearly did not vitiate the alliterative meter. It is also plausible, however, that the sociolect of the singers developed relatively late and was nevertheless capable of crossing the linguistic boundaries between the different Germanic dialects. This is possible to the extent that it was disseminated by traveling singers and appropriated on the spot by locals who, aware of the dialectal differences, were able to make the necessary changes.

The idea that one could learn the formulaic reservoir of alliterative verse by reading, and that the *Heliand* poet had done exactly that – just as, incidentally, Sievers himself had done it – cannot be dismissed out of hand, yet it is the product of a broad (or narrow) philological imagination. For the many formulas that the *Heliand* shares with Old English poetry alone, the poet would have needed an entire written inventory before him that he could draw from during the composition of every line, and this itself presupposes that he had access to a sufficiently large number of texts. In this way, according to Georg Baesecke, the poet would have been able to learn his "art from beginning to end" at Fulda, where the Old English poems *Christ III* (=*Christ* 868–1694), *Guthlac*, and *Phoenix* were readily available.[13] In reality – and Baesecke did not discount this – he would have had to come to Fulda with a great deal of his own knowledge, since these few Old English texts did not contain anywhere near the total number of formulas that the *Heliand* has in common with other alliterative poems. A somewhat more plausible hypothesis about the poet's training, then, would be that he – a *non ignobilis vates*, as the "Praefatio" to the *Heliand* calls him – was well rehearsed in the sociolect of Germanic singers, that he was thus a singer first of all,

---

13 Georg Baesecke, "Fulda und die altsächsischen Bibelepen," in *Kleinere Schriften zur althochdeutschen Literatur und Sprache*, by Baesecke, ed. Werner Schröder (Bern: Francke, 1966), 375f.: "Kunst von Anfang bis zu Ende."

and only later became a poet when confronted by the unfamiliar and slow-going task of transforming a written source.

To this singer turned poet, scholars have ascribed all the competence that would be necessary to mould Latin sources into the form that the *Heliand* represents. This is overly rash, in my opinion, and I would rather distribute this competence across a team, consisting of at least one additional collaborator and writer, in which the poet was responsible for only a part the total labor. Such an opinion leads to a fundamentally different estimation of his capabilities, knowledge, intentions, and innovations than is normally given to him. Alois Wolf, for instance, considers it beyond all doubt that the *Heliand* was consciously modeled after the example of Latin epics, since there were no long epic poems in Germanic tradition. Moreover, the form of such epics is naturally associated with literacy. According to Wolf, the poet distances himself from the traditional Germanic occasional poem "to underscore that the biblical material simply could not be conveyed in that medium."[14]

It is true that, with the exception of *Beowulf*, no long Germanic epic has come down to us, but this might have something to do with the conditions that would enable such vernacular poetry to be preserved in the first place. Surely the indications of epic composition in the *Heliand* and *Beowulf* could go back to a tradition of large-scale oral performances that had distinguished itself from that of the short occasional poem, beside which it represented a new genre.[15] As

---

14   Alois Wolf, *Heldensage und Epos: Zur Konstituierung einer mittelalterlichen volkssprachlichen Gattung im Spannungsfeld von Mündlichkeit und Schriftlichkeit*, ScriptOralia 68 (Tübingen: G. Narr, 1995), 72: "[...] um deutlich zu machen, daß der biblische Stoff eben nicht einfach in der Art eines traditionellen Ereignisliedes vermittelt werden dürfte."
15   John D. Niles, *Beowulf: The Poem and Its Tradition* (Cambridge, Mass.: Harvard UP, 1983), 57–63, discusses the expanding style of longer epics with a characteristic example, namely the description of heroes arming themselves, which takes up only one line in the *Finnsburg Fragment* – itself part of what seems to have been a shorter lay – and more than thirty lines in *Beowulf*.

Was the Heliand *Poet Illiterate?*

one can see in the *Heliand* and *Beowulf,* the content and style of this new tradition – Germanic heroic tales and, especially, enjambment (*Hakenstil*) and variation[16] – are completely independent from classical tradition, so that one should not even bother to look for Latin models.[17] The association between long epics and literacy, moreover, no longer seems to be a matter of course.

Like Johannes Rathofer, Wolf sees in the *Heliand* a thoroughly premeditated use of number symbolism. This, alongside a significantly new style – including a somewhat certain literary method of "carefully thought-out intensification" – led them to conclude that such a carefully planned composition would have been "unthinkable if it were not conceived as a literary text."[18] This would be convincing if it somehow did away the suspicion that such number symbolism is nothing but a scholarly flight of fancy, however learned,[19] and that this new style in no way represents an intentional break from the traditional alliterative verse form.[20] Although Wolf recognized

---

16   In accord with oral-formulaic theory, I understand these supposed characteristics of style as methods of composition that must have developed under the conditions of improvised performance. See Harald Haferland, "Mündliche Erzähltechnik im *Heliand,*" *Germanisch-Romanische Monatshefte* 52 (2002), 237–59.
17   Here I am also following Niles, *Beowulf: The Poem and its Tradition* [note 15], 63.
18   Wolf, *Heldensage und Epos* [note 14], 76, 77: "wohldurchdachter Steigerung," "ohne schriftliche Konzeption nicht zu denken ist."
19   To make such a statement in passing is not fair, but to take issue here with Rathofer's opinions would take me too far afield. See Johannes Rathofer, *Der Heliand. Theologischer Sinn als tektonische Form: Vorbereitung und Grundlegung der Interpretation*, Niederdeutsche Studien 9 (Cologne: Böhlau, 1962). Against Rathofer's views, see Willy Krogmann, *Absicht oder Willkür im Aufbau des Heliand*, Deutsches Bibel-Archiv: Abhandlung und Vorträge 1 (Hamburg: Friedrig Wittig, 1964); and Burkhard Taeger, *Zahlensymbolik bei Hraban, bei Hincmar und im Heliand? Studien zur Zahlensymbolik im Frühmittelalter*, Münchener Texte und Untersuchungen zur deutschen Literatur des Mittelalters 30 (Munich: Beck, 1970).
20   Wolf sees a dissolution of the alliterative technique whenever a hypermetric

through and through the influences of oral tradition on the form of the *Heliand*, he nevertheless strove to find evidence of its status as a literary and learned poem. A more simple approach was offered by Klaus Gantert. Also a proponent of the *Heliand*'s literariness, he explained the oral style of the poem as a missionary strategy to appeal to the expectations of the public.[21] In this case, the oral style of the *Heliand* was simply feigned. Certainly this possibility cannot be counted out, but it seems only to be proposed by those who either regard the literary origins of the poem as irrefutable or by those who, for whatever reason, really want this particular theory to be true.[22]

The recent approaches of Wolf and Gantert differ from my own. Instead of searching for evidence of the *Heliand* poet's learned deskwork, I think it is more reasonable to search yet again for signs of the constitutive role of orality in the origin of the poem. I say "yet

---

line contains a word that is especially important to the context. That this also betrays a movement away from oral heroic poetry does not seem tenable to me, neither does Wolf's attempt to demonstrate that the poet inserted calculated intensifications into the text and therefore worked in an entirely literary manner.

21   Gantert, *Akkommodation und eingeschriebener Kommentar* [note 3], 69f.
22   That the idea of feigned orality should be dealt with cautiously is made clear by the later medieval examples in Dennis H. Green, "Fictive Orality: A Restriction on the Use of the Concept," in *Blütezeit: Festschrift für L. Peter Johnson zum 70. Geburtstag*, ed. Joachim Heinzle et al. (Tübingen: Max Niemeyer, 2000), 161–74. From the fact that, in the *Heliand*, conventions and symptoms of oral tradition were written down, Franz H. Bäuml concludes that the poet wrote "a pseudo-oral text" (*einen pseudo-mündlichen Text*). See his "Verschriftlichte Mündlichkeit und vermündlichte Schriftlichkeit: Begriffsprüfungen an den Fällen 'Heliand' und 'Liber Evangeliorum'," in *Schriftlichkeit im frühen Mittelalter*, ed. Ursula Schaefer, ScriptOralia 53 (Tübingen: G. Narr, 1993), 254–66. In my opinion, this attempt at a compromise (or rather a concession) goes too far to one side and leaves the other side imprecisely defined. That orality and literacy were brought together in a single poet, as we shall see, is not the only possible way to explain the creation of poetry like that of the *Heliand*. Bäuml, it seems, has projected the typical working relationships of modern poets onto the past.

Was the Heliand *Poet Illiterate?*

again" because, a century ago, this was a fashionable discussion that has since been unjustly neglected and forgotten. On the basis of a long list of examples – which do not overlap but rather support and complement what I shall discuss below – Franz Jostes and Wilhelm Bruckner convincingly developed the opinion, for instance, that the poet had worked under the wing of an ecclesiastical advisor who provided him with his material. According to his custom, he in turn refashioned this material from memory.[23] We can see how, in this light, the *Heliand* poet needed neither a command of Latin nor the ability to read and write.

Word for Word Repetitions

The poet introduces the Sermon on the Mount with an independent – but appropriate – representation of the situation in which Jesus is about to speak. Here Jesus gathers his disciples and falls into a long silence before he begins (1279–1299). About the readiness of the disciples to listen attentively, the poem reads as follows (1281–1286):

> Stôdun uuîsa man,
> gumon umbi thana godes sunu   gerno suuîðo,
> uueros an uuilleon: uuas im thero uuordo niud,
> thâhtun endi thagodun,   huuat im thero thiodo drohtin,
> uueldi uualdand self   uuordun cûðien
> thesum liudiun te lioƀe

> [Wise men were very eager and willing to stand around God's Son, intent on His words. They thought and kept silent and

---

23   This idea is supported by a long list of imprecise translations – errors, in fact – and of various liberties that the poet takes with Tatian's text. See Franz Jostes, "Der Dichter des Heliand," *Zeitschrift für deutsches Altertum und deutsche Literatur* 40 (1896), 341-68; and Wilhelm Bruckner, *Der Helianddichter – ein Laie*, Wissenschaftliche Beilage zum Bericht über das Gymnasium in Basel, Schuljahr 1903/1904 (Basel, 1904).

wondered what the Chieftain of Peoples, the Ruler Himself, would want to say out of love for these people.]²⁴

After the Beatitudes and before Jesus continues, the seventeenth fitt begins with a description of the effects of the Sermon on the Mount, in which lines 1281b-1284a are repeated verbatim (1381–1387):

> So sprac he thô spâhlîco   endi sagda spel godes,
> lêrde the landes uuard   liudi sîne
> mid hluttru hugi. *Heliðos stôdun,*
> *gumon umbi thana godes sunu   gerno suuîðo,*
> *uueros an uuilleon: uuas im thero uuordo niud,*
> *thâhtun endi thagodun,*   gihôrdun thero thiodo drohtin
> seggean êu godes   eldibarnun [. . .]

[Thus he spoke wisely and told God's spell. The Guardian of the land taught His people with a clear mind. *Heroes were very eager and willing to stand around God's Son, intent on his words. They thought and kept silent.* They listened to the Chieftain of the People giving law to the nobly-born . . .]

The same passage is used yet again in lines 1580–1586:

> *Heliðos stôdun,*
> *gumon umbi thana godes sunu   gerno suuîðo,*
> *uueros an uuilleon: uuas im thero uuordo niud,*
> *thâhtun endi thagodun,*   uuas im tharf mikil,
> that sie that eft gehogdin,   that im that hêlaga barn
> an thana forman sið   filu mid uuordun
> torhtes getalde.

[*Heroes were very eager and willing to stand around God's Son, intent on his words. They thought and kept silent.* They needed very much

---

24   English translations of lengthy *Heliand* passages are from G. Ronald Murphy, trans., *The Heliand: The Saxon Gospel* (New York: Oxford UP, 1992).

to think about the many brilliant things that the holy Child had
told them this first time in words.]

Seen from the perspective of literary composition, the use of the same words to describe different situations is especially conspicuous; here there is a governing rule whose origins warrant consideration. The literary custom of not using the same words and phrases over and over and not simply repeating entire passages word for word might be related, essentially, to the image of the written script and the way in which this mediates the perception of a text. With written script, one is conscious of words as both words and word forms, that is, one does not recognize them simply for what they signify, but also as signifiers in their own right. This way of perceiving language is not natural or original, but rather an offshoot of learning how to write.[25] Yet if language is known only by oral transmission, then the listener is restricted to that which is being talked about. Thus repetitions seem not at all, or less, like linguistic repetitions – repetitions of individual words – but rather like repetitions in speaking about one thing or another. In this way they can serve a variety of functions – they can underscore, for example, the intensity of a statement – without sounding offensive or objectionable in their purely oral iteration.

Writing, on the other hand, favors the simultaneous perception of the written word and its meaning, and from this perspective repetitions appear both visually superfluous as well as redundant with respect to the goal of making information clear to the reader in an efficient way.[26]

---

25 See Ivan Illich, *Im Weinberg des Textes. Als das Schriftbild der Moderne entstand: Ein Kommentar zu Hugos Didascalicon* (Frankfurt am Main: Luchterhand, 1991), esp. 41–46, 99–107, where this is clearly demonstrated.

26 Wallace L. Chafe attributes this tendency toward higher integration and coherence in writing – and also the perception of redundancy – to the relative slowness of the writing process. See his "Integration and Involvement in Speaking, Writing and Oral Literature," in *Spoken and Written Language: Exploring Orality and Literacy*, ed. Deborah Tannen (Norwood: ABLEX, 1982), 36–38.

The *Heliand* poet does not seem to have these concerns, for repetition is an essential element of his style and, when it suits his story, he is not at all reluctant to repeat entire passages.[27] Once used, phrases faded away from memory; to use them again was to bring them back afresh to the imagination of the listener. In doing so, no attention was called to the passages as repetitions of individual words.

The Irregular Beginning of Fitts

Sentences in the *Heliand* begin three times more often in the middle of a long line (between the a- and b-verses) than they do at the head of one.[28] This is the result of a characteristic method of composing early Germanic alliterative poetry that has come to be called *Haken-* or *Bogenstil* (hooked- or arched-style). Despite these terms, the concept has nothing to do with a "style," but rather with a technique that facilitates the discovery and placement of alliterating words.[29] What is especially striking, however, is that fourteen of the seventy-one fitts begin at a caesura.[30] To begin fitts – sections of the story – in the middle of a verse clashes so flagrantly with the conventions of literary organization that the practice certainly requires an explanation. I am inclined to think that the answer lies in the poet's lack of familiarity with such conventions.

In manuscripts M and C, the placement of a new fitt in a caesura

---

27 The recurrence of lengthy passages in the *Heliand* is, admittedly, the exception, since most of the narrated situations are not as drawn out as the Sermon on the Mount. See however 1289f. and 1985f, 1693f. and 5360f, 3865f. and 4176f.

28 Dietrich Hofmann, *Die Versstrukturen der altsächsischen Stabreimgedichte Heliand und Genesis*, 2 vols. (Heidelberg: Carl Winter, 1991), 1:202f., has counted 2,150 sentence boundaries in the middle of a line and 688 at the end of a long line.

29 For an explanation of this technique, see Haferland, "Mündliche Erzähltechnik" [note 16], 248–59.

30 Namely fitts 15, 18, 22, 27, 33, 34, 36, 38, 39, 44, 55, 58, 61, and 69. On the conclusions that will be drawn from this below and for an extensive description of the manuscript relationships, see Taeger, *Der Heliand* [note 3], xx n47.

leads to a rather unusual consequence from which one can draw conclusions about the form of their common, but not immediate, archetype. The text in both manuscripts is written continuously throughout, that is, lines of verse are not distinguished, with the one exception that new fitts are begun with a new line and a large letter. In the cases where a new fitt begins at a caesura, the scribe of the direct *Vorlage* followed rather obviously the large initial of the archetype, which doubtless – as will become clear – stood incongruously at the beginning of the long line and not at the caesura, where the new fitt actually begins. The scribe, then, began his new line with a hemistich that contains the end of the previous sentence and not the beginning of the next one. We can conclude that the archetype, like our modern editions but unlike M and C, presumably broke the *Heliand* into lines of verse (that is, each manuscript line corresponded with a poetic long line), and that the scribe of the common exemplar copied the archetype faithfully to the extent that he left the initial letter where it had originally stood: at the beginning of the line. Thus he managed to preserve an entirely nonsensical division in the text that leaves the last sentence of the previous fitt incomplete and places the rest of it at the beginning of the next fitt.[31] Initials wielded a sort of graphic authority that the scribe simply could not disregard, so much so that he could not even place them where – especially in a continuous text – they rightly belonged.

The example of the fiftieth fitt will make all of this clear. This fitt, which begins after the story of the Lord's Passion and tells of the Last Supper, must have looked as follows in the archetype (4521–4528):[32]

---

31 It is also possible that the same decision was made independently by two different scribes of two different exemplars. It seems, also, that the decision was not made consistently; thus the scribe of M, for instance, indicates the beginning of fitts 33 and 38 with a large initial in the caesura. See Taeger, *Der Heliand* [note 3], figures 10b and 12a.

32 I have kept the spelling of the cited edition since I wish only to emphasize how the section division in the archetype might have looked. Images of the

          Iungaron Kristes,
  thene ambahtscepi erlos tholodun,
  thegnos mid githuldeon, sô huat sô im iro thiodan dede,
  mahtig thurh thea minnea, endi mênde imu al mêra thing
f irihon te gifrummienne. Friðubarn godes
  geng imu thô eft gisittien under that gesîðo folc
  endi im sagda filu langsamna râd. Uuarð eft lioht kuman,
  morgen te mannun.

[Christ's followers, His earls and thanes, suffered His serving of them in patience, whatever their Commander, the mighty One, did out of love. And He intended to do a much greater thing to be of service to the human race. God's Child of Peace went and sat down among the warrior-companions and gave them much long-lasting counsel. The light was coming back, morning was coming to mankind.]

The new fitt begins here in the caesura of line 4525 with the words *Friðubarn godes*, while the initial that marks the new fitt stands at the beginning of the long line. Such a layout is the only way to explain the section division and orthography of manuscripts M and C, which both begin the new fitt with *firihon te gifrummienne. Friðubarn godes* [. . .].

There can be little doubt that the division of the *Heliand* into fitts stems from the poet himself, just as the "Praefatio" informs us.[33] Often enough, his text indicates the section divisions of Tatian either with an independently expressed conclusion or an indepen-

---

beginning of this fitt in manuscripts M and C can be seen in Johannes Rathofer, "Zum Aufbau des Heliand," in *Der Heliand*, ed. Jürgen Eichhoff and Irmengard Rauch, Wege der Forschung 321 (Darmstadt: Wissenschaftliche Buchgesellschaft, 1973), 368 (figures 1 and 2).

33 Here we read: "Iuxta morem vero illius poematis omne opus per vitteas distinxit, quas nos lectiones vel sententias possumus appellare" [According to his custom he divided his entire work into fitts (*vitteas*), which we as readers are able to call sections of thought (*sententias*)].

Was the Heliand Poet Illiterate?

dent introduction to a fitt.[34] His arrangement of divisions, however, posed difficulties to the scribe of the archetype or original text. If it was uncustomary at that time to write down alliterative poetry, which derives from an exclusively oral medium, in separated verse lines (like Latin poetry),[35] then the irritating alternation of fitt beginnings between the onsets and caesuras of long lines must have been a problem with regard to the *mise en page*. Here the scribe decided to maintain the regularity of the layout and always to position the large letters at the beginning of a line, even if a new fitt does not begin until the caesura. Considering his presumed customs – only in exceptional cases, such as in a copy of a text of the Psalms, does he make use of small initials or capitals within a line[36] – this must have been a calculated decision. It begs the question why the poet did not anticipate this problem from the start and thus begin each new fitt at the beginning of a long line.

Measured by the conventions of written texts, according to which section divisions are designed to suit a particular layout, the placement of fitt-beginnings in caesuras is an especially conspicuous irregularity.[37] Of course the *Hakenstil*, which determines sentence

---

34 These places are cited in Haferland, "Mündliche Erzähltechnik" [note 16], 239–40n14–15.

35 Katherine O'Brien O'Keeffe, "Orality and the Developing Text of Caedmon's 'Hymn,'" *Speculum* 62 (1987), 1–20, points out that, in all the manuscripts of Bede's *Historia Ecclesiastica*, *Caedmon's Hymn* is written out continuously, whereas Bede's Latin poetry is written out in separate verse lines. Similarly, the manuscripts containing the *Hildebrandslied* or *Beowulf*, for instance, do not distinguish the alliterating lines. That this seems to have been done in the "original" *Heliand* manuscript may have had something to do with the fact that the poem was commissioned by the king, and thus plenty of parchment would have been made available for the project.

36 On the large letters in the *Heliand* manuscripts S and P, see Taeger, *Der Heliand* [note 3], xx n47.

37 Rathofer, "Zum Aufbau des Heliand" [note 31], 357, spoke of the irritation "that the modern observer derives from the indications of fitts in manuscript C" (*das der moderne Betrachter an der Fittenbezeichnung in C . . . nimmt*). How "the

Harald Haferland

boundaries, is also responsible for the location of the beginnings and endings of fitts, but why in these cases did the poet not deviate from his established method of composition in order to achieve a more perfect arrangement of the text? (That such things could be taken into consideration is evident in *Beowulf*, where none of the forty-three fitts begins in the middle of a line.)[38] I suspect it is because the *Heliand* poet, unlike the author of *Beowulf*, could not write and was therefore insensitive to such literary considerations. He left it to the scribe to deal with the unusual consequences of his composition, and the latter opted for a visual solution to these difficulties, never allowing a large initial to leap from the beginning of a line to its caesura, even if that is where a new fitt began.

Orality as a Medium

Nowhere in the *Iliad* or the *Odyssey* does Homer mention writing or script.[39] At the time when the *Heliand* was written, however, writing was too widely known to be overlooked. Nevertheless, whenever the *Heliand* poet mentions writing, he does so from an outsider's perspective, that is, from a perspective that an illiterate singer could well have adopted. Things are written *bi bôcstabon* 'with letters' (230), *mid handon* 'with hands' (7), *fingron* 'with fingers' (32), *an buok* 'in a book' (14), or *an brêf* 'in a letter' (352). It is unlikely that someone who could write would present such a detailed view of the act of writing.[40] To the illiterate observer, however, it would have been

---

search for the possible reasons behind this strange practice" (*die Frage nach den möglichen Gründen für diese fremd anmutende Eigenart*) necessarily leads to the numerological principles of the poem's composition (see pp. 360–99) is hard for me to comprehend.

38   See Neckel, ed., *Beowulf und die kleineren Denkmäler* [note 10], 2:vii.
39   See Georg Finsler, *Homer*, 2nd ed., 2 vols. (Leipzig: B. G. Teubner, 1913), 354. This fact had already caught the attention of Friedrich August Wolf.
40   It could of course be argued, however mildly, that these elaborate descriptions originated out of the need to find alliterating words.

fascinating to see what those who can write do and how they do it. In this case it would be relevant to state that writing is done with the fingers and that the script consists of individual letters that are written onto one type of writing material or another. In the work of Otfrid, a contemporary of the *Heliand* poet, one searches in vain for such a point of view.

Although the *Heliand* is based extensively on written sources and was composed in order to be written down, it is the circumstance of oral presentation that surfaces in the poem, not a writing process. Thus the poet says *Ik mag iu thoh gitellien* [. . .] 'I can tell you, however . . .' (4308), or *Ok mag ik iu gitellien, of gi thar to uuilliad huggien endi hôrien* [. . .] 'I can also tell you, if you are willing to think and listen' (3619), or *Hôriad nu* [. . .] 'Listen now!' (3661).[41] During a reading, each of such remarks would seem like a reflex of extempore story telling and thus stand in strange opposition to the established text. By considering later readings, the poet does not do away with the genuine characteristics of oral performance.[42] He never, in fact, betrays that he is translating Tatian, nor does he ever refer to the commentaries he has used, but rather uses the formula *Sô (Thô) gifragn ik* 'Thus (As) I have heard'.[43] As far as what it conveys, this

---

41 See also Gantert, *Akkommodation und eingeschriebener Kommentar* [note 2], 72–77.

42 Without a doubt, the poet could have simply feigned such situations, as happens in modern fiction, so that no strong conclusions can be drawn from this evidence alone.

43 The formula occurs at the beginning of fitts 8 (630), 13 (1020), 32 (2621), and 54 (4452). As a mark of new sections in the narrative, it appears in lines 288, 367, 3780, 3883, 3964, and 4065. Jesus himself uses it at line 3347. The formula has a similar function in *Beowulf* (see 1–2, 837, 2694, 2752), the *Hildebrandslied* (1), the *Wessobrunner Gebet* (1), and in the Old English poems *Andreas* (1), *Juliana* (1), *Genesis* (1960), *Exodus* (1), *Daniel* (1), *Christ II* (225), and *Phoenix* (1). It should be stressed that "formula" is used here in a different sense than how it is used above within the framework of oral-formulaic theory. A formula such as this is motivated by the narrative context alone and does not have any compositional function. See also Werner Hövelmann, *Die Eingangsformel in germanischer Dichtung*

formula is not really at odds with the way that the *Heliand* must have been composed; the poet probably learned his material by hearing it, so that he did not have to feign the seemingly genuine orality of his text at all. Admittedly he was surrounded by literacy; for the composition of the poem he was supplied with written sources and he, in return, supplied a dictation that was to be written down. Yet despite this literary milieu he was able to preserve the impression of exclusive orality with respect to the composition and presentation of his "text." This he could do as though the conditions for a *composition in performance* were still in place, even though he faced an entirely different situation. Listening and retelling – actions to which he returned again and again – remained both intact as elements of oral composition and isolated from reading and writing: A learned monk (or perhaps more than one) was responsible for preparing the material that was to be refashioned, and a scribe was responsible for writing the refashioned material down.

Although the *Heliand* was created on the model of written exemplars that must have lain open – at least before the collaborators – during the composition of the poem, the poet seems to have had no sense of the literary character of his work. What is meant by "orality as a medium" can be gauged by its differences from the written medium. Here it is fitting to draw comparisons to Otfrid, who made wide and conscious use of the latter.[44] Otfrid's goal was to write down that which would help him and his readers achieve salvation (*Nu will ih scríban unser héil*, 1.1.113), he speaks of his work often as "this book" (Salomo Episcopo Otfridus 23; Ad Ludowicum

---

(Bochum: H. Pöppinghaus, 1936).

44 On the following examples, see especially Dennis H. Green, "Zur primären Rezeption von Otfrids Evangelienbuch," in *Althochdeutsch*, ed. Rolf Bergmann et al., 2 vols. (Heidelberg: Carl Winter, 1987). 1:737–55, who provides much more evidence as well as meticulous analysis. My quotations of Otfrid are from Oskar Erdmann, ed., *Otfrids Evangelienbuch*, 5th ed., rev. Ludwig Wolff, Altdeutsche Textbibliothek 49 (Tübingen: Max Niemeyer, 1965).

Was the Heliand *Poet Illiterate?*

87; 3.1.11, and so on), he refers to his *giscrib* 'writing' (5.25.45), and thematizes the writing process quite extensively (4.1). This process takes place in the here and now and is Otfrid's solitary enterprise, but from the moment of writing – from the often repeated *nu* – he tunnels conceptually through time to the act of reading. The word *hiar*, which is stressed just as often,[45] also achieves this tunnel effect to the extent that it implicitly bears a temporal meaning; it unifies the moment of writing with the moment of reading the written passage. That Otfrid refers to the act of reading becomes clear when he addresses the similarly solitary reader in the second person singular,[46] as though his work is concretely directed towards a single person who always wants to be beside the holy and honorable Liutbert and Salomo, to whom the work is dedicated. Before the chapter on the temptation of Jesus in the desert, the moment of reading is underscored with the following announcement: *so thu thir hiar nu lesan scalt* 'as you will now here read' (2.3.68).

To perform this maneuver, Otfrid had to have faith in the textual permanence of his work and he had to develop a conception of his text as a *text* – something which can only be done once the durability of the written text has entered the imagination. This is so obvious to literary culture that it is difficult to distance oneself from the idea, but this was not so obvious to Otfrid; in one place he uses a phrase meant to stress something spoken: *Ih ságen iu hiar ubarlút* [. . .] 'I shall tell you very loudly' (3.20.159). One cannot, of course, say anything "very loudly" to a reader, so that in this case Otfrid has still, however involuntarily, understood literacy as a metaphor for speech.

Otfrid has organized his text as a written text, and his literary arrangement is a common theme of the work.[47] He frequently cites

---

45   See for instance 1.2.27 and 41, 1.3.45–47, 1.15.41, 1.19.25, 2.7.1, 3.1.27, 3.13.37, 3.22.3, 3.23.3. See especially 5.14.1–30.
46   See for instance 1.9.37, 1.17.67, 1.19.25, 1.22.13, 2.2.15, 3.15.39, 3.21.1–2. See especially 2.9.1–98.
47   See for instance 2.6.1–2, 3.1.1–14, 4.25.1–4, 4.35.44, 5.7.5, 5.8.1, 5.20.1–2,

the Bible, inviting his reader to read it independently,[48] and – what especially shows that he regards his text as a text – he refers again and again to things he has mentioned in the beginning, above, or earlier.[49] The adverbs of place evoke the permanence of the written form and steer the memory of the reader.

It is not necessary to undress and expose the medium of writing to the extent that Otfrid has, and so it proves nothing if this is not done. Yet it is noteworthy that the *Heliand* poet did not do the same thing. Since words vanish into thin air, one would expect to find anaphoric references just as often in oral compositions, but it seems that examples of this depend already on written texts. Two systems of reference can be differentiated: One suggests above all an oral presentation and relies on temporal deixis, and the other suggests a written presentation and relies on spatial deixis. They have long run beside one another and can often cross paths. Into the thirteenth century and beyond, temporal deixis would be used often exclusively in written texts that were designed to be read aloud.[50] In these cases, references activate the memory of the audience. They seem like such natural devices in textually supported oral presentations that one would expect to hear them in oral performances that do not rely on written texts. It is possible, however, that internal references presuppose an understanding of texts as texts and are simply imitating the literary procedure of establishing coherence. In any case, in the

---

5.23.1–3.
48   See for instance 1.23.17, 2.9.71, 2.24.2, 3.14.3, 3.14.51, 3.14.65, 3.19.16, 4.6.2, 4.7.92, 4.8.3, 4.15.59, 4.28.1, 4.28.18, 4.33.21, 5.6.22, 5.13.3.
49   See for instance 1.9.1, 1.17.3, 1.18.43, 2.2.6, 2.9.1, 4.22.33, 4.26.1, 5.4.6, 5.5.12, 5.12.4, 5.23.163. For additional examples of this phenomenon, see Manfred G. Scholz, *Hören und Lesen: Studien zur primären Rezeption der Literatur im 12. und 13. Jahrhundert* (Wiesbaden: F. Steiner, 1980), 123–25.
50   This can be seen, for example, in *Biterof und Dietleib* with the phrase *als ir wol ê habt vernomen* [as you have already heard] (5264; similarly in 6308, 6574, 13188, among others) and in Stricker's *Daniel* with the phrase *dâvon ich iu ê gesaget hân* [I spoke to you earlier about this] (3002; see also 404).

Was the Heliand *Poet Illiterate?*

Heliand – if it indeed reflects a state of unadulterated orality – such references are not made. The memory of what had been said was doubtless taken for granted, since no extra effort was made to evoke it again. The narration advances continuously without making references back or ahead, without making a theme of its organization, and without citing any sources (except the Evangelists, who are named in the beginning but never again). For the poet, the narration is always coinciding with the act of remembering what is about to be narrated. Only rare changes in tense, used to admonish and to address the salvation guaranteed through Christ – especially at the end of a fitt – stick out from the narrative flow, which otherwise shows nothing of Otfrid's literary methods.[51]

The language of the *Heliand* seems to vanish with the sound of its words; it functions as a window to the narrated events and is unconscious of its textuality. What stands out in the poem is only the permanent memory of events, not the permanence of a visualized linguistic form, a written text, that is detached from these events. Thus there can be no cross references either inside or outside of the poem. The *Heliand* does not present itself as a literary text but rather as fleeting speech. If this is so, it is natural that precautions are taken to ensure that the narrated events are organized in such a way that they are difficult to forget. In oral story telling, the conceptualizing of events allows for the retention of material and for the easy recollection of this material. When narrative patterns give a fixed wording to these event-concepts,[52] there are then higher structural rules that determine the organization of the material and make it memorable, that is, re-tellable. Three important rules can be formulated as follows: (1) Pieces of information about the characters and the setting are strung together according to the degree of their generality – from

---

51 See 2083–2087, 2227–2231, 3219–3223, 3665–3670, 4114–4117, and 4375–4377.
52 See Gantert, *Akkommodation und eingeschriebener Kommentar* [note 3], 77–85, who discusses the examples of the feast and the sea storm.

the general to the specific; (2) factually related events are put into an immediate narrative relationship; (3) complex events are told in a linear fashion.[53]

Take the beginning of the *Heliand*, for example: After the information about the four Evangelists there is a segment about the Word of God, which was at the beginning (38–45, following John 1.1/Tatian 1.1). Then there is information about the six ages of the world and how Jesus's birth initiated the sixth age (45–53). This is then supplemented by the independent remark about Rome's dominion over all kingdoms (53–60). Returning to Tatian, the poem mentions Herod's authority in Jerusalem (61–72), where Zechariah is serving in a temple of God (72–93), and now – in the second fitt – the angel comes to Zechariah with the announcement. We can see how a panoramic shot has almost become a close-up.

Especially significant are those places where the poet has rearranged or blended the sections of Tatian. For instance, immediately before John the Baptist begins his sermon on the banks of the Jordan (873–882, following Tatian 13.2), the poet inserts information from Tatian 4.19 about John's awakening in the desert (859–872). This is not even expressed hypotactically – "John, who had awakened in the desert, went to the Jordan to preach" – but rather with parataxis: "John awoke in the desert, where God's work had guided him. Then he went to the Jordan to preach." This is also an example of the second rule, though an even better demonstration would be the poet's treatment of parables. These the poet always connects immediately with their meaning, which is hardly the case in Tatian or the Gospels.[54]

---

53   Here I am following Walter J. Ong, *Oralität und Literalität: Die Technologisierung des Wortes*, trans. Wolfgang Schömel (Opladen: Westdeutscher Verlag, 1987), 42–61.

54   This is especially clear in the case of the parable of the wheat and the weeds (=Tatian 72.1–6), which is brought together with its meaning (=Tatian 76.3–5) in fitt 31. On the rearrangements and conflations of Tatian's text in the *Heliand*, see Windisch, *Der Heliand und seine Quellen* [note 7], 32–34; and Max H. Jellinek, Review of *Bruchstücke der altsächsischen Bibeldichtung aus der Bibliotheca Palatina*,

Was the Heliand *Poet Illiterate?*

Clearly the memory of the listeners, something of no concern to a writer, must not be unnecessarily strained.

Complex series of events pose fundamental difficulties to comprehension; when heard, they are usually simplified or forgotten. Much can be salvaged on paper, however, and the eye can jump from place to place, when necessary, and the hand can flip the pages. This is of course not so with the ear, which seems to rely much more on linearity during the reception of narrated events. Orality, then, tends always to reorganize narrative complexity in such a way that related events occur one after another. Thus, in Luke's Gospel (1.5–25; 1.26–38), the annunciation of the birth of John the Baptist and the birth of Jesus cannot be examples of oral composition since the events are related in strict parallelism. First the angel comes to Zechariah, then to Mary; then Mary makes her way to Elizabeth (as Jesus will later come to John the Baptist) and stays for three months. John is born after this, and then Jesus. This folding of events has a theological significance that a reader can easily grasp: John and Jesus stand in some relation to one another and belong together in God's plan for revelation. Aware of the limitations of his medium, the *Heliand* poet understood that he could not preserve the parallelism of these stories. In Old Saxon, the birth of John is announced in fitt 2, and John is born in fitt 3. Not long after this (*Thô ni uuas lang aftar thiu*), in fitt 4, Jesus's birth is announced, and He is born in the next fitt. This is, by Lukan standards, a simplified and falsified order of events that leaves nothing of theological meaning achieved by the original parallel arrangement. Other parallelisms between the lives of Jesus and John are similarly dissolved.

These are just a few examples – there are many more – of an oral reduction of literary narration that, in general, the poet carries out systematically. Of course, such reduction does not have to be restricted to the medium of orality, nor must this medium inevitably

---

by Karl Zangemeister and Wilhelm Braune, *Anzeiger für deutsches Altertum und deutsche Literatur* 21 (1895), 211–13.

lead to such reduction. In fact, the form of the *Heliand* might not prove the illiteracy of the poet at all, for it surely could have been premeditated in consideration of an illiterate audience. That said, the reduction of literary narration fits perfectly into a larger picture, according to which the poet seems to have been unfamiliar with writing and literacy.

Difficulties with the Spiritual Meaning of the Text

Only once does the *Heliand* poet venture an allegorical interpretation – something frequently met in Otfrid – and this is his explication of the healing of the blind men in Jericho (3588–3670 = fitt 44). The Venerable Bede, whose commentary on Luke's Gospel serves as the basis of this passage,[55] occasionally interprets the text allegorically to arrive at its spiritual meaning, as in his explanation of Luke 1.24-25 – "Post hos autem dies concepit Elisabeth uxor eius et occultabat se mensibus quinque dicens: Sic mihi fecit Dominus in diebus, quibus respexit auferre opproprium meum inter homines" [After those days his wife Elizabeth conceived, and for five months she remained in seclusion. She said, 'This is what the Lord has done for me when he looked favorably on me and took away the disgrace I have endured among my people']. Here Zechariah is thought to be an allegory for the Jewish kingdom of the Old Testament, and his wife an allegory for the old law.[56] If no one *ante legem et in lege* – that is, before the coming of Christ – could achieve a perfect life, then the five months of Elizabeth's seclusion, like the five books of Moses, signify the five ages of the world. Because the incarnation of Christ, in fulfillment of the law, inaugurates the sixth age of the world, for this reason the angel of the annunciation is sent to Mary during the sixth month of

---

55 See Windisch, *Der Heliand und seine Quellen* [note 7], 68–70.
56 Bede, *In Lucae evangelivm expositio* I, in D. Hurst, ed., *Bedae Venerabilis Opera. Pars II: Opera exegetica. 3: In Lvkae evangelivm expositio, In Marci evangelivm expositio*, CCSL 120 (Turnhout: Brepols, 1960), 28–30.

Was the Heliand *Poet Illiterate?*

Elizabeth's pregnancy, as happens later on in Luke's text.[57]

Though the doctrine of the ages of the world is mentioned in the *Heliand* (45–53),[58] Bede's efforts to identify the spiritual meaning of Luke 1.24–25, which draws upon this doctrine, are not.[59] The ages of the world had to be ignored for fear that, so early on, the spiritual interpretation might overtax the understanding of the intended audience (if not that of the poet himself), and overload the beginning of the story with difficult theology. Besides, the poet had already transplanted this doctrine from its place in Luke to the very beginning of the poem – just before mention of the Roman occupation of Jerusalem and the appointment of Herod – so that he could situate his poem within the broad framework of universal history and the "geography of power" (*Herrschaftsgeographie*).

For his only attempt at allegorical interpretation, the *Heliand* poet allows himself a great deal of time and fills up the entire forty-fourth fitt. Unlike the authors of Latin biblical commentaries, he cannot simply pepper his work with catchwords such as *significare, mystice designari, per allegoriam dici*, and so on; this would have clashed with his poetic style and made the forty-fourth fitt seem more out of place than it already does. The interpretation of the healing of the blind men in Jericho (in Luke there is only one blind man) unfolds in such an unconventional way that we are led to suspect one of two things: Either the poet, in accord with a missionary strategy, is trying to stoop to his audience's level of understanding,

---

57   Ibid., 29–31.
58   On this doctrine in general, see Hildegard L. C. Tristram, *Sex aetates mundi: Die Weltzeitalter bei den Angelsachsen und den Iren*, Anglistische Forschungen 165 (Heidelberg: Carl Winter, 1985).
59   On Bede's exegesis, see Henning Graf Reventlow, *Epochen der Bibelauslegung*, 4 vols. (Munich: C. H. Beck, 1990–2001), 2:121–27. It is likely that the mention of the ages of the world in the *Heliand* goes back to Bede's commentary on Luke, though this has been doubted. See Windisch, *Der Heliand und seine Quellen* [note 7], 47f.; and Baesecke, "Fulda und die altsächsischen Bibelepen" [note 13], 353f.

or he himself has misunderstood his source in a fundamental way. The first suspicion is improbable, for whoever could independently adopt and grasp, from a commentary on the Gospels, the method of allegorical interpretation would never in turn spurn this method for the sake of accommodating his audience. On the other hand, the second suspicion can be explained by a characteristic limitation of the poet's ingenuity. In Otfrid, too, the healing of the blind men is interpreted allegorically (*Evangelienbuch* 3.21). Yet while Otfrid, as with most of his allegorical excurses, makes it clear with his chapter title that he is about to discuss the spiritual meaning of the passage – and then does so – the similar interpretative effort by the *Heliand* poet loses its contours and lacks such definition.

In Bede, the text and interpretation of Luke 18.35–37 reads as follows:

> Factum est autem cum adpropinquaret Hiericho caecus quidam sedebat secus uiam mendicans. Et cum audiret turbam praetereuntem interrogabat quid hoc esset. Dixerunt autem ei quod Iesus Nazarenus transiret [Luke 18.35–37] – Caecus iste per allegoriam genus humanum significat quod in parente primo a paradisi gaudiis expulsum claritatem supernae lucis ignorans damnationis siue tenebras patitur. Sed cum Hiericho appropinquare Iesus dicitur caecus illuminatur. Hiericho quippe interpretatur luna. Luna autem in sacro eloquio pro defectu ponitur carnis quia dum menstruis momentis decrescit defectum nostrae mortalitatis designat. Dum igitur conditor noster approprinquat Hiericho caecus ad lumen redit quia dum diuinitas defectum nostrae carnis suscepit humanum genus lumen quod amiserat recepit. Qui videlicet caecus recte et iuxta uiam sedere et mendicans esse describitur. Ipsa enim ueritas dixit: Ego sum uia. Ergo qui aeternae lucis claritatem nescit caecus est; sed si iam in redemptorem credit, iuxta uiam sedet; si autem iam credit sed ut aeternam lucem recipiat rogare dissimulat atque a precibus cessat, caecus quidem iuxta uiam sedet sed minime mendicat; sic vero et credidit et exorat, et iuxta uiam sedet caecus et mendicat.

Was the Heliand Poet Illiterate?

[As he approached Jericho, a blind man was sitting by the roadside begging. When he heard a crowd going by, he asked what was happening. They told him, "Jesus of Nazareth is passing by" (Luke 18.35–37). This blind man designates allegorically the race of men who, denied the joys of paradise from the time of its earliest ancestor, is ignorant of the clarity of the heavenly light and suffer the damnation of darkness. Yet it is said that when Jesus approached Jericho, the blind man is illumined. Jericho, in fact, means moon (in Hebrew). In the Bible, however, the moon stands for the defects of the flesh because, as it wanes throughout the month, it represents the defects of our mortality. Therefore, as Our Maker approaches Jericho, the blind man turns toward the light. This is because, when God perceives the defects of our flesh, the race of men receives the light which had formerly lost it. As is clear to see, the blind man is described rightly as sitting beside the way and begging. Jesus, however, said truly: "I am the way." Therefore he is blind who is ignorant of the clarity of eternal light; but if he now believes in the Redeemer, he sits beside the way; yet if he now believes that, in order to receive the eternal light, he must conceal his begging and slacken with his prayers, he sits beside the way and begs little. Truly, he who has come to believe and pleads sits blind beside the way and begs.][60]

Over the course of his interpretation, and even during his summaries of the biblical passage, Bede consistently uses the present tense. This tense is used for describing the spiritual meaning of the Bible because it is the meaning of the text, and not the meaning of past events, that has to be interpreted.

In their rendition of the stories of the Bible, however, narrative biblical poems like the *Heliand* are compelled to use the preterit as

---

60 Bede, *In Lucae evangelivm expositio* V, in Hurst, ed., *Bedae Venerabilis Opera* [note 56], 331. A source for this passage other than Bede – namely a sermon by Haimos von Halberstadt – has been proposed by Bruckner, *Der Heliandichter* [note 23], 33f.

the tense of narration. The result is that a change of tense must accompany the leap from narration to interpretation. This is observable, for instance, in the *Evangelienbuch*: In chapter twenty of his third book, Otfrid tells the story of the blind man; in the next chapter, under the title *Spiritualiter*, he connects the story to its forthcoming interpretation with the following words:

> Firlíhe mir nu selbo Kríst,   ther únser liobo drúhtin ist,
> thaz íh nu hiar giméine,   wénan ther mán bizeine
> Ther blínter ward gibóraner [...]

> [May Christ himself, who is our dear Lord, allow me here to explain what that man signifies who was born blind.]

The semantic relationship between the blind man who figures in the Bible and the spiritual meaning that is attributed to him is independent of temporal constraints, and therefore the text moves into the present tense. Thus when writing about the spiritual meaning of a text, commentators will use, for instance, the form *significat* and not *significabat*,[61] and so in Otfrid we find *bizeinot* instead of *bizeinota*.

Otfrid can shift immediately back into the preterit to explain the origin of the blindness – the Fall – and the historical significance of the healing episode: Christ's deeds, after which we were able to see, benefited us (*Thie dáti uns wola tóhtun, joh sid giséhan mohtun* [3.21.21]). In doing so, Otfrid has historicized the soteriological meaning of the passage and thus deviated considerably from the interpretation put forth by Bede. Even measured against the rest of the *Evangelienbuch*,[62] the treatment of this passage is peculiar; not until the end of the chapter does this historicized explication revert to the present (3.21.33–36).

---

61   See for instance Hans-Jörg Spitz, *Die Metaphorik des geistigen Schriftsinns: Ein Beitrag zur allegorischen Bibelauslegung des ersten christlichen Jahrtausends*, Münstersche Mittelalter-Schriften 12 (Munich: W. Fink, 1972), s.v. *significare* in his index.
62   See 2.9, 3.7, 4.5, 4.25, 4.29, 5.6, 5.8, 5.14.

Was the Heliand *Poet Illiterate?*

After the *Heliand* poet has told the story of the blind man (3541–3588), he introduces his interpretation of the scene in the preterit (3588–3591):

> Thar uuas sô mahtiglîc
> biliði gibôknid,   thar the blindon man
> bi themu uuege sâtun,   uuîti tholodun,
> liohtes lôse [. . .]

[That was a powerful picture that was presented there where the blind men were sitting by the roadside. They were enduring suffering, they were deprived of light.]

This is reminiscent of the parables that the poet translated in earlier fitts, where *parabola* is rendered as *biliði*. It seems that he unintentionally mistook the healing of the blind man for a parable even though the scene is not a *biliði* like the many that Jesus had told, but rather a narrated event that would have to be converted into one. Whereas Jesus intends to demonstrate something metaphorically with his parables – *biliði* can refer to symbolic gestures besides parables, for instance at the Last Supper (4640–4651) – he is demonstrating something in the same way, according to the representation of the poet, in the simple action and circumstances of the healing scene. This is why the poet remains caught in the preterit.

He shifts to the correct tense, however, when he spells out the allegorical meaning of the event: *that mênid doch liudio barn* [That signifies, however, the children of the people (3591)].[63] What follows, in loose imitation of Bede,[64] is the creation story, the fall of man, the exile from paradise, and the darkness before the coming of Christ. Yet all of this is expressed again in the preterit tense, which – like Otfrid – the *Heliand* poet will abandon at the end of this section to

---

63 The pronoun *that* refers here to *biliði*.
64 In his commentary on this passage, Paul Piper points out its differences from Bede and Luke and proposes another source. See his *Die altsächsische Bibeldichtung (Heliand und Genesis)* (Stuttgart: I. G. Cotta, 1897).

declare the salvation for whoever *that giuuerkod, that he môti themu is uuege folgon* [so acts that he might follow His way (3670)].

It is of some interest that, in the section within the interpretation, the allegorical meaning of the passage is evoked two more times. These also occur in the preterit, which is highly abnormal. It is told how the blind men were sitting by the road, what it *meant* (!) that this took place in Jericho, what the people *meant* (!) who beckoned to Jesus, and how they then regained their sight with His help and praised Him. The semantic relationship between the event and its interpretation has thus become convoluted: What Jesus meant – though not in the form of a parable[65] [*That mênde that barn godes*... (3634)],[66] and what, after that, the blind men signified [*That mêndun thea blindun man*... (3654)]. In this case the healing is not historicized, as it is by Otfrid, but rather a categorical error has been committed. The error does not simply lie in the fact that, unlike in Bede, the meaning does not apply to biblical text but rather to the events narrated in the text. Such an "over-extension" of the allegorical method to a meaning that is not only there *in verbis* but also *in facto* is notorious and was known to Bede himself.[67] The error lies much more in the fact that the poet has historicized the allegory itself. Even this would not be an error if, in the Bible, the narrated event was already accompanied by an interpretation, as is the case, for instance, with Daniel's vision (Dan 7). Just as the *Annolied* renders this vision, the interpretation that is found in the Book of Daniel

---

65   The verb *mênian* is used in this sense in lines 3509 and 3445, among other places.

66   In this sense, *mênian* also occurs earlier at 3624, where Jesus "signified" something with his action.

67   So for instance in Augustine's *De trinitate* 15.9.15. Hartmut Freytag, *Die Theorie der allegorischen Schriftdeutung und die Allegorie in deutschen Texten besonders des 11. bis 13. Jahrhunderts*, Bibliotheca Germanica 24 (Bern: Francke, 1982), 24, cites a number of explanations made by the Church Fathers for such *allegoria facti*. Bede refers to the phenomenon in *De schematibus et tropis*; see Hennig Brinkmann, *Mittelalterliche Hermeneutik* (Tübingen: Max Niemeyer, 1980), 217–23.

can be related in the past tense: Thus the third animal, the Leopard, *beceichinôte* 'signified' Alexander, even if this is true in later Christian interpretation.[68] An interpretation of the animal as a future king, that is, was already present in the Book of Daniel (1.15–28), and thus the semantic relation, having already been expressed in the narration itself, is indeed historical. If such circumstances do not exist, however, then it must be explained why an author would stray from the customs of allegorical interpretation.[69]

It seems probable to me that the *Heliand* poet was put on the right track by his informants but that, while narrating the various components of the exegesis (the creation, the fall, the exile from paradise, the arrival of Christ), he lost himself in the momentum of his story-telling and annexed the allegory to the monopolizing tempo of his accustomed poetic form. It seems out of the question, moreover, that anyone capable of incorporating biblical commentary into his work without assistance would ever have made such a mistake. Granted we are dealing here with only two half-lines that can easily be overlooked, but they provide some insight into the mechanics of the oral medium: The poet is unfamiliar with the process of interpretation. He belongs to a world in which the conceptual and mental devices limit him, in general, to the representation of texts that have meaning and that can be given, on top of this, additional

---

68 *Annolied* 14.3, in Eberhard Nellmann, ed. and trans., *Annolied: Mittelhochdeutsch und Neuhochdeutsch*, 3rd ed. (Stuttgart: Reclam, 1986). See also 13.5, 16.2, and 17.1.

69 For an additional example, see the interpretation of the seven-branched lampstand (Ex 25.31–40) in the *Vorauer Moses*, where it somewhat abruptly reads *daz was alles bezeichenlich* [that was all symbolic], though the present tense is used exclusively throughout the rest of the interpretation. This text can be found in Joseph Diemer, ed., *Deutsche Gedichte des elften und zwölften Jahrhunderts* (Vienna: W. Braumüller, 1849; repr. Darmstadt: Wissenschaftliche Buchgesellschaft, 1968), 81. In one of his *mystice* sections, Otfrid seems to begin a similar interpretation when he relates the meaning of the Magi's gifts to the newborn Jesus: *thiz wás sus gibari theiz géistlichaz wári* [it was appropriate that it was spiritual (1.17.68)].

allegorical meaning. The world of orality is one in which, above all, actions and spoken words matter and are meaningful. It was in this light that, for the poet, Christ had presented the parable of the vineyard workers: *That mênde mahtic Krist, / barno that bezte, thô he that biliði sprac* [That is what powerful Christ meant, the best of the children of men, when he told that parable]. What Jesus meant by his actions is always of great significance,[70] and so it is also when he heals the blind men at Jericho. Here, meaning is given not only to Jesus but to the blind men themselves: They signified the hopeless history of mankind before the arrival of Christ, and their healing signified mankind's salvation.

A learned monk would hardly have gotten carried away with the oral medium to such an extent. He would have internalized the present tense in instances of allegorical interpretation, so that any indication of allegory would have prompted him to shift to that tense. If the *Heliand* poet was not a monk, however, but a singer unfamiliar with reading and writing, then the nature of the poem's composition should be reconsidered yet again, as should the circumstances that allowed this singer to become a poet who could transform a literary exemplar.

The Origin of the Heliand and the Legend of the Poet

Had the *Heliand* poet been educated as a traditional singer, he could not then have lived in a monastery from the time of early childhood. On the other hand, learning to read later in life is not that unusual, and we do not have to share Albert Lord's belief that a poet's ability to compose orally improvised verse would suffer after the poet had learned to write it down, or that the poetry would suffer somewhat even if it was composed as a dictation.[71] Nevertheless, it is not as obvious as scholars have long assumed that the poet possessed the

---

70   See also 2574–2577, 3444–3448, 3921–3925, among others.
71   Lord, *Der Sänger erzählt* [note 12], 184–205.

Was the Heliand *Poet Illiterate?*

means to familiarize himself extensively with learned Latin texts, something which would have been required to compose the *Heliand* independently.[72] Instead of the sensational idea that the poet was able to master two distinct talents equally well – composing poetry orally, that is, and reading Latin fluently – I think another possibility should be considered.

The model I have in mind is the Caedmon story in Bede's *Historia Ecclesiastica*, a legend with not a few unbelievable clichés, in which a swineherd gains the art of singing by divine providence as a gift from God.[73] Yet the form of his art and the entire context of the story – Caedmon was already old when he entered the monastery, where excerpts from the Bible were made accessible to him, the content of which he shaped into alliterative songs – illustrate a thoroughly believable case of a singer, or someone well versed in alliterative poetry, entering a monastery and using his abilities in the service of God. The credulity of the monks, especially with respect to miracles, and perhaps also Caedmon's incomplete education explain why no one was willing to accept that he had acquired his abilities by natural means and simply brought them along into the monastery.[74] From

---

72   Certain scholars in the nineteenth-century also believed the consensus of today; see for instance J. R. Köne, *Heliand oder das Lied vom Leben Jesu, sonst auch die altsächsische Evangelienharmonie. In der Urschrift mit nebenstehender Übersetzung, nebst Anmerkungen und einem Wortverzeichnisse* (Münster: Theissing, 1855), 368f., who doubted, though on flimsy grounds, that the *Heliand* poet needed any assistance. Objections to Köne's doubt would be made by Windisch, *Der Heliand und seine Quellen* [note 7], 84f., who always at least entertained the idea of learned collaborators. As mentioned above, this thought would find full support in Jostes, "Der Dichter des Heliand" [note 23] and Bruckner, *Der Heliandichter* [note 23], but has been out of favor in the twentieth century.

73   Bede, *Historia Ecclesiastica* 4.24, in Günter Spitzbart, ed. and trans., *Kirchengeschichte des englischen Volkes*, by Bede, 2nd ed. (Darmstadt: Wissenschaftliche Buchgesellschaft, 1997), 396–400.

74   On the belief in miracles as an impetus behind the creation of legends, see Heinrich Günter, *Psychologie der Legende: Studien zu einer wissenschaftlichen Heiligen-Geschichte* (Freiburg: Herder, 1949), 1–28. For a few additional references,

this originated the legend according to which he received divine instructions in a dream.[75] Nevertheless, there seems to be some truth in this legend, especially regarding the poet's skills. So it is said that he can take what he hears and transform it into a glorious song *rememorando secum et quasi mundum animal ruminando* [by his own memory and like an animal chewing the cud].[76] This rumination requires some time, so the poet works in the evenings to find the proper wording, stores this overnight in his memory – faithfully or only approximately? – and presents his work the next morning.[77] Having succeeded at this much, he is able to improvise and fill in the gaps of his song with supposedly spontaneous additions.[78] Certainly independent of the Caedmon legend, Cynewulf claims in *Elene* to have conceived of his poetry during practice sessions at night.[79] It is fundamentally convincing that a poet would take the time to lay out his composition and to practice in solitude before he performed an

---

see also Dieter von der Nahmer, *Die lateinische Heiligenvita: Eine Einführung in die lateinische Hagiographie* (Darmstadt: Wissenschaftliche Buchgesellscaft, 1994), 146–52. Francis P. Magoun, "Bede's Story of Caedmon: The Case History of an Anglo-Saxon Oral Singer," *Speculum* 30 (1955), 59f., takes Bede's description of the circumstances of the Caedmon tale at face value, as I do below.

75   In his dream, Caedmon is asked to sing about the creation of all things, and he begins by singing verses in praise of God. According to Bede, when Caedmon awoke he remembered everything he had sung (*Historia Ecclesiastica* 4.24, in Spitzbart, ed. *Kirchengeschichte* [note 73], 398). The legend, it seems, does everything in its power to support the possibility that Caedmon had a command over his art before the dream took place.

76   Ibid., 400.

77   Ibid., 398.

78   This can be assumed from the account that, after he awoke, Caedmon "soon added more verses in the same style to a song truly worthy of God" [*mox plura in eundem modum uerba Deo digni carminis adiunxit*]. Ibid., 398.

79   *Elene* 1236–1239, in George P. Krapp, ed., *The Vercelli Book*, Anglo-Saxon Poetic Records 2 (New York: Columbia UP, 1932), where *Elene* is printed on pages 66–102. Earl R. Anderson, *Cynewulf: Structure, Style, and Theme in his Poetry* (London: Associated University Presses, 1983), 42, relates this to the use of the epilogue in the "Vita sanctae Mariae meretricis."

alliterative song. A solitary composition that was meant to be written down later may have come about in the same way.

Of interest, too, is the way in which Caedmon comes to know the wording of the Bible. For this to happen, *doctores* and *interpretes* are needed to translate the text and explain it to him. He does not know any Latin and yet, by way of his unlearned memory, he refashions biblical stories and turns his learned assistants into an astounded audience.

This model is transferable.[80] Like Caedmon, the *Heliand* poet could have been supplied with material by learned collaborators, and so much, as mentioned above, had already been supposed by Jostes and Bruckner.[81] A commission from King Louis (the Pious?), as he is called in the "Praefatio," certainly would have ensured that every imaginable type of assistance be made available to the poet. The "Praefatio" makes no mention of such help whatsoever, and leaves the impression that the poet worked alone. Yet what determined this representation is above all the act of composition, which is the poet's own responsibility. The collaborators do not earn any mention – assuming that the author of the "Praefatio" knew of them at all – because they play no part in this act.

Under such circumstances the two distinct talents – again, a total command of the art and lexicon of Germanic singers and the ability to work independently with the Diatessaron and learned Latin commentaries – would not have been monopolized by the poet. One must rather understand the composition of the *Heliand* as a type of teamwork in which several hands participated, so that the many tasks that went into the production of the text were divided up. Though this might seem strange to authors today, it was not unusual in the Middle Ages.[82] In the *Heliand*, the clearly recognizable sections that

---

80 With special reference to the Caedmon legend, Niles, *Beowulf: The Poem and its Tradition* [note 15], 34–39, discusses the collaboration between illiterate poets or singers and learned scribes, something which, he assumes, must have taken place often during the composition of Anglo-Saxon poetry.
81 See above, note 23.
82 See for instance Otto Ludwig, "Vom diktierenden zum schreibenden Autor:

correspond to transitions in Tatian and the commentaries do not have to reflect the working process of the poet, as suggested above, but might rather be vestiges of teamwork that could only advance step by step. One sitting, of course, could not have produced the results that were achieved in the *Heliand*; the poet must have taken time beforehand to think about his work as a whole, since he managed to weave in some of his own material and, as shown above, rearrange certain passages from Tatian.[83] Thus the poem as it is recorded would reflect the final run through the composition, and the poet would have had plenty of opportunity in advance to think through what he wanted to say and how he wanted to say it.

I have tried above to find signs in the *Heliand* that indicate involuntary reflexes of orality on the part of the poet-singer, that bring to light his mnemonic practices, and that demonstrate his lack of learning. This is not to exclude the other possibility – namely, that the poet was doubly qualified, and remarkably so – but rather to make it seem less probable and matter of fact than scholars have supposed, without having gone through the alternatives and examined the text closely with these in mind. The inconspicuous signs that I have given as examples, which have not received much attention, seem especially meaningful: the word for word repetition of certain verses, the conclusion of fitts in the middle of a long line, and a distortion of the allegorical interpretation of a text. The verse and prose prefaces to the *Heliand*, moreover, represent two more (albeit more peripheral) signs that have not been taken very seriously, since they are usually considered to be either imitations of the Caedmon legend or retellings of a literary topos.[84] If there is a hagiographical

---

Die Transformation der Schreibpraxis im Übergang zur Neuzeit," in *Schreiben im Umbruch: Schreibforschung und schulisches Schreiben*, ed. Helmuth Feilke and Paul R. Portmann (Stuttgart: Klett, 1996), 16–28.

83   See Haferland, "Der Haß der Feinde" [note 8].

84   Von der Nahmer, *Die lateinische Heiligenvita* [note 74], 153–69, demonstrates that reference to the topos character of a legend is meaningless as far as source criticism is concerned. What is true, of course, is that one cannot take legends

Was the Heliand *Poet Illiterate?*

topos about a *puer senex*,⁸⁵ serious and hungry for knowledge as a boy – or so the thinking goes – then there is also a legendary topos about an uneducated man who, with some divine direction, exhibits unsuspected abilities and, in the case at hand, begins to compose inimitably fine poetry.⁸⁶

It is not entirely certain, however probable, that the "Praefatio" and the "Versus" even refer to the *Heliand* and belong together.⁸⁷ The dependence of the "Praefatio" on Bede's Caedmon story seems conceivable, since its author says that the *Heliand* poet was also entirely inexperienced with the art of alliterative poetry, and that it was in a dream that he was first called upon to sing of biblical stories in his own language. Upon close inspection, however, one cannot simply think about the core action of this story – the instructions in the dream – without also taking into account its broader context, namely that there are people who would report such a thing in the first place: *Ferunt eundem Vatem* [. . .] [They said there was a certain poet . . .].⁸⁸ If these people did indeed exist, they would be the very people to whom such a borrowing would be attributed. It is highly unlikely that they needed to borrow something of which they were already aware; rather, it is probably the case that they came up with the same legend, including the dream motif, without any knowledge

---

entirely for their word.

85   Ibid., 156–61.
86   On the motif of the dream admonition, see the index in Günter, *Psychologie der Legende* [note 74]. Karl-Heinz Schirmer, "Antike Traditionen in der versus-Vorrede zum Heliand," in *Festschrift für Gerhard Cordes zum 65. Geburtstag*, ed. Friedhelm Debus and Joachim Hartig, 2 vols. (Neumünster: Wachholtz, 1973–1976), 1:151f., refers to, among other things, classical parallels to the dream episode and stresses the difference between the Caedmon story and the "Versus."
87   Theodore M. Andersson, "The Caedmon Fiction in the 'Heliand' Preface," *PMLA* 89 (1974), 278–84, argues that the "Versus" is a sixteenth-century forgery. For a discussion of the older scholarship devoted to the "Praefatio" and the "Versus," see Willy Krogmann, "Die Praefatio in librum lingua Saxonica conscriptum," in *Der Heliand*, ed. Eichhoff and Rauch [note 32], 20–53.
88   Quoted from Behaghel, ed., *Heliand und Genesis* [note 6], 2.

of Bede. Moreover, that the author of the "Praefatio" borrowed the *Ferunt*-statement from Bede is also improbable since, for his purposes, the information about the dream was all that mattered. The possibility cannot be excluded that a legend like that about Caedmon developed independently about the *Heliand* poet.

Regardless of whether the author of the "Praefatio" knew anything about him, the remark is still significant – if it is true – that the poet was famous among the Saxons as a singer. This renown would be at odds, of course, with the legend that the poet's first experience as a singer was with biblical material, but this contradiction can be resolved, at least provisionally, if fame and legend are classified separately as secular and religious concepts, respectively. The verse preface also develops the story of the dream in detail. Here the picture is of a fortunate farmer who, distanced from the bustle of the world, is plowing his furrows until one day, after he has finished with his field and brought his cattle to pasture, falls into a deep sleep in which a divine voice reaches him (lines 24–26): *O quid agis Vates, cur cantus tempora perdis? / incipe divinas recitare ex ordine leges, / transferre in propriam clarissima dogmata linguam* [What are you doing, poet? Why are you squandering good singing time? Begin to recite the divine laws in their order and to translate the clearest of teachings into your own language!]. After this, the farmer miraculously became a poet who understood how to compose songs.

Certainly it would be unusual if such a legend – according to which, again, someone was converted late in life from the laity and, having been granted poetic talents from God, only then became acquainted with the Bible – were invented or adapted for the sake of a learned monk who taught himself to compose alliterative poetry from a book and, what is more, did so for missionary purposes. It is therefore safe to trust the word of the "Praefatio" and the "Versus," and that of the Caedmon legend too, that the singers in question first came into contact with spiritual matters later on and were supposedly enabled by God to render these matters into verse. Regarding the folkloric motif of the dream-visitation, this is described as a type of catalyst, before which the singers knew nothing of their art. Beyond the Caedmon story, the "Versus" suggests that the *Heliand* poet, his work in the field notwithstanding, could unlock the meaning of the Bible independently, which might explain why the "Praefatio" fails to mention any learned collaborator.

It goes without saying that the legendary aspects of this story need not be taken seriously. Just as Caedmon and the *Heliand* poet did not receive their artistic talents overnight from God, but had rather been cultivating them for a long time, so it can be safely assumed that they came into contact with the Bible only later on in life and that they could not understand it on their own – indeed, that they probably could not read at all. They required extensive instruction in order to perform their task, and only after a long time would they have been able to deal with such novel material independently.

The Hatred of Enemies:
Germanic Heroic Poetry and the Narrative Design of the *Heliand*[1]

Harald Haferland

(Translated by Erik Baumann)

Germanic heroic poetry – like all heroic poetry – tells of conflict and hostility, but its hero, oddly enough, is not a victorious one. On the contrary, he often must accept his own demise and the death of those close to him, and his heroism displays itself with decidedly greater clarity in demise than in victory. It is not necessary for him to fight successfully so that, in the end, victory will justify whatever means and courses of action have directed him. It is much more the case that he must conspicuously showcase the limitation of his possibilities; in fact, he seldom avoids such dilemmas that allow this very limitation to bring about his undoing. Indeed, it is dilemma that makes him a hero. In such circumstances, he acts in no way that might suggest any trace of cowardice, nor does he successfully extricate himself from his predicament by cunning or any other means; rather he places himself above danger and loss – in that he concedes to danger no power over his life and stands ready to face loss head on – even though these do, in fact, have power over him and will destroy his life.

---

1 Originally "Der Haß der Feinde: Germanische Heldendichtung und die Erzählkonzeption des *Heliand*," *Euphorion: Zeitschrift für Literaturgeschichte* 95 (2001), 237–56.

Hildebrand is driven to kill his own son, Gudrun and Kriemhild to sacrifice their own children. Next to her revenge against Sigurd, Brünhild's own life becomes of no consequence to her. Gunnar disregards death, which looms over him and Högni; both Brünhild's laughter and Gunnar's insouciance in the snake pit, into which Atli had him cast, demonstrate their refusal to have the pain of their loss – or concern over their lives – forced upon them.

Klaus von See has underscored the anarchic illogicality of such behavior; what fascinates him is the "exorbitant demonstration" of a person's own might and mettle who acts in exemplary situations in the story – this person's "independence, his irrationality and contrariness to the rules."[2] The hero is thus a "person who follows his impulses thoughtlessly and without restraint, who acts without concern for himself and others, who does the extraordinary and the exorbitant, not what is necessary, compulsory, or ethically exemplary."[3] By preferring to keep such concepts as "honor" and "fate" out of the discussion, Von See does well to prevent – with analytic distance – any superficial identification with such heroines and heroes.[4] That said, his standard of behavior – governed as it is by reason and accountability and ethics – is also inappropriate, even if it is only used to paint a negative picture.

However much heroics might be extraordinary, exorbitant, or an expression of individual power, there is still, unmistakably, some guiding principle behind it all. Such behavior does not result from

---

2 Klaus von See, "Was ist Heldendichtung?," in *Europäische Heldendichtung*, ed. Klaus von See, Wege der Forschung 500 (Darmstadt: Wissenschaftliche Buchgesellschaft, 1978), 1–38, here at 37–38: "exorbitante Demonstration," "Ungebundenheit, seine Unvernünftigkeit und Regel-widrigkeit."
3 Klaus von See, *Germanische Heldendichtung: Stoffe, Probleme, Methoden*, 2nd ed. (Wiesbaden: Athenäum, 1981), 69: "Mensch, der bedenkenlos, ungehemmt seinen Impulsen folgt, der ohne Rücksicht auf sich und andere handelt, der das Außergewöhnliche, das Exorbitante tut, nicht unbedingt das Notwendige, das Pflichtgemäße, das ethische Vorbildliche."
4 Ibid.

the irrational inspiration of the moment, nor from any spontaneous and thoughtless impulse – it is premeditated. To hazard a cursory sketch of what I mean: There is something that compels a hero or heroine to accept biting loss and demise, something that outweighs the expectation of both. Exorbitance is not sought after – it is rather to be endured – and any situation, which such exorbitance ultimately brings about, will necessarily be extraordinary. Readiness for heroic action, moreover, engenders an obligation to act accordingly and, at the same time, allows for this "obligation" to be perceived as such. Viewed as reasonable decision-makers, neither Hildebrand nor Gudrun/Kriemhild, neither Brünhild nor Gunnar, has to act as he or she does. Nevertheless, that they do so leads to the realization that, beyond simply seeking vengeance, they are ready to submit themselves to greater violence so as not to allow violence to triumph over them.

It is especially challenging to understand Gunnar's behavior in *Das Alte Atlilied*, upon which Von See has based his description. Gunnar sees no reason to trouble himself with a journey in response to Atli's apparently harmless invitation – in fact he scornfully declines it – yet when Gudrun's hidden warning makes it apparent that there is a threat of mortal danger, he quickly changes his mind. The exact opposite would be "rational," namely to consider accepting this seemingly friendly invitation but, upon recognizing possible danger, immediately to think better of it. Regarding his recognition of danger, to be sure, it is possible to misinterpret the motives to which Gunnar attributes his decision to act. Here he unambiguously denies that danger has anything to do with it, whether in his own eyes or those of his retainers.[5] That he goes out of his way to establish this point results from a "rationality" quite different from

---

5   Carola L. Gottzmann, *Das Alte Atlilied: Untersuchung der Gestaltungsprinzipien seiner Handlungs-struktur* (Heidelberg: Carl Winter, 1973), esp. 56–58. Gottzmann, however, detects a cool calculation behind Gunnar's decision: Since he can choose neither subjugation to Atli nor war against him, which would bring Gudrun over to Atli's side, he chooses his own death.

The Hatred of Enemies

that which concerns Von See, and is certainly not a simple reaction to the inspiration of the moment. This other "rationality" has to pay off in a world that, for its part, favors certain rules and values beyond simply staying alive.[6]

Analogous environments, in which an early death is more commonplace than it is for us – such as among Columbian drug dealers or Russian gangsters – and in which one has to impress and outclass an audience of friends and adversaries with actions contemptuous of death, must frequently produce a heroic pride that gives way to memorable action.[7] There is an unwillingness – understandable enough, given the "peaceful" and "enlightened" environments of those who express it – to admit the possibility that this type of behavior might be motivated by "rational" impulses.

It is not easy to recognize that from this heroic pride, or at least from this readiness to die, there is a bridge leading to the *Heliand*, whose author brought the Gospel home to the heathen Saxons. A hint at this connection, however, is provided by the twelfth-century baptismal font at Norum, which on one side shows Gunnar in the snake pit, plucking the harp – flauntingly and carefree – with his toes.[8] What business does Gunnar have on a baptismal font, and does he share any characteristics with Christ? There are other instances

---

6 I am following Gerd Wolfgang Weber, "'Sem konungr skyldi.' Heldendichtung und Semiotik: Griechische und germanische heroische Ethik als kollektives Normensystem einer archaischen Kultur," in: *Helden und Heldensage: Otto Gschwantler zum 60. Geburtstag*, ed. Hermann Reichert and Günter Zimmermann (Vienna: Fassbaender, 1990), 447–81, at 462–65.

7 In societies with state-run monopolies on violence, such action is largely forced into criminal mileus. Therefore the comparison need not be as odd as it might seem. It certainly does not apply, however, if the heroic behavior of so-called "heroic ages" is regarded by critics as a sort of collective norm. See Weber, "Som konunr skyldi" [note 6].

8 For an image of the baptismal font, see Otto Gschwantler, "Älteste Gattungen germanischer Dichtung," in *Europäisches Frühmittelalter*, ed. Klaus von See, Neues Handbuch der Literaturwissenschaft 6 (Wiesbaden: AULA, 1985), 91–123, at 112.

in the Nordic tradition where parallels to Christ have been sought and found; Thor's fight with the Midgard serpent, for instance, has been related to Christ's fight with the Leviathan.[9]

Gunnar evades death no more than Christ does; he accepts it to demonstrate something of higher value to him in a particular situation. Though Christ does not die so nonchalantly in the *Heliand*, and though the two figures differ fundamentally in what they show by their deaths, they do share the same fate, entered into of their own free will. Thus Gunnar provided a model for understanding Christ's behavior, and this model was used to endear such behavior to those who had not yet been converted (and to those "half-Christians" who were not yet entirely convinced).

While the *Heliand* poet does not openly draw such a far-reaching connection – he maintains a strict distance from his native tradition – it is nevertheless clear that he, too, needs and offers a model for understanding Christ's action, and that this model is based in Germanic heroic poetry, which was doubtless well-known to him. He employs certain narrative features that unmistakably stem from the heroic tradition and he tells, above all, of fighting and enmity. These things, admittedly, do not constitute the main theme of the Gospel or Tatian's Diatessaron, the primary source of the *Heliand*, but Jesus, of course, is not without enemies. In the end some of them succeed in bringing about his crucifixion. The *Heliand* poet was able to address this fact and thus to bring Jesus's message into accord with the spirit of heroic poetry with which he was familiar. That he does so – that he understands the message of meekness, preached at the risk of death, to be a special type of authority greater than that of any enemy's might – indicates his great debt to this tradition.

---

9   Otto Gschwantler, "Christus, Thor und die Midgardschlange," in *Festschrift für Otto Höfler zum 56. Geburtstag*, ed. Helmut Birkhan and Otto Gschwantler, 2 vols. (Vienna: Notring, 1968), 1:145–68; Aage Kabell, "Der Fischfang Thors," *Arkiv för nordisk filologi* 91 (1976), 123–29.

The Hatred of Enemies

Given that the poet makes no effort to scale back Jesus's meekness, however, it could just as easily be argued that he assimilated his medium entirely to the Christian message.[10] Indeed, the research of the last decades has preferred to do just this. The governing catch phrase of critics, then, is no longer the "Germanization of Christianity" – though this is perpetuated by Josef Weisweiler and Werner Betz,[11] whose interpretation of the *Heliand* recalls that of A. F. C. Vilmar[12] – but rather the "Christianization of *Germanentum*."[13] Scholarship has typically unfolded along only one of these two lines, as though they were mutually exclusive. Hulda Göhler, for example, took pains to demonstrate that, in the *Heliand*, Christ is portrayed as absolutely divine and in no way as an earthly king,[14] as if with her (admittedly relevant) evidence she had settled the matter once and for all. Yet the focus of her investigation was too narrow and she

---

10 See for instance Heinz Rupp, "Der Heliand: Hauptanliegen seines Dichters," in *Der Heliand*, ed. Jürgen Eichhoff and Irmengard Rauch, Wege der Forschung 321 (Darmstadt: Wissenschaftliche Buchgesellschaft, 1973), 247–69, at 260–64.
11 Josef Weisweiler and Werner Betz, "Deutsche Frühzeit," in *Deutsche Wortgeschichte*, ed. Friedrich Maurer and Heinz Rupp, 3rd ed., 2 vols. (Berlin: Walter de Gruyter, 1974), 1:55–133, at 70. On the use of these terms in the history of scholarship, see Albrecht Hagenlocher, *Schicksal im Heliand: Verwendung und Bedeutung der nominalen Bezeichnungen*, Niederdeutsche Studien 21 (Cologne: Böhlau, 1975), 1–27.
12 See A. F. C. Vilmar, *Deutsche Altertümer im Hêliand als Einkleidung der evangelischen Geschichte: Beiträge zur Erklärung des altsächsischen Hêliand und zur inneren Geschichte der Einführung des Christentums in Deutschland*, 2nd ed. (Marburg: N. G. Elwert, 1862). G. Ronald Murphy, who revived the question of the role of Germanicization in the *Heliand* – though with an inadequate command of earlier scholarship – justly focused on Vilmar's unnecessarily nationalistic perspective. See his *The Saxon Savior: The Germanic Transformation of the Gospel in the Ninth-Century Heliand* (New York: Oxford UP, 1989).
13 The expression first occurs in Walther Köhler, "Das Christusbild im Heliand," *Archiv für Kulturgeschichte* 26 (1936), 265–82, at 282.
14 Hulda Göhler, "Das Christusbild in Otrids Evangelienbuch und im Heliand," *Zeitschrift für deutsche Philologie* 59 (1934), 1–52, esp. 46.

left unaddressed certain details that might support the alternative. These details, of course, constituted the evidence upon which Vilmar – his focus equally narrow – had based his observations, which were similarly appropriate within the framework of his discussion. There is some truth to both sides. That Christ is portrayed as a chieftain in the *Heliand*, and his disciples as retainers, has never been a matter of debate – not even for Göhler.[15] Both Germanicizing and Christianizing tendencies are detectable in the *Heliand* and, as is the case with any process of acculturation,[16] nothing else is to be expected. With the acquisition of new cultural practices and religions, that is, there will always be some intertwining and overlapping between the familiar and the unfamiliar.

Working in another field, Jean Piaget has repeatedly identified such complementary processes in the development of human cognition. During the so-called sensorimotor period, he argues, infants develop reflexes by reacting passively to their physical environment and yet, at the same time, begin to act in such a way as to manipulate these very conditions. It is by way of such "circular reactions," which involve simultaneously the assimilation and accommodation of an environment, that a child comes to internalize the outside world.[17] With some reservation, it can be presumed that the cognitive development of children – as outlined by Piaget – is analogous to the way that a group of people (the Saxons) might come to understand what is unfamiliar (Christianity); in both cases, that is, there will always

15   Ibid., 35–40. See also Rupp, "Der Heliand" [note 10], 265–68.
16   The first to write on the process was Richard Thurnwald, "The Psychology of Acculturation," *American Anthropologist* 34 (1932), 557–69.
17   Jean Piaget, *Psychologie der Intelligenz*, trans. Lucien Goldmann and Yvonne Moser (Zurich: Rascher, 1948), 113–21; idem, *Nachahmung, Spiel und Traum: Die Entwicklung der Szmbolfunktion beim Kinde* (Stuttgart: Klett, 1969), 207–17 and *passim*. On Piaget's theory, see also Herbert Ginsberg and Sylvia Opper, *Piagets Theorie der geistigen Entwicklung* (Stuttgart: Klett, 1975), 32–34. It should be noted that Piaget uses the terms "assimilation" and "accommodation" in a way opposite both to the way I use them above and – with special respect to "accommodation" – to their use by missiologists.

be evidence of both assimilation and accommodation. Despite his efforts – and despite his access to learned Christian texts[18] – the poet could not do away with everything that might impede the Christian appropriation of his medium. He could do nothing but relate, to his fellow Saxons, the new and unfamiliar message along with those features of his native poetry that might contradict or vitiate the message itself. His achievement was great, however, and he managed to achieve his goal as thoroughly as possible.[19] This is so much the case that it is safe to assume certain aspects of his identity: Comfortable with native and Christian traditions, the *Heliand* poet was likely a converted singer who, having joined a monastic community, took pains to learn the theology of his day.

If the Gospel, retold in this radical new form, underwent a necessary degree of Germanicization, this is less the result of intentional accommodation – or even of basic reinterpretation – than it is an inevitable effect of the poetic style of the *Heliand*. Beyond featuring numerous rigid formulas, this style also brings with it a prefabricated narrative world – the world of heroic poetry in general – in which Jesus's story is made to take place.[20] As much as the poet admonishes against fighting and conflict,[21] his story involves much of the same: fighting, conflict, and above all the hatred of Jesus's enemies.

I would like here to approach the question of Germanicization and Christianization in the *Heliand* in terms of the poem's

---

18   Such material, which the poet might not have understood so well himself, was likely dictated to him by literate monks. See Harald Haferland, "War der Dichter des 'Heliand' illiterat?" *Zeitschrift für deutsches Altertum und deutsche Literatur* 131 (2002), 20–48.

19   For a more moderate opinion of the poet's achievement in this regard, see Johannes Rathofer, *Der Heliand: Theologischer Sinn als tektonische Form. Vorbereitung und Grundlegung der Interpretation*, Niederdeutsche Studien 9 (Cologne: Böhlau, 1962), 31–194.

20   Harald Haferland, "Mündliche Erzähltechnik im 'Heliand'," *Germanisch-Romanische Monatshefte* 52 (2002), 237–59.

21   See Rupp, "Der Heliand" [note 10], 260–61.

(somewhat elusive) narrative design, by which I mean, simply enough, what the poet has emphasized within the independent episodes of his own making. The goal will be to demonstrate the extent to which the narrative practices of Germanic heroic poetry – and the "ideology" that accompanies these practices – manifest themselves in the poem.

A conspicuous narrative feature of the *Heliand*, with roots in oral tradition, is the situational embedding of certain episodes that, in the Gospels, are given minimal scenic backdrop, if any at all. A prominent example is the embedding of the Sermon on the Mount into a scene – a crowd of attentive warriors – that is described before the beginning of the sermon (1279–1299), returned to twice throughout its course (1381–1388, 1580–1586) and described once more after its conclusion (1984–1993). More often, however, there are only brief indications that the poet's fidelity to narrative formulas has led him to divide his source into different situational frames.[22] This is made especially clear by the introductory formulas of the so-called fitts, the narrative units that divide the text. In this case, an event narrated in a previous fitt will be made the beginning of a new fitt, reintroduced with such formulas as *Sô sprac* (949, 1381), *Sô deda* (2284), *Sô hêlde* (2357), *Sô uuîsida* (2538), or *Sô lêrde* (3223, 3409).[23] What this suggests is that the fitts could not simply have been guidelines for reciting the poem – formal indications to start or stop reading – since these linking elements only make sense if the fitts are recited in immediate succession. Therefore the fitts are, above all, situational frames, within which parts of the story are mounted.

Such framing is evident in the treatment of just two sentences from the Diatessaron, corresponding to John 11.45–46, which relate the response of the Jews to Jesus's behavior:

---

22 See Haferland, "Mündliche Erzähltechnik" [note 20], 239–44.
23 On sentence-initial *sô*, see Otto Behaghel, *Die Sytax des Heliand* (Vienna: F. Tempsky, 1897), §422, II 2 B.

The Hatred of Enemies

> Multi ergo ex Iudæis qui venerunt ad Mariam et viderant quæ fecit, crediderunt in eum. Quidem autem ex ipsis abierunt ad Pharisaeos et dixerunt eis quæ fecit Ihesus.
>
> [Many of the Jews therefore, who had come with Mary and had seen what Jesus did, believed in him. But some of them went to the Pharisees and told them what he had done.][24]

This account of the Jews' divergent reaction, which in John and Tatian occurs in one breath, is interrupted in the *Heliand* with a fitt boundary. The poet underscores this interruption all the more by providing an independent ending to the one fitt (4114–4117) and an independent beginning to the other (4118–4125), thus separating further what belongs together. This is justified both by the situation and by the logic of its narration. In the scene, one group of Jews reacts to Lazarus's resurrection with amazement, while Jesus's enemies, embittered, go to Jerusalem to side against him before the Pharisees. In accord with the narrative practice of situational framing or embedding, the poet splits the reactions by assigning them to different scenes. They are separated, especially, by the enemy's relocation to Jerusalem, and the two settings reflect and emphasize the friend-enemy binary that the poet – fond of dualism – had already introduced earlier on.[25] Thus at the beginning of the forty-eighth

---

24 I have cited from Sievers's edition, though it is outdated, for its convenient division into sections: Eduard Sievers, ed., *Tatian: Lateinisch und Altdeutsch mit ausführlichem Glossar*, 2nd ed., Bibliothek des ältesten deutschen Literatur-Denmäler 5 (Paderborn: Ferdinand Schöningh, 1892; repr. 1966), section 135.27. The translation is from Bruce M. Metzger and Roland E. Murphy, eds., *The New Oxford Annotated Bible with Apocrypha: New Revised Standard Version* (New York: Oxford UP, 1994).

25 The friend-enemy binary appears most prominently in the poet's allusions to Matt 25.33–46, where the left hand is associated with hell (see 1772–1780, 3455–3460) and the right with heaven (4388–4390). Other common binaries in the poem include light and darkness, warmth and cold, abundance and lack, freedom and captivity, and so on (see especially fitt 53). On the significance of

fitt, for instance, the poet stresses that two parties have formed in response to Jesus's teachings, a group of friends (3932–3940) and a group of enemies (3927–3932).[26]

The boundary between the forty-ninth and fiftieth fitts does not fall exactly between the reaction of Jesus's friends and that of his enemies. After the poet has emphasized, at the end of fitt 49, Jesus's ability to protect people *uuið fiundo nîd* "against the hatred of enemies" (4116),[27] the theme is briefly reintroduced – as is typical – at the beginning of fitt 50. Here it is repeated that, having witnessed the awakening of Lazarus, many men became followers of the miracle worker. After this introductory sentence, however, the poet turns abruptly to describe the other camp, those who, against Jesus, *uunun mid iro uuordun* "fought with their words" (4124)[28]:

> Sô mag heƀenkuniges,
> thiu mikile maht godes   manno gehuilikes
> ferahe giformon   endi uuið fiund nîð
> hêlag helpen,   sô huemu sô he is huldi fargiƀid.

---

dualism for oral culture, see the contributions in Rodney Needham, ed., *Right & Left: Essays on Dual Symbolic Classification* (Chicago: U of Chicago Press, 1973).

26 Though these lines go back to Tatian 133.15–16 (John 10.19–21), they happen to be the only lines that the poet has taken from a large portion of the Diatessaron (from 129.7 to the beginning of 134). It suited the poet's context well and was, doubtless, very consciously selected.

27 Edward H. Sehrt – *Vollständiges Wörterbuch zum Heliand und zur altsächsischen Genesis*, Hesperia 14 (Göttingen: Vandenhoeck & Ruprecht, 1925), s.v. *fiund* – understands this occurrence of *fiund* to be in the plural and translates it as "the evil, hellish spirits" (die bösen, höllischen Geister). In this matter he is following Moritz Heyne, ed., *Hêliand: Mit ausführlichem Glossar*, 2nd ed. (Paderborn: F. Schöningh, 1873), s.v. *fiond*. Though the passage might admit such a translation, the basic meaning of the word and the broader context of the story seem to disqualify it.

28 The *Heliand* is cited from the following edition: Otto Behaghel, ed., *Heliand und Genesis*, 10th ed., rev. Burkhard Taeger, Altdeutsche Textbibliothek 4 (Tübingen: Max Niemeyer, 1996). English translations of lengthy quotations are taken from G. Ronald Murphy, trans., *The Heliand: The Saxon Gospel* (New York: Oxford UP, 1992).

The Hatred of Enemies

L.

Thô uuarð thar sô managumu manne   môd aftar Kriste,
gihuorƀen hugiskefti,   siðor sie is hêlagon uuerk
selƀon gisâhun,   huand eo êr sulic ni uuarð
uunder an uueroldi.   Than uuas eft thes uuerodes sô filu,
sô môdstarke man: ni uueldon the maht godes
antkennien kûðlîco,   ac sie uuið craft mikil
unnun mid iro uuordun: uuârun im uualdandes
lêra sô lêða . . . (4114–4125)

[Thus the King of Heaven, the mighty divine Power, can protect everyone's life-spirit and help everyone against the hatred of enemies – everyone to whom He grants His gracious favor. (. . .) Song 50 (. . .) The feelings of many men turned in favor of Christ, attitudes of mind changed, once they saw His holy works for themselves – such wondrous things never happened before in the world. Then again, there were also many people, people of very strong hostile feelings, who did not want to recognize knowledgeably the power of God; on the contrary, they fought against Him with their words. The Ruler's teachings were so loathsome to them . . .]

The struggle of Jesus's enemies against him and, in turn, his resistance against them, constitute the center of the poet's understanding of Jesus's acts and suffering. He was therefore compelled to draw a fitt boundary in such a place – of deciding importance to him – and thus to distinguish, with his narrative structure, Jesus's followers from his enemies. The latter, after all, are going off to Caiaphas to agitate for Jesus's execution, and this is a situation that deserves to be told on its own.

To show that the poet often relied on his own understanding of the Gospel story, based in terms of fighting and strife, I will concentrate below on the description of the Jews as Jesus's enemy and on certain passages – excluding the elaboration of fitt boundaries – in which the *Heliand* deviates from its source.[29] In the course of

---

29 These passages are cited in Haferland, "Mündliche Erzähltechnik" [note

paraphrasing Tatian, the poet often saw fit to insert independent material of his own: He portrays in detail, for instance, the lamentation of the mothers whose children are to be murdered on Herod's order (736–754); he takes time to interpret thoroughly the parable of the sower (2530–2537); he has Thomas's fearless loyalty, as Jesus's retainer, figure prominently (3992–4004); Peter's assault on Malchus during Jesus's arrest is presented as an act of heroics befitting the comitatus tradition (4865–4882). Moreover, with a seemingly firm understanding of levirate marriage, which the missionaries Corbinian and Cillian had forbidden among the Germanic tribes,[30] the *Heliand* poet tells in detail how John the Baptist lost favor with Herodias, the wife of Herod Antipas, who had previously been married to the latter's brother (2698–2727). The addition that their relationship began after the brother's death is not biblical and does not correspond to the facts.

Though most examples of narrative freedom are woven tightly into Tatian's story and, for the most part, cannot be set apart by verse, a few deviations clearly can. There are approximately sixty independent passages of three or more lines; some of these go back to biblical commentaries, while others lack an identifiable source.[31]

20], 239–40n14–15.

30 Regarding Cillian, who objected to the levirate marriage of the Thurigian Duke Gozbert - and was brought to death by the machinations of the Duke's wife - see the *Passio Kiliani martyris Wirzburgensis* 10–15, in Bruno Krusch and Wilhelm Levison, eds., *Passiones vitaeque sanctorum aevi merovingici*, MGH - Scriptorum Rerum Merovingicarum 5 (Hannover: Hahn, 1910), 722–28, at 727–28. On Corbinian, who similarly criticized the levirate marriage of the Bavarian Duke Grimoald, see the *Vita Corbiniani episcopi* 24–31, in Bruno Krusch, ed., *Arbeonis episcopi Frisingensis Vitae sanctorum Haimhrammi et Corbiniani*, MGH - Scriptores Rerum Germanicarum in Usum Scholarum 13 (Hannover: Hahn, 1920), 100–234, at 215–24.

31 Following Ernst Windisch, *Der Heliand und seine Quellen* (Leipzig: F. C. W. Vogel, 1868), the passages and their sources (if known) are as follows: Lines 5–37; 42–53 (Bede); 53–60; 288–295; 371–378; 478–480; 548–597; 645–648; 754–760; 790–794; 832–839; 868–872; 882–903; 941–943; 1032–1052 (Hrabanus);

The Hatred of Enemies

All told, the places where the poet does not rely on a source – independent fitt beginnings and conclusions included[32] – number some 600 verses, or roughly ten percent of the entire poem. While many of the independent passages are tied to narrow biblical contexts, others reflect the overarching narrative design with which the poet, as a Germanic singer, was better accustomed.[33] These verses tell of Jesus's (weaponless) struggles against his enemies and, even more so, of their struggles against him; they are woven in between tendentious translations and arrangements of Tatian that corroborate the poet's design.

1170–1172; 1199–1202; 1221–1243 (Hrabanus); 1325–1335; 1414–1419; 1472–1475; 1580–1586; 1613–1615; 1711–1720 (Hrabanus); 1724–1734; 1916–1928; 1962–1983; 1999–2012; 2142–2149; 2205–2212; 2238–2246; 2508–2514; 2574–2577; 2592–2595; 2634–2646; 2731–2742; 2760–2766; 2785–2793; 2807–2810; 2902–2908; 2941–2945; 3177–3182; 3208–3215; 3354–3359; 3444–3515 (Hrabanus); 2589–2670 (Bede); 3719–3727; 3780–3791; 3857–3867; 3895–3906; 3957–3963; 4167–4185; 4216–4229; 4243–4269; 4497–4501; 4660–4673; 4738–4743; 4748–4757; 5381–5394 (Hrabanus); 5487–5492; 5674–5682; and 5769–5781. This list does not reflect any consideration of which particular recension of the Diatessaron the *Heliand* poet had before him.

32   See above, note 29.

33   Among the independent passages cited in note 30, the following concern Jesus's enemies (the Jews) in one way or another: Lines 1227–1233; 2142–2149; 3719–3727; 3895–3906; 4167–4185; 4216–4224.; 4262–4269; 5381–5394; 5487–5492; 5674–5682; and 5769–5781. Additional examples appear in the following introductions or conclusions of fitts: Lines 2076–2087; 2285–2290; 2339–2345; and 3833–3839. Both Albrecht Hagenlocher – "Theologische Systematik und epische Gestaltung: Beobachtungen zur Darstellung der feindlichen Juden im Heliand und in Otfrids Evangelienbuch," *Beiträge zur Geschichte der deutschen Sprache und Literatur* 96 (1974), 33–58 – and Bernhard Sowinski – *Darstellungsstil und Sprachstil im Heliand*, Kölner germanistische Studien 21 (Cologne: Böhlau, 1985), 267–71 – discuss in detail the enmity between Jesus and the Jews in the *Heliand*. In contrast to Hagenlocher and Sowinski, who simply analyze the poet's negative characterization of the Jews, I will focus below on the narrative motives evident in the poet's independent episodes. Unlike both scholars, moreover, I will interpret these motives in terms of heroic poetry.

Jesus's enemies are the Jews and, from the outset, they are introduced as a people.[34] They are also mentioned in passages that, by way of Tatian, go back to the Synoptic Gospels, where they are not presented in a negative light. It is clear that the *Heliand* poet has relied especially on the Gospel of John – to which Tatian had also given preference – in order to amplify the negative characterization of the Jews.[35] To this end, too, the poet (and his collaborators) could make use of certain biblical commentaries.[36] His portrayal, therefore, is not based on any sort of anti-Semitism, but rather on the theological rejection of the Jews presented by contemporary exegetes and by the patristic authors before them.[37] In his commentary on Luke, for example, Bede blames first of all the Jewish high priests for Jesus's crucifixion, who – he adds – were not acting out of ignorance but rather out of hate.[38] Elsewhere he blames the Jews in general,[39] who are unwilling to acknowledge Jesus as their king,[40] who are blind,[41] and who have – up to the present day (*usque hodie*) – kept Jesus out

---

34   See line 61, for instance, where the poet speaks of *Iudeono folc* 'the Jewish people' instead of simply Judea, as is the case in Luke 1.5.

35   See Rudolf Bultmann, *The Gospel of John: A Commentary*, trans. G. R. Beasley-Murray (Oxford: Basil Blackwell, 1971), 86: "The term οἱ Ἰουδαῖοι, characteristic of the Evangelist [John], gives an overall portrayal of the Jews, viewed from the standpoint of Christian faith, as the representatives of unbelief (and thereby, as will appear, of the unbelieving 'world' in general). [. . .] This usage leads to the recession or to the complete disappearance of the distinctions made in the Synoptics between different elements of the Jewish people."

36   The poet relies most heavily on Bede's commentary on Luke, Alcuin's on John, and Hrabanus Maurus's on Matthew. See Windisch, *Der Heliand und seine Quellen* [note 31].

37   Hagenlocher, "Theologische Systematik" [note 33], 34, cites a few passages in Hrabanus and Alcuin.

38   D. Hurst, ed., *Bedae Venerabilis Opera. Pars II: Opera exegetica. 3: In Lvkae evangeivm*, CCSL 120 (Turnhout: Brepols, 160), 354.

39   Ibid., 394–95.

40   Ibid., 404.

41   Ibid., 407.

of their hearts.⁴² According to Bede, then, the servant of the high priest, whose severed ear Jesus restores (Luke 22.51–52), is an allegory for the Jewish people (*populus Iudaeorum*), for whom the possibility of salvation always remains.⁴³

The *Heliand* poet regards the Jews in a similar way, as is especially clear in the characterizations that pervade the second half of the poem.⁴⁴ The Jews are unrepentant and evil; they are *uulanca man* 'arrogant men' (3927 and elsewhere) or *uurêðe man* 'bitter men' (5121 and elswhere) and are characterized by a great number of pejorative adjectives: *grim* 'wrathful', *môdag* 'malicious', *derbi* 'evil', *dolmôd* 'audacious', *gêlmôd* 'unruly', *slidmôd* 'cruel', *gram* 'hostile', *mênhuat* 'criminal', *irri* 'furious', *ênhard* 'inimical', *gramhugdig* 'hostile', *baluhugdig* 'beligerent', and *hôti* 'hostile'. Moreover, their thought, behavior, and speech are associated with *gelp* 'scorn', *hosk* 'scorn', *bismersprâka* 'lampooning', *bihêtuuord* 'threatening words', *harmquiði* 'invective', *inuuid* 'enmity', *mordhugi* 'murderous intent', *nið* 'hatred', and so on. Despite all this, Jesus's covenant applies to them as well (see especially 2076–2087; also 5674–5682; 5769–5781).

The poet is able to use this theological condemnation of the Jews to bring his material into accord with the disposition of Germanic heroic poetry, according to which a hero becomes a hero through his downfall. The latter distinguishes himself by facing his enemies head on, an act that does not have to be accomplished – recall Gunnar – with the aid of arms. It is decisive, above all, for the hero to offer resolute resistance *uuið fiundo nîð* 'against the hatred of enemies', a formulaic expression in the *Heliand* (28, 52, 4116, 4210). The formula also occurs in the Old English *Seafarer*: *wið feonda nip* (75).⁴⁵ Though the *Seafarer* is not a heroic poem, it is likely that such independent

---

42   Ibid., 392.
43   Ibid., 388.
44   See Hagenlocher, "Theologische Systematik" [note 33], 34–38; and Sowinski, *Darstellungsstil und Sprachstil* [note 33], 269–71.
45   George P. Krapp and Elliott V. K. Dobbie, eds., *The Exeter Book*, Anglo-Saxon Poetic Records 3 (New York: Columbia UP, 1936), 143–47.

attestations of the formula derive from a common lexical repertoire of Germanic heroic poetry. As metrical and alliterative filler, the formula might have lost some of the contours of its original meaning; in the *Heliand*, therefore, it need not always refer to human adversaries.[46]

An admittedly remote parallel to Jesus's resistance to his enemies occurs in the *Battle of Maldon*, an Old English poem written around the year 1000 that relates the fight of Byrhtnoth and his men against the Viking invaders of Essex.[47] Byrhtnoth turns away a Viking messenger who expects the Anglo-Saxons to pay a tribute rather than to fight; instead of making any payment, he would rather have both sides come together in battle (60–61). He makes this choice, however, despite his awareness of having inferior numbers on his side, a fact that will turn out to decide the battle. What is more, he allows the slaughter to begin by granting the Vikings safe passage across the river Pante – by forfeiting his army's position – a gesture that, according to the poet, bears witness to his *ofermod* 'arrogance, pride (?)' (89).[48] After Byrhtnoth is mortally wounded, some of his men flee the battlefield but others remain and continue the hopeless fight. An old retainer, Byrhtwold, is made to sum up the heroic ideal just before the fragment breaks off: *Hige sceal þe heardra, heorte þe cenre, / mod sceal þe mare, þe ure mægen lytlað* "Our mind must be the firmer, our heart the bolder, our courage the greater, as our might diminishes" (312–13).

---

46 Thus the dictionary entries, s.v. *fiund*. See above, note 27.
47 For the text, see Elliot V. K. Dobbie, ed., *The Anglo-Saxon Minor Poems*, Anglo-Saxon Poetic Records 6 (New York: Columbia UP, 1942), 7–16.
48 On the meaning of *ofermod*, see Helmut Gneuss, *Die Battle of Maldon als historisches und literarisches Zeugnis* (Munich: C. H. Beck, 1976), 12–13, who defines it as *superbia* 'haughtiness, cruel arrogance, excessive pride', though the tenor of the poem seems not to support this. For another opinion, see Earl R. Anderson, "The Battle of Maldon: A Reappraisal of Possible Sources, Date, and Theme," in *Modes of Interpretation in Old English Literature: Essays in Honour of Stanley B. Greenfield*, ed. Phylllis R. Brown et al. (Toronto: U of Toronto Press, 1986), 247–72, at 264–65.

The Hatred of Enemies

It is only against the superior forces of his enemy, in the face of his undoing, that Byrhtnoth is able to muster heroic pride. Though the contempt for death that he demonstrates in dealing with the Vikings is not at all comparable to the message of the Sermon on the Mount, this message, in the *Heliand*, fulfills a comparable epic function. Here Jesus defines himself against the hatred of the Jews, just as Byrhtnoth does – though in a way altogether different – against the Vikings. It is precisely this type of hostility against the enemy with which the *Heliand* poet, keeping in step with his familiar heroic medium, embellishes his source material.[49] Jesus and Byrhtnoth (and Gunnar, too, in his own way) are ultimately killed, but each has an ethos of his own that allows him to triumph over death.

In his critique of Andreas Heusler's theory about the literary development of heroic legend, Walter Haug argues that heroic poetry can only mediate historical events by way of literary motifs; more generally, he stresses that "historical experience comes to be realized through literary patterns."[50] That literary patterns can be used to articulate historical experience is not disputed; at the same time, however, the patterns themselves developed during the process of articulating historical knowledge. Regarding the ethos of heroic poetry, it seems problematic to establish which came first. It should be kept in mind that Byrhtnoth and Gunnar share the same ethos, and that this is attributed to both of them by way of a sort of thematic rubric, namely the act of facing up against an insuperable challenge. This seemingly "literary" rubric, however, might just as well be a motif from everyday life. Certainly it is not "literary" if the

---

49 I do not interpret the hostility developed in the *Heliand* as a sort of literary antithesis required of an "epic" poem. Among others of this opinion, see Hagenlocher, "Theologische Systematik" [note 33], 36–41.

50 Walter Haug, "Andreas Heuslers Heldensagenmodell: Prämissen, Kritik und Gegenentwurf," *Zeitschrift für deutsches Altertum und deutsche Literatur* 41 (1975), 273–92, here at 282: "daß historische Erfahrung mittels literarischer Schemata zu sich selbst kommt."

historical Byrhtnoth really acted as he does in the *Battle of Maldon*; the poem claims that he did, after all, and there is little reason not to believe it. From time to time, then, heroic poetry deals with historical figures whose heroic action, on its own, does not require any "literary" stylization, and thus it makes use of narrative patterns in which there is no fixed distinction between literature and life.[51]

For the poet and audience of the *Heliand*, there would have been no doubt about the historicity of Jesus's actions, and Jesus's heroism is not schematized to the same extent as that of Byrhtnoth and Gunnar: As in Matthew (27.46, Tatian 207.2), for instance, he is permitted to express his despair on the cross (5631–5639); nor do the Jews, in the end, have any real power over Jesus's divine authority.[52] Nevertheless, Germanic heroic poetry provides a narrative mould for the portrayal of his life, and its contours are recognizable. Like alliteration and poetic formulas, the poet's narrative technique was an aspect of his medium that he impressed upon his new material without, at the same time, having some missionary strategy of accommodation in mind. There is thus an inevitable degree to which the *Heliand* poet has distorted the Gospel story by appropriating it to his own medium and – regardless of whether it was intended as such – the result of this distortion, a byproduct of assimilation, can be understood in terms of accommodation. It is only in this limited sense that we can speak of the poet's narrative design, since he does not openly stray from his exemplar to pour Jesus's life into the mold of heroic poetry.

When the twelve-year-old Jesus engages with the scribes in the temple (786–792), it is said that the Jews (*Iudeo liudi*) were there to

---

51   Narrative patterns should not be confused with literary or poetically stylized patterns. It can be assumed that all of our experiences can be fit into one narrative mould or another. See, for example, Daniel Dennent, *Philosophie des Menschlichen Bewußtseins*, trans. Franz Wuketits (Hamburg: Hoffmann und Campe, 1994), 532–51. Experiences, therefore, are not exactly "literarily" schematized; if narrative patterns are detectable in an example of oral "literature" – as in our case – this does not necessarily evidence a "literary" origin of the work, in Haug's sense of the word.

52   See Hagenlocher, "Theologische Systematik" [note 33], 40–41.

The Hatred of Enemies

serve "the god of their people" (*iro thiodgode*) and that a great crowd of Jews had gathered (*Iudeono gisamnod mancraft mikil*). None of this is mentioned in Tatian and Luke (2.41–51). Before the calling of the twelve disciples – in an episode taken from Hrabanus's commentary on Matthew – certain members of the "Jewish clan" (*Iudeono cunnies*) are identified as the main enemies of Jesus. Along with two other groups of people, they have come to hear Jesus speak, during his first visit to Galilee, and to witness his miracles:

> Sume uuârun sie im eft Iudeono cunnies,
> fêgni folcskepi: uuârun thar gefarana te thiu,
> that sie ûses drohtines dâdio endi uuordo
> fâron uuoldun, habdun im fêgnien hugi,
> uurêðen uuillion: uuoldun uualdand Crist
> alêdien them liudiun, that sie is lêron ni hôrdin,
> ne uuendin aftar is uuillion. (1227–1233)

[Some of them were of the Jewish clan, sneaky people. They had come there to spy on our Chieftain's deeds and words, they had a sneaky attitude of mind and ill-will. They wanted to make Ruling Christ loathsome to the people so that they would not listen to His teaching nor act according to His will.]

Neither in Hrabanus's commentary, nor indeed in Matthew, are the Jews called by name.[53] For the sake of his own story, however, the *Heliand* poet needs to identify, when he sees fit, exactly who Jesus's enemies are among the crowd.

---

53 In Hrabanus there are four groups, the last of which corresponds to that described in the lines cited above (1227–1233). About this group – without providing any additionaly information about its ethnicity – Hrabanus writes (PL 107, 793): "Quarta illorum erat, qui invidia ducti opus Domini dehonestare volebant, et ut eum in sermone comprehenderent, et ita apud principes accusarent, ut eum morti traderent, sicut et fecerunt quando ille permisit, non quando illi voluerunt" [There was a fourth group of people who, driven by envy, wanted to discredit the work of the Lord. So they tried to catch him in a word and accuse him to the princes so as to deliver him to death. They were able to do so when he allowed it, however, not when they wished].

The poet concludes the twenty-fourth fitt, which concerns the wedding in Cana, with a highly contrived account of Jesus's covenant with the Jews, according to which he promised them the kingdom of heaven *endi hellio gethuing uueride* "and protected them against the oppression of hell" (2081). Whereas the joys of the heavenly kingdom are enumerated here – a passage of the poet's own making (2076–2087) – a complementary episode, similarly independent and shortly thereafter, elaborates the great sufferings of hell, which threaten so many of the Jewish people (2142–2149). As highly as the poet praises Jesus's deeds (*diuran is dâdi*, 2228), so also does he make it readily apparent that, as a reward for their behavior, the Jews will be banished into hell (2285–2290), a fact that is hinted at early on in the preaching of John the Baptist (895–899). Toward the end of fitt 28, too, the Jews are granted this same *lêðlic lôngeld* 'miserable reward' for having "fought against his teachings" (*uunnun uuidar is uuordun*, 2339–2345).

While in Galilee, Jesus's conflict with his fellow countrymen intensifies to such an extent that he has to cease his mission. The poet expands to thirty lines (2669–2698) the mere three sentences from Luke's Gospel in which Jesus's townspeople drive him out of Nazareth and hope to cast him off a cliff, though he manages to escape "through the midst of them" (Luke 4.30; Tatian 78.9). The Jews draw up a retinue as if going to battle (*Hêtun thô iro uuerod cumen, gesiði tesamne*, 2669–2670). Unlike the disciples, they are not interested in Jesus's teachings (*ni was im is uuordo niud, spâhero spello*, 2672–2673), concerned as they are with throwing him to his death. Jesus disregards their threats, knowing that no harm can come to him before his time has come (2676–2681), and thus he vanishes from among them.[54] Those who do not believe in him – though he created heaven and earth (2884–2889)[55] – are labeled *uurêðe uuidarsacon*

---

54 Windisch, *Der Heliand und seine Quellen* [note 31], 60, detects here the influence of Bede's commentary on Luke, but the parallels seem rather vague.
55 In this passage, Windisch (ibid., 64) sees evidence of the poet's dependence

The Hatred of Enemies

'hostile adversaries' (2889; see also 3800, 3948, 5643). He knows that when he goes to Jerusalem, where the struggle will intensify, that the *Iudeo liudi* will not recognize his authority (3703–3705), a fact that is stated with more precision in the *Heliand* than it is in Luke 19.41–44 (Tatian 116.6). Moreover, it is hostile Jews – not simply Pharisees, as in Luke (19.39) – who grow distressed by the rowdy entrance into the city and demand that Jesus subdue the crowd (3719–3727).

After his skillful deflection of the question about imperial taxes, the Jews are forced to recognize that they cannot outdo Jesus with words; he speaks the truth, or *sôðspel* 'truthful speech' (3833–3839). This leads to a reintroduction of the binary friend-enemy theme during a transition between Tatian 120.7 (John 8.11) to 129.1 (Luke 19.47). Here the Jewish people begin to stir up animosity towards Jesus, but two separate parties take shape, the smaller of which has taken Jesus's side (3895–3906). Shortly after this, the poet returns to the theme, developing it further, in fitt 50. Jesus, who knows full well the hatred of the Jews among Caiaphas (4167–4185), encounters a gathering of enemies in Jerusalem who want to kill him (4216–4224). The small group of his supporters, however, manages to protect Jesus against his adversaries, who in turn avoid him (4224–4229). In an account of his preaching in the temple (4232–4256), Jesus gains the favor of much of the *folcscepi* 'people' (4256–4262), while some of the Jews continue to distrust his words and fight against him (4262–4269).

When Jesus is then taken prisoner, an explanation must be offered as to why he did not defend himself: He wants to save mankind by delivering them from hell into the kingdom of heaven (4918–4924). Further explanation is needed when the Jews triumph and take him away, bound: The disciples have not fled out of cowardice, but

---

on Alcuin's commentary on John. It is noteworthy, however, that the poet has rendered the concept of creation in Germanic terms, according to which creation encompassed *erde endi uphimil* 'earth and heaven above' (2886). For parallels in Germanic mythology, see Jan de Vries, *Altgermanische Religionsgeschichte*, 3rd ed., 2 vols. (Berlin: Walter de Gruyter, 1970), 2:360–61 (§571).

rather because their flight had been foretold (4931–4936). To be on the safe side, the poet neglects to relate Peter's self-reproaches: None should be surprised by Peter's behavior, since he was tested for the sake of illuminating human weakness and because God wanted it so (5023–5038). The apostle's earlier boasts, and boasting in general, is then said to be meaningless, since God is able to take away anyone's strength (5039–5049). Yet another explanation is given for why Jesus does not evade his sentence by making his divinity known: This is because, again, he wishes to save mankind, but also because, had he revealed himself to the Jews, he could not have carried out his work of salvation (5380–5394).

After receiving his sentence, Jesus is delivered into the hands of those who hate him; he patiently endures – though he feared death before (4748–4757) – what his enemies inflict upon him (5487–5492). The Jews set up a cross and hammer cold and sharp iron nails through his hands and feet, so that blood flows to the earth and drips down *fan ûson drohtine* 'from our Lord' (5532–5539). Jesus did not, however, want to avenge this wicked act of the Jews: "Hie ni uuelda thoh thia dâd uurecan grimma an then Iudeon" (5539–5540). This is in agreement with his teachings – which are to be followed even in distress (see 5302–5303) – and the graphic depiction of his execution allows for the heroic ethos, which Jesus is made to inspire, to come more clearly to the fore. Even the earthquake, brought about by Jesus's death, does not open the hardened hearts of the Jews (5674–5682). Moreover, though Jesus's resurrection reveals the light, unbars the door of hell, and prepares the way to heaven for all, still the Jewish guards at his tomb gain nothing from it (5769–5781).

There is nothing in Tatian's Diatessaron that corresponds to the lines cited above; each of which is from an independent passage of the poet's own design (or from an adaptation of a biblical commentary). Whenever the poet repeats the term *ûson drohtine* 'our Lord', he heightens his audience's identification with Jesus and, at the same time, underscores the blindness of Jesus's enemies. However

The Hatred of Enemies

much the poet has relied on the Gospels, his own design is not in full harmony with them; there are, after all, certain rifts between the New Testament and the ideological content of heroic poetry. Thus the poet, for instance, has a noticeably difficult time explaining the behavior of the disciples in the face of defeat. That Jesus did not defend himself could be justified, and the poet does so, but the flight of the disciples – and Peter's failure on all fronts – overtax the poet's understanding of things and lead to inventive justifications. Unlike Jesus's disciples, of course, most of Byrhtnoth's retinue follow their leader into death.[56]

It has often been remarked that the poet must have had difficulties here, especially since, until this point, the poem has unfolded in accord with his heroic conception of the story. About the poet's problem, for instance, Elisabeth Grosch has remarked that he had to make sense of these events, somehow, from the perspective of "the exacting ideal of Germanic heroism,"[57] and Franz Jostes described the poet's escape from this dilemma – his recourse to strict determinism – as a sort of un-Christian, "provincial fatalism" (*Bauernfatalismus*).[58] Johannes Rathofer rejected these interpretations and pointed instead to parallels in contemporary theology, in which light Jesus's "voluntary" submission in the *Heliand* can be understood to reflect his divine free will.[59] This was a common Christological belief at the time. What happens up to and including Jesus's death had taken place according to his own will; since he is acting as God, he is not to be measured by human or even heroic standards. After the lancing on the cross

---

56 On "suicidal fighting" for one's lord, see Anderson, "The Battle of Maldon" [note 48], 251–56.
57 Elisabeth Grosch, "Das Gottes- und Menschenbild im Heliand," *Beiträge zur Geschichte der deutschen Sprache und Literatur* 72 (1950), 90–120, at 115–17: "hochgespannten germanischen Heldenideals."
58 Franz Jostes, "Der Dichter des Heliand," *Zeitschrift für deutsches Altertum und deutsche Literatur* 40 (1896), 341–68, at 362.
59 Rathofer, *Der Heliand* [note 19], 150–60. See also Göhler, "Das Christusbild" [note 14], 30–31.

at the hands of "one of his hateful-minded enemies" (5703–5704), blood and water flow from Jesus's wound *all sô is uuillio geng* 'as he wanted it' (5710). About this, Rathofer remarks:

> [T]he poet follows the dogmatic sentiment of his time, which sees in the thrust of the lance the *benignitas propriae voluntatis (Christi)* 'the beneficence of Christ's will', which "preordained" all that he suffered *voluntate ac potestate* 'willingly and with authority'.[60]

That there exists here a fundamental explanatory problem is already evident in the divergent accounts of Jesus's death in the Gospels. His suffering on the cross is left unmentioned, for instance, in John's Gospel, which stresses instead the fulfillment of both Scripture and the divine plan (19.28–30).[61] From a Christological perspective, that is, even the New Testament authors had some difficulty explaining why Jesus allowed what he could have prevented. This is reason enough not pawn off the difficulties of the *Heliand* poet onto contemporary theology, which he may have to thank for his answer but certainly not for the interpretive difficulties themselves. These are not easily absorbed into his work but rather clash against it, and his somewhat desperate attempts to deal with them take him well beyond the content of the Diatessaron, with which he could have been content. Rathofer ignored this fact, and Grosch was in the right when she remarked that for the poet, as he was forced to tell it in the end, it came down to a narrative inconsistency between the ideology of heroic poetry and the behavior of Jesus and his disciples.[62]

---

60 Rathofer, *Der Heliand* [note 19], 160: "folgt der Dichter dem dogmatischen Empfinden seiner Zeit, das im Lanzenstich noch die 'benignitas propriae voluntatis (Christi)' am Werk sieht, die überhaupt alle Einzelheiten des Leidens 'vorherbestimmt' hat 'voluntate ac potestate'." As an analogue, Rathofer cites Agobard of Lyon's *Liber de correctione antiphonarii*; he also (ibid., 39n51) points to 1 Cor 2.7–9, which emphasizes the role of predestination through God's wisdom.
61 See Bultmann, *The Gospel of John* [note 35], 673–75.
62 Grosch, "Das Gottes- und Menschenbild" [note 57], 118–19.

The Hatred of Enemies

However, the disciples' failure does not differ entirely from what might occur in heroic poetry: Beowulf, too, was abandoned by his followers before he died in his fight with the dragon (2596–2599, 2845–2852). This hero suffers a fate comparable to that of Jesus,[63] at least in the sense that, by being deserted and overpowered, his courage is allowed to come that much more to the fore. It is within the framework of futile and thus heroic resistance – against the hatred of his enemies – that the *Heliand* poet was able to make sense of Jesus's actions and message and impress them upon his fellow Saxons. The contours of Germanic heroic poetry are still recognizable in the *Heliand* even if Jesus's death, upon closer inspection, is neither heroic nor the result of resistance – nor in any way futile.

---

63 The parallel has been noted by Robert E. Kaske, "Beowulf," in *Critical Approaches to Six Major English Works: Beowulf through Paradise Lost*, ed. Robert M. Lumiansky and Herschel Baker (Philadelphia: U of Pennsylvania Press, 1968), 3–40, at 31. Kaske presents additional parallels between Beowulf and Jesus on pp. 30–34.

IV

The Portrayal of the Jews in the *Heliand*

The Jews in the *Heliand*[1]

G. Ronald Murphy

In the beginning (of German literature) was the *Heliand*. There are a few other contenders for the honor – a few prayers, charms, and fragments – but the *Heliand* is our earliest epic. It is a unique work of literature in that it is the story of Jesus transposed, retold as if it had all occurred in the Viking-era world of Northern Europe. The author used Tatian's second-century harmony of the four Gospels as the basis for his epic and then re-imagined the whole story as if it had occurred in his own day. He recast the story in epic form, contemplatively integrating Northern European values, magic, sooth-saying, wizardry, contemporary Saxon history, warriors' courage, Germanic poetry, and personal mysticism with the Christian Gospel. The *Heliand* was written under the aegis of Louis the Pious around the year 830. Its purpose was to make the Christian Gospel accessible and less foreign to the Saxons, a people at that time recently and unhappily converted by the sword of Charlemagne and the Franks to Christianity after very bitter resistance, brutal warfare that continued over thirty years. The Saxons still vacillated between Christ and Woden. The war was still sporadically flaring up as the *Heliand*'s author worked on. His identity remains unknown, but he was an enormously gifted religious poet capable of profound intercultural communication. An ancient Latin preface maintains that he was a Saxon and an epic poet, a *vates*. Indeed he was.

---

1 Originally published in *German Literature Between Faiths: Jew and Christian at Odds and in Harmony*, ed. Peter Meister, Studies in German Jewish History 6 (Berlin: Peter Lang, 2004), 15–25, 179.

G. Ronald Murphy

It generally surprises readers that in a work so early as the *Heliand* there should be intense feeling expressed concerning the Jews, sometimes in the form of respect, as in the events surrounding the birth of John the Baptist and of Jesus, but in the main it is an unusually high degree of hostility. It is my purpose here to see why this was the case. There is of course hostility toward the Jews in the author's original text, in the four Gospels themselves, because the high priest, the Sanhedrin, and the crown rejected Jesus as messiah, and this is retained in the *Heliand*, but the *Heliand* goes further than the Gospels. This is something of a mystery, since it is difficult to imagine that Continental Saxons of the early ninth century would have had much contact with Jews. They had not even had familiar contact with Christianity. Why would the author have adopted such a negative attitude toward the Jews at such an early point in German Christian literary history?

My belief is that, first, the author of the *Heliand* was transforming the Gospel story of Christ into a Germanic heroic epic. Effective epic form required him to create a consistent, powerful opposing force to provide a decisive contest with the hero of his epic, especially in the final battle scene. Second, the author's pastoral intent in the *Heliand* was to exalt the traditional heroic epic value of loyalty, *triuue*, in order to have a native argument for steadiness of loyalty to Christ instead of the persistent vacillation of his Saxon converts between Christ and Woden.[2] He thus also needed an antagonistic force associated with disloyalty. Third, the author is deeply immersed in the cultural heroic world's adulation of generosity, of the throne as the "chair of giving," the *gifstol*, of chieftainly munificence with jewels and treasure. He sees money, and especially usury, as an approaching threat to his concept of wealth, and he associates the threat with Jews because of his reading of the scene in which Jesus drives moneylenders from

---

2   For an extensive discussion of this point, see my *The Saxon Savior: The Germanic Transformation of the Gospel in the Ninth-Century Heliand* (New York: Oxford UP, 1989), esp. chapter 2

The Jews in the Heliand

the temple. In each case, then, it was the Jews in the Gospel story who would provide him with what is epic required.

Jews are treated with respect in the infancy narratives in the synoptic Gospels and also in the *Heliand*. Joseph is depicted in the Christmas story as a Saxon nobleman whose horse guards are in the fields at night when the angel appears to announce the birth of Christ in Bethlehem. There are no shepherds. The author takes great pains, more than in Luke, to describe Mary and Joseph as noble Jews, descendants of King David:

> Thô giuuêt im ôc mid his hîuuisca
> Ioseph the gôdo, sô it god mahtig
> ualdand uuelda: sôhta im thiu uuânamon hêm
> thea burg an Bethleem, thar iro beiðero uuas,
> thes heliðes handmahal endi ôc thera hêlagun thiornun,
> Mariun thera gôdun. Thar uuas thes mâreon stôl
> an êrdagun, aðalcuninges,
> Dauides thes gôdon, than langa the he thana druhtskepi thar,
> erl under Ebreon êgan môsta,
> haldan hôhgisetu. Siu uuârun is hîuuiscas,
> cuman fon is cnôsla, cunneas gôdes,
> bêðiu bi geburdiun. (356–367)

[The good Joseph went also with his household, just as God, ruling mightily, willed it. He made his way to his shining home, the hill-fort at Bethlehem. This was the assembly place for both of them, for Joseph the hero and Mary the good, the holy girl. This was the place where in olden days the throne of the great and noble good King David stood for as long as he reigned, enthroned on high, an earl of the Hebrews. Joseph and Mary both belonged by birth to his household, they were of good family lineage, of David's own clan. (15)]³

---

3 Quotations of the *Heliand* are from Otto Behaghel, ed., *Heliand und Genesis*, 10th ed., rev. Burkhard Taeger, Altdeutsche Textbibliothek 4 (Tübingen: Max

G. Ronald Murphy

In order to further identify the Saxons with the events of the coming of Christ, Saxon negative feeling concerning foreign Frankish governors (the *missi*, or "those sent" by Charlemagne to the rule the conquered Saxon homeland) finds a thinly disguised place in the description of Jewish feelings toward Herod:

>   habdun fan Rûmuburg   rîki geuunnan
>   helmgitrôsteon,   sâton iro heritogon
>   an lando gihuem,   habdun liudeo giuuald,
>   allon elitheodon.   Erodes uuas
>   an Hierusalem   oƀer that Iudeono folc
>   gicoran te kuninge,   sô ina thie kêser tharod,
>   fon Rûmuburg   rîki theodan
>   satta undar that gisîði.   Hie ni uuas thoh mid sibbeon bilang
>   aƀaron Israheles,   eðiligiburdi,
>   cuman fon iro cnuosle,   neuan that hie thuru thes kêsures thanc
>   fan Rûmuburg   rîki habda,
>   that im uuârun sô gihôriga   hildiscalcos,
>   aƀaron Israheles   elleanruoƀa:
>   suiðo unuuanda uuini,   than lang hie giuuald êhta (57–70)

[... those helmet-lovers from hill-fort Rome had won an empire. Their military governors were in every land and had authority over the people of every noble race. In Jerusalem, Herod was chosen to be king over the Jewish people. Caesar, ruling the empire from hill-fort Rome, placed him there – among the warrior-companions – even though Herod did not belong by clan to the noble and well-born descendants of Israel. He did not come from their kinsmen. It was only thanks to Caesar in hill-fort Rome, who ruled the empire, that the descendants of Israel, those fighting men renowned for their toughness, had

Niemeyer, 1996), cited by line number. English translations are from G. Ronald Murphy, trans., *The Heliand: The Saxon Gospel* (New York: Oxford UP, 1992), and are cited by page number.

The Jews in the Heliand

to obey him. They were Herod's unwavering friends – as long as he held power ... (5-6)]

As in the Gospels, the *Heliand* author refers to "the Jews" in a negative tone where they are found in opposition to Christ; this is primarily in the scenes of open debate in the middle part of the story and especially in the Passion and Crucifixion accounts. The feeling in the *Heliand*, however, seems to spread backward from the Passion account so that it is simply the Jews who are everywhere in the story acting in opposition to Christ. What has the author done to cause this impression?

One of the changes clearly necessary in writing the *Heliand* version of the Gospel story was to simplify the Jewish parts of the story. The endless contentions about what is or is not allowed on the Sabbath are left out of the *Heliand* – for good reason: northern European converts to Christianity would simply not understand the need for such debate. Far more significant, however, would be the elimination of the sub-groups of Pharisees, Sadducees, and the Scribes (in many translations called "lawyers" since they were the experts in Torah, the law). Since differences between these groups would have no meaning for the Saxons, the author of the *Heliand* simply refers to all of them as Jews. This has the good effect of making the opposition simple and straightforward for the Saxon neophyte to understand, and of providing a single enemy for the epic plot line, but it has the very bad effect of reducing all the hostile sub-groups to one: "the Jews." Lacking mention of any religious sub-groups (Pharisees, Sadducees, etc.), "the Jews" become responsible for the opposition to Christ on almost every page of the story.[4]

---

4 See Lawrence E. Frizzell, "Jew and Christian in the New Testament," in *German Literature Between Faiths: Jew and Christian at Odds and in Harmony*, ed. Peter Meister, Studies in German Jewish History 6 (Berlin: Peter Lang, 2004), 1–13, 177–78.

G. Ronald Murphy

When Christ is seized after the agony in the garden, the mixture of respect for the power of the Jewish clan and disrespect for its handling of Christ are expressed in terms that echo a brave Germanic chieftain's last stand:

> Uuerod sîðode thô
> antat sie te Criste   kumane uurðun,
> grim folc Iudeona,   thar he mid is iungarun stôd,
> mâri drohtin: bed metodogiscapu,
> torhtero tîdeo.   Thô geng imu treulôs man,
> Iudas tegegnes   endi te themu godes barne
> hnêg mid is hôbdu   endi is hêrron quedde,
> custe ina craftagne   endi his quidi lêste,
> uuîsde ina themu uuerode,   al sô he êr mid uuordun gehêt.
> That tholode al mid githuldiun   thiodo drohtin,
> uualdand thesara uueroldes   endi sprak imu mid is uuordun tô,
> frâgode ine frôkno: 'behuî kumis thu sô mid thius folcu te mi,
> behuî lêdis thu mi sô these liudi tô   endi mi te thesare lêðan thiode
> farcôpos mid thînu kussu   under thit kunni Iudeono,
> meldos mi te thesaru menegi?' (4824–4839)

[The warriors went forward, the grim Jewish army, until they had come to Christ. There He stood with His followers, the famous Chieftain. He was awaiting the workings of fate, the glorious time. Judas the man without loyalty went up to Him, bowed his head to God's Child, and spoke to his Lord. He kissed the Mighty One, keeping his word, and indicated Christ to the warriors just as he had said earlier in his words. The Chieftain of Peoples, the Ruler of this world, bore all that with patience, spoke to Judas in His words and asked him frankly, "Why are you coming to Me like this with an army? Why are you leading these people to Me and selling Me to this loathsome Jewish clan, and with your kiss identifying me to this crowd? (159)]

The Jews in the Heliand

As the scene goes on, the crowd asks which one is Jesus and when Jesus says, "It is I," they fall to the ground. The Gospels say little more, but the *Heliand* gives grudging respect to the Jewish warriors who, despite fear, manage to seize the Chieftain:

>Geng imu thô uuið thea man sprekan,
>uuið that uuerod ôðar   endi sie mid is uuordun fragn,
>huene sie mid thiu gesîðiu   sôkean quâmin
>sô niudlico an naht,   'so gi uuillean nôd frummien
>manno huilicumu.'   Thô sprak imu eft thiu menegi angegin,
>quâðun that im hêleand thar   an themu holme uppan
>geuuîsid uuâri,   'the thit giuuer frumid
>Iudeo liudiun   endi ina godes sunu
>selƀon hêtid.   Ina quâmun uui sôkean herod,
>uueldin ina gerno bigeten: he is fan Galileo lande,
>fan Nazarethburg.'   Sô im thô the neriendio Crist
>sagde te sôðan,   that he it selƀo uuas,
>sô uurðun thô an forhtun   folc Iudeono,
>uurðun underbadode,   that sie under bac fellun
>alle efno sân,   erðe gisôhtun,
>uuiðeruuardes that uuerod: ni mahte that uuord godes,
>thie stemnie antstandan: uuârun thoh sô strîdige man,
>ahliopun eft up an themu holme,   hugi fastnodun,
>bundun briostgithâht,   gibolgane gengun
>nâhor mid nîðu,   anttat sie thene neriendion Crist
>uuerodo biuurpun. (4838–4858)

[Then He went to speak to the other men, the (Jewish) warriors, and asked them in His words why they had come looking for Him at night, bringing their warrior-companions with them, "as if you want to cause trouble for someone." The crowd spoke back to Him and said that they had been told that the Healer was up here on the hill, the one who creates mobs among the Jewish people and calls Himself God's Son. "We have come here looking for Him, we are anxious to find Him. He is from

> Galileeland, from Nazareth." As the rescuing Christ told them in soothsaying that He was the one, the Jewish people became frightened; they were so terrified that they instantly fell backwards and every one of them was on the ground. The army of warriors pulled back in retreat – they could not stand up to the Word, the voice, of God. But there were some real fighting men among them who ran back up the hill, strengthened their resolve, controlled their inner feelings, and went raging forward in hatred until they had Christ the Rescuer surrounded by their men. (159; italics mine)]

There is more than a little admiration expressed for so brave a Jewish enemy that they would rush forward to arrest someone who speaks with the voice of God. Then, too, the bravery of a protagonist is estimated by the impressiveness of the antagonist, as can be seen in the Anglo-Saxon epics, especially *Beowulf.*

In accord with his purpose of Saxonizing the Gospel story, the *Heliand* poet everywhere depicts Jesus as a Saxon chieftain, and consequently, never as a Jew. Jesus is taken captive in the manner in which pagan Saxons were by Christian Franks: he is loaded with body chains and manacles as were Saxon prisoners of war (in the Gospels Jesus is occasionally referred to as bound, never as chained). Jesus and Peter are annoyed by an arrogant earl asking for the head tax as were the conquered Saxons. The Jews in the *Heliand*, however, outside of the infancy narrative, are always described as non-Saxons, as a foreign army, as a different people, and their behavior toward Christ is seen both as something unfit for a Saxon – the authors point! – and as betrayal of clan loyalty for their own chieftain. In an especially artistic stroke, the word for the high priest Caiaphas, who is the one who arranges for the condemnation and death of Christ, is not a local Germanic word. The author takes no chance on using a word from the Germanic world that might lend itself to a reading that Christ was condemned by Saxons. Caiaphas is called a bishop – Christ is condemned by "bishop Caiaphas," thus suggesting instead

The Jews in the Heliand

that Christ's execution is associated with Christian political power (lines 4147, 4469). Frankish behavior in the Saxon wars might, it is suggested, have been opposed to Christ. Onto the Jews, ironically, is loaded the resentment that Saxons must have harbored against Christian Franks after their thirty-year war of conquest and submission, a war still sporadically flaring up during the time of the writing of the *Heliand*. The author attempts to divert the negative feelings that Saxons must have had about their forced conversion away from Christ and onto the Franks/Jews in his narrative.

The adjectives used for the Jews in the *Heliand* are thus so condemnatory and strong as to shock the reader. The Jews are "a different kind of people" *mislike man*, they are "evil-minded," "slithery-hearted" *slithmodag*. Even more ominously for Northern Europe, Jews are "hostile," "cruel" *grimmig*, "people from the South" *sutharliudi*. The adjectives serve to get actual feelings and prejudices of the Saxons, whether against Franks or people from the Mediterranean South, into the text of the Gospel story and thus render it emotionally closer to them and less emotionally foreign. The cry of the Jewish mob, "His blood be upon us and upon our children," is made into a dangerous magic curse in the *Heliand*: "Let his gore pour over us, his blood and his death-curse, his *ban-edi*."

The sad thing for real Jews in all this, however, is that about fifty years after the writing of the *Heliand*, the Ottonian Saxon line took over the throne of Charlemagne's Frankish empire. From that point on there would no longer be that complex ambiguity in reading the role of the "evil-minded" Jews in the *Heliand* as being, at least in part, an allusion to the behavior of the imperial Franks. It would all be read as Jewish behavior.

Curiously enough, the place in the *Heliand* where the Jews are most condemned, perhaps more than in the Passion, as engaging in "injustice, pure and simple," *unreht ênfald*, is in the pericope of driving the money changers out of the temple. Before looking at the background of this text, it will be good to look at the incident in the Gospel text which we believe the poet had before him, Tatian's Diatessaron:

> Et intravit Ihesus in templum dei, et cum fecisset quasi flagellum de funiculis, eiciebat omnes vendentes et ementes in templo, oves quoque et boves et mensas nummulariorum, effudit aes, et cathedras vendentium columbas evertit, Et dicit eis: auferte ista hinc, et nolite facere domum patris mei domum negotiationis. Scriptum est: domus mea domus orationis vocabitur omnibus gentibus, vos autem fecistis eam speluncam latronum.

> [And Jesus went into the temple of God, and when he had made a kind of whip of ropes he threw out all the sellers and buyers in the temple, the sheep too and the oxen and he threw over the tables of the money changers (nummulariorum), dumped the coins, and overturned the chairs of the dove sellers. And he says to them: "Take this stuff (ista) out of here, and do not make my father's house a sales' house. It is written: My house will be called a house of prayer for all peoples – you have made it a den of thieves."][5]

In the *Heliand* this scene becomes one of more severe condemnation. Nowhere else does the author insert a phrase as strong as "pure injustice" *unreht ênfald*. It is a phrase that even Jesus is not depicted in the Gospels as using, angry though he might have been. The same scene in the *Heliand* becomes:

> Thô he an thene uuîh innen,
> geng an that godes hûs: fand thar Iudeono filu,
> mislike man,   manage atsamne,
> thea im thar côpstedi   gikoran habdun,
> mangodun im thar mid manages huî: muniterias sâtun

---

5   The Latin text is quoted from Eduard Sievers, ed., *Tatian: Lateinisch und altdeutsch mit ausführlichem Glossar*, 2nd ed., Bibliothek des ältesten deutschen Literatur-Denkmäler 5 (Paderborn: Ferdinand Schöningh, 1892; repr. 1966), 167 (ch. 117).

an themu uuîhe innan, habdun iro uuesl gidago
garu te geɓanne. That uuas themu godes barne
al an andun: drêf sie ut thanen
rûmo fan themu rakude, quað that uuâri rehtara dâd
that thar te bedu fôrin barn Israheles
'endi an thesumu mînumu hûse helpono biddean,
that sia sigidrohtin sundiono tuomie,
than hêr theoɓas an thingstedi halden,
thea faruuarhton uueros uuehsal driɓan,
unreht ênfald. (3733–3747)

[Then He went into the holy shrine, the house of God. There He found many Jews, a different kind of people (*mislike man*), gathered – they had chosen this place as their business place (*côpstedi*). They were buying and selling all manner of things. Moneylenders (*muniterias*, a foreign word, from Latin *moneta*) were sitting inside the shrine; every day they had their exchange money ready to give. That was completely repulsive to God's Son. He drove them out of there, away from the shrine. He said it would be a much better thing for the sons of Israel to come there to pray, to ask for help (a Germanic lord's feudal obligation) in My house, to ask that the victorious Chieftain (*sigidrohtin*, a Germanic title) take away their sins rather than come here to an assembly of thieves, the perverted people who practice usury, plain injustice! (122–23)]

While other passages suggest at least partial displaced hostility against the Franks, the hostility here may genuinely target contemporary Jews. In the original Diatessaron the word *Jew* does not occur even once in this passage. In the original, it is solely the inappropriateness of the place where the business is occurring that is the problem, not the business itself. The *Heliand* author has removed the whip from the scene, but has made it clearly Jewish (twice mentioning them by name), and has condemned the practice of money changing as a business done by a "different kind of people," who engage in a practice which is itself a perversion and an act of pure injustice! What stands between the Diatessaron's and the *Heliand*'s versions of the story is the passage of seven hundred years of time, the Christian church's intervening condemnation of usury, understood broadly, and the poet's anger at the Jews for making a business of charging money for money: usury.[6] Significantly, the Old Testament also strongly condemns and forbids taking interest on a loan or exchange as sinful. The prohibition is to be found in three places:

> And if thy brother be waxen poor and his means fail with thee [...] Take no interest of him or increase; but fear they God [...] Thou shalt not give him they money upon interest. (Leviticus 25.35–37)

> If thou lend money to any of my people [...] thou shalt not be to him as a creditor (nosheh), neither shall ye lay upon him interest. (Exodus 22.24)

> Thou shalt not lend upon interest to thy brother: interest of money, interest of victuals, interest of anything that is lent upon interest. Unto a foreigner thou mayest lend upon interest; but unto thy brother thou shalt not lend upon interest; that the Lord thy God may bless thee in all that thou puttest thy hand unto. (Deuteronomy 23.20–21)

There are two sources for the author's anger at the Jews for the practice of taking interest on money loaned or exchanged: both the church's universal condemnation of the practice and the author's own condemnation based on his notion of wealth (jewels and conquered treasure) from the world of Germanic epic tradition, as being the expression of inner worth and the source of generosity.[7]

---

6 S.v. "usury" in the *Encyclopedia Judaica*, ed. Cecil Roth and Geoffrey Wigoder (Jerusalem: Keter, 1971–72).
7 Aristotle also condemned the practice of taking any money above the

The Jews in the Heliand

The church never clearly defined usury but first condemned the practice officially in a letter of Pope Leo the Great in the year 443 as something done by those who are held captive by desire for filthy profit (*lucri turpis cupiditate captatos*), who wish to get rich off usury (*faenore velle ditescere*).⁸ The church thus at that time forbade making money off money on the basis of the avoidance of the sin of avarice (unless condemnation of usury arose from anger at the Jews) rather than any New Testament dictum, and it did so especially for clerics – who more, even, than most Christians should not resemble Jews. At the time of the *Heliand*, four hundred years later, the capitularies of Charlemagne forbade usury to everyone, not merely ecclesiastics, citing both Pope Leo's letter and also the "law of the folk,"⁹ that is, Germanic tradition – something that would identify usurers as "foreign," "a different kind of people."

> Money had no place in the epic poems of Homer, just as it had no place in the lives of his heroes. In the words of Voltaire, "Agamemnon might have had treasure, but certainly no money." Commerce did not appear in Homer's poetry in which men pursued honor, not [monetary] wealth [...] They did not negotiate, compromise, or argue over the value of worldly goods. The strongest demanded that goods be given to them as tribute for use in their campaigns; they did not deign to haggle with shopkeepers. [...] Commerce had little meaning for Odysseus and his comrades because they lived in a world that did not yet know money.¹⁰

---

amount in the principal. Aristotle, however, was not really that well known in Europe until the High Middle Ages, some four hundred years after the writing of the *Heliand*.

8 Heinrich Denzinger, *Kompendium der glaubensbekenntnisse und kirchlichen Lehrentscheidungen*, 37th ed., rev. Peter Hünermann (Freiburg: Herder, 1991), 131.

9 John T. Noonan, *The Scholastic Analysis of Usury* (Cambridge, Mass.: Harvard UP, 1957), 11–17.

10 J. McIver Weatherford, *The History of Money: From Sandstone to Cyberspace*

This is the world of the Saxon North, as well, of *Beowulf* and the *Heliand*, a world now threatened by the intrusion of the exchange of money instead of the gift of wealth. The author is so concerned with the thought that the Gospel story might actually justify usury that he completely eliminates the parable of the talents from his book. In this parable (Matt 25.14–30, similarly Luke 19.12–27), Jesus depicts a lord giving three servants different amounts of money. The lord is very happy with the first two because each of them multiplied their money while he was away. The third servant is condemned for doing nothing with the amount he was given (he buried it out of fear). The lord then says to him that he could have at least given it to the bankers so that he could have earned some interest on it. Even though this parable could be understood metaphorically, the *Heliand* author chooses instead to suppress it completely in his version of the Gospel.

The reason for the suppression is the differing notion of wealth in the epic tradition of the North.[11] In the language of this tradition, Jesus has treasure, as does God, but no money. When Jesus is born in the *Heliand*, he is wrapped in swaddling clothes and jewels. Whenever the poor are presented in the *Heliand*, it is with a certain suspicion that they have come not so much to be enriched by Jesus's teaching but rather because they know that rich people will be around to give them alms. When Jesus dies on the cross, the veil of the temple is split in two and, in the *Heliand*, the people can see the "treasure hoard" hidden so long in the holy of holies. Wealth is, as in the book of Revelation and in the description of the heavenly Jerusalem, radiant like jewels and precious stones. From

---

(New York: Crown, 1997), 28–29.

11   For an excellent study of the rational concept of wealth in the North, I recommend Mark Dreisonstok, *The Pagan-Christian Concept of Wealth and its Relationship to Light in the* Heliand *and in* Beowulf, *with Consideration of Other Anglo-Saxon Works* (PhD diss., Georgetown University, 2000). Much of what I say here is based on this study.

this comes the view that wealth radiates itself, it does not gather in. The prime analogy for wealth, then, is the jewel – which refracts and reflects light outward, unlike the dark coin. In *Beowulf*, for example, it is only the murky light of Grendel's home that does not radiate outward. His spoils and his light are forever confined by the gloomy walls of the underwater cave. Like money, Grendel and his dam aim at accumulating in darkness, attracting to themselves, at interest, at keeping and increasing. It is no wonder that the author of the *Heliand* sees using money to acquire more money as a perversion of his notion of wealth as radiant; he sees wealth as goodness was seen in the medieval commonplace: radiant of itself – *diffusivum sui*. Beowulf radiates his wealth in chieftain-like style, giving to those who help, such as to the coast guard who watched over his ship as he fought the monster. In the *Heliand* even the poor woman who gives her two small coins to the temple treasury is praised to the heavens because, though poor, she is "wealthy." She radiates what she has, like a jewel.

It may have been that both the Saxon poet and the Carolingian capitularies saw the coming of money and usury as a serious threat to the Germanic-Christian tradition of treating wealth in jewels and gold as the basis for generosity and munificence. The cultural threat to this ideal lay concealed even in those very capitularies of Charlemagne that prohibited usury: Penalties and fines against the Saxons are given in terms of the Byzantine *solidus*, a coin. The enemy was not at the gates but already within. Within the author's apologetic purpose, attributing the desire to commit the sin of acquisitive usury to the Jews, the "sons of Israel," was a telling way to make a stand against usury. The practice is described as being that of the opponents of Christ, something done only by *mislike man* "a different kind of people," a people not familiar with the ancient heroic custom and the "law of the folk." Then, calling on the ancient prejudice of those Northern climes against the slippery slyness, real or imagined, of those from warmer climes: all these things against Christ are only done by Southern people, *sutharliuti*.¹² The Jews in the *Heliand* are made to play a complex role whose detailed characteristics come from the ninth century as well as from the first.

Last of all we must not imagine that the *Heliand* author wants us to think Jesus died for the sins and because of the sins of the Jews alone. In his description of the Crucifixion he lets the reader known at the end that the Jews in the story of Christ are really, when all is said and done, a stand-in for the whole human race and its behavior, and not just acting for themselves:

> Uuerod Iudeono
> sô manag mislîc thing   an mahtigna Crist
> sagdun te sundium.   Hie suîgondi stuod
> thuru ôðmuodi,   ne antuuordida niouuiht
> uuið iro uurêðun uuord: uuolda thesa uuerold alla
> lôsian mid is lîƀu: bithiu liet hie ina thia lêðun thiod
> uuêgian te uundron,   all sô iro uuillio geng:
> ni uuolda im opanlîco   allon cûðian
> Iudeo liudeon,   that hie uuas god selƀo;
> huand uuissin sia that te uuâron,   that hie sulica giuuald haƀdi
> oƀar theson middilgard,   than uurði im iro muodseƀo
> giblôðit an iro briostun: thann ne gidorstin sia that barn godes
> antlocan liohto mêst   liudio barnon.
> Bethiu mêð hie is sô an muode,   ne lêt that manno folc
> uuitan, huat sia uuarahtun. (5379–5394)

[The Jewish people said many different sinful things about mighty Christ. He stood there, keeping silent in patient humility. He did not answer their hostile words, He wanted to free

---

12   Jews were not religiously bound by Christian injunctions against the practice of usury. Did the author possibly have contact with Jews in the ninth century who would have exchanged money for livestock, or money for money and charged a fee? The question is impossible to answer but finds later literary resonance, of course, in Shakespeare's Shylock.

the whole world with His life – that is why He let the evil clan subject him to whatever terrible torture they desired. He did not want to let all the Jewish people know openly that He was God Himself. For, if they really knew how much power He had over this middle world, their feelings would turn cowardly within their breasts and they would never dare to lay their hands on the Son of God, and then the kingdom of heaven, the brightest of the worlds, would never be unlocked to the sons of men. Because of this He hid it in his heart and did not let the human clan know what they were doing. (177)]

That is the ultimate role that the Jews in the *Heliand* play: They are the human race in its treatment of its God-with-us. Perhaps this accounts as well for the intensity of the author's treatment of the Jews.

Jesus Christ between Jews and Heathens:

The Germanic Mission and the Portrayal of Christ in the Old Saxon *Heliand*[1]

Martin Friedrich

(Translated by Ariane Fischer and James Pasternak)

I

In 1934, the Berlin missiologist Johannes Witte wrote a brochure entitled *How did Christianity Come to the Germanen?*[2] Contrary to the position of the nationalist movement (*völkische Bewegung*) of the time, he wanted to show that Christianity had been a blessing for them. The *Germanen*, he thought, were ripe for the Gospel, and could therefore quickly internalize it and forge a Germanic

---

1 Originally "Jesus Christus zwischen Juden und Heiden: Das Christusbild in der Germanenmission, dargestellt am *Heliand*," *Zeitschrift für Kirchengeschichte* 113 (2002), 313–28.
2 Johannes Witte, *Wie kam das Christentum zu den Germanen?* (Gotha: L. Klotz 1934). On Witte, see for instance G. Rosenkranz, "Witte, Johannes," in *Die Religion in Geschichte und Gegenwart: Handwörterbuch für Theologie und Religionswissenschaft*, ed. Kurt Galling, 3rd ed., 7 vols. (Tübingen: Mohr, 1957–65), 6:1781. [The translators of this chapter have at times preferred to use the German word *Germanen* of the original text, which lacks the awkwardness present in available English renderings such as "early Germanic tribes" or "Teutons." -Ed.]

Jesus Christ between Jews and Heathens

Christianity.³ In the Middle Ages, the Germanization of Christianity supposedly found its realization in Martin Luther, though it was still colored by Roman influences. Among other things, according to Witte, this meant that "in the case of Luther [. . .] even the slightest hint of Judaic law, which is so present in Paul, is absent from the depiction of Christ's sacrifice [. . .]."⁴ This example is enough to show that, on various occasions, peculiar ideas have formed around this ideologically charged topic. Representatives of popular religiosity, such as Mathilde Ludendorff, associated Christianity and Judaism closely with one another, and spoke therefore of the crime of Christianization, by which an essentially alien Semitic religion was forced upon the *Germanen*.⁵ Clerics, for their part, defended Christianization as something that purified both Germanness (*Germanentum*) as well as Christianity, allowing them to fulfill their destiny. According to this reading, Christianity was purged, in the course of Germanization, of its offensive features, foremost among which were its Roman qualities, though its Jewishness was not far behind.

Given the nature of the debate, it is not surprising that discussion of the Germanic mission, which was lively in the first half of the twentieth century, ebbed appreciably after 1945. The two German Church historians of today who have dealt most intensively with this period, Knut Schäferdiek and Arnold Angenendt, have rejected the thesis of the Germanization of Christianity,⁶ and only in recent years

---

3   See ibid., 26–31: "Die Schaffung eines deutschen Christentums" [The creation of a Germanic Christianity].
4   Ibid., 28: "bei Luther [. . .] auch der leiseste Hauch des Jüdisch-Juridischen in der Auffassung des Sühnentodes Christi [fehlt], das bei Paulus vorhanden ist [. . .]."
5   A historiographic assessment of the debate sparked by the nationalist movement [*völkische Bewegung*] over the mission to the *Germanen* is lacking. For the best overview, see Kurt Dietrich Schmidt, *Die Bekehrung der Ostgermanen zum Christentum: Der ostgermanische Arianismus* (Göttingen: Vandenhoeck & Ruprecht, 1939), 11–62.
6   See Knut Schäferdiek, "Germanen. § 46: Christianisierung," in *Reallexikon*

have Anglophone researchers dared to broach the topic. In doing so, they have renewed the argument – a portentous gesture – that the Germanization of Christianity brought with it a corruption of the Christian message, the consequences of which, they claim, could be felt into the twentieth century.[7]

Generalizations regarding the conversion of the *Germanen*, of course, are hardly possible. It is debatable whether the Germanic peoples who adopted Christianity between the fourth and the twelfth centuries shared anything more in common with one another than certain linguistic connections. In any event, there was a vast di-

---

der germanischen Altertumskunde, ed. Johannes Hoops et al., 2nd ed., vol. 11 (Berlin: Walter de Gruyter, 1998), 388–395, at 388–90; and Arnold Angenendt, *Das Frühmittelalter: Die abendländische Christenheit von 400 bis 900*, 2nd ed. (Stuttgart: W. Kohlhammer, 1995), 36–42. Both works contain a short summary of the discussion with an analysis of the problems. For a history of the literature, see Hermann Dörries, "Zur Frage der Germanisierung des Christentums," in *Wort und Stunde*, by Dörries, 3 vols. (Göttingen: Vandenhoeck & Ruprecht 1966–70), 2:190–209.

7   See especially James C. Russell, *The Germanization of Early Medieval Christianity: A Sociohistorical Approach to Religious Transformation* (New York: Oxford UP, 1994); and Samuel P. Scheibler, *Golgotha and Götterdämmerung: German Religious Paradigm Shifts and the Proclamation of the Gospel* (New York: Peter Lang, 1996). Russell speaks of a contradiction between, on the one hand, the Germanic religion, which being Indo-European was characterized by its *Volk*-orientation and affirmation of the secular and, on the other hand, Christianity as an anti-secular Asiatic religion of salvation. In the mission to the *Germanen*, Christianity took on the features of the Germanic religion because its message was conveyed in a diluted manner. Although this was meant to be temporary, it established itself through the influence of the Ottonian rulers on the entire Western Church. The negative consequences were partially reversed in the reform movements of the Middle Ages, in the Reformation, and at the Second Vatican Council. Scheibler also postulates that the *Germanen* (mis-)understood Christian concepts in light of their religious beliefs and that this resulted in a "commingling of the *Edda* and the Gospel." In this regard, both borrow Heinrich Böhmer's thesis, which he formulated as early as 1913. See Dörries, "Zur Frage der Germanisierung" [note 6], 197–98; and Angenendt, *Das Frühmittelalter* [note 6], 38.

vide separating the nomadic tribes of the migration era from the highly developed kingdoms of Scandinavia on the threshold of the High Middle Ages. Practically all we know about the pre-Christian Germanic religion is from Old Norse sources, and even these should be approached with great reservation.[8] Finally, our knowledge of the history of the Christianization is itself is filled with numerous gaps. The sources allow few definitive statements regarding the ways in which Christianity was introduced to the *Germanen*, and so it is no coincidence that good general surveys continue to be rare.[9]

Below I shall concern myself with an old question, namely: What role can be attributed to Judaism in the type of Christianity that emerged in this new world? In this matter, as in every church-historical approach to this loaded relationship, two errors are to be avoided. The first is that dark pessimism which depicts the entire history of Christianity, in an undifferentiated manner, as nothing but a series of disenfranchisements and persecutions of the Jews. The second is the opposite of the first, that is, a whitewashing of history that projects contemporary perceptions, as we like them, onto the past. (The evaluation of the Germanic mission by church historians in the 1920s and 30s provides, of course, a striking example of this.) In addition, certain avenues of investigation will also be avoided: (1) The status of the Jews in the early Middle Ages will not enter my discussion. While it is true that the popularity enjoyed by the Jews

---

8   It is above all due to the work of Walter Baetke, who demonstrated Christian influences in medieval Icelandic literature, that the problem of the sources was placed in a new light. See his *Kleine Schriften: Geschichte, Recht und Religion in germanischem Schrifttum*, ed. Kurt Rudolph and Ernst Walter (Weimar: Böhlau, 1973), esp. 206–46, 319–50, and 370–74.

9   Aside from Russell's work [note 7], a less ideological treatment of the subject is Carole M. Cusack's *Conversion among the Germanic Peoples* (London: Cassell, 1998). Despite her use of sociological and psychological categories, Cusack's work produces hardly any new conclusions. In German, there is Lutz E. von Padberg's *Die Christianisierung Europas im Mittelalter* (Stuttgart: Reclam, 1998), which is intended for non-specialists.

at the Carolingian court, for example, accords with the warm image of them living in harmony with Christians before the Crusades,¹⁰ the harsh and violent attempts to convert them, undertaken in the Frankish and Visigothic kingdoms, would also have to be addressed.¹¹ Here, however, I have omitted the entire external history; only at the end will an explanation be offered for the ambivalent attitude of the Germanic peoples and the increasing anti-Semitism in the High Middle Ages. (2) The thesis associated with so-called Germanic Arianism is untenable, namely that there existed a Germanic inclination toward a human conception of Christ that deviated from the Greek idea of the Trinity.¹² Arian – or rather Homoian – Christianity happened to have gained currency in Byzantium when the Goths converted to Christianity and was not retained among the latter on account of some special theological compatibility.¹³ Homoianism

---

10   See for example Bernhard Blumenkranz, "Die Entwicklung im Westen zwischen 200 und 1200," in *Kirche und Synagoge: Handbuch zur Geschichte von Christen und Juden*, ed. Karl Heinrich Rengstorf and Siegfried von Kortzfleisch (Stuttgart: Klett, 1968), 84–135, esp. 109–10; Marianne Awerbuch, *Christlich-jüdische Begegnung im Zeitalter der Frühscholastik*, Abhandlung zum christlich-jüdischen Dialog 8 (Munich: Kaiser, 1980), 13–17; and Angenendt, *Das Frühmittelalter* [note 6], 377–78.

11   See Blumenkranz, "Die Entwicklung" [note 10], 102–07; Angenendt, *Das Frühmittelalter* [note 6], 165–75; and Amnon Linder, "Christlich-Jüdische Konfrontation im kirchlichen Frühmittelalter," in *Die Kirche des früheren Mittelalters*, ed. Knut Schäferdiek, Kirchengeschichte als Missionsgeschichte 2 (Munich: Kaiser, 1978), 397–441, esp. 418–20, 429–30.

12   See Helmut Lother, *Die Christusauffassung der Germanen* (Gütersloh: C. Bertelsmann 1937), 19–20: "The human-heroic image, according to which Christ became a demi-god, was accessible for the Germanic tribes, whereas Greek speculation was alien to them" [Die menschlich-heldische Vorstellung, nach der Christus zum Halbgott wurde, war den Germanen zugänglich, griechische Spekulation war ihnen fremd]. Schmidt argued similarly in *Die Bekehrung der Ostgermanen* [note 5], 275–76, 431–38.

13   See Hanns Christof Brennecke, "Christianisierung und Identität: Das Beispiel der germanischen Völker," in *Missionsgeschichte, Kirchengeschichte, Weltgeschichte: Christliche Missionen im Kontext nationaler Entwicklungen in Afrika, Asien und*

itself, incidentally, was a product of the Greek imagination,[14] and can hardly be regarded as an extension of Judeo-Christian Christology – just as little as Spanish Adoptionism can, which was combated by the court theologians at Aachen in the era of Charlemagne.[15] (3) Of slight significance, too, is the esteem of the Old Testament that was held early on among the Franks.[16] This had at its heart statutory provisions of the law, and of course the royal ideology as well, and had little to do with an understanding of the person and work of Christ. Only one detail is worthy of mention, namely the introduction of the Festival of the Circumcision that appeared in the sixth and seventh centuries among the Franks and the Visigoths.[17] This can be considered the earliest evidence of the fact that the *Germanen* had a deeper appreciation of Christ's roots in Judaism than did the Roman Christians, in whose festival calendar the date appeared much later. The specific background, however, is unclear.

Instead of these approaches, the focus below – though generally concerned with the transformation of Christianity – will be narrowed to the sub-question of how the *Germanen* perceived Christ at the time of their conversion. Thus the old debate will be renewed of whether, during the mission to the Germanic tribes, the Gospel was falsified or asserted with new clarity. To be precise: Did the *Germanen*, in their appropriation of the figure of Christ, see only the immortal

---

Ozeanien, ed. Ulrich van der Heyden and Heike Liebau, Missionsgeschichtliches Archiv 1 (Stuttgart: F. Steiner, 1996), 239–247, at 244–247; Knut Schäferdiek, "Die geschichtliche Stellung des sogenannten germanischen Arianismus," in *Die Kirche des früheren Mittelalters* [note 11], 79–90.

14 Hermann Dörries, "Germanische Nationalkirchen," in *Wort und Stunde* [note 6], 2:76–111, here 2:81–84.
15 See Angenendt, *Das Frühmittelalter* [note 5], 349.
16 See for instance Raymund Kottje, *Studien zum Einfluss des Alten Testaments auf Recht und Liturgie des frühen Mittelalters (6.-8. Jahrhundert)*, 2nd ed., Bonner historische Forschungen 23 (Bonn: Ludwig Röhrscheid, 1970); and Awerbuch, *Christlich-jüdische Begegnung* [note 10], 71–73.
17 Kottje, *Studien zum Einfluss des Alten Testaments* [note 16], 84–86.

God, the ruler and king, and thereby advance the detachment of Christianity from its Judaic roots?[18] Or did they possess a deeper understanding of the biblical narrative and thus contribute not to the removal of the Jewish presence from the story (*Entjudaisierung*) but rather, in some respects, to its reassertion?

Christian poetry from the latter years of the conversion could serve as the basis of such an examination. However, I will exclude the Anglo-Saxon songs, in which Christ is depicted as a warrior against otherworldly forces.[19] It might also be worth examining Scandinavian poetry, especially since the role of the mission in this literature has been somewhat neglected in scholarship.[20] The *Niðrstigningar saga* (Gospel of Nicodemus), for instance, celebrates Christ as lord over the powers of hell – like some Old English poetry – but also inserts, unlike its Latin original, passages from the Book of Job.[21] Gamli

---

18 This is the prevalent view in both the older and newer literature. See Kurt Dietrich Schmidt, *Die katholische Mission unter den Westgermanen* (Göttingen: Vandenhoeck & Ruprecht, 1939), 62–66, 151–62; idem, *Germanischer Glaube und Christentum: Einzeldarstellungen aus dem Umbruch der deutschen Frühgeschichte* (Göttingen: Vandenhoeck & Ruprecht 1948), esp. 51–65, 74–76; Régis Boyer, *Le Christ des barbares: Le monde nordique (IXe-XIIIe S.)* (Paris: Cerf, 1987), 145–150; Angenendt, *Das Frühmittelalter* [note 6], 421–23.

19 See Schmidt's interpretation of the literature in *Die katholische Mission* [note 18], 151–62; idem, *Germanischer Glaube* [note 18], 53–58; Heinrich Bornkamm, *Christus und die Germanen* (Berlin: Verlag des Evangelischen Bundes, 1936), 6–8; Lother, *Die Christusauffassung der Germanen* [note 12], 29–34.

20 Boyer's *Le Christ des barbares* [note 18], which promises much at first glance, provides only an overview of the old Germanic religion and the conversion of Scandinavia in order to show, through the saga literature, how Christ was understood during the period of pagan-Christian syncretism. The spiritual poems are only briefly touched upon on page 136. For a study especially focused on the representation of Christ in Old Norse literature, see Fredrik Paasche, "Kristusskikkelsen i gammalnordisk lære, liv og lov," in *Artikler og taler*, by Paasche (Oslo: Aschehoug, 1948), 107–119.

21 Ibid., 108–110; Fredrik Paasche, *Norges og Islands litteratur inntil utgangen av middelalderen,* rev. Anne Holtsmark, Norsk litteratur historie 1 (Oslo: Aschehoug, 1957), 298–99, 334.

kanóki's *Harmsól* and the anonymous *Leiðarvísan* sing about Christ in the traditional skaldic form, and yet manage to incorporate biblical motifs, including some from the Old Testament.[22] However, this literature, written in the eleventh and twelfth centuries, belongs already to the High Middle Ages, with its new Christian piety.[23] Below, therefore, I will consider only that great work pertaining to the Christianization of the Saxons, namely the Old Saxon *Heliand*, a poetic retelling of the Gospels. After surveying the scholarship, I will outline, by way of several examples, how the *Heliand* represents Christ in relation to his – the Jewish – people, and finally I will attempt to determine the specific role of the Germanic mission in the relationship between the Church and Judaism.

II

The *Heliand*, an alliterative poem of almost 6,000 lines, is not only regarded as the most significant Germanic linguistic monument of the ninth century, but has also served as the paradigm for the Germanization of Christianity.[24] August Vilmar, in an influential

---

22   See ibid., 313–15, 335; Wolfgang Lange, *Studien zur christlichen Dichtung der Nordgermanen, 1000–1200*, Palästra 222 (Göttingen: Vandenhoeck & Ruprecht, 1958), 143–57; idem, *Christliche Skaldendichtung* (Göttingen: Vandenhoeck & Ruprecht, 1958), 30–45 (German translations of both poems). In *Harmsól* one detects echoes of the Isaiah 50–66 (the so-called *Gottesknechtlieder*) in stanzas 17, 19, 21 and 27, and echoes of the Psalms in stanzas 35, 38 and 57. In *Leiðarvísan*, which incorporates the old tradition of divine authorship (*Himmelsbrief*), it is not only noteworthy how the Flood and Exodus accounts are featured in the story of salvation, but also how the story of Christ himself is given an Old Testament background (see esp. stanzas 24 and 29).

23   See Paasche, "Kristusskikkelsen" [note 20], 111–12; and idem, *Norges og Islands litteratur* [note 21], 295–96.

24   On the history of scholarship, see Heinz Rupp, *Forschung zur althochdeutschen Literatur 1943–1962* (Stuttgart: Metzler, 1965), 39–50, 54–55; Johannes Rathofer, *Der Heliand. Theologischer Sinn als tektonische Form: Vorbereitung und Grundlegung der Interpretation*, Niederdeutsche Studien 9 (Cologne: Böhlau, 1962), 3–51,

study, was the first to celebrate the *Heliand* as a Germanic refashioning of the Gospel story, in which Christian ideas were overshadowed by the heroic ideal and pagan mythology.[25] The Gospel story, according to Vilmar, appears "as the glorious procession of the German king through his land."[26] This interpretation defined the image of the *Heliand* for nearly a century until Walther Köhler, in the 1930s, formulated an opposing theory; it was, he thought, "not the Germanization of Christianity but the Christianization of Germanness," that characterized the poem.[27] Köhler pointed out, justly, that much of what had been interpreted enthusiastically as Germanic was in fact already present in the poet's sources.

The scholarship after 1945 followed this course for some time, emphasizing the poet's orthodoxy.[28] More and more, however, a

---

205–63; Albrecht Hagenlocher, *Schicksal im Heliand: Verwendung und Bedeutung der nominalen Beziehungen*, Niederdeutsche Studien 21 (Cologne: Böhlau, 1975), 1–8, 13–22. For a more recent survey, see Wolfgang Haubrichs, "Heliand und altdeutsche Genesis," in *Reallexikon der germanischen Altertumskunde*, ed. Johannes Hoops et al., 2nd ed., vol. 14 (Berlin: Walter de Gruyter, 1998), 297–308.

25   On Vilmar, see Rathofer, *Der Heliand* [note 24], 31–32; and G. Ronald Murphy, *The Saxon Savior. The Germanic Transformation of the Gospel in the Ninth-Century Heliand* (New York: Oxford UP, 1989), 3–7.

26   A. F. C. Vilmar, *Deutsche Altertümer im Heliand als Einkleidung der evangelischen Geschichte* (Marburg: N. G. Elwert, 1845), 54: "als der glorreiche Zug eines deutschen Volkskönigs durch sein Land."

27   Walther Köhler, "Das Christusbild im Heliand," *Archiv für Kulturgeschichte* 26 (1936), 265–82, here at 282: "Nicht Germanisierung des Christentums, sondern Christianisierung des Germanentums." He draws partially on the work of Hulda Göhler, "Das Christusbild in Otfrieds Evangelienbuch und im Heliand," *Zeitschrift für deutsche Philologie* 59 (1934–35), 1–52. On Göhler's work, see Rathofer, *Der Heliand* [note 24], 32–36; and Hagenlocher, *Schicksal im Heliand* [note 24], 5–6, 14. Hermann Wicke would follow a similar thread in his little known yet valuable *Das wunderbare Tun des Heiligen Krist nach der altsächsischen Evangelienharmonie: Eine Einführung in das Verständnis des "Heliand"* (Göttingen: Vandenhoeck & Ruprecht, 1935).

28   See for example Heinz Rupp, "Der Heliand: Hauptanliegen seines Dichters," in *Der Heliand*, ed. Jürgen Eichhoff and Irmengard Rauch, Wege der Forschung 321 (Darmstadt: Wissenschaftliche Buchgesellschaft, 1973), 247–69 (originally

Jesus Christ between Jews and Heathens

central question emerged, namely how the poet, probably a monk in the Frankish-Saxon borderland, communicated the Gospel, which in his eyes was unambiguous, to the newly converted Saxon tribe. In other words, the problem of accommodation – or acculturation – rose to the fore. Johannes Rathofer made an important contribution by comparing the adaptation of the Gospel material in *Heliand* with that of Marcan material in the Gospel of Luke.[29] Just as one has to limit any assertion of Hellenization in the case of Luke, so too, in the case of the *Heliand*, one can speak of a Germanization only in a restricted sense. Whatever Germanization might be detected, he thought, remained peripheral and in the service of the orthodox theology of the Carolingian era. In the main part of his work, Rathofer interprets the *Heliand* as a masterfully structured work of art, in which numerical symbolism is the key to understanding. Though he demonstrates his great knowledge of the numerical theories of Carolingian theology, he fails to pursue the question of whether Jewish numerology might have provided a model.[30] Doubtful, too, is his general conclusion, according to which the message of the *Heliand* can be reduced to a narrative reflection of both the doctrine of the Trinity and that of Christ's dual nature (*Zweinaturenlehre*). He perceived the *Heliand* as

---

published in 1956); idem, "The Adoption of Christian Ideas into German, with Reference to the 'Heliand' and to Otfrid's 'Evangelienbuch'," *Parergon* 21 (1978), 33–41; the discussion of the works of Elisabeth Grosch and Gertrud Eberhard in Rupp, *Forschung zur althochdeutschen Literatur* [note 24], 44–45; Rathofer, *Der Heliand* [note 24], 37–50; and Hagenlocher, *Schicksal im Heliand* [note 24], 6, 14–15. This interpretation is further supported, with evidence from Old Norse literature, in Walter Baetke, *Die Aufnahme des Christentums durch die Germanen: Ein Beitrag zur Frage der Germanisierung des Christentums* (Darmstadt: Wissenschaftliche Buchgesellschaft, 1959), 27–38.

29   Rathofer, *Der Heliand* [note 24], 51–194. For appraisal and criticism of Rathofer's ideas, see Rupp, *Forschung zur althochdeutschen Literatur* [note 24], 47–50; and Hagenlocher, *Schicksal im Heliand* [note 24], 6–8, 15–22.

30   In one passage, Rathofer, *Der Heliand* [note 24], 516, mentions the meaning of the Talmud and "Kaballa" (sic), but only in passing.

a product of the learned theology of its time and, in doing so, largely suppressed its Germanic origins.

It is this matter – the Germanic features of the poem – that is reexamined by G. Ronald Murphy, an American Jesuit. In his study of the *Heliand*, he explicitly evokes Vilmar, but not in the unhistorical and uncritical manner of older scholarship.[31] While earlier scholars would interpret putative Germanic features of the *Heliand* without consulting the likely source of the poem, Murphy specifically makes comparisons with Tatian's *Diatessaron*. This work, a Gospel harmony that originated in Syria around 170 and was widely known in the West, has long been recognized as the most important source of the *Heliand*.[32] However, because the *Heliand* was written for the Saxons, he also takes into account the historical background of the work – the violent conversion to Christianity just two generations before – as well as native religious beliefs. His thesis is that the *Heliand* poet produced a true synthesis of Christian and Saxon elements: "The *Heliand* author possessed a deeply respectful attitude toward the values of Germanic religion and culture, but an equally careful regard for his Christianity"; he was capable, therefore, "of transforming the Gospel into the traditional religious imagery and values of his people."[33]

In several essays, the Dutch patristic scholar Gilles Quispel has presented a rather idiosyncratic interpretation.[34] He assumes that

---

31 Murphy, *The Saxon Savior* [note 25]. See also Murphy's English translation of the poem: G. Ronald Murphy, trans., *The Heliand: The Saxon Gospel* (New York: Oxford UP, 1992). It appears that a certain interpretation is gaining popularity in the Anglo-Saxon world that, by going beyond Murphy, can be seen as reverting back to Vilmar's view. See for example Cusack, *Conversion among the Germanic Peoples* [note 9], 129–30, and the literature discussed there.

32 For the history of the literature in the nineteenth century, see William L. Petersen, *Tatian's Diatessaron: Its Creation, Dissemination, Significance, and History in Scholarship*, Supplements to Vigiliae Christianae 25 (Leiden: E. J. Brill, 1994), 105–10.

33 Murphy, *The Saxon Savior* [note 25], ix.

34 Gilles Quispel, "Some Remarks on the Gospel of Thomas," *New*

the *Heliand* is dependent upon a version of the *Diatessaron* that, in contrast to the rest of the Western tradition, has a special affinity with the lost Syriac original and, therefore, reflects the latter's relation to the Gnostic Gospel of Thomas. Thus the *Heliand*, he supposes, preserves certain extra-canonical and – to some degree – authentic Judeo-Christian biblical readings. If this were true, it would be immensely significant to the topic of the Jews and the Germanic mission, but Quispel's complicated argumentation has failed to convince.[35] He offers, incidentally, only a textual comparison – removing a number of individual phrases from their context – and he does not provide any systematic interpretations of the *Heliand*. His assertion that, because of its connection to the Syriac *Diatessaron*, the *Heliand* is more un-Germanic than Germanic should be taken lightly.[36]

III

It is not necessary to refer to the Gospel of Thomas or other apocryphal literature to understand the *Heliand* as a text particularly intimate with the Jewish background of the story of Christ, an intimacy hardly expected in the time of the Germanic mission. The author of the *Heliand* was a highly learned and talented poet who competently shaped his material and struggled to explain the figure of Jesus to his Germanic contemporaries. It remains to be asked how

---

Testament Studies 5 (1959), 276–90, esp. 283–86; idem, "Der Heliand und das Thomasevangelium," *Vigiliae Christianae* 16 (1962), 121–50; idem, "Jewish Influences on the 'Heliand'," in *Religions in Antiquity, Essays in Memory of Erwin Ramsdell Goodenough*, ed. Jacob Neusner (Leiden: E. J. Brill, 1968), 244–250. Concerning his thesis, in which the Heliand is relevant only indirectly, see also Petersen, *Tatian's Diatessaron* [note 32], 272–81, 327–38.

35   From the perspective of a Germanist, Willy Krogmann offered the most significant objections; see his "Heliand, Tatian und Thomasevangelium," *Zeitschrift für neutestamentliche Wissenschaft* 51 (1960), 255–68. Regarding Quispel's other critics, see Petersen, *Tatian's Diatessaron* [note 32], 281–300. A student of Qusipel, Petersen agrees with his teacher.

36   Quispel, "Jewish Influences" [note 34], 249.

the Old Testament background manifests itself in his representation of Christ, and whether he leaves any room for Jesus *qua* Jew among depictions of him as a Germanic king or orthodox Godhead.

To begin with there is the issue of geography. It is quite clear in the *Heliand* that the Gospel originated in the land of the Jews. Though the poet, indeed, eliminated a number of Semitisms and modified the setting of the work to accord with that of his northern homeland, such modifications are relatively minor.[37] The apostles, for instance, travel on Lake Genezareth in a high-keeled longboat,[38] and it is suggested that houses should not be built on sand for fear of the North Sea tides.[39] Nevertheless, he leaves no doubt that Jesus was born in Bethlehem, where David had ruled over the Hebrews,[40] and in the temple of Jerusalem he behaves "according to the custom of the people."[41] In Galilee, moreover, he was raised "in a dignified manner,"[42] and his influence begins at the river Jordan, by the Sea of Galilee, and ends in Jerusalem, the capital of the Jewish people.[43] Such comments, of course, do not exhaust the relationship of Christ to his people. Already in the prophecy of his birth that is related to

---

37 See Rathofer, *Der Heliand* [note 24], 82–114. Despite the following two examples – of the *Heliand* poet's consideration for his pagan audience – Rathofer's chapter title, "Weitgehende Tilgung des jüdischen Hintergrundes," is far from justified.

38 See lines 2265–2266 and 2906–2908. The *Heliand* is cited from the following edition: Otto Behaghel, ed., *Heliand und Genesis*, 10th ed., rev. Burkhard Taeger, Altdeutsche Textbibliothek 4 (Tübingen: Max Niemeyer, 1996). Lengthy translations below are based on Murphy, *The Heliand* [note 31]. For an interpretation of lines 2906–2908, see Murphy, *The Saxon Savior* [note 25], 65–67.

39 Lines 1801–1824. For commentary, see Rathofer, *Der Heliand* [note 24], 90–91.

40 Lines 356–365.

41 Line 454: "thero liudeo landsidu."

42 Line 1137: "tîrlîco atogan."

43 Line 3543. This small selection of place names, which can easily be expanded, is enough to illustrate that, contrary to the impression left Rathofer, only a few place names have been removed.

Jesus Christ between Jews and Heathens

Herod, Christ is referred to as the "beloved protector of the country, [. . .] the mighty counselor who will rule the Jewish people."[44] In the temple, Simeon makes the following remark to the child Jesus (lines 489–492):

> Thîna cumi sindun
> te dôma endi te diurðon,   drohtin frô mîn,
> aƀarun Israhelas,   êganumu folke,
> thînum lioƀun liudun.

[Your coming, my Lord Chieftain, brings glory and honor to the sons of Israel, Your own clan, Your own dear people.]

In his description of when the twelve-year-old Jesus was in the Temple, moreover, the poet adds certain details not found in his sources. In the *Heliand* (lines 808–811), Jesus is found:

> an them uuîha innan,   thar the *uuîsa* man,
> suuîðo glauuua gumon   *an* godes êuua
> lâsun ende lînodun,   huô sie lof scoldin
> uuirkean mid iro uuordun   them, the thesa uuerold giscôp.

[inside the temple, where wise and intelligent men read and learn in God's law how to praise the One who made the world with human words.]

In the Gospel of Luke, as in Tatian, neither the law nor the praise of God is mentioned,[45] yet such things are fundamental to the teaching and learning that took place at Temple. These additions correspond well with a general feature in the *Heliand*, which tends to emphasize

---

44   Lines 626-628: "liof landes uuard [. . .] the rihtien scal Iudeono gumskepi."
45   See Tatian, ch. 12, in Achim Masser, ed., *Die lateinisch-althochdeutsche Tatianbilingue Stiftsbibliothek St. Gallen Cod. 56*, Studien zum Althochdeutschen 25 (Göttingen: Vandenhoeck & Ruprecht, 1994), 99.

Christ's teaching over his performance of miracles – it is largely through his teaching, in other words, that Jesus is presented as the Savior.[46] Though Rathofer was quick to notice this point,[47] he failed to draw a connection to the Gospel of Matthew, in which Jesus is portrayed, from a Jewish-Christian perspective, as an ideal teacher of the Torah.[48]

Examples of Jesus's rabbinic behavior in the poem could be multiplied, as can those of his messianic presence. His most common appellation, after all, is *Crist* 'messiah', and he is also called *sunu Dauides* 'the son of David' and *friðubarn godes* 'God's child of peace'.[49] The Hellenistic titles Son of God and Savior are also used, but not preferred, and such Germanic terms as *landes uuard* 'guardian of the land' and *mundboro* 'protector' are not especially common. Finally, the title *kuning* 'king', which appears so frequently in the work, has clear messianic undertones.[50]

---

46   See Bernhard Sowinski, *Darstellungsstil und Sprachstil im Heliand,* Kölner germanistische Studien 21 (Cologne: Böhlau, 1985), 274–75.
47   Rathofer, *Der Heliand* [note 24], 447, remarks that, to Jesus's teaching, the *Heliand* poet assigns "die entscheidene soteriologische Funktion" [the deciding soteriological function].
48   See Alexander Sand, *Das Matthäus-Evangelium,* Erträge der Forschung 275 (Darmstadt: Wissenschaftliche Buchgesellschaft, 1991), esp. 34, 62, 103–4.
49   See Sowinski, *Darstellungsstil und Sprachstil* [note 46], 272–73, for a list of Christ's titles in the *Heliand*. For examples of *sunu Dauides*, see lines 2991 (which has no precedent in Tatian), 3563, and 3682; for *friðubarn godes*, which has no parallel in the Diatessaron, see lines 667, 983, and 2099.
50   The implications of this word to the Saxons will be considered below. In scholarship, the relationship between temporal and spiritual kingdoms in the *Heliand* is an issue of its own. See for example Köhler, "Das Christusbild im Heliand" [note 27], 272–78; Wicke, *Das wunderbare Tun* [note 28], 100–01; and Rathofer, *Der Heliand* [note 24], 39–40, 401–15. Linked to this is also the question of whether the disciples' relationship to Christ is understood in terms of the *comitatus,* a matter that features strongly in older *Heliand* research; see for example Baetke, *Die Aufnahme des Christentums* [note 28], 30–36; and Dörries, "Zur Frage der Germanisierung" [note 6], 264–266.

Jesus Christ between Jews and Heathens

At the same time, it cannot be denied that the poet views the Jews' relationship to their Messiah as extremely antagonistic. After the calling of the first disciples, the poet places Christ in the company of Jews with wicked intentions (lines 1227–1230):

>   Sume uuârun sie im eft Iudeono cunnies,
> fêgni folcskepi: uuârun *thar gefarana* te thiu,
> that sie ûses drohtines   dâdio endi uuordo
> fâron *uuoldun*,   habdun im *fêgnien* hugi,
> uurêðen uuillion: uuoldun uualdand Crist
> alêdien them liudiun.

[Some of them were of the Jewish clan, sneaky people. They had come there to spy on our Chieftain's deeds and words, they had a sneaky attitude of mind and ill-will. They wanted to make Ruling Christ loathsome to the people.][51]

Such statements recur as a leitmotif throughout the text. Often without precedent in either the Gospels or Tatian, observations about the hostility of the Jews feature in nearly every scene.[52] The negative depiction of the Jews increases steadily and reaches its peak at the Passion, for which the *Heliand* holds the Jews solely responsible. (In this regard the poet follows the tendency of the Gospels, which exaggerate the responsibility of the Jews – over that of the Romans – for Christ's death. In the *Heliand*, however, the Crucifixion itself has become solely the work of the Jews, the Romans playing no part

---

51 There is no corresponding passage in Tatian.
52 See the discussion in Rathofer, *Der Heliand* [note 24], 336–43, 380–89; and Sowinski, *Darstellungsstil und Sprachstil* [note 46], 267–271. Albrecht Hagenlocher seems off the mark in his opinon that, in the *Heliand*, the enmity of the Jews arises from their ignorance; the lines just cited seem to indicate the opposite. See his "Theologische Systematik und epische Gestaltung: Beobachtung zur Darstellung der feindlichen Juden im Heliand und in Otfrids Evangelienbuch," *Beiträge zur Geschichte der deutschen Sprache und Literatur* (Tübingen) 96 (1974), 33–58, esp. 44, 57. Moreover, his assertion that Jewish hostility, for the poet, served an epic function void of theological relevance fails to persuade.

at all.)⁵³ While the stereotype of the Jewish rejection of Christ had made its way from John's Gospel into the *Diatessaron*, the rejection is emphasized even further by the *Heliand* poet. About the lasting guilt of the Jews, for instance, his comments are more radical than any found in the New Testament (lines 2284-2290):

> Sô deda the drohtines sunu   dago gehuilikes
> *gôd uuerk* mid is iungeron,   sô neo Iudeon umbi that
> an thea is *mikilun craft*   thiu mêr ne gelobdun,
> that he alouualdo   alles uuâri,
> landes endi liudio: thes sie noh lôn nimat,
> uuîdana uuracsîð,   thes sie thar that geuuin dribun
> uuið *selban* thene *sunu drohtines.*

[The more the Chieftain's Son did good work every day with His followers, the more the Jews did not believe at all in His mighty power because of that! Nor did they believe that He was the All-Ruler of everything, people and country. They are still receiving their reward for that – farflung journeying in exile – because they fought against the Son of the Chieftain Himself.]⁵⁴

Here the author is clearly following a model of salvation, grounded in belief in Christ, that he also makes use of elsewhere. In the story of the centurion at Capernaum, for instance, he underscores in strong terms the faith of the pagan, which he places in stark contrast to the disbelief of the Jews. The poet's embellishment of Matt 8.11-12, where Jesus describes the joys of the heathens and the punishment of the Jews, reads as follows (lines 2131-2144):

> [. . .] noh sculun elitheoda   *ôstane* endi *uestane*,
> mancunnies cuman   manag tesamne,

---

53   See esp. lines 5532-5535, where it is the Jewish people (*folc Iudeono*) who built the site of execution and nailed Christ to the cross. See also Rathofer's remarks on the third foretelling of the Passion (fitt 43) in *Der Heliand* [note 24], 380-81.
54   See also lines 2339-2345. Again, there is no corresponding passage in Tatian.

Jesus Christ between Jews and Heathens

> *hêlag folc godes   an heḃenrîki*:
> thea môtun thar an Abrahames   endi an Isaakes sô self
> endi *ôc* an Iacobes,   gôdoro manno,
> barmum restien   endi bêðiu *gethologean*,
> uuelon endi uuilleon   endi *uuonodsam* lîf,
> gôd lioht mid gode.   Than scal *Iudeono* filu,
> theses rîkeas suni   berôḃode uuerðen,
> *bedêlide* sulicoro diurðo,   endi sculum an dalun thiustron
> an themu alloro ferristan   ferne liggen.
> Thar mag man gehôrien   heliðos quîðean,
> thar sie iro torn manag   tandon bîtad;
> thar ist *gristgrimmo*   endi grâdag fiur [. . .]

[There are still many foreign peoples from the East and the West, many of the clans of men, who are to come together, the holy people of God, in the kingdom of heaven. There they can rest in the lap of Abraham, of Isaac himself, and of Jacob too – those good men – and can enjoy welfare and happiness, a life of pleasure, good life in God's light! Then many of the Jews, the sons of this kingdom, will be robbed, deprived of these glories, and will lie in dark valleys at the farthest ends of the infernal regions. There you will hear those heroes lamenting, there they continually bite their teeth in their anger. There the guest rages in pain and the fire is greedy.]

It is easy to see the poet's motivation here: By emphasizing the faith that Jesus expected in strangers and in foreign lands,[55] he hopes to embolden the will of his fellow Saxons, whom the Franks had looked down upon for centuries as pagans.[56] At the same time, of course, he wished to issue his countrymen a keen warning to heed the Christian message, lest they lose any chance of salvation. To this end, the Jews function for him as "the archetype of all who doubt

---

55 For further documentation of this, see Sowinski, *Darstellungsstil und Sprachstil* [note 46], 268.
56 See Murphy, *The Saxon Savior* [note 25], *passim*, but esp. 25–26.

the divinity of Christ."[57] It is, on the one hand, difficult to accuse him of denigrating contemporary Jews, since there were hardly any Jews living among the Saxons. On the other hand, the *Heliand* surely contributed to their demonization – to the reputation of Jews, which would later become more common, as the enemies of God and murderers of Christ.

It should be stressed, however, that the so-called "substitution theory"[58] – that is, the idea that the Jews forfeited their status as God's people and were replaced by pagan converts to Christianity – is offset by a "model of participation" (*Teilnahmemodell*),[59] according to which the pagan world is incorporated into the Covenant with Israel. As we have just seen in the *Heliand*, people from East and West are expected to rest in the heavenly kingdom on the bosom of the Jewish patriarchs Abraham, Isaac, and Jacob. This ambivalent attitude is even more evident in the account of the Canaanite woman (Matt 15.21–28), to which the *Heliand* poet has also added

---

57 Rathofer, *Der Heliand* [note 24], 343: "Typus aller an der Göttlichkeit Christi zweifelnden Menschen."

58 "Substitution theory" (*Substitutionstheorie*) has been used in numerous works to define the relationship of the Church to Israel since the beginning of Christianity. On this phenomenon, see for instance Wolfram Liebster, "Umkehr und Erneuerung im Verhältnis von Christen und Juden," in *Umkehr und Erneuerung: Erläuterungen zum Synodalbeschluß der Rheinischen Landessynode 1980 „Zur Erneuerung des Verhältnisses von Christen und Juden"*, ed. Bertold Klappert and Helmut Starck (Neukirchen-Vluyn: Neukirchener Verlag, 1980), 55–65, at 56–58; Hans-Joachim Barkenings, "Das eine Volk Gottes: Von der Substitutionstheorie zur Ökumene mit Israel," in ibid., 167–181, at 167–174; and Leonore Siegele-Wenschkewitz, "Mitverantwortung und Schuld der Christen am Holocaust," *Evangelische Theologie* 42 (1982), 171–190, at 189. That the doctrine of a disinheritance of Israel was in fact propagated – and that it was highly influential – is not a matter of debate. One should be careful, however, to avoid generalizations that gloss over subtleties and fail to recognize that, more often than not, this idea had as its hope the conversion of Jews to Christianity.

59 See Bertold Klappert, "Die Wurzel trägt dich," in *Umkehr und Erneuerung* [note 58], 23–54, at 28; for further clarification, see idem, "Jesus Christen zwischen Juden und Christen," in ibid., 138–66, esp. 161–63.

Jesus Christ between Jews and Heathens

embellishments of his own. In contrast to the Gospel story, in which Jesus crosses the border simply to avoid unrest, that of the *Heliand* is introduced with a positive description of Jesus's relations with foreigners (lines 2975–2982):

> Elithioda quam,
> *imu gumon* tegegnes: uuârun is gôdun uuerk
> ferran gefrâgi,   that he sô filu sagde
> uuâroro uuordo: *imu uuas* uuillio mikil,
> that he sulic folcskepi   frummien môsti,
> that sie simla gerno   gode thionodin,
> uuârin gehôrige   heḃencuninge
> mankunnies manag.

[Foreigners came to Him, they came to meet Him. From far away they had heard tell of His good works and that He said so much in wise words. He had a great desire to do something for such people so that they would always serve god gladly and so that many of the clans of mankind would be under obedience to heaven's King.]⁶⁰

In doing so, the poet deprives the story of its main point, namely that, in the encounter with the pagan woman, Jesus comes to a realization and for the first time decides to extend his mission beyond his own people.⁶¹ Despite this introduction, the *Heliand* goes on to tell the story in its usual form: The woman begs for her daughter to be healed, but Jesus ignores her entirely. As in Matthew, Jesus,

---

60   There is, of course, no corresponding passage in Tatian. On the entire pericope, see Rathofer, *Der Heliand* [note 24], 127–28.
61   See for instance the commentaries by Ulrich Luz, *Das Evangelium nach Matthäus*, 4 vols., Evangelisch-Katholischer Kommentar zum Neuen Testament 1 (Zurich: Benziger, 1985–2002), 2:437–438; and Wolfgang Wiefel, *Das Evangelium nach Matthäus*, Theologischer Handkommentar zum Neuen Testament 1 (Leipzig: Evangelische Verlagsanstalt, 1998), 284–87. Luz's commentary is available in English as *Matthew: A Commentary*, trans. James E. Crouch, 3 vols. (Minneapolis: Fortress, 2001–2005).

when the disciples arrive, explains his treatment of the woman in the following way (lines 3000–3002):

> êrist scal ik Israheles　aƀoron uuerðen,
> folcskepi te *frumu*,　that sie ferhtan hugi
> hebbian te iro hêrron.

> [I am to take care of Israel's hereditary clansmen first, to see that they have a proper attitude toward their Lord.]

This is followed by an amplification of the poet's, in which Christ cites the wickedness and disbelief of the Jews as the reason why they, in particular, are in need of his teaching (lines 3002–3005):

> 　　　　　　　　　im is helpono tharf,
> thea liudi sind farlorane,　farlâten habbiad
> uualdandes uuord,　that uuerod is getuîflid,
> driƀad im dernean hugi [. . .]

> [The people (the Jew) are lost; they have abandoned the Ruler's word; the warriors have doubts; people are driven by evil thoughts . . .]

In a final act of ambivalence, however, Jesus concludes this speech with another unprecedented remark (lines 3007–3008): "thoh scal thanen helpe cumen / allun elithiodun" [though it is from here that help is to come for all foreign peoples!]. In other words, it is from the Jews – their wickedness aside – that salvation will reach the rest of mankind.[62]

IV

The image that the *Heliand* presents of the Jews and of Christ's relationship to them vacillates enigmatically between the love and

---

62　Wicke, *Das wunderbare Tun* [note 27], 86 emphasizes this fact and then attempts to excuse the *Heliand* for a doctrine which was difficult for a German, writing in 1935, to accept.

hatred of Judaism. This is, indeed, somewhat due to Tatian's harmonization of the four Gospels; here, Matthew's positive assessment of the Torah and his representation of Jesus as the savior of Israel is intertwined with John's often black-and-white depiction of the Jews as the enemies of Christ, and both attitudes must have left an impression on the poet. There is, however, an additional explanation for such ambivalence in the *Heliand*, key to which is a term that appeared twice in the passage cited just above. Here, Christ is willing to champion both pagans and the people of Israel, and the same word is used for both, namely *folcskepi*, which can denote a 'sense of community' (*Volkschaft*), the 'customs of a people' (*Volkstum*), or simply 'people, tribe, nation' (*Volk*). What does this imply?

Given its various appropriations throughout history, the concept of *Volk* must be evoked with caution. The use of the term in the 1920s and 1930s, of course, is inadequate with regard to the mission to the *Germanen*. It is just as true, however, that without some notion of *Volk* the mission cannot be fully understood. Though, after many centuries, Christianity would be adopted by individuals, the missionary activity of the early Middle Ages focused – almost exclusively – on entire tribes and peoples. In the case of the *Germanen*, it was typical for a king to accept baptism and then, in turn, to be followed by his people.[63] This was natural because their politics were inseparable from their religion – "a cultic religion rooted in political unity," as Walter Baetke described it.[64] Christian missionaries, preaching a universal

---

63   On this characteristic of the Germanic mission, see Baetke, *Die Aufnahme des Christentums* [note 28], 20–24; Lutz E. von Padberg, *Mission und Christianisierung: Formen und Folgen bei Angelsachsen und Franken im 7. und 8. Jahrhundert* (Stuttgart: F. Steiner, 1995), esp. 51–52, 56–60, and 95–102; and Cusack, *Conversion among the Germanic Peoples* [note 9], 175–78.
64   Walter Baetke, "Religion und Politik beim Übergang der germanischen Stämme zum Christentum," in his *Kleine Schriften* [note 8], 351–69, here at 356: "eine auf den politischen Verband bezogene Kultreligion." See also Russell, *The Germanization of Early Medieval Christianity* [note 7], 47–48, who defines the Germanic faith as "folk religion" in contrast to a "universal religion." This distinction is key to his understanding of a transformation of Christianity.

religion of redemption, often had problems with the alien thinking of the converted and the converted to be, and such misunderstandings resulted in various conflicts.[65] However, these differences in thought also yielded new ways of understanding the Gospel.

To return to our theme: The Germanic poet applies the concept of the *Volk* to both sides – to that of the pagan foreigners, who represent his Saxons, and to that of the Jews. This might seem theologically questionable but, historically speaking, it is not incorrect, at least not initially. Even if Judaism was not a folk-religion in the sense of the old Germanic faith, the Jews certainly formed a cultic community. This is reflected as late as the New Testament stories and therefore also in the *Heliand*,[66] and is something that the poet could use to his advantage. As much as the chief purpose of his work was to make the Gospel part of Saxon culture, it was also obvious to him that Jesus, as a Jew, was there above all for the Jewish people. He is there for them both as a teacher and a king, a term with sacred and secular connotations. The *Heliand* poet could not hold it against the Jews for having a political or national conception of salvation and for therefore misunderstanding Jesus's mission – a Christian allegation to the present day – because the medieval *Germanen* also conflated religion and politics, as is clear in the dual function of the Germanic king.

---

65   See Lutz E. von Padberg, "Odin oder Christus? Loyalitäts- und Orientierungskonflikte in der frühmittelalterlichen Christianisierungsepoche," *Archiv für Kulturgeschichte* 77 (1995), 249–78, esp. 256–58.
66   The account of the twelve-year-old Jesus in the Temple, discussed above, can be cited as evidence of such a community. So it is too, I think, when the Jews are said to gather in Jerusalem, "thar sie scoldun iro gode thionon" [where they were supposed to serve their God] (line 4465). This does not mean, as Sowinski believes (*Darstellungsstil und Sprachstil* [note 45], 270), that the Jews worshipped a god different from that of Christians, but rather that Jerusalem is the cultic site of the Jews. As such, this site does not first appear in the Passion story, but already in the accounts of Jesus's childhood, where it is mentioned in a similar phrase: "thar te Hierusalem, Iuðeo liudi iro thiodgode thionon scoldun" [there at Jerusalem, where the Jews were supposed to serve the God of their people] (lines 789–90).

Jesus Christ between Jews and Heathens

Clearly it was of great interest to the *Heliand* poet that the salvation brought by Christ was universal and available to all,[67] yet this could not be taken for granted at his time, as it could at the earliest stages of Christianity. Throughout the poem one detects a sense of gratitude for a salvation that left its source, having emanated from the Jews to the other peoples of the world. However, just as the poet, a Germanic Christian, was able to appreciate Jesus's Jewishness in an entirely new way, he was also at a loss as to why the majority of Jews denied Jesus's message. While he does not maintain that all Jews rejected Christ – he is aware that the twelve disciples were Jews – he does emphasize the rejection by the vast majority. He cannot comprehend why the Jews did not listen to Jesus but rather persecuted and killed him, a man of their own flesh and blood who grew up in their midst and upheld their laws, who would bring their Covenant to fulfillment, and who was thus to be their protector and king. And so the poet's originally positive attitude is reversed. Since it was inconceivable to him that Jews did not understand Jesus, he could only explain the Jewish rejection of Christ as something inimical. Who, he must have thought, could have understood Jesus better? Who could have had a greater feeling of solidarity with him than his own people? In the poet's mind, such animosity and depravity must be punished, and the disenfranchisement of the Jews satisfied his sense of justice.

This attitude, which had already existed for centuries, gained new momentum within the context of the Germanic mission. It would go on to contribute to the negative perception of contemporary Jews and to their subsequent cruel treatment, as could be shown with numerous examples. In this light, the *Heliand* and the entire epoch of the Germanic mission can be seen as exemplifying a great part

---

67   Aside from the two pericopes discussed immediately above, the poet also expresses this universality through the character of Simeon, who praises the child Christ not only as the savior of Israel but also – like the Gospel of Luke – as a great light for all peoples of the earth: "Thu bist lioht mikil allun elithiodun" (lines 487–488).

of Church history: It was largely not indifference toward the Jews that led to horrible consequences – as is often read – but rather a sense of unrequited love that manifested itself as anti-Semitism; this is especially recognizable in Luther, among other examples. The tragedy of Christianity is such that its very closeness to Judaism would, again and again, drive the two religions apart.

V

The Discovery of the Leipzig Fragment (2006)

A New *Heliand* Fragment
From the Leipzig University Library[1]

Hans Ulrich Schmid

(Translated by Valentine A. Pakis)

On April 20, 2006, Mr. Thomas Döring and Dr. Falk Eisermann informed me over the telephone about the discovery of an early, clearly vernacular fragment in the Leipzig University Library that had been used as a cover for a seventeenth-century book.[2] According to Mr. Döring, the small volume belonged to the holdings of the Leipzig Thomaskirche, which is now stored in the university collection. My first glance revealed clues

---

1 Originally published as "Ein neues 'Heliand'-Fragment aus der Universitätsbibliothek Leipzig," *Zeitschrift für deutsches Altertum und deutsche Literatur* 135 (2006), 309–23.
2 The following works are combined in the volume, which measures 12.8 by 7.5 cm, with a 3 cm spine: IANITORES LOGICI BINI. Hoc est, Exercitationes duæ ad Organum Aristotelis viam & januam aperientes: I. DE NATURA LOGICÆ. II. DE QUINQUE UNIVERSALIBUS. Quibus omnes de hac materia Quæstiones numero 500. apprimè utiles mirâ brevitate enucleantur: Et præcipuæ Rameorum exerationes dereguntur, Auctore & Præside CASPARO BARTHOLINO Malmogio Dano. Editio altera priore castigatior. Cum Indice Quæstionum perspicuo. Wittebergæ, Prælo Gormaniano. M.DC.IX (36 and 198 pages), and JACOBI MARTINI Professoris academici LOGICÆ PERIPATETICÆ PER DICHOTOMIAS IN GRATIAM RAMISTARVM RESOLUTÆ LIBRI DVO. Secundò editi distinctius, emaculatius, auctius. WITTEBERGÆ, Ex officina Henckeliana, Sumptibus Zachariæ Schureri, Anno M.DC.VIII (192 pages).

about the text and language of the fragment. The words *sten* 'stone', *idise* 'women', *giungarom* 'disciples', and *ik uuet* 'I know', written in ninth-century Carolingian minuscule, indicated at once that what I had before me was Old Saxon, and it was easy to recognize that the language was alliterating. It followed that the text could hardly be any but an excerpt from the *Heliand*, and specifically the story about the women at the empty tomb of Christ (based on Luke 24). Comparison with the corresponding passage in Eduard Sievers's edition of the *Heliand* confirmed this assumption: On its only visible side (at the time), the fragment contained lines 5823–5845 of the *Heliand*. In a conversation with the director of the library, Prof. Dr. Ulrich Johannes Schneider, it was agreed that the fragment should be detached from the seventeenth-century book by the restoration staff in order to see what was written on the side that had been glued down. The detached side brought the conclusive passage to light, namely the rest of line 5845, lines 5846–5869, and the beginning of line 5870, and in unusually good condition at that. The edition and the first philological evaluation of the fragment – which will be known by siglum L after the place of its discovery and will keep the shelf mark "Leipzig, Universitätsbibliothek, Thomas 4073 (Ms)" – were entrusted to me, for which I am grateful to Prof. Schneider. My thanks are also due to Dr. Eisermann and especially to the actual discoverer, Mr. Döring, without whose sharp eye the fragment would have remained hidden in the library catalogue. Such gratitude does not belong in a footnote.

Fragment L

The detached vellum manuscript page measures approximately 24 by 16.6 cm. Nothing can be said, of course, about the original size of the leaf, the margins of which were cut by the book binder. The text area measures 19.5 by 12.5 cm. The beginnings of lines that coincide with the beginnings of manuscript lines are marked with

A New Heliand Fragment from the Leipzig University Library

slightly enlarged initial letters (lines 2, 6, 12, 23 recto, and 38, 39, 40 verso; see the transcription in Diplomatic Rendition below as well as the images of the MS), and this results in an extended line length of 13.5 cm. Both sides contain 23 lines. The script bears clear signs of the ninth century: Word separation is not consistently carried out (see the text in Diplomatic Rendition, lines 9 *faNthem*, 23 *anfundigaro*, but line 7 *uuill fpell* written separately), ascenders are thickened at the top, and the descenders of *f, f,* and *r* are lengthened. The letter *d* appears only in its straight form, and capital N occurs word medially and word finally.[3] Its size, arrangement, and script raise the possibility that L was taken as waste paper from the same manuscript as the Prague fragment P (now kept in Berlin),[4] which agrees with L down to the details of its layout (and wear!); each also contains 23 lines per page. The text area of P and – as far as can I can tell – its page size are also identical to the those of L. Moreover, as is the case in L, enlarged lowercase letters appear in the left margins of P when the beginnings of verse and manuscript lines coincide. It is the case, admittedly, in all *Heliand* manuscripts – in both codices as well as the fragments[5] – that enlarged letters will introduce the beginning of a verse line, but the placement of these in the margin occurs only in L and P. The similarity extends even to some especially distinctive letter forms: the *E* in *ENdi* (text in Diplomatic Rendition,

---

3   Karin Schneider, *Paläographie und Handschriftenkunde für Germanisten: Eine Einführung* (Tübingen: Max Niemeyer, 1999), 21f.
4   On MS P, see Hans Lambel, "Ein neuentdecktes Blatt einer Heliandhandschrift," *Sitzungsberichte der kaiserlichen Akademie der Wissenschaften in Wien: Philosophisch-historische Classe* 97 (1880), 613–24. Black and white images of P can be seen in Burkhard Taeger, ed., *Der Heliand: Ausgewählte Abbildungen zur Überlieferung*, Litterae 103 (Göppingen: Kümmerle, 1985), 15f. For an excellent color image of its back side, see Peter J. Becker and Eef Overgaauw, eds., *Aderlass und Seelentrost: Die Überlieferung deutscher Texte im Spiegel Berliner Handschriften und Inkunabeln* (Mainz: P. von Zabern, 2003), 29.
5   See the images in Taeger, *Der Heliand* [note 4].

line 30; see the image) exhibits the same conspicuous form, with the uppermost cross-stroke slanting upward, that P has (line 998, in *En alouualdand*). On the other hand, P has a unique form of enlarged *g* that resembles the number 3 (P 995 *gisehan*). In comparable positions L exhibits more closed forms (text in Diplomatic Rendition, line 6 *gibada*; see the image). Different too is the form of enlarged *a*; whereas P has an uncial form that clearly stands out from the minuscule-*a* of the rest of the text (e.g., *an* 1003 and 1006), L simply uses, at the beginning of a verse line, an enlarged form of the *a* that it exhibits elsewhere (see the text in Diplomatic Rendition, lines 28 and 29 *an* and the image).

According to Bernhard Bischoff, the provenance of P cannot be determined with certainty.[6] Though a more detailed comparative paleographical examination of L and P must be left to the specialists, the agreements in the structure and language of both fragments (on the language, see The Language of L below) – at least as they appear to someone without expertise in paleography – suggest that L and P belonged either to the same manuscript or to affiliated manuscripts from the same scriptorium.

THE TEXT

The text is presented below, first of all in a diplomatic transcription that hopes to be as true to the manuscript as possible. After that will follow a lightly normalized version, divided and numbered according to verse lines, with modern punctuation and capitalization.

---

6   Bernhard Bischoff, "Paläographische Fragen deutscher Denkmäler der Karolingerzeit," in *Mittelalterliche Studien: Ausgewählte Aufsätze zur Schriftkunde und Literaturgeschichte*, by Bischoff, 3 vols. (Stuttgart: Anton Hiersemann, 1981), 3:104. Bischoff classifies the fragment as "Niederdeutschland, um oder nach 850" in his *Katalog der festländischen Handschriften des neunten Jahrhunderts (mit Ausnahme der wisigotischen), Teil I: Aachen – Lambach* (Wiesbaden: Harrassowitz, 1998), 70.

A New Heliand *Fragment from the Leipzig University Library*

Diplomatic Rendition

Examples of long <ſ> and majuscule <N> are reproduced. Italics indicate where the text has been filled out with readings from MS C. Word separation corresponds with the manuscript evidence, as does punctuation. On both sides of the manuscript there are interlinear glosses that are printed in their proper place below. They have been written in a slightly darker ink, probably during a round of correcting. Whether these are in the same hand that wrote the body of the text cannot be made out for sure on paleographic grounds, though a linguistic detail suggests that they were inserted by a different scribe: Whereas the spelling *sc* is used more often than not in the body of the text, an interlinear gloss on the verso side of L reads *skir*.

Line 41 (the outset of fitt 70) begins with a large initial <H> whose upper part was colored in red and whose lower part in yellow. As mentioned above, the beginnings of verse lines are marked by slightly enlarged minuscules. The word *engil* (line 8) is no longer clearly legible; presumably, the <e> of this word was also slightly enlarged.[7]

Recto

1   *ast*andan iú eNdi ſind theſa ſtedi lárea.
2   thit graf an theſuN griota Nu muguN gi gangaN
3   herod. Nahor mikilo ik uuet that iſ iu iſ Niod

---

[7] The text presented here has been updated to accord with that of Professor Schmid's revised transcription, published in "Nochmals zum Leipziger 'Heliand'-Fragment," *Zeitschrift für deutsches Altertum und deutsche Literatur* 136 (2007), 376–78. This revision was prompted, in part, by the publication of two other editions of the fragment, namely: Irmengard Rauch, "The Newly Found Leipzig *Heliand* Fragment," *Interdisciplinary Journal for Germanic Linguistics and Semiotic Analysis* 11 (2006), 1–17; and Heike Sahm, "Neues Licht auf alte Fragen: Die Stellung des Leipziger Fragments in der Überlieferungsgeschichte des „Heliand"," *Zeitschrift für deutsche Philologie* 126 (2007), 81–98 [-Ed.].

4   ſehaN. an theſaN ſtén innaN hier ſind Noh thiu
5   ſtediſkina. thar iſ líchamo lag lungra fenguN.
6   gibada an iro brioſtuN. blecoN idiſe. uuliteſco
7   nio uuif. uuaſ im that uuill ſpell mikil tegi
8   hóreanna that im fan iro hérroN ſagda engil
9   thaſ alouualdoN. hiet ſia eft thanaN. faNthem
10 graua gangan endi faraN te them giungarom
11 xristaſ. ſeggian them iſ giſídoN ſuođon uuord*on*
12 that iro drohtin uuaſ. fan dođe aſtandaN. hiet
13 ok anſundron ſymoN petrusa. uillſpell mikil
14 uuorduN kuđeaN. kumi drohtinas io that
15 xriſt ſelƀo uuaſ *aN* galileo land thar *ina* eft
16 iſ giungaroN ſculuN. geſehaN iſ geſiđoſſo hie im
17 er ſelƀo giſprak uuarom uuorduN reht ſo thúo
18 thia uuif thanaN. gangaN uueldun ſo ſtuoduN *im*
19 tegegnaſ thar engiloſ tueNa aNalohuitoN u*u*ana
20 moN giuuadeom eNdi ſprakuN im mid iro uuor
21 d*oN* tuo. hélaglico hugi uuarđ giblódid. them
22 id*i*ſoN an egiſoN Nimahtun aN thia engiloſ godaſ
            ſcauuoN   ſcone
23 bi them uulite uulitaN uuaſ im thiu uuaname te

VERSO

         t ſkir
24 ſtrang. te ſúikle teſehanna. thúo ſprákun *im san*
25 aNgegiN. uualdandaſ bodoN endi thea uuif fra
26 goduN. tehui ſia criſta tharod. quicaN mid dó
27 duN. ſuno drohtinaſ ſuókian quámiN. ferahaſ
28 fullaN Nú gi ina Neſídat hier. an theſuN ſteNgra
29 ua ac hie iſ aſtandaN giu. aN iſ líchamon theſ
30 gí giloƀeaN ſculuN. Endi gehuggiat thero uuor
31 do the hie iu teuuaraN oft. ſelƀo ſagda thann hie

32 aN iuuuoN geſíđea uuaſ. aN galileo landa hu hie
33 ſcoldi gigeƀen uuerđaN. giſald ſelbo anſundigaro
34 manno. hetteandero hand helag drohtiN. that
35 ſea ina queledin endi aN crucea ſlúogiN. dóđaN
36 gidádiN endi that hie ſcoldi thuruh drohtinaſ
37 craft. an thriddioN daga thioda teuuilleaN.
38 libbeaNdi aſtandaN Nú habat hie all gileſtid ſó.
39 gefrumid miđ firihoN ileat gí nú forđ hinaN.
40 gangat gahlico. eNdi giduat it them iſ giungarom kúđ.
41 Hie haƀat ſia giu farfarana. endi iſ im forđ
42 hinaN. angalileoland thar ina eft iſ giunga
43 roN ſculuN. giſehan iſ geſíđoſ thuo uuarđ ſaN af
44 tar thiu. thém uuiboN aN uuilleoN. that ſia gihór
45 duN ſulic uuord ſprekaN. kuđeaN thia craft godaſ.
46 uuaruN im ſó akumaNa thúo noh. ia forohta

Normalized Rendition

The text ought to be presented a second time according to verse lines for the sake of readability and easier comparison with the editions. Here a problem is posed by the interlinear glosses (see The Interlinear Glosses in L and P below); I have followed the wording in the body of the text.

5823 *ac hie ist ast*andan iú, endi sind thesa stedi lárea,
5824 thit graf an thesun griota.   Nu mugun gi gangan herod
5825 nahor mikilo   – ik uuet that is iu is niod sehen
5826 an thesan stén innan –   hier sind noh thiu stedi skina
5827 thar is líchamo lag.   Lungra fengun
5828 gibada an iro briostun   blecon idise,
5829 uulitesconio uuif: uuas im that uuillspell mikil
5830 te gihóreanna   that im fan iro hérron sagda

5831　engil that alouualdon.　　Hiet sia eft thanan
5832　fan them graua gangan　　endi faran te them giungarom xristas,
5833　seggian them is gisídon　　suodon uuord*on*,
5834　that iro drohtin uuas　　fan dode astandan.
5835　Hiet oc an sundron　　simon petrusa
5836　uillspell mikil　　uuordun cudian,
5837　kumi drohtinas,　　io that xrist selƀo
5838　uuas an galileo land　　'thar *ina* eft is giungaron sculun
5839　gisehan is gesidos,　　so hie im er selƀo gisprak
5840　uuarom uuordun.'　　Reht so thúo thia uuif thanan
5841　gangan uueldun,　　so stuodu*n* *im* tegegnas thar
5842　engilos tuena　　an alohuiton
5843　uu*an*amon giuuadeom　　endi sprakun im mid iro uuordon tuo
5844　hélaglico:　　hugi uuard gibló did
5845　them i*d*ison an egison:　　nimahtun an thia engilos godas
5846　bi them uulite uulitan:　　uuas im thiu uuaname te strang,
5847　te suikle tesehanna.　　Thúo sprákun *im san* angegin
5848　uualdandas bodon　　endi thea uuif fragodun,
5849　te hui sia crista therod　　quican mid dódun,
5850　suno drohtinas　　suókian quámin
5851　ferahas fullan;　　'nú gi ina nefídat hier
5852　an thesun stengraua,　　ac hie is astandan giu
5853　an is líchamon:　　thes gí giloƀean sculun
5854　endi gehuggiat thero uuordo,　　the hie iu teuuaran oft
5855　selƀo sagda,　　thann hie an iuuuon gesidea uuas
5856　an galileo landa,　　hu hie scoldi gigeƀen uuerdan,
5857　gisald selbo　　an sundigaro manno,
5858　hetteandero hand,　　helag drohtin,
5859　that sea ina queledin　　endi an crucea slúogin,

5860 dóđan gidádin   endi that hie scoldi thuruh drohtinas craft
5861 an thriddion daga   thioda teuuillean
5862 libbeandi astandan.   Nu habat hie all gilestid só
5863 gefrumid mið firihon: ileat gí nú forð hinan,
5864 gangat gahlico   endi giduat it them is giungarom kúð.
5865 Hie haƀat sia giu farfarana   endi is im forð hinan
5866 an galileoland,   thar ina eft is giungaron sculun,
5867 gisehan is gesíðos.'   Thuo uuarð sán aftar thiu
5868 thém uuibon an uuilleon,   that sia gihórdun sulic uuord sprekan,
5869 kuðean thia craft godas;   uuarun im só akumana thúo noh
5870 ia forohta

Of the other extant *Heliand* manuscripts, only Cotton Caligula A VIII at the British Library in London (=C) contains the lines preserved in L. Since C was written in the second half of the tenth century in southern England[8] – thus at some distance, in time and space, from the original – it is clear that L contains a text that is much closer to the archetype. It seems reasonable, then, to present variant readings of L and C side by side.[9] The accent marks in L, which in general have no correspondence in C, are not taken into account.

5824 L *thesun*: C *theson*, L *griota*: C *griote*, 5825 L *mikilo*: C *mikilu*, L *is*: C *ist*, L *niod*: C *niud*, 5826 L *thesan*: C *theson*, L *stén*: C *stene*, L *thiu*: C *thia*, L *skina*: C *scina*, 5828 L *briostun*: C *brioston*, L *blecon*: C

---

8 On the tradition as a whole, see Taeger, *Der Heliand* [note 4]. On the provenance and date of C, see ibid., viii.

9 Readings of C are taken from Eduard Sievers, ed., *Heliand: Titelauflage vermehrt um das Prager Fragment des Heliand und die Vaticanischen Fragmente von Heliand und Genesis*, Germanistische Handbibliothek 4 (Halle: Waisenhaus, 1935).

bleca, 5829 L *uulitesconio*: C *ulitisconi*, L *uuif*: C *uuiƀ*, L *that*: C omits, L *uuillspell*: C *uilspell*, 5830 L *gihóreanna*: C *gihorianne*, L *hérron*: C *heren*, 5831 L *thas*: C *thes*, L *alouualdon*: C *alouualden*, 5832 L *graua*: C *graƀe*, L *giungarom*: C *iungron*, L *xristas*: C *Cristes*, 5833 L *seggean*: C *seggian*, L *gisíđon*: C *gisithon*, L *suođon*: C *suothon*, 5835 L *petrusa*: C *Petruse*, 5836 L *uuorđun*: C *uuordon*, L *cuđian*: C *cuthian*, L *io*: C *gie*, 5837 L *kumi*: C *cumi*, L *drohtinas*: C *drohtines*, 5838 L *giungaron*: C *iungron*, 5839 L *gesiđos*: C *gisithos*, L *gisprak*: C *gisprac*, 5840 L *uuarom*: C *uuaron*, L *uuorđun*: C *uuordon*, L *thia*: C *thiu*, L *uuif*: C *uuiƀ*, 5841 L *tegegnas*: C *tegegnes*, 5842 L *alohuiton*: C *alahuiton*, 5843 L *giuuadeom*: C *giuuadion*, L *sprakun*: C *spracun*, L *im*: C omits,[10] L *mid*: C *mid*, 5844 L *uuarđ*: C *uuarth*, L *giblóđid*: C *giblothid*, 5845 L *them*: C *then*, L *idison*: C *idision*, L *nimahtun*: C *ne mahtun*, L *godas*: C *godes*, 5846 L *them*: C *themo*, L *uulitan*: C *scauuo*, L *uuaname*: C *uuanami*, 5847 L *sehanna*: C *sehanne*, L *sprákun*: C *spracun*, 5848 L *uualdandas*: C *uualdandes*, L *bodon*: C *bodun*, L *thea*: C *thiu*, L *uuif*: C *uuib*, 5849 L *crista*: C *Cristan*, L *dódun*: C *dodon*, 5850 L *drohtinas*: C *drohtines*, 5851 L *ferahas*: C *ferahes*, L *nefíđat*: C *ni findat*, 5852 L *thesun*: C *theson*, L *stengraua*: C *stengraƀe*, L *giu*: C *nu*, 5853 L *lichamon*: C *lichamen*, L *giloƀean*: C *gilobian*, 5854 *gehuggiat*: C *gehuggian*, L *teuuaran*: C *te uuaron*, 5855 L *selƀo*: C *selbo*, L *gesiđea*: C *gisithe*, 5856 L *galileo landa*: C *Galilealande*, L *hu*: C *huo*, L *gigeƀen*: C *gigeban*, L *uuerđan*: C *uuerthan*, 5858 L *hetteandero*: C *hetandero*, 5859 L *sea*: C *sia*, L *queledin*: C *quelidin*, L *crucea*: C *cruci*, L *slúogin*: C *slogun*, 5860 L *drohtinas*: C *drohtines*, 5861 L *daga*: C *dage*, L *uuillean*: C *uuillion*, 5862 L *libbeandi*: C *libbiandi*, L *habat*: C *habit*, 5863 L *gefrumid*: C *gifrumid*, 5864 L *mid*: C *mid*, L *ileat*: C *iliat*, L *forđ*: C *forth*, L *giduat*: C *duot*, L *giungarom*: C *iungron*, L *kúđ*: C *cuth*, 5865 L *haƀat*: C *habit*, L *giu*: C *iu*, L *farfarana*: C *furfarana*, L *is*: C *ist*, L *forđ*: C *forth*, 5866 L *galileoland*: C *Galileo land*, L *giungaron*: C *iungron*, 5867 L *gesíđos*:

---

10 Rückert's conjecture of *im* is thus confirmed; see Heinrich Rückert, ed., *Heliand* (Leipzig: F. A. Brockhaus, 1876).

A New Heliand *Fragment from the Leipzig University Library*

C *gisithos*, L *uuarđ*: C *uuarth*, L *sán*: C omits,[11] L *aftar*: C *after*, 5868 L *uuilleon*: C *uuillon*, L *sprekan*: C *sprecan*, 5869 L *kuđean*: C *cuthian*, L *godas*: C *godes*, L *akumana*: C *acumana*, 5870 L *gie*: C *ia so*, L *forohta*: C *forahta*.

THE LANGUAGE OF L

In the following analysis no attempts will be made to relate the language of L to that of the original text[12]; rather I have limited the discussion to those features that can be considered characteristic of the fragment itself. Of special interest in this regard are the linguistic features that L shares with P against the rest of the tradition.

a. In contrast to C, <th> occurs only word initially in L (e.g., 5823 *thesa*, 5831 *thanan*). Medially and finally, <đ> is used,[13] as is also the case in P.[14]

b. Medially, the voiced labial fricative is represented by <ƀ> (so, for instance, 5839 *selƀo*, 5856 *gigeƀen*), and finally by <f> (e.g. 5829 *uuif*). In M the grapheme <ƀ> occurs very inconsistently; in C the stroke across the ascender of <b> is much more common.[15] In this regard, the consistency of P is similar to that of L. In contrast with L, the corresponding text of C repeatedly evidences *uuiƀ*.[16] Comparable in P is 984 *liof*. Only in the dative singular of 'grave' (5832 *graua* and 5852 *stengraua*) is the letter <u> used for

---

11 This confirms the conjecture made by Moritz Heyne, ed., *Heliand, nebst den Bruchstücken der altsächsischen Genesis*, 4th ed. (Paderborn: F. Schöningh, 1905).
12 On the question of the language of the archetype, see Hans Steinger, "Die Sprache des Heliand," *Jahrbuch des Vereins für niederdeutsche Sprachforschung* 51 (1925), 1–54.
13 Johan H. Gallée, *Altsächsische Grammatik*, 3rd ed., rev. Johannes Lochner and Heinrich Tiefenbach (Tübingen: Max Niemeyer, 1993), 133–39.
14 Lambel, "Ein neuentdecktes Blatt" [note 4], 616f.
15 Ibid., 616.
16 Gallée, *Altsächsische Grammatik* [note 13], 125–29.

this sound. The situation in the Vatican fragment (V) is similar: Medial <ƀ> (e.g., 1304 *fargeƀan*), occasionally <u> (1286 *líoua*), final <f> (1289 *lóf*). All in all, the spelling of fragments L, P (and also V) seems closer to the original than that of M and C does.[17]

c. The distribution of <k> and <c> seems lexically dependent. In this case there is striking agreement between L and P: <k> appears in forms of the verb *sprekan* (5839, 5843, 5847, 5868, P 974 *spraki*), in *mikilo* (5825), <c> in the cluster <sc>, above all in forms of *sculan* (5838, 5853, 5856, 5860, 5866, P 972 *scolda*), in *craft* (5850, 5869, P 1004 *craftu*), in the suffix *-lîc* (5844 *hélaglico*, 5864 *gahlico*, 5868 *sulic*, P 967 *diurlico*, 1001 *uuarlico*), and also once in the name of Christ (5849, P 979, 982 *Crist*), for which L twice has <x> (5832 *xristas*, 5837 *xrist*).

d. As in C and P – but not in M – reflexes of Germanic *ē$_2$[18] appear in L either as <ie> (5831 *hiet*, 5839, 5860 *hie*, P 969, 985 *thie*) or <ia> (5840, 5845 *thia*). However, P also evidences the monophthongized variant of the personal pronoun *he* (993), while L uses *hie* exclusively (5839, 5852, and so on).

e. In L, Germanic *ō[19] appears almost universally as <uo>, with or without an accent, e.g., 5841 *stuodun*, 5850 *suókian*, 5859 *slúogin*, though once as <ua>, in 5864 *giduat*.[20] L agrees here with P and C.[21] In 5833 *suođon*, the <uo> diphthong occurs for secondary Germanic *ō (<*a after the loss of a nasal and compensatory

---

17 Steinger, "Die Sprache des Heliand" [note 12], 11f.
18 Ibid., 28–30.
19 Ibid., 24–28. On the idea that spelling <uo> in P, C, and V represents that of the archetype – as opposed to the spelling <o> in M – see Thomas Klein, *Studien zur Wechselbeziehung zwischen altsächsischem und althochdeutschem Schreibwesen und ihrer sprach- und kulturgeschichtlichen Bedeutung*, Göppinger Arbeiten zur Germanistik 205 (Göppingen: Kümmerle, 1977), 334.
20 On the peculiarities specific to the verb *dôn*, see Gallée, *Altsächsische Grammatik* [note 13], 68f.
21 Ibid., 66–69; and further Lambel, "Ein neuentdecktes Blatt" [note 4], 615.

lengthening), for which P offers nothing comparable.

f. Long *ī* (written <í>) originated from the loss of a nasal in 5851 *nefíđat* (compare *ni findat* in C).[22] This form agrees with the practice of M and disagrees with the corresponding text in C; P contains no comparable form.

g. As in P, inflectional <a> predominates in L,[23] for example in the genitive singular of masculine and neuter *a*-stems: 5837 *drohtinas* (so also P 961 *drohtinas* but M 961 *drohtines*). The dative singular ends in -*a*, e.g., 5824 *griota*, 5832 *graua*, and 5834 *petrusa*. To compare are P 965 *stroma* and 989 *barna*, while M and C exhibit the readings *strome* and *barne*. In agreement too is the peculiar accusative *crista* in L 5849 and P 991.[24] Elsewhere only M 657 contains an isolated parallel to this (the name of Christ occurs approximately 50 times in the poem).[25] Word final -*a* is, as in P,[26] frequent in other forms – in pronouns (e.g., 5823 *thesa*), adjectives (e.g., 5827 *lungra*), verbs (e.g., 5855 *sagda*), and numerals (5842 *tuena*).

h. As in P,[27] <o> repeatedly occurs in inflectional endings of the weak declension, thus in L 5828 *blecon*, 5830 *hérron*, 5831 *alouualdon*, 5833 *gisíđon*. In the dative plural of vowel stems, on the other hand, <u> is read: 5836, 5840 *uuordun* (so too in P 969). In the same

---

22   Gallée, *Altsächsische Grammatik* [note 13], 157–59; and Steffen Krogh, *Die Stellung des Altsächsischen im Rahmen der germanischen Sprachen*, Studien zum Althochdeutschen 29 (Göttingen: Vandenhoeck & Ruprecht, 1996), 218.
23   For details on the Old Saxon tradition (also beyond that of the *Heliand*), see Steinger, "Die Sprache des Heliand" [note 12], 13–17; and Klein, *Studien zur Wechselbeziehung* [note 19], 344, 366. Seen as a whole, L and P represent what Klein calls the "(a, o)-System" type (see esp. 399–414).
24   Steinger, "Die Sprache des Heliand" [note 12], 7.
25   See the collection of evidence in Edward H. Sehrt, *Vollständiges Wörterbuch zum Heliand und zur altsächsischen Genesis* (Göttingen: Vandenhoeck & Ruprecht, 1925), 733.
26   On the ratio in P, see Lambel, "Ein neuentdecktes Blatt" [note 4], 615.
27   Ibid., 616.

Hans Ulrich Schmid

way <u> features in the present and preterit tense conjugational endings of second and third person plural verbs (5824 *mugun*, 5841 *uueldun*, 5843 *sprakun*, P 985 *anthlidun*).

i. The nominative singular of the word "son" is in L 5850 *suno*, as it is in P 961, 992. Elsewhere in the *Heliand* tradition the form *sunu* predominates.[28]

j. Striking too is the occasional preservation of final *-m* in the dative plural, as in L 5832, 5864 *giungarom* (as opposed to *iungron* in C), 5843 *giuuadeom* (C *giuuadion*), and so also in the strong masculine adjective 5840 *uuarom* (C *uuaron*). Again, corresponding forms occur in P,[29] such as the noun 996 *mannom* (but C *mannon*, M *mannun*), and adjectives P 981 *beztom* and 990 *hohom* (but M *bezton*, C *beston*, and MC *hohon*).

k. Pre-Old Saxon *j* before *o* and *u* appears several times as *gi-*, e.g., 5838, 5866 *giungaron*, 5832, 5864 *giungarom*. Comparable in P 965 (among other places) *Giohannes* and 965 *Giordana*.[30] In the corresponding passages, M and C have *iungron*, *Iohannes*, and *Iordana*. Hans Steinger considers the spelling <gi>, which also occurs in V, that of the original.[31]

l. With reference to the usage in P and V, Steinger considers the spelling out of final geminate consonants characteristic of the *Heliand* archetype.[32] This spelling also occurs in L in the cases of 5829 *uuillspell* and 5855 *thann*.

m. Unique is the form L 5829 *uulitesconio uuif*. The adjective is in the nominative plural of the strong neuter declension. In C the corresponding form is *ulitisoni uuiƀ*, which is to be expected.[33] Unfortunately, P lacks any comparative evidence. The simplest explanation for this *-io* in L is of course that it is a scribal error.

---

28 Sehrt, *Vollständiges Wörterbuch* [note 25], 733.
29 Lambel, "Ein neuentdecktes Blatt" [note 4], 617.
30 Ibid., 617; and Steinger, "Die Sprache des Heliand" [note 12], 17f.
31 Ibid., 2f., 11.
32 Ibid., 11.
33 Gallée, *Altsächsische Grammatik* [note 13], 225.

A New Heliand Fragment from the Leipzig University Library

The ending could also go back to -*iu* and be explained by the influence of the pronominal inflection (compare the demonstrative *thiu*).[34] In Old High German the ending -*iu* is regular for the nominative neuter plural of the strong adjectival declension (e.g., *scōniu*).[35] The word final change *o* < *u* is evidenced by 5850 *suno* (so too P 967, 1005); moreover, the pronominal form *thiu* is attested several times in L (5826, 5846, 5867).

There are, then, rather many linguistic agreements between L and P that, taken by themselves, might demonstrate little, but taken together with the similarities of script and layout can be used to support the thesis that the two fragments stem from a common manuscript. There are noteworthy differences between the two, however, and these are enumerated below:

n. It is very clear to see that the accent marks in L are used to indicate vowel length, and that this practice has no correspondence in P, e.g., 5826 *stén*, 5827 *líchamo*, 5868 *gihórdun*. Occasionally these clear, hooked accent marks stand over diphthongs as well, as in 5859 *slúogin* and 5869 *thúo*.

There are also cases in which words and spellings differ in L and P:

o. In agreement with corresponding forms in C and M, L 5853 exhibits an infinitive *giloƀean*, whereas P 958 has the form *giloƀon*, which fails to reflect Germanic **j*.[36]

p. The dative singular *thioda* at L 5861 is an isolated form; the corresponding form in P 963 reads *thiodo*, which is in accord with M *thiedo* and C *thiodu*. However, P 981 does contain the form *beda*,

---

34 Ibid., 238.
35 Wilhelm Braune, *Althochdeutsche Grammatik I*, 15th ed., rev. Ingo Reiffenstein (Tübingen: Max Niemeyer, 2004), 220–24.
36 All the forms are presented in Sehrt, *Vollständiges Wörterbuch* [note 25], 347f.

the morphology of which can be compared to that of *thioda*.³⁷

q. The clearly Hellenistic spelling *xrist*, which has no parallel in P, has been discussed in another context above (see § c.).

The divergences between L and P listed above are within the bounds of what can regularly be observed in manuscripts of this age. Even indications of vowel length do not need to be applied consistently throughout an entire codex. If L and P do indeed stem from the same manuscript, they would represent parts of the text that are very far removed from one another, a fact which might explain the divergent spelling practices. All in all, there are strong codicological and linguistic arguments in support of the idea that L and P are fragments of the same codex, though it is impossible to know for sure. In any case, Hans Lambel's 1880 assessment of fragment P holds true for the new discovery as well, namely that it "surpasses the other extant manuscripts in the consistent and careful presentation of sounds, indeed also to some degree in its phonological and morphological antiquity."³⁸ By the "other extant manuscripts" M and C are meant, for Lambel's assessment predates the discovery of the Vatican and Straubing fragments.

THE INTERLINEAR GLOSSES IN L AND P

As mentioned above, there are two interlinear glosses in L (see the lowermost line in image 1 and the first line in image 2). In P, too, a word has been written above the line. How are these additions to be judged?

a. 5846.: Here L exhibits the following original wording: *nimahtun*

---

37 In C and M, the dative singular of *beda* 'prayer' is almost universally *bedu*. See Gallée, *Altsächsische Grammatik* [note 13], 203f. The form *thioda* attested in L also has a parallel in the Vatican fragment; see Steinger, "Die Sprache des Heliand" [note 12], 30f.

38 Lambel, "Ein neuentdecktes Blatt" [note 4], 618: "an Consequenz und Sauberkeit der Lautgebung, zum Theil wohl auch in der Alterthümlichkeit in Lauten und Formen [. . .] beide anderen Hss. übertraf."

A New Heliand *Fragment from the Leipzig University Library*

an thia engilos godas / bi them uulite uulitan: uuas im thiu uuaname te strang. Striking here is the verb *uulitan* 'look at', which is otherwise unattested in Old Saxon. One could interpret *uulitan* as a dittographical error made under the influence of the immediately preceding *uulite*, but since Old English has the verb *wlītan* and Old Norse has *líta* – both of which corresponding exactly with Old Saxon *uulîtan*[39] – and, furthermore, since Gothic evidences the weak form *wlaiton*, which is based on the stem of the preterit singular of the primitive Germanic strong verb, there is then no reason not to take the Old Saxon word seriously. Above this word, however, in darker ink and in a contemporary (though perhaps different) hand, the verb *scauuon* is written. One finds, instead of *uulitan*, the very same *scauuon* at the corresponding place in C. This latter verb, which was certainly more common, can be understood as a correction in L, but also as an explanatory gloss. Another interlinear entry was made above the same line, namely *scone*, which happens to alliterate with *scauuon*. This gloss, however, has no parallel in C, whose entire line reads as follows: *bi themo uulite scauuon: uuas im thiu uuanami te strang.* There is, then, only partial agreement between the secondary reading of L and the passage in C. An explanation for this seemingly contradictory situation might be that the form *scauuon* was adopted as the better reading in an intermediary text between L and C. There was no need, however, to replace *uuaname* with *scone* for the sake of alliteration because, even if *scauuon* has replaced *uulita*, the alliterative pair *uulite* and *uuaname* would still have remained. Though it cannot be proved, it is conceivable that the interlinear entries were adopted from a *Heliand* manuscript that, instead of *uulitan* and *uuaname*, already contained *scauuon* and *scone*.

---

39 The verb represents the same root that underlies the preceding *uulite*. See Elmar Seebold, *Vergleichendes und etymologisches Wörterbuch der germanischen starken Verben*, Janua Linguarum: Series Practica 85 (The Hague: Mouton, 1970), 563f.

b. 5847: The original a-verse in L was *te úikle tesehanna*, which makes no sense. C reads *suithi* at the corresponding place but provides no further help. Before the *ú*, the hand of the corrector inserted an *f*. The simplest explanation for this is that the *Vorlage* of L had *suikle*, and that the scribe of L rendered it falsely out of sloppiness. The adjective meaning 'light, shining, gleaming' occurs only twice in the *Heliand* (3577 and 5625) and has variant forms in the tradition: In C it appears both times as *suigle*, whereas in M 3577 it appears as *suikli* (line 5625 is not attested in M). As far as etymology is concerned, *suigli* seems to be the "correct" form.[40] The existence of the *k*-variant in M allows the possibility, however, that the original *úikle* of L is an error for *suikle* (what prompted the scribe to put an acute accent above the consonantal *u*, a mark elsewhere reserved for long vowels and diphthongs, must remain unsettled). It seemed perfectly appropriate to the correcting scribe that, to ensure the understanding of the originally corrupt word, he should add the explanatory word *skir* 'pure' above the line.

c. Fragment P also contains an interlinear gloss. Here above the word *lungras* in line 987 – *uuas im an gelicnessa lungras fuglas* 'it had the likeness of a powerful bird' – the word *gitalas* has been entered, with which the likeness would then be of a "fast bird." At this place C also has *lungras*, and M has the faulty *iungres*, which makes no sense (see also M 1287 *iungaro* for *lungro*). The erroneous variants in M can be explained by the scribe having no knowledge of the original word, and this leads to the speculation that the glossator of P – regardless of whether this hand was also responsible for the body of the text – similarly considered the word *lungras* obscure and thus explained it with the more common *gitalas*. The difference in meaning between the gloss and

---

40   Frank Heidermanns, *Etymologisches Wörterbuch der germanischen Primäradjektive*, Studia linguistica Germanica 33 (New York: Walter de Gruyter, 1993), 575.

the interpretamentum, which is not slight, suggests that *lungras* might have been misunderstood entirely and simply "explained" by a word compatible with the context.[41] If one wanted to interpret the inserted word not as an explanatory addition – not as a gloss per se – but rather as an alternative reading for *lungras*, one would either have to view it as alliterating with *gelicnessia*, which would vitiate the rules of alliteration, or accept that the line would lack alliteration altogether.

At first glance, the interlinear entries in L and P seem very similar. They are written in a somewhat smaller script than that of the text body, with a darker ink, and certainly after the completion – of the first draft, that is – of the entire codex. They serve different functions: The first case might represent an alternative to the original reading, the next case remedies a corruption in the text, and the entry in P is presumably to be understood as an attempt to clarify the meaning of a word, though the possibility that an alternative reading was meant cannot be excluded with total confidence. Assuming again that L and P belonged to the same manuscript – P toward its beginning, L toward its end – these interlinear entries would indicate a subsequent revision of the work. In this regard, what comes to mind are the revisions made by Otfrid's own hand in the Viennese Codex 2687.[42]

---

41   This is Lambel's position in "Ein neuentdecktes Blatt" [note 4], 619. In Sehrt's dictionary [note 25], 192, the discussion is similarly about a "gloss," as is also the case in Willy Krogmann, "Studien zum Altwestfälischen," *Niederdeutsches Jahrbuch* 77 (1954), 13. Steinger, "Die Sprache des Heliand" [note 12], 2 interprets the entry as an addition that "is meant to assist the interpretation of the word."

42   For an edition of this text, see Wolfgang Kleiber and Ernst Hellgardt, eds., *Evangelienbuch*, by Otfrid von Weißenburg, 3 vols. (Tübingen: Max Niemeyer, 2004).

Hans Ulrich Schmid

The Relationship of L and C

Most of the readings in which L and C differ (see Normalized Rendition above) are of a graphemic, phonetic-phonological, or morphological sort. Such deviations are to be expected because of the spatial and temporal distance, mentioned already above, between the two manuscripts, and they are of little relevance to establishing a genealogical relationship between the texts. However, there are a few divergent wordings and syntactical structures, and these may involve readings in L that are closer to the archetype than the variants in C. The following examples are noteworthy:

a. 5829: L *uuas im that uuillspell mikil*: C *uuas im uuilspell mikil*. In contrast to C, L exhibits the pronoun *that*. The context suggests that the pronoun represents the more original reading, since *that uuillspell* 'that welcome message' makes clear the anaphoric reference to the words of the angel sitting in the empty tomb.

b. 5843: L *endi sprakun im mid iro uuordon tuo*: C *endi spracun mid iro uuordon tuo*. Here the personal pronoun is lacking in C that had been supplied – rightfully, as is now clear – by Rückert and subsequent editors.

c. 5852: L *ac hie is astandan giu*: C *ac hie ist astandan nu*. As far as semantics is concerned, the adverb *giu* 'already' is far more accurate than *nu* 'now'. It is met also, though with a different spelling, in the parallel first line of L (5823) – *ac hie ist astandan* – which happens to agree with C.

d. 5852–54: L *ac hie is astandan giu / an is líchamon thes gí gilobean sculun. / endi gehuggiat thero uuordo*: C *ac hie ist astandan nu / an is lichamen: thes gi gilobian sculun endi gehuggian thero uuordo*. With the imperative *endi gehuggiat*, L evidences a change in syntactical construction, whereas the *endi gihuggian* of C, an infinitive governed by *sculun*, works as a parallel to *gilobian*. Whichever reading is more original cannot be decided in absence of additional witnesses. However, when an a-verse is used in apposition to the preceding b-verse in alliterative poetry, the variation is normally lexical and not syntactic, and this fact might endorse the idea that the infinitive – the C variant – is the older of the two. In accord with this tendency, on the other hand, the scribe of C could have smoothed over the construction that remains in L. In any event, the syntax of L is entirely sensible; with *endi gehuggiat* a new fact is introduced, as the angel reminds the women of the words that Jesus spoke before His death.

e. 5867: L *thuo uuard sán aftar thiu*: C *Thuo uuarth after thiu*. The editor Moritz Heyne added the word *san* at this place, and the reading of L has confirmed his conjecture.

Despite a sample of fewer than fifty lines, it can be seen that C deviates from L not only in graphemic and phonological matters but also in its wording. Nevertheless, because neither the Munich *Heliand* manuscript M nor any of the other known fragments contains the same text as L, no conclusions can be drawn with any certainty about the relationship of L and C as regards their relationship to the archetype or original. The fact that one of the three interlinear entries in L corresponds with the text of C speaks for a certain proximity between the two. On the other hand, the fact that L evidences a corruption that was later corrected in a manner that disagrees with C suggests – along with the other variants – that at the least there is no direct affiliation between L and C. If L indeed stems from the same *Heliand* codex as P – and many things, as we have seen, point in this direction – then, genealogically, L and P would lead back to a preliminary stage *CP/L,[43] the path from which to C must have taken an unknown number of intermediate steps.

---

43 See Burkhard Taeger's stemma in Otto Behaghel, ed., *Heliand und Genesis*, 10th ed., rev. Burkhard Taeger, Altdeutsche Textbibliothek 4 (Tübingen: Max Niemeyer, 1996), xxiv.

Some Additional Remarks

Another question that can be raised here – but not answered – is whether L (possibly together with P) belonged to that enigmatic manuscript which enjoyed popularity within the Humanist and Reformation circles of Naumburg, Leipzig, and Wittenberg, and from which Flacius Illyricus possibly took the Latin "Praefatio" printed in his *Catalogus testium veritatis*.[44] With great caution, Kurt Hannemann considered the possibility that P could be a remnant of this manuscript.[45] That a fragment has been discovered, of all places, among the former holdings of the Thomaskirche at the Leipzig University Library that exhibits codicological and linguistic similarities with P lends an entirely new perspective to this complex of questions. The Church of St. Thomas took over the library collection of the monastery at Pergau, which for its part had been settled by monks from the Abbey of Corvey. Could this be an indirect path from Leipzig to the original home of the *Heliand*? And could this manuscript also be identical with the so-called Luther-*Heliand*, about which we know nothing beyond the brief mention of it by Melanchthon? And could Flacius really have taken his "Praefatio" from this very manuscript? These questions go beyond the scope of the present publication, the goal of which was to provide the first textual analysis of MS L.

---

44 The "Praefatio" is printed in the majority of *Heliand* editions. A reproduction of its first printing can be seen in Taeger, *Der Heliand* [note 4], 33f.

45 Kurt Hannemann, "Die Lösung des Rätsels der Herkunft der Heliandpraefatio," in *Der Heliand*, ed. Jürgen Eichhoff and Irmengard Rauch, Wege der Forschung 321 (Darmstadt: Wissenschaftliche Buchgesellschaft, 1973), 1–13.

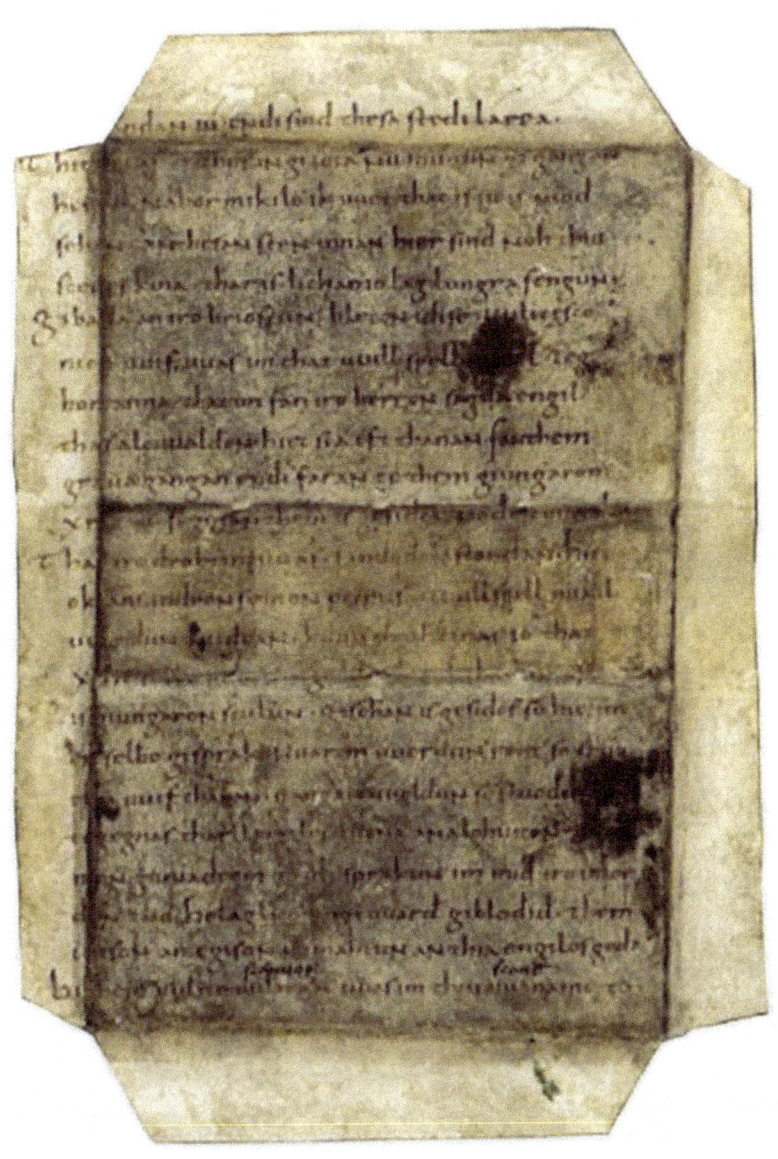

Image 1: Leipzig, Universitätsbibliothek, Thomas 4073 (MS), outer side: Heliand (L)

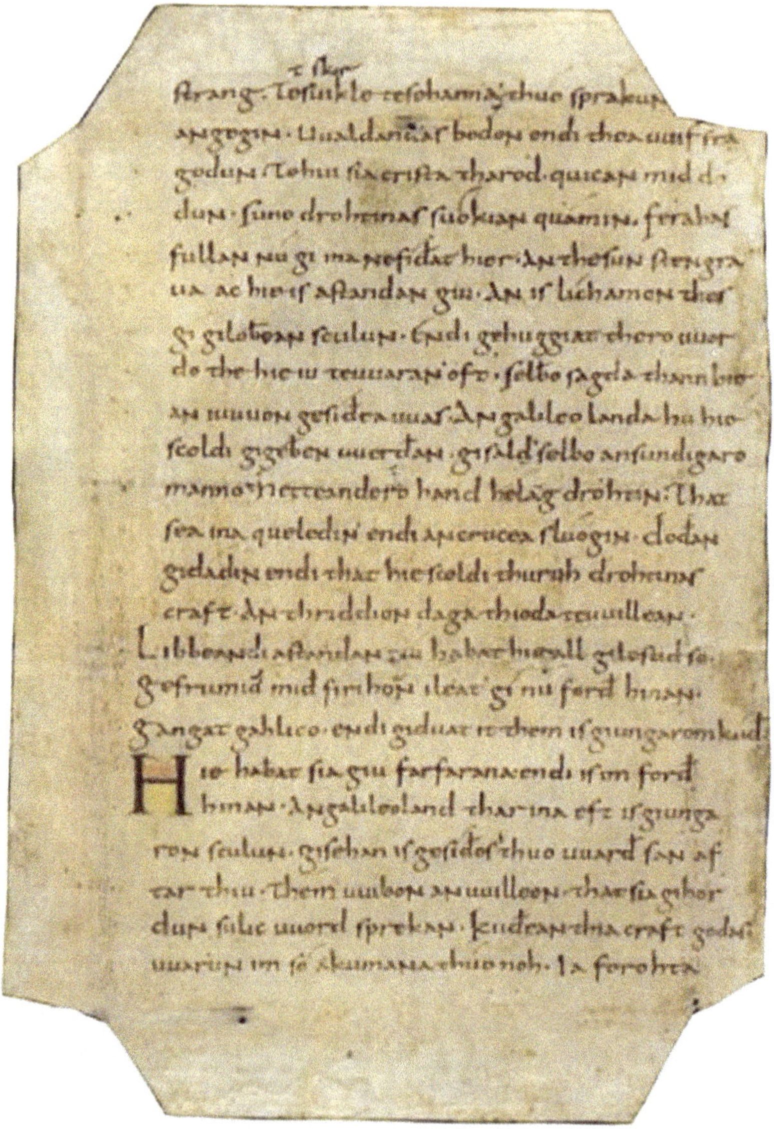

strang. Tosulelo tesohanna; thuo sprakun
angegin. Uualdandas bodon endi thea uuiffra
godun. Tohun sixcrista tharod. quicapi mid d-
dun. suno drohtinas subkian quamin. ferahas
fullan nu gi managefidac hier an thesun stengra
ua ac hie is astandan giu. An is lichamon thes
& gilotean sculun. Endi gehuggiat thero uuer
do the hie iu teuuaran ofto. selbo sagda than lio
an nuuon gesidea uuas an galileo landa hu hie
scoldi gigeben uuerdan. gisald selbo ansundigaro
manno herreandero hand helig drohtin. That
sea ina queledin endi an erucea sluogin. dodan
gisladin endi that hie soldi thurah drohtines
craft an thriddion daga thioda teuuillean.
Libbeandi astandan zu habar hies all getsid sa.
gefrumid mid firihon. ilear gi nu ferd hinan
gangat gahlico. endi giduat it them is giungaron kud

Hie habat siu giu farfaran. endi is in forð
hinan angalileo land. thar ina eft is giunga
ron sculun. gisehan is gesidos. thuo uuard san af
tar thiu them uuibon an uuilleon. that sia ghor
dun salic uuord sprekan. kudean thia craft godas
uuarun im so skumana. thio noh. Ia forohtea

Image 2: Leipzig, Universitätsbibliothek, Thomas 4073 (MS), inner side: Heliand (L)

Works Cited

"114 in Coptic Script of 'Thomas Gospel' Described Here." *New York Times.* March 19, 1959. 1.
Aland, Barbara, et al., eds. *The Greek New Testament.* 4th ed. Nördlingen: C. H. Beck, 2001. Repr. 2004.
Anderson, Earl R. "The Battle of Maldon: A Reappraisal of Possible Sources, Date, and Theme." In *Modes of Interpretation in Old English Literature: Essays in Honour of Stanley B. Greenfield.* Ed. Phyllis R. Brown et al. Toronto: U of Toronto Press, 1986. 247–72.
Anderson, Earl R. *Cynewulf: Structure, Style, and Theme in his Poetry.* London: Associated University Presses, 1983.
Andersson, Theodore M. "The Caedmon Fiction in the 'Heliand' Preface." *PMLA* 89 (1974): 278–84.
Angenendt, Arnold. *Das Frühmittelalter: Die abendländische Christenheit von 400 bis 900.* 2nd ed. Stuttgart: W. Kohlhammer, 1995.
"Apostolic Authorship Denied." *New York Times.* October 7, 1956. 34.
Appiah, Kwame Anthony. "Race." In *Critical Terms for Literary Study.* Ed. Frank Lentricchia and Thomas McLaughlin. 2nd ed. Chicago: U of Chicago Press, 1995. 274–87.
Arnett, Carlee. "A Cognitive Approach to the Old Saxon Processual Passive." *American Journal of Germanic Linguistics and Literatures* 12 (2000): 81–99.
Arnett, Carlee. "Perfect Selection in the Old Saxon *Heliand*." *American Journal of Germanic Linguistics and Literatures* 9 (1997): 23–72.
Auerbach, Erich. *Mimesis: The Representation of Reality in Western Literature.* Trans. Willard R. Trask. Princeton: Princeton UP, 1953. Repr. 1991.
Augustyn, Prisca. *The Semiotics of Fate, Death, and the Soul in Germanic Culture:*

The Christianization of Old Saxon. Berkeley Insights in Linguistics and Semiotics 50. New York: Peter Lang, 2002.

Awerbuch, Marianne. *Christlich-jüdische Begegnung im Zeitalter der Frühscholastik*. Abhandlung zum christlich-jüdischen Dialog 8. Munich: Chr. Kaiser, 1980.

Baarda, Tjitze. "'Chose' or 'Collected': Concerning an Aramaism in Logion 8 of the Gospel of Thomas and the Question of Independence." *Harvard Theological Review* 84 (1991): 373–97.

Baarda, Tjitze. "Clement of Alexandria, and the Parable of the Fisherman: Matthew 13.47–48 or Independent Tradition?" In *The Synoptic Gospels: Source Criticism and the New Literary Criticism*. Ed. Camille Focant. Leuven: Leuven UP, 1993. 582–98.

Baarda, Tjitze. "Het Evangelie van Thomas: Vier korte studies." In *Het Evangelie van Thomas*. By Tjitze Baarda et al. VU-segmenten 5. Zoetermeer: Meinema, 1999. 9–46.

Baarda, Tjitze. "Op zoek naar de tekst van het Diatessaron." *Vox Theologica* 32 (1962): 107–19

Baarda, Tjitze. "The Parable of the Fisherman in the *Heliand*: The Old Saxon Version of Matthew 13:47–50." *Amsterdamer Beiträge zur älteren Germanistik* 36 (1992): 39–58.

Baarda, Tjitze. "Philoxenus and the Parable of the Fisherman: Concerning the Diatessaron Text of Matthew 13.47–50." In *The Four Gospels, 1992: Festschrift Frans Neirynck*. Ed. Frans van Segbroeck et al. 3 vols. Leuven: Leuven UP, 1992. 2:1403–23.

Baarda Tjitze. "Thomas and Tatian." In *Early Transmission of Words of Jesus: Thomas, Tatian and the Text of the New Testament*. Ed. J. Helderman and S. J. Noorda. Amsterdam: VU Boekhandel, 1983. 37–49. Originally "Thomas en Tatianus." In *Het Evangelie van Thomas*. By R. Schippers and Tjitze Baarda. Kampen: Kok, 1960.

Baesecke, Georg. "Fulda und die altsächsischen Bibelepen." In *Kleinere Schriften zur althochdeutschen Literatur und Sprache*. By Baesecke. Ed. Werner Schröder. Bern: Francke, 1966. 348–76.

Baesecke, Georg. *Die Überlieferung des althochdeutschen Tatian*. Hallische Monographien 4. Halle: Max Niemeyer, 1948.

Works Cited

Baetke, Walter. *Die Aufnahme des Christentums durch die Germanen: Ein Beitrag zur Frage der Germanisierung des Christentums*. Darmstadt: Wissenschaftliche Buchgesellschaft, 1959.

Baetke, Walter. *Kleine Schriften: Geschichte, Recht und Religion in germanischem Schrifttum*. Ed. Kurt Rudolph and Ernst Walter. Weimar: Böhlau, 1973.

Baetke, Walter. "Religion und Politik beim Übergang der germanischen Stämme zum Christentum." *Kleine Schriften: Geschichte, Recht und Religion in germanischem Schrifttum*. Ed. Kurt Rudolph and Ernst Walter. Weimar: Böhlau, 1973. 351–69.

Bal, Mieke. *Lethal Love: Feminist Literary Readings of Biblical Love Stories*. Indiana Studies in Biblical Literature. Bloomington: Indiana UP, 1987.

Bammesberger, Alfred. "As. *thimm*: Wortbildung und phonologische Entwicklung." *Amsterdamer Beitrage zur älteren Germanistik* 52 (1999): 3–9.

Bammesberger, Alfred. "The Etymology of Germanic **idis-*." *NOWELE: North-Western European Language Evolution* 52 (2007): 81–89.

Barkenings, Hans-Joachim. "Das eine Volk Gottes: Von der Substitutionstheorie zur Ökumene mit Israel." In *Umkehr und Erneuerung: Erläuterungen zum Synodalbeschluß der Rheinischen Landessynode 1980 „Zur Erneuerung des Verhältnisses von Christen und Juden"*. Ed. Bertold Klappert and Helmut Starck. Neukirchen-Vluyn: Neukirchener Verlag, 1980. l67–181.

Barnes, Mervin R. "Old High German Umlaut." In *Interdigitations: Essays for Irmengard Rauch*. Ed. Gerald F. Carr et al. New York: Peter Lang, 1999. 239–46.

Bartsch, H.-W. "Das Thomas-Evangelium und die synoptischen Evangelien." *New Testament Studies* 6 (1960/1961): 249–60.

Bäuml, Franz H. "Verschriftlichte Mündlichkeit und vermündlichte Schriftlichkeit: Begriffsprüfungen an den Fällen 'Heliand' und 'Liber Evangeliorum'." In *Schriftlichkeit im frühen Mittelalter*. Ed. Ursula Schaefer. ScriptOralia 53. Tübingen: G. Narr, 1993. 254–66.

Becker, Peter J., and Eef Overgaauw, eds. *Aderlass und Seelentrost: Die Überlieferung deutscher Texte im Spiegel Berliner Handschriften und Inkunabeln*. Mainz: P. von Zabern, 2003.

Works Cited

Behaghel, Otto., ed. *Heliand und Genesis*. 9th ed. Rev. Burkhard Taeger. Altdeutsche Textbibliothek 4. Tübingen: Max Niemeyer, 1984.

Behaghel, Otto, ed. *Heliand und Genesis*. 10th ed. Rev. Burkhard Taeger. Altdeutsche Textbibliothek 4. Tübingen: Max Niemeyer, 1996.

Behaghel, Otto. *Die Syntax des Heliand*. Vienna: F. Tempsky, 1897.

Belkin, Johanna, and Jürgen Meier, eds. *Bibliographie zu Otfrid von Weißenburg und zur altsächsischen Bibeldichtung (Heliand und Genesis)*. Bibliographien zur deutschen Literatur des Mittelalters 7. Berlin: Erich Schmidt, 1975.

Berr, Samuel. *Etymological Glossary to the Old Saxon Heliand*. New York: Peter Lang, 1971.

Bessinger, J. B., ed. *A Concordance to the Anglo-Saxon Poetic Records*. Ithaca: Cornell UP, 1978.

Bischoff, Bernhard. *Katalog der festländischen Handschriften des neunten Jahrhunderts (mit Ausnahme der wisigotischen), Teil I: Aachen – Lambach*. Wiesbaden: Harrassowitz, 1998.

Bischoff, Bernhard. "Paläographische Fragen deutscher Denkmäler der Karolingerzeit." In *Mittelalterliche Studien: Ausgewählte Aufsätze zur Schriftkunde und Literaturgeschichte*. By Bischoff. 3 vols. Stuttgart: Anton Hiersemann, 1981. 3:73–111.

Bischoff, Bernhard. Review of *Werden und der Heliand: Studien zur Kulturgeschichte der Abtei Werden und zur Herkunft des Heliand*. By Richard Drögereit. *Anzeiger für deutsches Altertum* 66 (1952): 7–12.

Bischoff, Bernhard. "Die Schriftheimat der Münchener Heliand-Handschrift." *Beiträge zur Geschichte der deutschen Sprache und Literatur* [Tübingen] 101 (1979): 161–70. Reprinted in *Mittelalterliche Studien: Ausgewählte Aufsätze zur Schriftkunde und Literaturgeschichte*. By Bischoff. 3 vols. Stuttgart: Anton Hiersemann, 1981. 3:112–19.

Bischoff, Bernhard. "Die Straubinger Fragmente einer Heliand-Handschrift." *Beiträge zur Geschichte der deutschen Sprache und Literatur* 101 (1979): 171–80.

Blumenkranz, Bernhard. "Die Entwicklung im Westen zwischen 200 und 1200." In *Kirche und Synagoge: Handbuch zur Geschichte von Christen und Juden*. Ed. Karl Heinrich Rengstorf and Siegfried von Kortzfleisch. Stuttgart: Klett, 1968. 84–135.

Works Cited

Bonnard, Pierre. *L'Évangile selon Saint Matthieu*. Commentaire du Nouveau Testament 1. Neuchâtel: Delachaux & Niestlé, 1963.

Bornkamm, Heinrich. *Christus und die Germanen*. Berlin: Verlag des Evangelischen Bundes, 1936.

Bostock, J. Knight. *A Handbook on Old High German Literature*. Oxford: Clarendon, 1955.

Bostock, J. Knight. *A Handbook on Old High German Literature*. 2nd ed. Rev. K. C. King and D. R. McLintock. Oxford: Clarendon, 1976.

Boutkan, Dirk. "II. Pre-Germanic Fish in Old Saxon Glosses: On Alleged Ablaut Patterns and Other Formal Deviations in Gmc. Substratum Words." *Amsterdamer Beiträge zur älteren Germanistik* 52 (1999): 11–26.

Boutkan, Dirk. "Pre-Germanic Fishnames I: Gmc. 'bream'." *Amsterdamer Beiträge zur älteren Germanistik* 51 (1999): 5–22.

Boutkan, Dirk. "Pre-Germanic Fishnames III: A New Etymology of 'herring'." *Amsterdamer Beiträge zur älteren Germanistik* 53 (2000): 5–22.

Boyer, Régis. *Le Christ des barbares: Le monde nordique (IXe-XIIIe S.)*. Paris: Cerf, 1987.

Braune, Wilhelm. *Althochdeutsche Grammatik*. 9th ed. Rev. Walter Mitzka. Tübingen: Max Niemeyer, 1959.

Braune, Wilhelm. *Althochdeutsche Grammatik I*. 15th ed. Rev. Ingo Reiffenstein. Tübingen: Max Niemeyer, 2004.

Braune, Wilhelm. *Althochdeutsches Lesebuch*. 17th ed. Rev. Ernst A. Ebbinghaus. Tübingen: Max Niemeyer, 1994.

Bredehoft, Thomas. "Old English and Old Saxon Formulaic Rhyme." *Anglia* 123 (2005): 204–29.

Brennecke, Hanns Christof. "Christianisierung und Identität: Das Beispiel der germanischen Völker." In *Missionsgeschichte, Kirchengeschichte, Weltgeschichte: Christliche Missionen im Kontext nationaler Entwicklungen in Afrika, Asien und Ozeanien*. Ed. Ulrich van der Heyden and Heike Liebau. Missionsgeschichtliches Archiv 1. Stuttgart: F. Steiner, 1996. 239–247.

Brinkmann, Hennig. *Mittelalterliche Hermeneutik*. Tübingen: Max Niemeyer, 1980.

van den Broek, Roelof. "A Latin Diatessaron in the 'Vita Beate Marie et Salvatoris Rhythmica'." *New Testament Studies* 21 (1974): 109–32.

Works Cited

Bruckner, Wilhelm. *Der Helianddichter – ein Laie.* Wissenschaftliche Beilage zum Bericht über das Gymnasium in Basel, Schuljahr 1903/1904. Basel, 1904.

Bultmann, Rudolf. *The Gospel of John: A Commentary.* Trans. G. R. Beasley-Murray. Oxford: Basil Blackwell, 1971.

Burchhardt, Clemens, ed. *Heliand: Die Verdener altsächsische Evangelium-Dichtung von 830 übertragen ins 21. Jahrhundert.* Verden: Wirtschaftsförderkreis des Domherrenhauses, 2007.

Callender, Craig J. *Gemination in West Germanic.* Doctoral Diss. University of South Carolina, 2006.

Carr, Gerald F. Review of *The Saxon Savior: The Germanic Transformation of the Gospel in the Ninth-Century Heliand* and *The Heliand: The Saxon Gospel.* By G. Ronald Murphy. *American Journal of Germanic Linguistics and Literatures* 6 (1994): 95–105.

Cathey, James E. "Give Us This Day Our Daily *râd*." *Journal of English and Germanic Philology* 94 (1995): 157–175.

Cathey, James E., ed. *Hêliand: Text and Commentary.* Medieval European Studies 2. Morgantown: U of West Virginia Press, 2002.

Cathey, James E. "Interpretatio Christiana Saxonica: Redefinition for Re-education." In *Interdigitations: Essays for Irmengard Rauch.* Ed. Gerald F. Carr et al. New York: Peter Lang, 1999. 163–72.

Cathey, James E. *Old Saxon.* Languages of the World 252. Munich: Lincom Europa, 2000.

Cathey, James E. Review of *The Semiotics of Fate, Death, and the Soul in Germanic Culture: The Christianization of Old Saxon.* By Prisca Augustyn. *Interdisciplinary Journal of Germanic Linguistics and Semiotic Analysis* 10 (2005): 251–260.

Cathey, James E. "Die Rhetorik der Weisheit und Beredtheit im *Hêliand*." *Literaturwissenschaftliches Jahrbuch* 37 (1996): 31–46.

Cerquiglini, Bernard. *Éloge de la variant: Histoire critique de la philologie.* Paris: Seuil, 1989.

Chafe, Wallace L. "Integration and Involvement in Speaking, Writing and Oral Literature." In *Spoken and Written Language: Exploring Orality and Literacy.* Ed. Deborah Tannen. Norwood: ABLEX, 1982. 35–53.

Works Cited

Chase, Frederic Henry. *The Lord's Prayer in the Early Church.* Cambridge: Cambridge UP, 1891.

Coffey, Michael P. *Autosegmental Processes in Early Germanic: Evidence from Northwest Germanic.* Doctoral diss. University of California-Berkeley, 2005.

Conrady, Karl Otto. "Reminiszenzen und Reflexionen." In *Wie, warum und zu welchem Ende wurde ich Literaturhistoriker?* Ed. Siegfried Unseld. Frankfurt: Suhrkampf, 1972. 39–78.

Cordes, Gerhard. Review of *Der Heliand: Theologischer Sinn als tektonische Form. Vorbereitung und Grundlegung der Interpretation.* By Johannes Rathofer. *Anzeiger für deutsches Altertum* 78 (1967): 55–79.

Cordes, Gerhard, and Ferdinand Holthausen. *Altniederdeutsches Elementarbuch: Wort- und Lautlehre.* Heidelberg: Carl Winter, 1973.

Cusack, Carole M. *Conversion among the Germanic Peoples.* London: Cassell, 1998.

D'Alquen, Richard. 1994. Review of *The Old Saxon Language: Grammar, Epic Narrative, Linguistic Interference.* By Irmengard Rauch. *American Journal of Germanic Linguistics and Literatures* 6 (1994): 89–95.

Dart, John. *The Laughing Savior: The Discovery and Significance of the Nag Hammadi Coptic Library.* New York: Harper & Row, 1976.

Dennett, Daniel. *Philosophie des menschlichen Bewußtseins.* Trans. Franz Wuketits. Hamburg: Hoffmann und Campe, 1994.

Dentan, Robert C. "From the Gospel of Thomas." Review of *The Secret Sayings of Jesus.* By Robert M. Grant and David Noel Freedman. *New York Times.* April 3, 1960. BR26.

Denzinger, Heinrich. *Kompendium der glaubensbekenntnisse und kirchlichen Lehrentscheidungen.* 37th ed. Rev. Peter Hünermann. Freiburg: Herder, 1991.

Dewey, Tonya Kim. *The Origins and Development of Germanic V2: Evidence from Alliterative Verse.* Doctoral diss. University of California-Berkeley, 2006.

Dewey, Tonya Kim. Review of *The Metre of Old Saxon Poetry: The Remaking of Alliterative Tradition.* By Seiichi Suzuki. *Interdisciplinary Journal of Germanic Linguistics and Semiotic Analysis* 11 (2006): 278–281.

Dibelius, Otto. *Die echte Germanisierung der Kirche.* Berlin: Kranz, 1935.

Works Cited

Diemer, Joseph, ed. *Deutsche Gedichte des elften und zwölften Jahrhunderts.* Vienna: W. Braumüller, 1849. Repr. Darmstadt: Wissenschaftliche Buchgesellschaft, 1968.

Doane, Alger N., ed. *The Old Saxon Genesis: An Edition of the West Saxon Genesis B and the Old Saxon Vatican Genesis.* Madison: U of Wisconsin Press, 1978.

Dobbie, Elliott V. K., ed. *The Anglo Saxon Minor Poems.* Anglo-Saxon Poetic Records 6. New York: Columbia UP, 1942.

Dörries, Hermann. "Zur Frage der Germanisierung des Christentums." In *Wort und Stunde.* By Dörries. 3 vols. Göttingen: Vandenhoeck & Ruprecht 1966–70. 2:190–209.

Dreisonstok, Mark. *The Pagan-Christian Concept of Wealth and its Relationship to Light in the* Heliand *and in* Beowulf, *with Consideration of Other Anglo-Saxon Works.* Doctoral diss. Georgetown University, 2000.

Drögerheit, Richard. "Die Heimat des *Heliand.*" *Jahrbuch der Gesellschaft für niedersächsische Kirchengeschichte* 49 (1951): 1–18. Repr. in *Sachsen, Angelsachsen, Niedersachsen: Ausgewählte Aufsätze in einem dreibändigem Werk.* By Drögereit. Ed. Carl Röper and Herbert Huster. 3 vols. Hamburg: Commercium, 1978. 3:51–68.

Drögerheit, Richard. "Die schriftlichen Quellen zur Christianisierung der Sachsen und ihre Aussagefähigkeit." In *Die Eingliederung der Sachsen in das Frankenreich.* Ed. Walther Lammers. Darmstadt: Wissenschaftliche Buchgesellschaft, 1970. 451–69.

Drögerheit, Richard. *Werden und der Heliand: Studien zur Kulturgeschichte der Abtei Werden und zur Herkunft des Heliand.* Essen: Fredebeul & Koenen, 1951.

Ebbinghaus, E. A. Review of *The Old Saxon Language: Grammar, Epic Narrative, Linguistic Interference.* By Irmengard Rauch. *General Linguistics* 33 (1993): 123–25.

Ehrismann, Gustav. *Geschichte der Deutschen Literatur bis zum Ausgang des Mittelalters. Erster Teil: Die althochdeutsche Literatur.* Munich: C. H. Beck, 1918.

Eichhoff, Jürgen, and Irmengard Rauch, eds. *Der Heliand.* Wege der Forschung 321. Darmstadt: Wissenschaftliche Buchgesellschaft, 1973.

Works Cited

Erdmann, Oskar, ed. *Otfrids Evangelienbuch*. 5th ed. Rev. Ludwig Wolff. Altdeutsche Textbibliothek 49. Tübingen: Max Niemeyer, 1965.

Eska, Joseph F. Book Notice of *Old Saxon*. By James E. Cathey 2000. *Language* 79 (2003): 836.

"Excerpts From Talk on Jesus' Sayings." *New York Times*. March 19, 1959. 12.

Finsler, Georg. *Homer*. 2nd ed. 2 vols. Leipzig: B. G. Teubner, 1913.

Fischer, Bonifatius, et al., eds. *Biblia Sacra iuxta Vulgata versionem*. 4th ed. Stuttgart: Württemburgische Bibelanstalt, 1994.

Fleischer, Jürg. "Das prädikative Adjektiv und Partizip im Althochdeutschen und Altniederdeutschen." *Sprachwissenschaft* 32 (2007): 279–348.

Flint, Valerie. *The Rise of Magic in Early Medieval Europe*. Princeton: Princeton UP, 1991.

Flowers, Stephen E. *Runes and Magic, Magical Formulaic Elements in the Older Runic Tradition*. New York: Peter Lang, 1986.

Foerste, William. "Otfrids literarisches Verhältnis zum Heliand." *Niederdeutsches Jahrbuch: Jahrbuch des Vereins für niederdeutsche Sprachforschung* 71/73 (1950): 40–67.

Foley, John Miles. *The Odyssey, Beowulf, and the Serbo-Croatian Return Song*. Berkeley: U of California Press, 1990.

Frantzen Allen J. *Desire for Origins: New Language, Old English, and Teaching the Tradition*. New Brunswick: Rutgers UP, 1990.

Freytag, Hartmut. *Die Theorie der allegorischen Schriftdeutung und die Allegorie in deutschen Texten besonders des 11. bis 13. Jahrhunderts*. Bibliotheca Germanica 24. Bern: Francke, 1982.

Friedrich, Martin. "Jesus Christus zwischen Juden und Heiden: Das Christusbild in der Germanenmission, dargestellt am *Heliand*." *Zeitschrift für Kirchengeschichte* 113 (2002), 313–28.

Frizzel, Lawrence E. "Jew and Christian in the New Testament." In *German Literature Between Faiths: Jew and Christian at Odds and in Harmony*. Ed. Peter Meister. Studies in German Jewish History 6. Berlin: Peter Lang, 2004. 1–13, 177–78.

Fulk, Robert D. Review of *The Metre of Old Saxon Poetry: The Remaking of Alliterative Tradition*. By Seiichi Suzuki. *Journal of Germanic Linguistics* 17 (2005): 149–153.

Fuss, Martin. *Die religiose Lexik des Althochdeutschen und Altsächsischen.* Frankfurt: Peter Lang, 2000.

Gallée, Johan H. *Altsächsische Grammatik.* 2nd ed. Rev. Johannes Lochner. Halle: Max Niemeyer, 1910.

Gallée, Johan H. *Altsächsische Grammatik.* 3rd ed. Rev. Heinrich Tiefenbach. Tübingen: Max Niemeyer, 1993.

Gantert, Klaus. *Akkommodation und eingeschriebener Kommentar: Untersuchungen zur Übertragungsstrategie des Helianddichters.* Tübingen: Narr, 1998.

Garitte, Gerard. "Bibliographie." *Le Muséon* 73 (1960): 210–22.

Genzmer, Felix, ed. and trans. *Heliand und die Bruchstücke der Genesis.* Stuttgart: Reclam, 1955. Repr. 1977 and 1989.

Ginsberg, Herbert, and Sylvia Opper. *Piagets Theorie der geistigen Entwicklung.* Stuttgart: Klett, 1975.

Gneuss, Helmut. *Die Battle of Maldon als historisches und literarisches Zeugnis.* Munich: C. H. Beck, 1976.

Goblirsch, Kurt G. *Lautverschiebungen in den germanischen Sprachen.* Heidelberg: Carl Winter, 2005.

Goblirsch, Kurt G. "The Voicing of Fricatives in West Germanic and the Partial Consonant Shift." *Folia Linguistica Historica* 24 (2003): 111–152.

Göhler, Hulda. "Das Christusbild in Otfrieds Evangelienbuch und im Heliand." *Zeitschrift für deutsche Philologie* 59 (1934–35): 1–52.

Gottzmann, Carola L. *Das Alte Atlilied: Untersuchung der Gestaltungsprinzipien seiner Handlungsstruktur.* Heidelberg: Carl Winter, 1973.

Green, Dennis H. "Fictive Orality: A Restriction on the Use of the Concept." In *Blütezeit: Festschrift für L. Peter Johnson zum 70. Geburtstag.* Ed. Joachim Heinzle et al. Tübingen: Max Niemeyer, 2000. 161–74.

Green, Dennis H. "Zur primären Rezeption von Otfrids Evangelienbuch." In *Althochdeutsch.* Ed. Rolf Bergmann et al. 2 vols. Heidelberg: Carl Winter, 1987. 1:737–55.

Grein, C. W. M. *Die Quellen des Heliand. Nebst einem Anhang: Tatians Evangelienharmonie herausgegeben nach dem Codex Cassellanus.* Cassel: Theodor Kay, 1869.

Works Cited

Grosch, Elisabeth. "Das Gottes- und Menschenbild im Heliand." *Beiträge zur Geschichte der deutschen Sprache und Literatur* 72 (1950): 90–120.

Gschwantler, Otto. "Älteste Gattungen germanischer Dichtung." In *Europäisches Frühmittelalter*. Ed. Klaus von See. Neues Handbuch zur Literaturwissenschaft 6. Wiesbaden: AULA, 1985. 91–123.

Gschwantler, Otto. "Christus, Thor und die Midgardschlange." In *Festschrift für Otto Höfler zum 65. Geburtstag*. Ed. Helmut Birkhan and Otto Gschwantler. 2 vols. Vienna: Notring, 1968. 1:145–68.

Guillaumont, A., et al., eds. *The Gospel According to Thomas: Coptic Text Established and Translated*. Leiden: E. J. Brill, 1959.

Günter, Heinrich. *Psychologie der Legende: Studien zu einer wissenschaftlichen Heiligen-Geschichte*. Freiburg: Herder, 1949.

Haferland, Harald. "Der Haß der Feinde: Germanische Heldendichtung und die Erzählkonzeption des *Heliand*." *Euphorion* 95 (2001): 237–56.

Haferland, Harald. "Mündliche Erzähltechnik im *Heliand*." *Germanisch-Romanische Monatshefte* 52 (2002): 237–59.

Haferland, Harald. *Mündlichkeit, Gedächtnis und Medialität: Heldendichtung im deutschen Mittelalter*. Göttingen: Vandenhoeck & Ruprecht, 2004.

Haferland, Harald. "War der Dichter des 'Heliand' illiterat?" *Zeitschrift für deutsches Altertum und deutsche Literatur* 131 (2002): 20–48.

Hagenlocher, Albrecht. *Schicksal im Heliand: Verwendung und Bedeutung der nominalen Beziehungen*. Niederdeutsche Studien 21. Cologne: Böhlau, 1975.

Hagenlocher, Albrecht. "Theologische Systematik und epische Gestaltung: Beobachtung zur Darstellung der feindlichen Juden im Heliand und in Otfrids Evangelienbuch." *Beiträge zur Geschichte der deutschen Sprache und Literatur* (Tübingen) 96 (1974): 33–58.

Hannemann, Kurt. "Die Lösung des Rätsels der Herkunft der Heliandpraefatio." In *Der Heliand*. Ed. Jürgen Eichhoff and Irmengard Rauch. Wege der Forschung 321. Darmstadt: Wissenschaftliche Buchgesellschaft, 1973. 1–13.

Hartman, Megan. "Kuhn's Laws, Old Saxon, and the Hypermetric Line." Paper presented at GLAC 14. Madison, Wisconsin, 2008.

Haubrichs, Wolfgang. "Heliand und altdeutsche Genesis." In *Reallexikon der germanischen Altertumskunde*. Ed. Johannes Hoops et al. 2nd ed. Vol. 14. Berlin: Walter de Gruyter, 1998. 297–308.

Haubrichs, Wolfgang. "Die Praefatio des Heliand: Ein Zeugnis der Religions- und Bildungspolitik Ludwigs des Deutschen." In *Der Heliand*. Ed. Jürgen Eichhoff and Irmengard Rauch. Wege der Forschung 321. 400–35.

Haubrichs, Wolfgang. "Von den Anfängen bis zum hohen Mittelalter." In *Geschichte der deutschen Literatur von den Anfängen bis zum Beginn der Neuzeit*. 2nd ed. Ed. Joachim Heinzle. Tübingen: Max Niemeyer, 1995.

Haug, Walter. "Andreas Heuslers Heldensagenmodell: Prämissen, Kritik und Gegenentwurf." *Zeitschrift für deutsches Altertum und deutsche Literatur* 104 (1975): 273–92.

Heidermanns, Frank. *Etymologisches Wörterbuch der germanischen Primäradjektive*. Studia linguistica Germanica 33. New York: Walter de Gruyter, 1993.

Hellgardt, Ernst. "Die *Praefatio in librum Antiquum lingua Saxonica conscriptum*, die *Versus de poete & interprete huius codicis* und die altsächsische Bibelepik." In *Entstehung des Deutschen: Festschrift für Heinrich Tiefenbach*. Ed. Albrecht Greule and Eckhard Meineke. Heidelberg: Carl Winter, 2004. 173–230.

Henß, Walter. "Zur Quellenfrage im Heliand und ahd. Tatian," *Niederdeutsches Jahrbuch: Jahrbuch des Vereins für niederdeutsche Sprachforschung* 77 (1954): 1–7.

Heyne, Moritz, ed. *Hêliand: Mit ausführlichem Glossar*. 2nd ed. Paderborn: F. Schöningh, 1873.

Heyne, Moritz, ed. *Heliand, nebst den Bruchstücken der altsächsischen Genesis*. 4th ed. Paderborn: F. Schöningh, 1905.

Hofmann, Dietrich. *Die Versstrukturen der altsächsischen Stabreimgedichte Heliand und Genesis*. 2 vols. Heidelberg: Carl Winter, 1991.

den Hollander, August, and Ulrich Schmid. "Middeleeuwse bronnen van het Luikse «Leven van Jezus»." *Queeste* 6 (1999): 127–46.

Holthausen, Ferdinand. *Altsächsisches Elementarbuch*. Heidelberg: Carl Winter, 1900.

Works Cited

Holthausen, Ferdinand. *Altsächsisches Elementarbuch*. 2nd ed. Heidelberg: Carl Winter, 1921.

Hopper, Paul J., and Elizabeth Closs Traugott. *Grammaticalization*. 2nd ed. Cambridge Textbooks in Linguistics. Cambridge: Cambridge UP, 2003.

Hoptman, Ari. *Verner's Law, Stress, and the Accentuation of Old Germanic Poetry*. Doctoral diss. University of Minnesota-Minneapolis, 2002.

Hövelmann, Werner. *Die Eingangsformel in germanischer Dichtung*. Bochum: H. Pöppinghaus, 1936.

Huber, Wolfgang. *Heliand und Matthäusexegese: Quellenstudien insbesondere zu Sedulius Scottus*. Münchener Germanistische Beiträge 3. Munich: M. Hueber, 1969.

Huisman, J. A. Afterword to "Der Heliand und das Thomasevangelium." By Gilles Quispel. *Vigiliae Christianae* 16 (1962): 151–52.

Hunzinger C.-H. "Unbekannte Gleichnisse Jesu aus dem Thomas-Evangelium." In *Judentum, Urchristentum, Kirche: Festschrift für Joachim Jeremias*. Ed. Walther Eltester. Berlin: A. Töpelmann, 1960. 209–20.

Hurst, D., ed. *Bedae Venerabilis Opera. Pars II: Opera exegetica. 3: In Lvkae evangelivm expositio, In Marci evangelivm expositio*. CCSL 120. Turnhout: Brepols, 1960.

Illich, Ivan. *Im Weinberg des Textes. Als das Schriftbild der Moderne entstand: Ein Kommentar zu Hugos Didascalicon*. Frankfurt am Main: Luchterhand, 1991.

Isakson, Bo. "How Primary was the OHG Primary Umlaut?" *NOWELE: North-Western European Language Evolution* 41 (2002): 99–104.

Iscrulescu, Cristian. *The Phonological Dimension of Grammatical Markedness*. Doctoral diss. University of Southern California, 2006.

Jeep, John M. 2004. Review of *Hêliand: Text and Commentary*. By James E. Cathey. *Speculum* 79 (2004): 147–149.

Jellinek, Max H. Review of *Bruchstücke der altsächsischen Bibeldichtung aus der Bibliotheca Palatina*. By Karl Zangemeister and Wilhelm Braune. *Anzeiger für deutsches Altertum und deutsche Literatur* 21 (1895): 204–25.

Jones, George Fenwick. Review of *The Heliand*. By Mariana Scott. *Modern Language Notes* 82 (1967): 488–90.

Jostes, Franz. "Der Dichter des Heliand." *Zeitschrift für deutsches Altertum und deutsche Literatur* 40 (1896): 341–68.

Jülicher, Adolf. "Der echte Tatiantext." *Journal of Biblical Literature* 43 (1924): 132–71.

Kabell, Aage. "Der Fischfang Thors." *Arkiv för nordisk filologi* 91 (1976): 123–29.

Kacandes, Irene. "German Cultural Studies: What Is at Stake?" In *A User's Guide to German Cultural Studies*. Ed. Scott Denham, Irene Kacandes, and Jonathan Petropoulos. Ann Arbor: U of Michigan Press, 1997. 2–28.

Kartschoke, Dieter. *Bibeldichtung: Studien zur Geschichte der epischen Bibelparaphrase von Juvencus bis Otfrid von Weißenburg*. Munich: Fink, 1975.

Kartschoke, Dieter. *Geschichte der deutschen Literatur im frühen Mittelalter*. 2nd ed. Munich: Dtv, 1994.

Kaske, Robert E. "Beowulf." In *Critical Approaches to Six Major English Works: Beowulf through Paradise Lost*. Ed. Robert M. Lumiansky and Herschel Baker. Philadelphia: U of Pennsylvania Press, 1968. 3–40.

Kawasaki, Yasushi. *Eine graphematische Untersuchung zu den HELIAND-Handschriften*. Munich: Iudicium, 2004.

Kehr, Dave. Review of *The Green Pastures*. Directed by Marc Connelly. *The Chicago Reader*. http://onfilm.chicagoreader.com/movies/capsules/4254_GREEN_PASTURES (accessed April 19, 2004).

Kellogg, Robert L. "The South Germanic Oral Tradition," in *Franciplegius: Medieval and Linguistic Studies in Honor of F. P. Magoun, Jr*. Ed. Jess B. Bessinger and Robert P. Creed. New York: New York UP, 1965.

Klappert, Bertold. "Jesus Christen zwischen Juden und Christen." in *Umkehr und Erneuerung: Erläuterungen zum Synodalbeschluß der Rheinischen Landessynode 1980 „Zur Erneuerung des Verhältnisses von Christen und Juden"*. Ed. Bertold Klappert and Helmut Starck. Neukirchen-Vluyn: Neukirchener Verlag, 1980. 138–66.

Klappert, Bertold. "Die Wurzel trägt dich." In *Umkehr und Erneuerung: Erläuterungen zum Synodalbeschluß der Rheinischen Landessynode 1980 „Zur Erneuerung des Verhältnisses von Christen und Juden"*. Ed. Bertold Klappert and Helmut Starck. Neukirchen-Vluyn: Neukirchener Verlag, 1980. 23–54.

Works Cited

Kleiber, Wolfgang, and Ernst Hellgardt, eds. *Evangelienbuch*. By Otfrid von Weißenburg. 3 vols. Tübingen: Max Niemeyer, 2004.

Klein, Thomas. *Studien zur Wechselbeziehung zwischen altsächsischem und althochdeutschem Schreibwesen und ihrer sprach- und kulturgeschichtlichen Bedeutung*. Göppinger Arbeiten zur Germanistik 205. Göppingen: Kümmerle, 1977.

Köhler, Walther. "Das Christusbild im Heliand." *Archiv für Kulturgeschichte* 26 (1936): 265–82.

Köne, J. R. *Heliand oder das Lied vom Leben Jesu, sonst auch die altsächsische Evangelienharmonie. In der Urschrift mit nebenstehender Übersetzung, nebst Anmerkungen und einem Wortverzeichnisse*. Münster: Theissing, 1855.

Kottje, Raymund. *Studien zum Einfluss des Alten Testaments auf Recht und Liturgie des frühen Mittelalters (6.-8. Jahrhundert)*. 2nd ed. Bonner historische Forschungen 23. Bonn: Ludwig Röhrscheid, 1970.

Krapp, George P., ed. *The Vercelli Book*. Anglo-Saxon Poetic Records 2. New York: Columbia UP, 1932.

Krapp, George P., and Elliott V. K. Dobbie, eds. *The Exeter Book*. Anglo-Saxon Poetic Records 3. New York: Columbia UP, 1936.

Krogh, Steffen. *Die Stellung des Altsächsischen im Rahmen der germanischen Sprachen*. Studien zum Althochdeutschen 29. Göttingen: Vandenhoeck & Ruprecht, 1996.

Krogmann, Willy. *Absicht oder Willkür im Aufbau des Heliand*. Deutsches Bibel-Archiv: Abhandlung und Vorträge 1. Hamburg: Friedrig Wittig, 1964.

Krogmann, Willy. "Eine 'Ackermann'-Handschrift zwischen Urschrift und Archetypus." *Zietschrift für deutsche Philologie* 86 (1967): 80–90.

Krogmann, Willy. *Der althochdeusche 138. Psalm: Forschungsgeschichtlicher Überblick und Urfassung*. Hamburg: F. Wittig, 1973.

Krogmann, Willy. "Apokryphes im Heliand?" *Niederdeutsches Jahrbuch: Jahrbuch des Vereins für niederdeutsche Sprachforschung* 79 (1956): 15–35.

Krogmann, Willy. "Eine fremde Fitte im Heliand." *Niederdeutsches Jahrbuch: Jahrbuch des Vereins für niederdeutsche Sprachforschung* 78 (1955): 1–27.

Krogmann, Willy. *Goethes 'Urfaust'*. Berlin: Emil Ebering, 1933.

Krogmann, Willy. *Die Heimatfrage des Heliand im Lichte des Worschatzes*. Wismar: Hinsdorff, 1937.

Krogmann, Willy. "Heliand, Tatian, und Thomasevangelium." *Zeitschrift für die neutestamentliche Wissenschaft* 51 (1960): 255–68.

Krogmann, Willy. "Heliand und Thomasevangelium." *Vigiliae Christianae* 18 (1964): 65–73.

Krogmann, Willy. *Das Hildebrandslied: In der langobardischen Urfassung hergestellt*. Berlin: Erich Schmidt, 1959.

Krogmann, Willy. *Die Kultur der alten Germanen*. Konstanz: Athenaion, 1960.

Krogmann, Willy. *Der Name der Germanen*. Wismar: Hinsdorff, 1933.

Krogmann, Willy. "Die Praefatio in librum aniquum lingua Saxonica Conscriptum." In *Der Heliand*. Ed. Jürgen Eichhoff and Irmengard Rauch. Wege der Forschung 321. Darmstadt: Wissenschaftliche Buchgesellschaft, 1973. 20–53.

Krogmann, Willy. *Der Rattenfänger von Hameln: Eine Untersuchung über das Werden der Sage*. Berlin: Emil Ebering, 1934.

Krogmann, Willy. "Studien zum Altwestfälischen." *Niederdeutsches Jahrbuch* 77 (1954): 7–15.

Krogmann, Willy. *Untersuchungen zum Ursprung der Gretchentragödie*. Wismar: Willgeroth & Menzel, 1928.

Krogmann, Willy. "Die Vorlage des 'Reynke de Vos'." *Niederdeutsches Jahrbuch: Jahrbuch des Vereins für niederdeutsche Sprachforschung* 87 (1964): 29–55.

Krusch, Bruno, ed. *Arbeonis episcopi frisingensis Vitae Sanctorum Haimhrammi et Corbiniani*. Monumenta Germaniae Historica: Scriptores Rerum Germanicarum in Usum Scholarum 13. Hannover: Hahn, 1920.

Krusch, Bruno, and Wilhelm Levison, eds. *Passiones vitaeque sanctorum aevi merovingici*. Monumenta Germaniae Historica: Scriptorum Rerum Merovingicarum 5. Hannover: Hahn, 1910.

Kuhn, Thomas. *The Structure of Scientific Revolutions*. 2nd ed. Chicago: U of Chicago Press, 1970.

Kyes, Robert L. Review of *The Heliand*. By Mariana Scott. *The Modern Language Journal* 52 (1968): 46–47.

Works Cited

Labib, Pahor, ed. *Coptic Gnostic Papyri in the Coptic Museum at Old Cairo*. Cairo: Government Press, 1956.

Lagenpusch, Emil. "Walhallklänge im Heliand." In *Festschrift zum siebzigsten Geburtstage Oskar Schade, dargebracht von seinen Schülern und Verehrern*. Königsberg: Hartung, 1896. 135–52.

Lambel, Hans. "Ein neuentdecktes Blatt einer Heliandhandschrift." *Sitzungsberichte der kaiserlichen Akademie der Wissenschaften in Wien: Philosophisch-historische Classe* 97 (1880): 613–24.

Lange, Wolfgang. *Christliche Skaldendichtung*. Göttingen: Vandenhoeck & Ruprecht, 1958.

Lange, Wolfgang. *Studien zur christlichen Dichtung der Nordgermanen, 1000–1200*. Palästra 222. Göttingen: Vandenhoeck & Ruprecht, 1958.

Layton, Bentley, ed. *Nag Hammadi Codex II, 2–7*. Nag Hammadi Studies 20. Leiden: E. J. Brill, 1989.

Lehmann, Ruth P.M. Review of *Zur Heliandmetrik: Das Verhältnis von Rhythmus und Satzgewicht im Altsächsischen*. By Ingeborg Hinderscheidt. *Speculum* 56 (1981): 391–393.

Lehmann, Winfred P. *The Alliteration of Old Saxon Poetry*. Norsk Tidsskrift for Sprogvidenskap, Suppl. Bind 3. Oslo: H. Aschenhoug, 1953.

Lehmann, Winfred P. "The Alliteration of Old Saxon Poetry." In *Der Heliand*. Ed. Jürgen Eichhoff and Irmengard Rauch. Wege der Forschung 321. Darmstadt: Wissenschaftliche Buchgesellschaft, 1973.

Leloir, L., ed. *Saint Éphrem. Commentaire de l'évangile concordant: Texte Syriaque (Mss. Chester Beatty 709)*. Chester Beatty Monographs 8. Dublin: Hodges & Figgis, 1963.

Leube, Achim. "Die Sachsen." In *Die Germanen: Geschichte und Kultur der germanischen Stämme in Mitteleuropa*. Ed. Bruno Krüger. 2 vols. Berlin: Akademie, 1979–83. 2:443–85.

Liberman, Anatoly. "Ernst A. Ebbinghaus (1926–1995): Portrait of the Linguist as an Old Man." *American Journal of Germanic Linguistics & Literatures* 9 (1997): 117–29.

Liberman, Anatoly. "Heliand." In *Dictionary of Literary Biography*. Vol. 148. Ed. Will Hasty and James Hardin. New York: Gale Research, 1995. 189–95.

Works Cited

Liebster, Wolfram. "Umkehr und Erneuerung im Verhältnis von Christen und Juden." In *Umkehr und Erneuerung: Erläuterungen zum Synodalbeschluß der Rheinischen Landessynode 1980 „Zur Erneuerung des Verhältnisses von Christen und Juden"*. Ed. Bertold Klappert and Helmut Starck. Neukirchen-Vluyn: Neukirchener Verlag, 1980. 55–65.

Linder, Amnon. "Christlich-Jüdische Konfrontation im kirchlichen Frühmittelalter." In *Die Kirche des früheren Mittelalters*. Ed. Knut Schäferdiek. Kirchengeschichte als Missionsgeschichte 2. Munich: Kaiser, 1978. 397–441.

Liuzza, R. M., ed. *The Old English Version of the Gospels*. EETS Original Series 304. Oxford: Oxford UP, 1994.

Lord, Albert B. *Der Sänger erzählt: Wie ein Epos entsteht*. Trans. Helmut Martin. Munich: C. Hanser, 1965.

Lother, Helmut. *Die Christusauffassung der Germanen*. Gütersloh: C. Bertelsmann, 1937.

Ludwig, Otto. "Vom diktierenden zum schreibenden Autor: Die Transformation der Schreibpraxis im Übergang zur Neuzeit." In *Schreiben im Umbruch: Schreibforschung und schulisches Schreiben*. Ed. Helmuth Feilke and Paul R. Portmann. Stuttgart: Klett, 1996. 16–28.

Luz, Ulrich. *Das Evangelium nach Matthäus*. 4 vols. Evangelisch-Katholischer Kommentar zum Neuen Testament 1. Zurich: Benziger, 1985–2002.

Luz, Ulrich. *Matthew: A Commentary*. Trans. James E. Crouch. 3 vols. Minneapolis: Fortress, 2001–2005.

Magoun Francis P. "Bede's Story of Caedmon: The Case History of an Anglo-Saxon Oral Singer." *Speculum* 30 (1955): 49–65.

Magoun, Francis P. "The *Praefatio* and *Versus* Associated with some Old-Saxon Biblical Poems." In *Mediaeval Studies in Honor of Jeremiah Denis Matthias Ford, Smith Professor of French and Spanish Literature, Emeritus*. Ed. Urban T. Holmes and Alex J. Denomy. Cambridge, Mass.: Harvard UP, 1948. 107–36.

Markey, Thomas L. *Germanic Dialect Grouping and the Position of Ingvæonic*. Innsbruck: Institut für Sprachwissenschaft, 1976.

Markey, Thomas L. *A North Sea Germanic Reader*. Munich: Fink, 1976.

Works Cited

Masser, Achim, ed. *Die lateinisch-althochdeutsche Tatianbilingue Stiftsbibliothek St. Gallen Cod. 56*. Studien zum Althochdeutschen 25. Göttingen: Vandenhoeck & Ruprecht, 1994.

Masser, Achim. "Tatian." In *Die Deutsche Literatur des Mittelalters: Verfasserlexikon*. Ed. Wolfgang Stammler et al. 2nd ed. Vol. 9. Berlin: Walter de Gruyter, 1995. 620–28.

McLintock, David R. "Heliand." In *Dictionary of the Middle Ages*. Ed. Joseph R. Strayer et al. 13 vols. New York: Scribner, 1982–1989. 6:150–51.

Metzger, Bruce M., and Roland E. Murphy, eds. *The New Oxford Annotated Bible with Apocrypha: New Revised Standard Version*. New York: Oxford UP, 1994.

Meyer, Marvin W. Preface to *The Nag Hammadi Library in English*. Ed. Marvin W. Meyer et al. Leiden: E. J. Brill, 1977. ix-xi.

Mierke, Gesine. *Memoria als Kulturtransfer: Der alsächsische »Heliand« zwischen Spätantike und Frühmittelalter*. Studien zur Literatur und Gesellschaft des Mittelalters und der frühen Neuzeit 11. Cologne: Böhlau, 2008.

Murphy, G. Ronald. *The Heliand: The Saxon Gospel*. New York: Oxford UP, 1992.

Murphy, G. Ronald. "The Jews in the *Heliand*." In *German Literature Between Faiths: Jew and Christian at Odds and in Harmony*. Ed. Peter Meister. Studies in German Jewish History 6. Berlin: Peter Lang, 2004. 15–25, 179.

Murphy, G. Ronald. "The Light Worlds of the *Heliand*." *Monatshefte* 89 (1997): 5–17.

Murphy, G. Ronald. "Magic in the *Heliand*." *Monatshefte* 83 (1991): 386–97.

Murphy, G. Ronald. *The Saxon Savior: The Germanic Transformation of the Gospel in the Ninth-Century Heliand*. New York: Oxford UP, 1989.

von der Nahmer, Dieter. *Die lateinische Heiligenvita: Eine Einführung in die lateinische Hagiographie*. Darmstadt: Wissenschaftliche Buchgesellschaft, 1994.

Neckel, Gerhard, ed. *Beowulf und die kleineren Denkmäler der altenglischen Heldensage: Mit Text und Übersetzung, Einleitung und Kommentar sowie einem Konkordanz-Glossar. In drei Teilen*. Germanistische Bibliothek, Reihe 4: Texte. Heidelberg: Carl Winter, 1976.

Needham, Rodney, ed. *Right & Left: Essays on Dual Symbolic Classification.* Chicago: U of Chicago Press, 1973.
Nellmann, Eberhard, ed. and trans. *Annolied: Mittelhochdeutsch und Neuhochdeutsch.* 3rd ed. Stuttgart: Reclam, 1986.
Nielsen, Hans F. Review of *The Old Saxon Language: Grammar, Epic Narrative, Linguistic Interference.* By Irmengard Rauch. *Word* 46 (1995): 442–444.
Niles, John D. *Beowulf: The Poem and Its Tradition.* Cambridge, Mass.: Harvard UP, 1983.
Noonan, John T. *The Scholastic Analysis of Usury.* Cambridge, Mass.: Harvard UP, 1957.
North, Richard. *Pagan Words and Christian Meanings.* Amsterdam: Rodopi, 1991.
O'Keeffe, Katherine O'Brien. "Orality and the Developing Text of Caedmon's 'Hymn'." *Speculum* 62 (1987): 1–20.
Olson, Mike, and Shannon Dubenion-Smith. "Towards a Typology of Relativization Strategies in Old Saxon." Paper presented at the 18th International Conference on Historical Linguistics. Montreal, 2007.
Ong, Walter J. *Oralität und Literalität: Die Technologisierung des Wortes.* Trans. Wolfgang Schömel. Opladen: Westdeutscher Verlag, 1987.
Paasche, Fredrik. "Kristusskikkelsen i gammalnordisk lære, liv og lov." In *Artikler og taler.* By Paasche. Oslo: Aschehoug 1948. 107–119.
Paasche, Fredrik. *Norges og Islands litteratur inntil utgangen av middelaldere.* Rev. Anne Holtsmark. Norsk litteratur historie 1. Oslo: Aschehoug, 1957.
von Padberg, Lutz E. *Die Christianisierung Europas im Mittelalter.* Stuttgart: Reclam, 1998.
von Padberg, Lutz E. *Mission und Christianisierung: Formen und Folgen bei Angelsachsen und Franken im 7. und 8. Jahrhundert.* Stuttgart: F. Steiner, 1995.
von Padberg, Lutz E. "Odin oder Christus? Loyalitäts- und Orientierungskonflikte in der frühmittelalterlichen Christianisierungsepoche." *Archiv für Kulturgeschichte* 77 (1995): 249–78.
Pagels, Elaine. *The Gnostic Gospels.* New York: Random House, 1979.
Pakis, Valentine A. "(Un)Desirable Origins: The *Heliand* and the Gospel of

Works Cited

Thomas." *Exemplaria: A Journal of Theory in Medieval and Renaissance Studies* 17 (2005): 215–53.

Palviainen, Santeri. "The Gender of the Old Saxon Suffix *-skepi*." *Harvard Working Papers in Linguistics* 12 (2007): n.p.

Parry, Milman. "Studies in the Epic Technique of Oral Verse-Making." In *The Making of Homeric Verse: The Collected Papers of Milman Parry*. Ed. Adam Parry. Oxford: Clarendon Press, 1971. 266–364.

Penzl, Herbert. Review of *Altniederdeutsches Elementarbuch: Wort- und Lautlehre*. By Gerhard Cordes. *Language* 52 (1976): 511–514.

Petersen, William. "The Diatessaron of Tatian." In *The Text of the New Testament in Contemporary Research: Essays on the Status Quaestionis*. Ed. Bart D. Ehrman and Michael W. Holmes. Grand Rapids: W. B. Eerdmans, 1995. 77–96.

Petersen, William L. "New Evidence for a Second Century Source of the *Heliand*." In *Medieval German Literature: Proceedings from the 23rd International Congress on Medieval Studies*. Ed. Albrecht Classen. Göppingen: Kummerle, 1989. 21–38.

Petersen, William L. *Tatian's Diatessaron: Its Creation, Dissemination, Significance, and History in Scholarship*. Supplements to Vigiliae Christianae 25. Leiden: E. J. Brill, 1994.

Piaget, Jean. *Nachahmung, Spiel und Traum: Die Entwicklung der Symbolfunktion beim Kinde*. Stuttgart: Klett, 1969.

Piaget, Jean. *Psychologie der Intelligenz*. Trans. Lucien Goldmann and Yvonne Moser. Zurich: Rascher, 1948.

Pickering, Frederick P. "Christlicher Erzählstoff bei Otfrid und im Heliand." *Zeitschrift für deutsches Altertum und deutsche Literatur* 85 (1954/1955): 262–91.

Pierce, Marc. "Constraints on Syllable Structure in Early Germanic." *Journal of Indo-European Studies* 28 (2000): 17–29.

Piper, Paul, ed. *Die altsächsische Bibeldichtung (Heliand und Genesis)*. Stuttgart: I. G. Cotta, 1897.

PL = Migne, J.-P., ed. *Patrologiæ cursus completes. Series Latina*. 221 vols. Paris, 1844–1864.

Pretzel, Ulrich. "Krogmann." In *Neue deutsche Biographie*. Vol. 13. Berlin: Duncker & Humblot, 1982. 67–68.

Priebsch, R. *The Heliand Manuscript Cotton Caligula A. VII in the British Museum: A Study*. Oxford: Clarendon, 1925.

Quispel, Gilles. "L'Évangile selon Thomas et le Diatessaron." In *Gnostic Studies II*. By Quispel. Istanbul: Nederlands Historisch-Archaeologisch Instituut, 1975. 31–55.

Qusipel, Gilles. "Gnosis and the New Sayings of Jesus." *Eranos Jahrbuch* 38 (1969): 271–96.

Qusipel, Gilles. *Het Evangelie van Thomas in de Nederlanden*. Amsterdam: Elsevier, 1971. Repr. Baarn: Tirion, 1991.

Quispel, Gilles. "Der Heliand und das Thomasevangelium" *Vigiliae Christianae* 16 (1962), 121–51. Repr. in *Gnostic Studies II*. By Quispel. Istanbul:Nederlands Historisch-Archaeologisch Instituut, 1975. 70–97.

Quispel, Gilles. "Jewish Influences on the 'Heliand'." In *Religions in Antiquity: Essays in Memory of Erwin Ramsdell Goodenough*. Ed. Jacob Neusner. Leiden: E. J. Brill, 1968. 244–50.

Quispel, Gilles. "The Latin Tatian or the Gospel of Thomas in Limburg." *Journal of Biblical Literature* 88 (1969): 321–30.

Quispel, Gilles. "Liudger en het Evangelie van Thomas." *Rondom het Woord* 13 (1971): 207–18.

Quispel, Gilles. "Some Remarks on the Gospel of Thomas." *New Testament Studies* 5 (1958/1959): 276–90.

Quispel, Gilles. "The Syrian Thomas and the Syrian Macarius." *Vigiliae Christianae* 18 (1964): 226–35.

Quispel, Gilles. *Tatian and the Gospel of Thomas: Studies in the History of the Western Diatessaron*. Leiden: E. J. Brill, 1975.

Ranke, Ernst, ed. *Codex Fuldensis: Novum Testamentum latine interprete Hieronymo ex manuscripto Victoris Capuani*. Marburg & Leipzig: N. G. Elwert, 1868.

Rasmussen, Jens Elmgård. "The Growth of i-Umlaut in Norse and West Germanic: Thoughts on a Recent Book." *Acta Linguistica Hafniensia* 32 (2000): 143–59.

Rathofer, Johannes. "Die Einwirkung des Fuldischen Evangelientextes auf den althochdeutschen *Tatian*: Abkehr von der Methode der Diatessaronforschung." In *Literatur und Sprache im europäischen Mittelalter*:

Works Cited

Festschrift für Karl Langosch zum 70. Geburtstag. Ed. Alf Önnerfors, Johannes Rathofer, and Fritz Wagner. Darmstadt: Wissenschaftliche Buchgesellschaft, 1973. 256–308.

Rathofer, Johannes. *Der Heliand: Theologischer Sinn als tektonische Form. Vorbereitung und Grundlegung der Interpretation.* Niederdeutsche Studien 9. Cologne: Böhlau, 1962.

Rathofer, Johannes. "Realien zur altsächsischen Literatur." *Niederdeutsches Wort* 16 (1976): 4–62.

Rathofer, Johannes. "Zum Aufbau des Heliand." In *Der Heliand.* Ed. Jürgen Eichhoff and Irmengard Rauch. Wege der Forschung 321. Darmstadt: Wissenschaftliche Buchgesellschaft, 1973. 344–99.

Rauch, Irmengard. "A Newly Found Leipzig *Heliand* Fragment." *Interdisciplinary Journal for Germanic Linguistics and Semiotic Analysis* 11 (2006): 1–17.

Rauch, Irmengard. *The Old Saxon Language: Grammar, Epic Narrative, Linguistic Interference.* Berkeley Models of Grammars 1. New York: Peter Lang, 1992.

Rauch, Irmengard. "Paralanguage: Evidence from Germanic." *Semiotica* 135 (2001): 147–56.

Rauch, Irmengard. "What Can Generative Grammar Do for Etymology? An Old Saxon Hapax." *Semasia: Beiträge zur germanisch-romanischen Sprachforschung* 2 (1975): 249–60.

Reventlow, Henning Graf. *Epochen der Bibelauslegung.* 4 vols. Munich: C. H. Beck, 1990–2001.

Richardson, Peter. "The Consolation of Philology." *Modern Philology* 92 (1994): 1–13.

Riecke, Jörg. "Anatomisches und Heilkundliches in altsächsischen Glossaren." *Amsterdamer Beiträge zur älteren Germanistik* 52 (1999): 207–25.

Robinson, James M. Introduction to *The Nag Hammadi Library in English.* Ed. Marvin W. Meyer et al. Leiden: E. J. Brill, 1977. 1–25.

Robinson, James M. "The Jung Codex: The Rise and Fall of a Monopoly." *Religious Studies Review* 3 (1977): 17–30.

Robinson, Orrin W. *Old English and its Closest Relatives.* Stanford: Stanford UP, 1992.

Rosenkranz, G. "Witte, Johannes." In *Die Religion in Geschichte und Gegenwart: Handwörterbuch für Theologie und Religionswissenschaft*. Ed. Kurt Galling et al. 3rd ed. 7 vols. Tübingen: Mohr, 1957–65. 6:1781.

Roth, Cecil, and Geoffrey Wigoder, eds. *Encyclopedia Judaica*. Jerusalem: Keter, 1971–72.

Rückert, Heinrich, ed., *Heliand*. Leipzig: F. A. Brockhaus, 1876.

Rupp, Heinz. "The Adoption of Christian Ideas into German, with Reference to the 'Heliand' and Otfrid's 'Evangelienbuch'." *Parergon* 21 (1979): 33–42.

Rupp, Heinz. *Forschung zur althochdeutschen Literatur 1943–1962*. Stuttgart: Metzler, 1965.

Rupp, Heinz. "Der Heliand: Hauptanliegen seines Dichters." In *Der Heliand*. Ed. Jürgen Eichhoff and Irmengard Rauch. Wege der Forschung 321. Darmstadt: Wissenschaftliche Buchgesellschaft, 1973. 247–69.

Russell, James C. *The Germanization of Early Medieval Christianity*. Oxford: Oxford UP, 1994.

Russom, Geoffrey. "A Bard's-Eye View of the Germanic Syllable." *Journal of English and Germanic Philology* 101 (2002): 305–328.

Russom, Geoffrey. *Beowulf and Old Germanic Metre*. Cambridge: Cambridge UP, 1998.

Russom, Geoffrey. Review of *The Metre of Old Saxon Poetry: The Remaking of Alliterative Tradition*. By Seiichi Suzuki. *Anglia* 123 (2005): 702–05.

Sahm, Heike. "Neues Licht auf alte Fragen: Die Stellung des Leipziger Fragments in der Überlieferungsgeschichte des *Heliand*." *Zeitschrift für deutsche Philologie* 126 (2007): 81–98.

Sahm, Heike. "Wiederholungen über Wiederholungen: Zur Variation in der „Altsächsischen Genesis"." *Zeitschrift für deutsche Philologie* 123 (2004): 321–40.

Said, Edward W. *Orientalism*. New York: Pantheon, 1978.

Sand, Alexander. *Das Matthäus-Evangelium*. Erträge der Forschung 275. Darmstadt: Wissenschaftliche Buchgesellschaft, 1991.

Schäferdiek, Knut. "Germanen. § 46: Christianisierung." In *Reallexikon der germanischen Altertumskunde*. Ed. Johannes Hoops et al. 2nd ed. Vol. 11. Berlin: Walter de Gruyter, 1998. 388–395.

Works Cited

Schäferdiek, Knut. "Die geschichtliche Stellung des sogenannten germanischen Arianismus." In *Die Kirche des früheren Mittelalters*. Ed. Knut Schäferdiek. Kirchengeschichte als Missionsgeschichte 2. Munich: Kaiser, 1978. 79–90.

Scheibler, Samuel P. *Golgotha and Götterdämmerung: German Religious Paradigm Shifts and the Proclamation of the Gospel*. New York: Peter Lang, 1996.

Scherer, Wilhelm. *Geschichte der deutschen Litteratur*. 10th ed. Berlin: Weidmann, 1905.

Schiller, Friedrich. *Über die ästhetische Erziehung des Menschen in einer Reihe von Briefen*. Stuttgart: Reclam, 1965.

Schirmer, Karl-Heinz. "Antike Traditionen in der versus-Vorrede zum Heliand." In *Festschrift für Gerhard Cordes zum 65. Geburtstag*. Ed. Friedhelm Debus and Joachim Hartig. 2 vols. Neumünster: Wachholtz, 1973–1976. 1:136–59.

Schmid, Hans Ulrich. "Ein neues 'Heliand'-Fragment aus der Universitätsbibliothek Leipzig." *Zeitschrift für deutsches Altertum und deutsche Literatur* 135 (2006): 309–23.

Schmid, Hans Ulrich. "Nochmals zum Leipziger 'Heliand'-Fragment." *Zeitschrift für deutsches Altertum und deutsche Literatur* 136 (2007): 376–78.

Schmid, Ulrich B. "In Search of Tatian's Diatessaron in the West." *Vigiliae Christianae* 57 (2003): 176–99.

Schmidt, Henry J. "What is Oppositional Criticism? Politics and German Literary Criticism from Fascism to the Cold War." *Monatshefte* 79 (1987): 292–307.

Schmidt, Kurt Dietrich. *Die Bekehrung der Ostgermanen zum Christentum: Der ostgermanische Arianismus*. Göttingen: Vandenhoeck & Ruprecht, 1939.

Schmidt, Kurt Dietrich. *Die katholische Mission unter den Westgermanen*. Göttingen: Vandenhoeck & Ruprecht, 1939.

Schuhmacher, W. Wilfried. "LG (Velbert) *jot* 'ihr' < **jut* (oder OS *git*)?" *NOWELE: North-Western European Language Evolution* 45 (2004): 59–60.

Schwink, Frederick W. 2004. *The Third Gender: Studies in the Origin and History of Germanic Grammatical Gender*. Heidelberg: Carl Winter, 2004.

Schneider, Karin. *Paläographie und Handschriftenkunde für Germanisten: Eine Einführung.* Tübingen: Max Niemeyer, 1999.

"Scholars Study a 'Fifth Gospel': 13 Volumes Dug Up in Egypt Are Only Apocryphal Works, Coptic Expert Says Here." *New York Times.* October 7, 1956. 34.

Scholz, Manfred G. *Hören und Lesen: Studien zur primären Rezeption der Literatur im 12. und 13. Jahrhundert.* Wiesbaden: F. Steiner, 1980.

Schönbach, Anton E. "Deutsches Christentum vor tausend Jahren." *Cosmopolis* 1 (1896): 605–21.

Schwab, Ute. "Ansätze zu einer Interpretation der altsächsischen Genesisdichtung 1." *AION-Sezione Germanica* 17 (1974): 111–86.

Schwab, Ute. *Einige Beziehungen zwischen altsächsischer und angelsächsischer Dichtung.* Spoleto: Centro italiano di studi sull'alto Medioevo, 1988.

Schwab, Ute, et al., eds. *Die Bruchstücke der altsächsischen Genesis und ihrer altenglischen Übertragung: Einführung, Textwiedergabe, und Übersetzung, Abbildung der gesamten Überlieferung.* Göppinger Beiträge zur Textgeschichte 29. Göppingen: Kümmerle, 1991.

Scott, Mariana, trans. *The Heliand: Translated from the Old Saxon.* University of North Carolina Studies in the Germanic Languages and Literatures 52. Chapel Hill: U of North Carolina Press, 1966.

von See, Klaus. *Germanische Heldensage: Stoffe, Probleme, Methoden.* 2nd ed. Wiesbaden: Athenäum, 1981.

von See, Klaus. "Was ist Heldendichtung?" In *Europäische Heldendichtung.* Ed. Klaus von See. Wege der Forschung 500. Darmstadt: Wissenschaftliche Buchgesellschaft, 1978. 1–38.

Seebold, Elmar. *Vergleichendes und etymologisches Wörterbuch der germanischen starken Verben.* Janua Linguarum: Series Practica 85. The Hague: Mouton, 1970.

Sehrt, Edward H. *Vollständiges Wörterbuch zum Heliand und zur altsächsischen Genesis.* Hesperia 14. Göttingen: Vandenhoeck & Ruprecht, 1925.

Sehrt, Edward H. *Vollständiges Wörterbuch zum Heliand und zur altsächsischen Genesis.* 2nd ed. Hesperia 14. Göttingen: Vandenhoeck & Ruprecht, 1966.

Siegele-Wenschkewitz, Leonore. "Mitverantwortung und Schuld der Christen am Holocaust." *Evangelische Theologie* 42 (1982): 171–90.

Works Cited

Sievers, Eduard, ed. *Heliand*. Halle: Waisenhaus, 1878.

Sievers, Eduard, ed. *Heliand: Titelauflage vermehrt um das Prager Fragment des Heliand und die Vaticanischen Fragmente von Heliand und Genesis.* Germanistische Handbibliothek 4. Halle: Waisenhaus, 1935.

Sievers, Eduard, ed. *Tatian: Lateinisch und altdeutsch mit ausführlichem Glossar*. 2nd ed. Bibliothek des ältesten deutschen Literatur-Denkmäler 5. Paderborn: Ferdinand Schöningh, 1892. Repr. 1966.

Sievers, Paul. *Die Accente in althochdeutschen und altsächsischen Handschriften*. Berlin: Mayer & Müller, 1906.

Simms, Douglas P. A. *Reconstructing an Oral Tradition: Problems in the Comparative Metrical Analysis of Old English, Old Saxon and Old Norse Alliterative Verse*. Doctoral diss. University of Texas-Austin, 2003.

Skvairs, Ekaterina. "Altsächsisch-altniederfränkisches Kontakterbe und sein Fortleben im Niederdeutschen." *Amsterdamer Beiträge zur älteren Germanistik* 55 (2001): 27–60.

Smith, Laura Catharine. *Cross-Level Interactions in West Germanic Phonology and Morphology*. Doctoral diss. University of Wisconsin-Madison, 2004.

Smith, Laura Catharine. "The Resilience of Prosodic Templates in the History of West Germanic." In *Historical Linguistics 2005*. Ed. Joseph C. Salmons and Shannon Dubenion-Smith. Amsterdam: John Benjamins, 2007. 351–65.

Sowinski, Bernhard. *Darstellungsstil und Sprachstil im Heliand*. Kölner germanistische Studien 21. Cologne: Böhlau, 1985.

Spitz, Hans-Jörg. *Die Metaphorik des geistigen Schriftsinns: Ein Beitrag zur allegorischen Bibelauslegung des ersten christlichen Jahrtausends*. Münstersche Mittelalter-Schriften 12. Munich: W. Fink, 1972.

Spitzbart, Günter, ed. and trans. *Kirchengeschichte des englischen Volkes*. By Bede. 2nd ed. Darmstadt: Wissenschaftliche Buchgesellschaft, 1997.

Stapel, Wilhelm, ed. *Der Heliand*. Münster: C. Hanser, 1953.

Steinger, Hans. "Die Sprache des Heliand." *Jahrbuch des Vereins für niederdeutsche Sprachforschung* 51 (1925): 1–54.

Stevens, Christopher M. "The Derivational Suffixes and Suffixoids of Old Saxon: A Panchronic Approach to a Linguistic Category." *American Journal of Germanic Linguistics and Literatures* 12 (2000): 53–79.

Stevens, Christopher M. "More Prefixes and Prefixoids of Old Saxon and Further Examples of the Grammaticalization of the Old Saxon Root." *Leuvense Bijdragen* 91 (2002): 301–18.

Stevens, Christopher M. "The Prefixes and Prefixoids of Old Saxon: On the Grammaticalization of the Old Saxon Adverbs and Prepositions." *Leuvense Bijdragen* 93 (2004): 151–78.

Stevens, Christopher M. "Revisiting the Affixoid Debate: On the Grammaticalization of the Word." In *Grammatikalisierung im Deutschen*. Ed. Torsten Leuchner et al. Berlin: De Gruyter, 2005. 71–84.

Strecker, Karl. "Studien zu den karolingischen Dichtern IV." *Neues Archiv der Gesellschaft für ältere deutsche Geschichtskunde* 44 (1922): 209–51.

Sundquist, John D. "Case Attraction and Relative Clause Variation in the Old Saxon *Hêliand*." Paper presented at GLAC 13. State College, PA, 2007.

Suzuki, Seiichi. "Anacrusis in the Meter of the *Heliand*." In *Interdigitations: Essays for Irmengard Rauch*. Ed. Gerald F. Carr et al. New York: Peter Lang, 1999. 189–99.

Suzuki, Seiichi. *The Metre of Old Saxon Poetry: The Remaking of Alliterative Tradition*. Cambridge: D.S. Brewer, 2004.

Suzuki, Seiichi. *The Metrical Organization of Beowulf: Prototype and Isomorphism*. Berlin: De Gruyter, 1996.

Suzuki, Seiichi. "The Metrical Organization of the *Heliand*: Gradation and Harmonization." *Interdisciplinary Journal for Germanic Linguistics and Semiotic Analysis* 6 (2001): 11–39.

Suzuki, Seiichi. "The Metrical Reorganization of Type E in the *Heliand*." *American Journal of Germanic Linguistics and Literatures* 12 (2000): 281–90.

Szemerényi, Oswald J. L. "A New Leaf of the Gothic Bible." *Language* 48 (1972): 1–10.

Taeger, Burkhard. "Heliand." In *Die Deutsche Literatur des Mittelalters: Verfasserlexikon*. Ed. Wolfgang Stammler et al. 2nd ed. Vol. 3. Berlin: Walter de Gruyter, 1981. 959–63.

Taeger, Burkhard, ed. *Der Heliand: Ausgewählte Abbildungen zur Überlieferung*. Litterae 103. Göppingen: Kümmerle, 1985.

Works Cited

Taeger, Burkhard, "Das Straubinger 'Heliand'-Fragment II." *Beiträge zur Geschichte der deutschen Sprache und Literatur* 103 (1981): 402–24.

Taeger, Burkhard. "Das Straubinger 'Heliand'-Fragment: Philologische Untersuchungen I." *Beiträge zur Geschichte der deutschen Sprache und Literatur* 101 (1979): 181–228.

Taeger Burkhard. "Ein vergessener handschriftlicher Befund: Die Neumen im Münchener *Heliand*." *Zeitschrift für deutsches Altertum und deutsche Literatur* 107 (1978): 184–93.

Taeger, Burkhard. *Zahlensymbolik bei Hraban, bei Hincmar und im Heliand? Studien zur Zahlensymbolik im Frühmittelalter.* Münchener Texte und Untersuchungen zur deutschen Literatur des Mittelalters 30. Munich: Beck, 1970.

Thurnwald, Richard. "The Psychology of Acculturation." *American Anthropologist* 34 (1932): 557–69.

Tiefenbach, Heinrich. "Altsächsisch und Altniederländisch." *Amsterdamer Beiträge zur älteren Germanistik* 57 (2003): 61–76.

Tiefenbach, Heinrich. "Anmerkungen zu einem Altniederdeutschen Elementarbuch." *Beiträge zur Namenforschung (N.F.)* 10 (1975): 64–75.

de Tischendorf, Constantinus, ed. *Evangelia Apocrypha.* 2nd ed. Leipzig: Hermann Mendelssohn, 1876.

Toller, T. Northcote. Supplement to *An Anglo-Saxon Dictionary.* By Joseph Bosworth. London: Oxford UP, 1955.

Trager, George. "Paralanguage: A First Approximation." *Studies in Linguistics* 13 (1958): 1–12.

Tristram, Hildegard L. C. *Sex aetates mundi: Die Weltzeitalter bei den Angelsachsen und den Iren.* Anglistische Forschungen 165. Heidelberg: Carl Winter, 1985.

Vanneufville, E., trans. *Héliand. L'évangile de la Mer du Nord.* Turnhout: Brepols, 2008.

Vennemann, Theo. "Key Issues in English Etymology." In *Sounds, Words, Texts, and Change.* Ed. Teresa Fanego, Belén Méndez-Naya, and Elena Seoane. Amsterdam: Benjamins, 2002. 227–52.

Vilmar, A. F. C. *Deutsche Altertümer im Heliand als Einkleidung der evangelischen Geschichte.* Marburg: N. G. Elwert, 1845.

Vilmar, A. F. C. *Deutsche Altertümer im Hêliand als Einkleidung der evangelischen Geschichte*. 2nd ed. Marburg: N. G. Elwert, 1862.
Vogels, Heinrich J. *Beiträge zur Geschichte des Diatessaron im Abendland*. Neutestamentliche Abhandlungen 8:1. Münster: Aschendorff, 1919.
de Vries, Jan. *Altgermanische Religionsgeschichte*. 2nd ed. 2 vols. Berlin: Walter de Gruyter, 1956–57.
de Vries, Jan. *Altgermanische Religionsgeschichte*. 3rd ed. 2 vols. Berlin: Walter de Gruyter, 1970.
Wackernagel, Jacob. "Über ein Gesetz der indogermanischen Wortstellung." *Indogermanische Forschungen* 1 (1892): 333–436.
Wadstein, Elis, ed. *Kleinere altsächsische Sprachdenkmäler mit Anmerkungen und Glossar*. Leipzig: D. Soltau, 1899.
Weatherford, J. McIver. *The History of Money: From Sandstone to Cyberspace*. New York: Crown, 1997.
Weber, C. A. "Der Dichter des Heliand im Verhältnis zu seinen Quellen." *Zeitschrift für deutsches Altertum und deutsche Literatur* 64 (1927): 1–76.
Weber, Gerd Wolfgang. "„Sem konungr skyldi". Heldendichtung und Semiotik: Griechische und germanische heroische Ethik als kollektives Normensystem einer archaischen Kultur." In *Helden und Heldensage: Otto Gschwantler zum 60. Geburtstag*. Ed. Hermann Reichert and Günter Zimmermann. Vienna: Fassbaender, 1990. 447–81.
Weisweiler, Josef, and Werner Betz. "Deutsche Frühzeit." In *Deutsche Wortgeschichte*. Ed. Friedrich Maurer and Heinz Rupp. 3rd ed. 2 vols. Berlin: Walter de Gruyter, 1974. 1:55–133.
fon Weringha, Juw. *Heliand and Diatessaron*. Studia Germanica 5. Assen: Van Gorcum, 1965.
Whitman, Cedric H. *Homer and the Heroic Tradition*. Cambridge, Mass.: Harvard UP, 1958.
Wicke, Hermann. "Wollte der Dichter des Heliand nichts anderes als ein Künder germanischen Lebensgefühles sein?" *Zeitschrift der Gesellschaft für niedersächsische Kirchengeschichte* 42 (1937): 227–38.
Wicke, Hermann. *Das wunderbare Tun des Heiligen Krist nach der altsächsischen Evangelienharmonie: Eine Einführung in das Verständnis des "Heliand"*. Göttingen: Vandenhoeck & Ruprecht, 1935.

Works Cited

Wiefel, Wolfgang. *Das Evangelium nach Matthäus.* Theologischer Handkommentar zum Neuen Testament 1. Leipzig: Evangelische Verlagsanstalt, 1998.

Wilson, Joseph. Review of *The Heliand: The Saxon Gospel.* By G. Ronald Murphy. *Journal of English and Germanic Philology* 94 (1995): 454–56.

Windisch, Ernst. *Der Heliand und seine Quellen.* Leipzig: F. C. W. Vogel, 1868.

Witte, Johannes. *Wie kam das Christentum zu den Germanen?* Gotha: L. Klotz, 1934.

Wolf, Alois. "Beobachtungen zur ersten Fitte des Heliand." *Niederdeutsches Jahrbuch* 98/99 (1975/76): 7–21.

Wolf, Alois. *Heldensage und Epos: Zur Konstituierung einer mittelalterlichen volkssprachlichen Gattung im Spannungsfeld von Mündlichkeit und Schriftlichkeit.* ScriptOralia 68. Tübingen: G. Narr, 1995.

Zahn, Theodor. *Tatian's Diatessaron.* Forschungen zur Geschichte des neutestamentlichen Kanons und der altkirchlichen Literatur 1. Erlangen: A. Deichert, 1881.

Zangmeister, Karl, and Wilhelm Braune. "Bruchstücke der altsächsischen Bibeldichtung aus der Bibliotheca Palatina." *Neue Heidelberger Jahrbücher* 4 (1894): 205–94.

Zanni, Roland. 1985. "Wortbildung des Altniederdeutschen (Altsächsischen)." In *Sprachgeschichte: Ein Handbuch zur Geschichte der deutschen Sprache und ihrer Erforschung.* Vol. 2. Ed. Werner Besch et al. Berlin: De Gruyter, 1985. 1094–1102.

Zurla, Cynthia. *Medium and Message: The Confluence of Saxon and Frankish Values as Portrayed in the Old Saxon Heliand.* Doctoral diss. McGill University, 2005.

www.ingramcontent.com/pod-product-compliance
Lightning Source LLC
Chambersburg PA
CBHW052144300426

44115CB00011B/1513